PARTICIPATION WITHOUT DEMOCRACY

PARTICIPATION WITHOUT DEMOCRACY

Containing Conflict in Southeast Asia

Garry Rodan

CORNELL UNIVERSITY PRESS   ITHACA AND LONDON

First published 2018 by Cornell University Press

Printed in the United States of America

Library of Congress Cataloging-in-Publication Data

Names: Rodan, Garry, 1955– author.
Title: Participation without democracy : containing conflict in Southeast Asia / Garry Rodan.
Description: Ithaca : Cornell University Press, 2018. | Includes bibliographical references.
Identifiers: LCCN 2017049686 (print) | LCCN 2017055324 (ebook) | ISBN 9781501720130 (pdf) | ISBN 9781501720123 (ret) | ISBN 9781501720109 | ISBN 9781501720109 (cloth ; alk. paper) | ISBN 9781501720116 (pbk. ; alk. paper)
Subjects: LCSH: Political participation—Southeast Asia—Case studies. | Representative government and representation—Southeast Asia—Case studies. | Democracy—Southeast Asia—Case studies. | Social conflict—Southeast Asia—Case studies. | Southeast Asia—Politics and government—21st century.
Classification: LCC JQ750.A91 (ebook) | LCC JQ750.A91 .R625 2018 (print) | DDC 323/.0420959—dc23
LC record available at https://lccn.loc.gov/2017049686

Cornell University Press strives to use environmentally responsible suppliers and materials to the fullest extent possible in the publishing of its books. Such materials include vegetable-based, low-VOC inks and acid-free papers that are recycled, totally chlorine-free, or partly composed of nonwood fibers. For further information, visit our website at cornellpress.cornell.edu.

Contents

Abbreviations and Acronyms

ABAMIN	Abante Mindanao
ACT Teachers	Alliance of Concerned Teachers
Amanah/PAN	Parti Amanah Negara (Amanah/PAN, National Trust Party)
AMP	Association of Muslim Professionals
AWARE	Association of Women for Action and Research
Bayan	Bagong Alyansang Makabayan (New Patriotic Alliance)
Bersih	Gabungan Philihantaya Bersih dan Adil (Coalition for Clean and Fair Elections)
BN	Barisan Nasional (National Front)
BS	Barisan Sosialis (Socialist Front)
BUB	bottom-up budgeting
CCT	conditional cash transfer
CDAC	Chinese Development Assistance Council
CDD	community-driven development
CEAC	Community Empowerment and Activity Cycle
CGG	Coalition for Good Governance
CODE-NGO	Caucus of Development Non-Governmental Organizations
Comelec	Commission on Elections
ConCom	Constitutional Commission
CONPAC	Coalition of Non-Governmental Organisations and Professional Appointed Councilors
CPP	Communist Party of the Philippines
CSO	civil society organization
DAP	Democratic Action Party
DBM	Department of Budget and Management
DEPAN	Dasar Ekonomi Untuk Pembangunan Negara (Economic Policy for National Development)
DILG	Department of Interior and Local Government
DSWD	Department of Social Welfare and Development
EC	Election Commission
eCP	e-consultation paper
EPU	Economic Planning Unit
ETP	Economic Transformation Program
FB	Facebook

FU	Feedback Unit
Gabriela	General Assembly Binding Women for Integrity, Equality, Leadership, and Action
Gerakan	Parti Gerakan Rakyat Malaysia (Malaysian People's Movement Party)
GLC	government-linked companies
GRC	group representation constituency
GTP	Government Transformation Program
HINDRAF	Hindu Rights Action Front
INCITEGov	International Center for Innovation, Transformation and Excellence in Governance
ISA	Internal Security Act
Kalahi-CIDSS	Kapit-Bisig Laban sa Kahirapan (Linking Arms Against Poverty)—Comprehensive and Integrated Delivery of Social Services
KMU	Kilusang Mayo Uno (May First Movement)
LGU	Local Government Unit
LPRAP	Local Poverty Reduction Action Plan
LPRAT	Local Poverty Reduction Action Team
MCA	Malaysian Chinese Association
MIC	Malayan Indian Congress
MOP	mode of participation
MP	member of parliament
NAPC	National Anti-Poverty Commission
NCMPs	non-constituency member/s of parliament
ND	National Democratic
NEAC	National Economic Advisory Council
NECC (I & II)	National Economic Consultative Council
NEM	New Economic Model
NEP	New Economic Policy
NGO	nongovernmental organization
NKRAs	National Key Result Areas
NMP	nominated members of parliament
NSS	Nature Society of Singapore
NTUC	National Trades Union Congress
1MDB	One Malaysia Development Bank
OSC	Our Singapore Conversation
PAP	People's Action Party
PAS	Parti Islam Se-Malaysia (Pan-Malaysian Islamic Party)
PASC	Public Administration Select Committee

PDAF	Priority Development Assistance Fund
Pemandu	Performance Management and Delivery Unit
PH	Pakatan Harapan (Coalition of Hope)
PKR	Parti Keadilan Rakyat (People's Justice Party)
PLS	Party-List System
PMO	Project Management Office
PO	people's organization
PPBM	Parti Pribumi Berastu Malaysia (Malaysia United Indigenous Party)
PR	Pakatan Rakyat (People's Alliance)
PSC	Parliamentary Select Committee
PSWs	Policy Study Workshops
REACH	Reaching Everyone for Active Citizenry @ Home
RPRATs	Regional Poverty Reduction Action Teams
SBF	Singapore Business Federation
SINDA	Singapore Indian Development Association
SMF	Singapore Manufacturers' Federation
SRI	Strategic Reform Initiatives
SUARAM	Suara Rakyat Malaysia (Voice of the Malaysian People)
TUCP	Trade Union Congress of the Philippines
UMNO	United Malays National Organization
WP	Workers' Party

Acknowledgments

The ambitious scale and nature of this book project required significant resources, made possible by generous funding from the Australian Research Council (ARC) for the Discovery Project "Representation and Political Regimes in Southeast Asia" (DP1093214). I am grateful to the ARC and the anonymous peer referees who strongly endorsed my application. Additional support from Murdoch University was also important and appreciated.

The cooperation of an extensive range of interviewees involved in designing, supporting, or opposing different forms of political participation and/or representation in Singapore, the Philippines, and Malaysia also provided crucial insights. I sincerely thank them for their contributions. The book benefited too from an array of colleagues and other academics whom I engaged with on the project, or who supported it indirectly, at some point. Especially important were Kanishka Jayasuriya, Richard Robison, Kevin Hewison, Jane Hutchison, Caroline Hughes, Khoo Boo Teik, Lee Jones, Vedi Hadiz, Chua Beng-Huat, Jeffrey Wilson, Nicole Curato, and Shahar Hameiri. Thanks as well to Kelly Gerard, Dani Arlow, and Charlotte Pham for excellent research assistance at different stages, and to Michelle Hackett for the same over a longer period. Sia Kozlowski's outstanding administrative support at the Asia Research Centre was also appreciated.

I am grateful to Cornell University Press's anonymous referees, who made numerous suggestions that were acted on to enhance the manuscript. A special thanks to Roger Haydon for his expert guidance and advice in the processes leading to this book's publication—what a pleasure to work with him and the production team at Cornell University Press.

Throughout the challenges of researching and writing this book, it was Jane Tarrant who suffered most from my obsession with "struggles over political representation" and who also remained my most important supporter. I cannot thank her enough.

PARTICIPATION WITHOUT DEMOCRACY

STRUGGLES OVER POLITICAL REPRESENTATION

In this book, two simple propositions are made. First, the development of market capitalism with its deepening inequalities and its disruption of established patterns of social power and interest generates new political challenges for both entrenched elites and those at the political margins. Second, the struggles for power unleashed within these processes do not simply take the form either of elites ramping up the instruments of authoritarian control or of broader populations seeking to enforce and to extend existing models of representative democracy. Rather, both elites and their opponents are moving beyond these institutional paradigms to construct or pursue their own models of participation, representation, and democracy with vastly different objectives in mind. For many entrenched elites, these initiatives are designed as political instruments to enforce and consolidate deepening concentrations of power and wealth and to domesticate opposition. For those on the margins of power, they are intended as the political vehicles for these concentrations to be dismantled.

This study examines the central paradox in this general institutional recalibration of politics; namely, that expanded political representation—in both its democratic and nondemocratic forms—is serving more to constrain political contestation than enhance it. It will refer specifically to Southeast Asia, where these broad processes have been an important aspect of recent institutional change. Here, it is argued, structures of increased political participation have tended to intensify political fragmentation among anti-elite forces, militating against broad reformist coalitions. Ideologies favoring a depoliticization of conflicts either emanating from

1

the uneven effects of capitalist development or compounded by them have also been institutionalized.

The Study's Wider Significance

Southeast Asia presents as an excellent locus for this study not because it is distinctive or different. On the contrary, it can serve as a theoretical laboratory for understanding dynamics between capitalist development and political regimes in general. These dynamics are not just shaping conflicts in Southeast Asia but across the globe. Political and social crises linked to the effects of capitalist development are being played out in the populist politics that have characterized Donald Trump's controversial presidential victory in the United States and in the majority support in Britain to withdraw from the European Union. They are also at the heart of the rise over recent decades of right-wing anti-immigration populist parties in Europe and left-wing redistributive populist movements in Latin America, the anti-globalization Occupy Wall Street movement in the United States, and equivalents elsewhere following the global financial crisis of 2007–2008.

Analysts identify a "hollowing out" or diminishing of democracy in Western Europe (Hay 2007; Mair 2013; Streeck 2014) and a fundamental "disconnect" in the United States between an unrepresentative political class and citizens (Fiorina and Abrams 2011). Meanwhile, delayed but sweeping capitalist transformations elsewhere have failed to generate the democratization anticipated. Indeed, capitalism and authoritarianism in China and Russia, among other places, have become a demonstrably viable combination for the foreseeable future.

In an analysis encompassing both established liberal democracies of advanced capitalist societies and those in Spain, Brazil, and Turkey, where capitalist development and democracy have more recently combined, Tormey (2015) provocatively hypothesized the "end of representative politics." It is argued in this book, however, that the emergence of new nondemocratic forms of representation as a mechanism for narrowing the space for political contestation is at least as significant as, if not more than, the bypassing of representation altogether.

Across a wide range of democratic and authoritarian regimes around the world there has been a proliferation of diverse new forms of political participation and assorted exhortations about "active citizenship," "empowerment," "participatory democracy," and "delegative democracy." However, meanings and purposes attached to these concepts vary, as competing forces struggle over the extent and nature of permissible political conflict through these new institutions. Different ideologies of political representation are integral to the aims, strategies, and outcomes between contending forces.

The global rise of participatory budgeting over recent decades is emblematic of this struggle. In various ways, this has created opportunities for citizen involvement in decisions about how public budgets are spent. This includes in established liberal democracies such as in the United Kingdom, the United States, Canada, France, and Germany, as well as in more recent democracies and postauthoritarian societies such as Brazil, Argentina, Indonesia, and the Philippines, and even in authoritarian regimes such as China, Mozambique, and Albania. However, who can participate in these deliberations, how, and on what particular questions about the budget are contested and/or tightly controlled matters within these countries.

The same applies to myriad other creative—often distinctive—initiatives in public policy consultation or feedback involving popular forces and/or technical experts outside of government. In the process, democratic representation can either be bolstered, introduced, or substituted with nondemocratic alternatives.

Populism's recent resurgence has exposed the limits of many new forms of public political participation to contain conflict. It has also intensified unresolved normative contention over appropriate political participation and representation in complex, globalized capitalist market systems, and their increasingly unequal material and social outcomes. Recent radical institutional reform prescriptions from egalitarian, elitist, and other worldviews highlight this.

In *Against Elections*, van Reybrouck (2016) attributes widespread political resentment, cynicism, and/or disinterest among citizens to the dominance of powerful elite interests over electoral politics and institutions of representative democracy. Van Reybrouck's solution lies in a return to the principles of Athenian participatory democracy to ensure direct and meaningful popular power. By contrast, in *Against Democracy*, Brennan (2016) advocates the introduction of a structured epistocracy to restrict the influence of what he sees as ignorant and irrational voters. His critique of democracy has partial resonances with the meritocratic elitism championed by former Singapore prime minister Lee Kuan Yew, which has long enjoyed some appeal in the West from varying interests and technocratic and conservative ideological perspectives (Rodan 1996b; Micklethwait 2011).

Meanwhile, libertarians have seized on populism and the concerns underlying it, their solution being to radically shrink the ambit of state authority to make government—and democracy—less relevant to individual goals or decision making. This is especially evident in the United States, where the ideas and strategies of the Heritage Foundation think tank have been influential. Trump appointments to the executive, statutory bodies, his economic advisory councils, and his budget reflect this (T. Anderson 2017). This influence should not be overstated, however, since it is mediated by the complex and contradictory coalitional interests—including those aligned with economic nationalism—surrounding the Trump administration. Indeed, in August 2017, Trump dissolved two advisory business councils—the Strategic and Policy Forum and the White House Manufacturing Jobs Initiative—after seven corporate leaders resigned in protest over the president's failure to condemn white supremacists involved in a violent demonstration at Charlottesville that month (Jacobs 2017).

This book is intended therefore as a contribution to analysis of a general phenomenon where elites and popular forces alike are searching for new institutional solutions to new political problems. It draws on examples from Southeast Asia, where innovative forms of political participation and representation are being generated both to serve consolidation of power and to break open the doors of privilege. This study looks in particular at three specific forms or models of this process.

In the first, technocratic elites seek to politically absorb and contain increasingly diverse social forces so as to contain independent civil society. Here, Singapore has led the way in the most extensive and creative formal and informal initiatives in state-controlled avenues for increased political participation and public policy feedback.

In a second model, perhaps best illustrated in the case of the Philippines, powerful private oligarchs struggle with both technocratic and more popular reform forces in the battle to reconstruct democracy following the authoritarian phase under Ferdinand Marcos. The latter variously look to local-level community participation, party lists for congressional elections, and populist leaders to transcend the limitations of existing elite rule—including authoritarian populists such as President Rodrigo Duterte.

Yet it is in another model, Malaysia, where the struggle over political institutions is most polarized and elite options most constrained. The continued centrality of race, ethnicity, and religion to rationalizing authoritarian elite rule limits the scope for innovative state-based initiatives in popular political participation. Instead, direct political participation through independent civil society activism and street protests demanding reform to electoral institutions has escalated.

Limits of Existing Theory

Of course, this book's central propositions fly in the face of entrenched theories that link democratization with a deepening of market capitalism or explain seeming diversions as aberrations and hybrid regime political systems. However, it is argued here that this presumed link is not so clear. Capitalism may mature and flourish in a varied range of political institutions—including those that are authoritarian in nature. Nor, it is argued, do democratic or representative institutions naturally serve the values or goals of equality and accountability. These institutions take many and varied forms and can just as easily be the instruments of oligarchy and despotism (see Robison and Hadiz 2004).

To be sure, since Huntington's (1991) influential thesis on a "third wave" of democratizations accompanying capitalist globalization, there has been a reassessment of the pace, scale, and prospects of such transitions. However, it is one thing to declare the end of the democratic transitions paradigm—a declaration grounded in various conscious and unconscious assumptions about how liberal democracy constitutes "real" and "natural" political change—as Carothers (2002) did a decade and a half ago. It is quite another thing to develop an adequate theoretical and conceptual framework to better identify, understand, and explain regime diversity—especially the emergence of various new forms of political representation.

There has been no more influential concept in trying to grapple with the reality of regime diversity at odds with earlier modernization theory than that of the "hybrid regime," understood as a mixture of authoritarian and democratic elements (Case 1996, 2002; Levitsky and Way 2002, 2010; Schedler 2002, 2006; Ottaway 2003; Croissant and Merkel 2004; Merkel 2004). However, here the influence of the transition paradigm persists through evaluation of predominantly formal institutions against liberal democratic ideal types. This also diverts analysis from how wider political economy relationships and conflicts concerning the ownership, control, and distribution of resources help shape institutions.

A major limitation of the hybrid regime approach is that we learn much about what these regimes *do not* do, but much less about what they actually *do*. By contrast, this book poses more fundamental and open questions than those preoccupying hybrid regime theorists, namely: What forms of political participation and associated representation are emerging, why, and what does this mean for regime directions? Integral to such inquiry are the questions of who promotes, supports, or opposes specific initiatives in, or reforms to, political representation and why. We need to understand particularly the significance of new forms and ideologies of representation for the ways that political regimes set the boundaries of institutionalized conflict.

Precisely because institutions structure political participation, they invariably privilege some interests and conflicts over others (Schattschneider 1975; Mair 1997). This includes whether independent collective organizations are incorporated or bypassed in favor of attempts to promote more individualized and/or seemingly less politicized forms of group representation. Indeed, what is fundamentally at stake everywhere in struggles over institutions of political participation and representation is not the democratic integrity or functionality of political institutions per se. It is instead which interests these institutions serve.

A New Approach

The distinctive theoretical approach of this book conceptualizes political regimes as comprising modes of participation (MOPs) shaped by the following fundamental interrelated dynamics: social conflicts over power and the interest coalitions that form around them under capitalist development; the institutional manifestations of these struggles as contending forces variously attempt to contain or expand the scope for legitimate political conflict; and the mediating influence of ideology shaping the conduct and outcomes of these struggles.

In sharp contrast with liberal pluralist understandings, the MOP framework views political institutions within the context of a wider exercise of state power inseparable from deeply rooted social conflicts. These conflicts of course vary in nature and intensity across and within countries. However, the framework emphasizes that tensions over, and coalitions of interest attached to, historically specific forms of capitalist development are pivotal in struggles over participation and representation. We cannot understand which conflicts emerge as most contentious, nor the key battle grounds over institutional and ideological responses to them, without this analytical emphasis.

Therefore, the MOP framework inquires into how and why institutional structures and ideologies shape the way different actors and conflicts are included or excluded from parliamentary and extraparliamentary politics. These modes condition who gets what, when, and how—the definitive questions of politics everywhere, according to Lasswell (1936). They are pivotal to whether and how conflict over material inequalities, corruption, environmental degradation, or human rights abuses, for example, is addressed, contained, or compounded. The MOP framework particularly highlights the rise of new state-sponsored or state-controlled modes that have emerged in both democratic and authoritarian regimes, and their fundamental importance to influencing these different possible outcomes (Jayasuriya and Rodan 2007).

An especially original aspect of the MOP framework developed here is the introduction of two concepts of nondemocratic ideologies—consultative and particularist—alongside more established categories of democratic and populist ideologies. Consultative ideologies are imbued with a technocratic, apolitical notion of participation as problem solving, and eschew political competition. Particularist ideologies emphasize the rights to representation of discrete identities and communities based on ethnicity, race, religion, geography, gender, and culture. These ideologies loom large in elite strategies to foster depoliticization and the political fragmentation of their critics and opponents. Typically, the sorts of institutions that these two ideologies give rise to eschew independent class-based organizations, such as independent trade unions, or seek to dilute class conflict by fostering different bases of political representation, for example with region-based identities.

Consultative ideologies principally provide support for a wide range of state-based or state-sponsored advisory and public policy feedback bodies as well as local level participatory institutions established in conjunction with international aid agencies to address problems of social and economic development. These ideologies have a remarkably wide appeal and tactical political utility. Technocratic authoritarians, liberals, and leftist radicals alike have either embraced or sought to exploit consultative ideologies to reproduce or recast the institutional limits to political contests.

This book provides detailed analyses of these ideological strategies and con-tests within Southeast Asia to demonstrate the general analytical power of the MOP framework. Comparable contests over institutions for participatory budgeting and other feedback mechanisms occur across regions and regimes around the world. Local strategic partnerships in the United Kingdom, for example, routinely incorporate business and community activists, local agencies, and voluntary organ-izations in public service delivery consultations. Initiatives in public policy consul-tation can also take a concentrated one-off form. The 2008 two-day 2020 Summit in Australia under Prime Minister Kevin Rudd is such an example, attracting a mix of business leaders, experts, and prominent public figures—including actors Kate Blanchett and Hugh Jackman—to advise on policy challenges.

Particularist ideologies have been important in rationalizing the incorporation into parliamentary institutions of assorted discrete ethnic, religious, and other groups, both through elected party-list systems and various forms of appointed membership of parliament. Parliamentary seats have been reserved for ethnic minorities or indigenous communities in Croatia, Singapore, Jordan, Western Samoa, Colombia, Pakistan, the Palestinian Authority, New Zealand, Norway, Finland, and Denmark. In Belgium, Canada, Northern Ireland, and the Nether-lands, there is also guaranteed parliamentary representation for regional, linguis-tic, and religious-based interests (Bird 2005; Protsyk 2010; Bird, Saalfeld, and Wüst 2011; Simon 2012).

Particularist ideologies also provide the basis for select inclusion into various public policy consultative institutions, such as those established to maintain reli-gious or ethnic harmony, which can isolate wider social forces from deliberations over the causes and solutions to ethnic and religious friction. No less importantly, these ideologies can be pitted too against institutional initiatives promoted by incumbent elites. Separatist movements, such as Muslim demands for an au-tonomous Bangsamoro region of Mindanao in the Philippines and similar calls by Muslim minorities in southern Thailand, are examples of this.

To be sure, consultative mechanisms or particularist affirmative action can serve as a complement, or an alternative, to democratic representation. Yet, while various new modes of participation may fall short on democratic criteria, this in no way diminishes their importance. They are vitally important precisely because in many instances they are integral to strategies by elites to perpetuate their rule and/ or to intra-elite struggles that shape the boundaries of permissible conflict. These new modes can also have unintended consequences, such as heightened scrutiny of, and pressures on, elite governance strategies, as some forces attempt to exploit official ideologies about opening up politics. Because specific sociopolitical coalitions of interest and ideology vary across models of capitalist development, though, so too do the forms and outcomes of different struggles over representation.

Book Structure and Chapters

There are good reasons for the focus on a selection of countries from Southeast Asia for demonstrating the general explanatory power of the MOP framework. First, the region occupies an important and growing place within the burgeoning hybrid regime literature (see, for example, Morlino, Dressel, and Pelizzo 2011). Second, parliamentary and extraparliamentary political institutions are both understudied and yet to be subjected to sustained comparative analysis in the literature on Southeast Asia. Third, Singapore, the Philippines, and Malaysia have sufficiently different histories and/or political economies to demonstrate the universal applicability of a framework meant to explain the variation in institutions and ideologies of political participation and representation that have emerged and the reasons for that variation.

Methodologically the book examines institutional innovations to provide separate chapters on parliamentary and extraparliamentary institutions for each country and the struggles thereof. Interviews with actors involved in these institutions have been important to many of the analyses. They are often essential for trying to more fully understand who promotes, supports, or opposes specific initiatives in, or reforms to, political participation and why.

Before proceeding with case studies of initiatives in parliamentary and extraparliamentary modes of participation, chapter 1 more fully explains the rationale for, and distinctive elements of, the theoretical approach referred to above and adopted throughout this book. The chapter draws analytical links between social conflicts, political institutions, and the dynamic, contradictory, and socially transformative impacts of capitalism. This is complemented by chapter 2, where the MOP conceptual framework of analysis is detailed and illustrated. It explains the importance of different ideologies of representation—nondemocratic and democratic—to the mediation of struggles over who should be represented, how, and why in parliamentary and extraparliamentary political institutions.

How do we apply these insights to the three countries of this book where there are significant points of intersection and departure in the extent and nature of recourse to new MOPs? In chapter 3 it is explained that in Singapore, the Philippines, and Malaysia legacies of Cold War political repression, reinforced by the impacts of economic globalization, have been conducive to the political fragmentation of social forces seeking political participation. Consequently, strong independent collective organizations and coalitions thereof have been conspicuously absent from formal representative party politics and civil society more generally. To the extent that this vacuum has been filled, it has tended to be by small, single-issue nongovernmental organizations (NGOs) and a plurality of political identities, including in articulation with race, religion, region, and gender. Yet, there are also profoundly important differences to the ways that capitalism is organized and the interests most benefiting from these arrangements. Consequently, there are variations in the nature and intensity of conflicts over the distribution of the benefits and costs of capitalist development in each country. Elite political strategies attempting to contain this conflict through new MOPs, and their effectiveness, also necessarily diverge.

In particular, as specific concerns over rising material and social inequalities have mounted in each country, recourse to and the impact of consultative and particularist institutions and ideologies of representation are far from uniform. Consultative ideologies resonate strongest with the interests of technocratic politico-bureaucrats under state capitalism and authoritarian rule in Singapore, where state-sponsored participation has most proliferated. In the Philippines, private concentrations of wealth and power by capitalist oligarchs enable these interests to exploit electoral institutions and ideologies of representation, sometimes fused with particularist ideological appeals. Yet acute oligarchic political dominance also periodically fuels coalitions of liberal technocratic elites and middle-class NGO activists pursuing governance reform and community participation, variously embracing or tactically exploiting consultative representation ideologies. In Malaysia, particularist ideologies of ethnicity, race, and religion are pivotal to rationalizing a coalition of interests between ethnic Malay political, bureaucratic, and economic elites. The primacy of ethnic Malay political supremacy and related state patronage of a Malay bourgeoisie have rendered technocratic institutions and ideologies of consultative representation much more problematic for the Malaysian political regime.

Nowhere has it been more emphatically demonstrated that capitalist development and authoritarian rule can be viable partners than in Singapore. Yet the partnership has faced challenges and involved creative new elite strategies to contain

conflict. Capitalist development combining economic globalization and state capitalism had, by the 1980s, resulted not just in extended resources and powers of
politico-bureaucrats across economic, social, and political spheres. There was also
significant expansion of the professional middle class. Meanwhile, competitive
pressures on labor and domestic business associated with Singapore's niche in
global manufacturing processes were exposing the limitations of established forms
of political co-option. The People's Action Party (PAP) therefore introduced new
structures and ideologies of consultative representation to reduce the attraction
of opposition parties and to bypass or control independent intermediary organizations in general. This was a project of expanding the political space of the PAP
state, as chapters 4 and 5, respectively, analyze through case studies on the introduction of nominated members of parliament (NMPs) and then on new
mechanisms for policy feedback and suggestions by the public.

Introduced in 1990, Singapore's NMPs are appointed by a parliamentary committee after receiving public nominations meeting specified criteria. The scheme
reflected PAP concerns about rising electoral support for opposition parties, a
pattern that appeared to be subsequently arrested or contained. However, rising
material and social inequalities and questions about the environmental sustainability accompanying capitalist growth would lead to increased opposition electoral support by the turn of the century. NMPs nevertheless remain an integral
and effective part of the PAP's broader and evolving strategy of consolidating
political fragmentation in order to organizationally and ideologically contain
political conflict through consultative representation.

That strategy includes the public policy feedback institution—the Feedback
Unit, which was introduced in 1985 and renamed Reaching Everyone for Active
Citizenry @ Home (REACH) in 2006—providing individuals and selected social
groups opportunities for participation. Following the 2011 election, a new initiative in state-controlled public policy dialogue also emerged—Our Singapore
Conversation (OSC)—in an attempt to bolster the avenues for, and appeal of,
consultative representation. Government policy adjustments to arrest its electoral
drift were depicted by PAP leaders as informed by OSC feedback—not a response to greater voter support for opposition parties. Interpreting a 9.8 percent
swing back to the PAP at the 2015 polls as evidence of the success of these strategies, the PAP has projected more expansive and diverse forms of state-
sponsored and state-controlled public feedback.

In the postauthoritarian Philippines, oligarchic elites have sought not to
consolidate a cohesive and tightly controlled form of state power as technocratic
elites did in Singapore. Their challenge is instead how to blunt reformist forces
critical of informal networks of oligarchic power over state power. The new MOPs

that have emerged, though, are as much sites of struggle *between* reformers of different ideological orientations as they are for attempts to rein in oligarchic powers.

Unlike in Singapore, the introduction in the Philippines of a Party-List System (PLS) of representation in congress involved democratically elected rather than appointed representation. Yet the PLS was, and remains, an institutional initiative for both containing and expanding the extent and scope of permissible conflict under democratic politics: a compromise by elites in the face of popular disenchantment with the rapid reassertion of oligarchic elite power following the collapse of the Marcos administration and authoritarian rule. As chapter 6 explains, elites looked to the PLS to contain the possibility of unpredictable populist alternatives amidst widespread popular concerns about acute poverty and corruption accompanying capitalist development in the Philippines. Moderate and radical reformist forces, by contrast, hoped to eke out some influence within congress to air these concerns. Entrenched elite interests have generally prevailed in this struggle, exploiting the PLS to increase their representation and power in congress. Meanwhile reformist forces have politically divided through multiple small parties and policy foci promoted by the PLS.

The tightened grip of oligarchic power over congress and the limits this places on economic and social reform help explain the emergence of new modes of extraparliamentary participation in the Philippines. Poverty alleviation strategies of the World Bank and other multilateral aid agencies struck a chord particularly with select technocratic reformers in government and elements of the NGO community seeking opportunities for direct participation in development projects. With the 2010 election of Benigno Aquino III as president and the introduction of Bottom-up Budgeting (BUB), this direction was reinforced through popular participation in the selection of publicly funded local government projects to combat corruption. However, chapter 7 demonstrates that BUB supporters differed over which civil society forces should be empowered, how much, and on what issues. Particularly contentious was the extent to which organizations representing workers and peasants and advocating radical reforms were encouraged or excluded from participation. Significantly, one of the first decisions in 2016 under the presidency of Rodrigo Duterte was to abandon BUB. In Duterte's populist ideology, greater store is placed on his direct representation of the poor rather than on the building up of intermediary organizations, whether justified through democratic or consultative ideologies.

Significantly, in struggles over representation in both authoritarian Singapore and in the Philippines, where there is more contested political space, consultative ideologies have been and remain integral to struggles over representation. This is despite the challenge elites face in both regimes of trying to manage or avert unintended consequences from promoting consultative ideologies and institutions of representation. In sharp contrast, though, these technocratic ideologies have not sat comfortably with the interests and racial rationale underlying economic and political regimes in Malaysia. Elites have thus been less adept at depoliticizing conflict through new MOPs. This has been exposed with increased urbanization, rising material inequalities, and intensified public concerns about state corruption accompanying capitalist deepening.

To be sure, Malaysia's Barisan Nasional (BN, National Front) governments have undertaken significant but failed experiments in consultative representation, most notably through the 1989–1990 and 1999–2000 National Economic Consultative Councils (NECCs). The NECCs—the main focus of chapter 8—incorporated a range of party-political, NGO, and civil society organization (CSO) actors to advise the cabinet on major development plans. However, the cabinet acted very selectively on NECC recommendations, eschewing governance reform proposals that could compromise the discretionary powers and patronage systems integral to the political supremacy of the BN lead party, the United Malays National Organization (UMNO), and the promotion of an ethnic Malay bourgeoisie. By the end of the first NECC, popular expectations and hopes for reform through this new mode of participation had diminished. The second NECC confirmed this. Thereafter, the institutional and ideological significance of consultative representation for engaging popular forces was substantially reduced, although it would retain some periodic importance for managing intra-elite conflict over economic governance. Technocratic administrative incorporation of select experts into state policy deliberations would also be explored under President Najib Razak to try and contain wider conflict and structural problems of the capitalist development model, but with no greater success.

The failure of the NECCs increased the likelihood of alternative MOPs emerging to contest the limits of political contestation intended by the BN. This is exactly what transpired, and in such a way that it was doubly threatening for the existing authoritarian regime—as chapter 9 explains. Not only would reformers focus on the need to ensure the democratic integrity of electoral institutions, but mass demonstrations would also become an integral alternative MOP for advancing this agenda. Most alarmingly for the BN, when the independent civil society movement Bersih (Gabungan Philihantaya Bersih dan Adil, Coalition for Clean and Fair Elections) emerged in 2007, it comprised new multiethnic coalitions of BN opponents and critics. There was also a push from various civil society and party political forces for the reintroduction of local government elections, discontinued in 1965 in favor of state-appointed councilors.

Yet both the Bersih movement and the local elections reform coalition contained their own contradictions that made it difficult to forge a sustainable ideological agreement on the purpose and content of democratic political representation reform. Focus on procedural reform to electoral and related institutions could not resolve underlying tensions between liberal emphasis of meritocracy and political liberties on the one hand, and concerns about social and material inequality on the other. In the absence of an alternative social redistributive reform agenda, ethnic Malay support for Bersih, as well as for the reintroduction of local elections, remained vulnerable to the appeal of particularist ideologies and ethnic-based affirmative action policies of the BN government. Consequently, Bersih fractured in 2015 at the very moment that a corruption scandal involving Prime Minister Najib Razak and a state development company generated political crisis and polarization.

Individually and collectively, the case study chapters highlight how the emergence, reproduction, and attempts to change modes of participation within the state can only be understood in relation to wider social conflict over what interests should be advanced or blocked through political institutions. They also show that ideologies of political representation are integral to the struggle between competing social and political forces over containing or expanding the space and nature of conflict permissible within those institutions. In particular, these case studies shed light on how and why a range of nondemocratic institutions and ideologies often enjoy support from various forces—within and beyond elites. These institutions may appear to be dysfunctional from a "quality of democracy" perspective, but certainly not to the forces and interests instigating and/or defending them.

The conclusion returns to the wider applicability beyond Southeast Asia of the MOP framework adopted in this book. This includes its relevance for analyzing struggles over representation in established democracies of early developing capitalist societies and for understanding the rise and significance of populism, which, by definition, is less about reforming or creating political institutions—the particular focus in this study—than about bypassing them.

THEORIZING INSTITUTIONS OF POLITICAL PARTICIPATION AND REPRESENTATION

It is now clear that the expansion of market capitalism has not uniformly produced liberal democracy and its forms of political representation. However, attempts to explain this seeming puzzle have largely failed where they regard this as a problem of transition rather than recognizing that the different and illiberal regime forms that have emerged have their roots in capitalism itself and are its natural products. In other words, regimes that diverge from earlier liberal democratic forms are not just in a process that is stuck, marooned, hijacked, hybridized, or even entering a gray zone. No less misleading is the idea that we are in a formative transitional phase, to be completed once democratic institutions take root and are consolidated.

This chapter elaborates on these points to explain why the various transition theories cannot provide us with the tools to understand what is mistakenly conceived of as a puzzle. Departing from this ascendant paradigm, this chapter offers an alternative account of how to understand divergences among political regimes and their institutions as capitalism has transformed late developing countries. It outlines a distinctive political economy approach and the related modes of participation (MOPs) framework adopted throughout this book.

Southeast Asia offers an ideal focus for demonstrating the pitfalls of the transition paradigm and its derivatives, and the advantages of this MOP framework. As capitalist development has intensified in Southeast Asia, analyses of political institutions in the region have increasingly emphasized how differently these operate from counterparts in established liberal democracies. The concept of hybrid regime has been among the most widely adopted in attempts to characterize and scrutinize this pattern. Yet while use of the concept has helped highlight the democratic shortfalls of many institutions, a comprehensive identification and analysis of nondemocratic parliamentary and extraparliamentary institutions and ideologies has generally eluded hybrid regime analysts. Why hybrid regimes emerged in the first place and how institutions relate to broader social conflicts is also underdeveloped in the prevailing literature.

In this study, by contrast, institutions are viewed as inseparable from the way that state power is generated, reproduced, and conditioned by dynamic conflicts between social forces and interests. The question is: How are institutions harnessed in these power struggles and why? After all, conflict is managed in different institutional ways across regimes, with varying mixes and natures of parliamentary and extraparliamentary institutions involved. This requires explanation, especially as it involves new modes of political participation and representation in struggles over how conflict is institutionally managed in Southeast Asia.

Toward such an explanation, this chapter examines in depth the strengths and weaknesses of the existing literature for understanding political institutions and regime dynamics in what are generally referred to as hybrid and nondemocratic or authoritarian regimes. Thereafter, it elaborates on the MOP framework applied in this study to understand the relationship between political institutions, social structure, and history. This framework is intended to provide for a more decisive break from the democratic transition's problematic, toward more open inquiry into where political regimes are headed and why.

The MOP framework is defined by its emphasis on the following four core interrelated political economy relationships:

1. Capitalism is inherently dynamic and conflict ridden. Interests among elites can change with development, resulting in intra-elite conflicts; the emergence of new social forces and unequal distribution of the rewards and costs of development also lay foundations for new conflicts.
2. These conflicts exert pressures and opportunities for elites and their opponents, respectively seeking to contain or advance conflict over the distribution of power and resources. Adjustments to, and innovations in, political strategies and institutions of participation thus follow.
3. Ensuing struggles over permissible conflict through political participation are mediated by ideologies of political representation and their attempted tactical exploitation.
4. However, different models of capitalism are more or less conducive to the institutionalization and dominance of particular ideologies of representation and MOPs. Ideological mobilizations are variously constrained and facilitated by historically specific coalitions of interest accompanying capitalist development processes.

Ideologies of representation are thus not complementary or supplementary to the MOP—they are integral to it. And the MOP and capitalism are endogenous and mutually conditioning.

It would be tempting to try and extrapolate simple cause-and-effect relationships to explain what sorts of MOPs prevail in what categories of countries. Instead, the power of this framework lies principally in identifying the universal and complex processes shaping political regime directions under capitalist development.

Transition Paradigm's Persistence

Over time, there have been refinements and revisions by theorists expecting a subsequent repeat of the supposed uniform historical link between capitalist development and liberal democracy among early industrializing countries.[1] Initial democratic optimism by modernization theorists starting in the 1950s was tempered by interventions from the mid-1980s that emphasized leadership, tactical, and other factors mediating democratic transitions from authoritarian rule (O'Donnell, Schmitter, and Whitehead 1986). Subsequently, Huntington (1991) reasserted a more classical modernization theory stance, positing a late twentieth-century "third wave" of democratization linked to economic globalization. However, Huntington exaggerated the scale of such transitions, often conflating institutional appearances of electoral democracy with their reality (Doorenspleet 2000; Møller and Skaaning 2013). An exhaustive study by Przeworski et al. (2000) also concluded that economic development does not tend to generate democracies, but democracies were much more likely to survive in wealthy societies. Consequently, in the post–Cold War years, as multiparty elections became even more widespread but "real" democracy seemed still remote, the concept of "hybrid regime" was increasingly harnessed to scrutinize these very institutions.[2]

In early variants of the concept of hybrid regime the emphasis was on trying to highlight adaptive aspects of either democratic or authoritarian regimes. In Diamond's (1989) original use of "semi-democracies" and "pseudo-democracies," for example, the purpose was to identify the emergence of new forms of authoritarian rule. As he argued, "the existence of formally democratic political institutions, such as multiparty electoral competition, masks (often, in part, to legitimate) the reality of authoritarian domination" (xvii–xviii). O'Donnell (1994), by contrast, posited that newly installed regimes in Argentina, Brazil, Peru, Ecuador, Bolivia, South Korea, and the Philippines satisfied Dahl's (1956) definition of polyarchy without necessarily leading to representative democracy. His concept of "delegative democracy" was meant to capture this "new species" of democracy (O'Donnell 1994, 60).[3]

Subsequently, attempts to further characterize and distinguish hybrid regimes took many and varied directions. In Zakaria's (1997, 2003) characterization of "illiberal democracy," he noted a post–Cold War expansion of regimes combining elections and authoritarianism, involving varying degrees of limits on political competition (Zakaria 2003, 99). Levitsky and Way (2002, 52) also submitted "competitive authoritarianism" as a distinctive form of hybrid regime, appearing to concede a little more contentious political space than under illiberal democracy. Here "democratic institutions are widely viewed as the principal means of obtaining and exercising political authority" (52). However, formal rules of electoral competition are considered so systematically violated that the regime "fails to meet conventional minimum standards for democracy," unlike in O'Donnell's delegative democracy (Levitsky and Way 2002, 52, 53).[4]

Significantly, the dynamics assumed by transition theorists shaping democratic prospects evolved too. Alongside the earlier emphasis on the importance of strategies and bargains between elites (O'Donnell, Schmitter, and Whitehead 1986), the role of institutions assumed increased attention. Zakaria (1997, 40), for instance, argued that the prospects of transition from hybrid to "genuine democracy" rested on the institutionalization of constitutional liberalism to preserve liberty and law in the first instance (28). Linz (1997, 408) made a related but broader argument about the centrality of institutions to democratic consolidation, observing that "even bad democracies are better than authoritarian rule since we can assume that they may undergo processes of re-equilibration, and with improved conditions and leadership may become fully consolidated." This assumed that agency could triumph over structure to craft the requisite institutions for similar forms of representative democracy as had historically emerged in Western Europe, Britain, and North America (Robison and Hadiz 2004, 258).

Paradoxically, though, the volume and variety of applications of the concept of hybrid regime only escalated following Carothers's (2002) declaration that the transition paradigm was dead.[5] He observed that many countries thought to be in a process of democratic transition had entered a "gray zone" that could be an indefinite regime condition (9–11). Certainly his acknowledgment of the possibility of sustainable alternatives to liberal democracy underlined the importance of conceptually distinguishing and explaining nondemocratic institutions. However, Carothers did not outline the beginnings of a new framework to that end, nor submit a new theorization of the relationship between capitalist development and political institutions. Consequently, the requisite departures from transition theory assumptions and genuine conceptual breakthroughs needed to meet the challenge set by Carothers failed to emerge from hybrid regime theorists.

Nomenclature adopted in characterizations of hybrid regimes highlights how focus remains on accounting for what regimes are *not* (namely, not quite democracies), against an idealized benchmark. This includes "partial democracies" (N. Robinson 2003; Epstein et al. 2006; Zinecker 2009), "pseudo-democracies" (Volpi 2004), "semi-democracies" (Rich 2002), "defective democracies" (Croissant and Merkel 2004; Merkel 2004; Boggards 2009), "deviant democracies" (Seeberg 2014), "illiberal democracies" (Zakaria 2003), "limited democracies" (Haynes 2001), "competitive authoritarianism" (Levitsky and Way 2002, 2010), "electoral authoritarianism" (Diamond 2002), and "semi-authoritarianism" (Ottaway 2003). In particular, terms like "defective," "deviant," "semi," and "pseudo" democracy can only make sense in relation to a fully democratic ideal type (Rodan and Jayasuriya 2012, 178). Indeed, many hybrid regime analyses embrace this benchmark in quality of democracy evaluations of political institutions (Beetham 2004), including detailed descriptions and typologies of hybrid regime variants (Morlino 2004; Roberts 2005).

This normative concern with democracy is understandable and it has led in many cases to analyses powerfully highlighting the exploitation by elites of formally democratic institutions. Analytical sophistication also continues to build in this quality of democracy literature, notably by contributions emphasizing the multidimensional, hence often uneven, levels of "democratic qualities" among various institutions within a single political regime (Morlino, Dressel, and Pelizzo 2011; Morlino 2012).[6] Nevertheless, analytical priority is still given to the question of whether there has been, or can be, genuine democratic transition. Yet to fully take up the challenge inferred by Carothers's (2002) pronouncement, different and more open questions demand attention: What is the nature and direction of political institutions and why?

Among other things, therefore, we should be looking to literature taking the durability of authoritarian regimes more seriously. However, while there are impressive works from varying theoretical perspectives doing just that, the insights they offer are uneven and partial with regard to overcoming problems described above pertaining to the popular use of the hybrid regime concept.

Rational choice institutionalist analyses, for example, have not abandoned but reinforced transition theory assumptions about the analytical primacy attached to the strategic choices of incumbent elites (see Geddes 2006; Gandhi and Przeworski 2007; Gandhi 2008). Meanwhile, Brownlee's (2007, 2008) historical institutionalist approach illuminates various social structural and historical factors conditioning the options available to incumbent elites in institutional strategies. Yet he shares with most of the former authors an analytical focus on a comparatively narrow range of political institutions—political parties and elections.[7]

This general analytical bias toward formal political institutions is explained by Gandhi (2008, 1) on the basis that "the institutional inventiveness of dictators is most apparent when they govern with nominally democratic institutions, such as legislatures and political parties," while Brownlee (2007, 42) asserted that "elections are the autocrat's latest fashion."[8] Undoubtedly, the harnessing of elections and parties by elites in strategies of political co-option is of major importance to understanding regime directions, but whether this is the only fashion—or even the most important or innovative fashion—is open to question. Moreover, Gandhi's (2008, xxiv) observation that legislatures and parties within authoritarian regimes offer "little in the way of representation and accountability to participants and ordinary citizens" is arrived at without consideration or analysis of nondemocratic institutions and ideologies on their own terms.

In short, these authors are motivated by an important but different set of questions from this book. Principally they want to explain why authoritarian leaders bother with elections and whether or not these institutions render authoritarian regimes more stable. This leaves other critical questions unexplored.

Indeed, alternatives to opposition parties and electoral competition have been emerging in the political strategies of elites in authoritarian and postauthoritarian regimes—often accompanied by nondemocratic ideologies of representation and accountability.[9] To differing degrees these innovations can be observed from the world's most populous authoritarian regime, China, to one of the world's least populous, in Singapore, as well as among diverse regimes and capitalist transformation experiences in Southeast Asia, Latin America, and Africa.

Such innovations are many and varied in recent decades, as illustrated by the following examples. In China, this has included public hearings and comment procedures (Horsley 2006); deliberative participatory budgeting and other public policy consultative mechanisms (Leib and He 2006; Fishkin et al. 2010; He 2014, 2015; Almén 2016; Yan and Xin 2016); homeowners' action groups (Cai 2005); and other forms of institutionalized contention (Perry and Goldman 2007). In Singapore, the ruling party introduced unelected members of parliament to try and limit the appeal of elected opposition representatives (Rodan 2009). Prior to the Arab Spring, a range of unelected public policy consultative councils were established in Bahrain, Oman, Qatar, Saudi Arabia, and the United Arab Emirates (Bensahel 2004). Under a 250-member Citizens' Assembly in Ecuador, networks of social organizations and sectoral councils were also incorporated into government economic policy deliberations (Youngs 2015), while varying forms of public participation and consultation in budget planning and decision making have also been introduced in Brazil, the Philippines, Mozambique, and Kenya (Wampler

2007; Buur 2009; Dressel 2012; *Business Daily* 2015). In Peru, the Roundtable for the Fight against Poverty also incorporated religious and other nongovernmental organizations and civil society groups into public policy coordination strategies (McNulty 2011).

Appreciation of the importance of extraparliamentary innovations is most evident in literature over the last decade focusing on political participation in Latin America outside, or in articulation with, formal electoral institutions. These studies have examined diverse initiatives to promote popular participation by governments in Brazil, Venezuela, Uruguay, Bolivia, Ecuador, Mexico, and Peru—including the introduction of grassroots participatory budgeting, community councils for local development projects, and assorted government policy advisory bodies (Selee and Peruzzotti 2009; Cameron and Sharpe 2010, 2012; McNulty 2011; Avritzer 2013; Balderacchi 2016).

This literature is especially valuable in highlighting the contested meaning of democracy and the institutions for achieving it, not least as this involves the relationship between participatory and formal representative democracy (Selee and Peruzzotti 2009; Houtzager and Lavalle 2010; Baiocchi, Heller, and Silva 2011; Avritzer 2013). Studies of participatory budgeting in particular acknowledge the importance of struggles over the design of such informal political institutions for political regime directions (see Goldfrank and Schneider 2006; Wampler 2007). Nevertheless, the break with the transition paradigm is arguably incomplete, since analytical emphasis is still on trying to understand the nature and preconditions for improving the "quality of democracy" (Cameron and Sharpe 2012, 17).[10]

Clearly the transition paradigm continues to exert a pervasive influence within and beyond the hybrid regime literature, affecting the sorts of questions asked about political institutions and influencing which institutions are privileged in those inquiries. A framework for understanding the emergence and significance of political institutions for regime directions thus needs not just to transcend prevailing conceptual dependence on a linear authoritarian-democratic continuum and to encompass parliamentary and extraparliamentary institutions. It also requires greater acknowledgment that institutions have social foundations. Explicit or implicit institutional design prescriptions to enhance or promote democracy (see, for example, N. Robinson 2003; Henderson 2004; Reilly 2007) reflect an overly technical conception of institutions, raising expectations that, with requisite understanding and political will, elites can suitably adjust institutions. Why hybrid regimes emerged in the first place and how institutions relate to broader social conflicts are generally not part of these analyses.

Social Conflict and Political Institutions

In contrast with much of the hybrid regime literature, the question to be asked about institutions is not whether they function according to some technical or idealized conceptions of institutions, but for whom they function and why. This necessitates explaining the emergence of institutions, the interests they serve, and how. More precisely, it means understanding political institutions as the embodiment of deeply rooted conflict over social and economic power, from which they should be analytically inseparable. Institutions are created to structure and limit the permissible bounds of participation and representation in deliberations and decisions concerning that social and economic power. As such, they are themselves sites of dynamic social and political conflict.

The particular theoretical approach adopted here in analyzing institutions has been variously referred to as a social conflict approach (Rodan, Hewison, and Robison 1997, 2001, 2006), a social foundations approach (Rodan and Jayasuriya 2012), and the Murdoch School of political economy (Rasiah and Schmidt 2010, 16; Jones 2014; Pepinsky 2014).[11] This approach occupies a distinctive place among attempts to situate institutions in their social and historical contexts. It includes, but goes beyond, the notion that political institutions are affected by social, structural, and historical factors, an insight that has been the basis of a range of previous sophisticated and illuminating studies (see Capoccia and Ziblatt 2010; Slater and Simmons 2010; Møller 2013).

To be sure, there are approaches within both the hybrid and broader regimes literature fruitfully examining relationships between institutions, social structure, and history (see, for example, Ottaway 2003; Hawthorne 2004; Carothers 2006; Brownlee 2008; Levitsky and Way 2010, 321; Slater 2010). Nevertheless, political institutions in these works are ultimately viewed as instruments to elevate political engagement beyond societal or intraparty conflict, thereby regularizing and shaping political competition and/or sustaining the functionality of elite-dominated institutions (Rodan and Jayasuriya 2012; Pepinsky 2014). In essence, and by contrast, institutions are viewed here as inseparable from social conflict and related struggles over state power shaping access to, and control over, resources. The approach is consistent with Sangmpam's (2007, 201) call for nothing less than analytically subordinating institutions to "society-rooted politics, the preeminent explanatory variable." From a similar perspective, Poulantzas (1974, 63) explained: "Institutions do not determine social antagonisms: it is the class struggle which governs the modifications in the State apparatuses."

In particular, this approach gives special emphasis to dynamic political economy relations—notably capitalist development—in analyzing social conflicts and associated coalitions of social and political forces struggling over state power and related political institutions. This is not to suggest that social conflicts are limited to contests between different social classes and fractions thereof, nor to deny that ethnic, religious, and other identities with precapitalist roots continue to form the basis of important political struggles over state power. However, the conditions under which these conflicts play out, and the coalitions that are possible in the process, are fundamentally influenced by the transformative and contradictory nature of capitalist development (Poulantzas 1973; Jessop 1982, 1983a, 1983c, 1990).

Concepts of "state" and "state power" are central to this approach, but what do they mean? The state in this approach is "an amalgam of social, political, ideological and economic elements organized in a particular manner. In this sense, the state is not so much a set of functions or a group of actors, as an expression of power" (Hewison, Rodan, and Robison 1993, 4). This theoretical position aligns with Jessop (1983b, 273) who argues that "the state is not a real subject that exercises power, [but] state power certainly exists." State power refers to a complex and dynamic set of social relationships, at all times influencing the use of the state apparatus, namely the prevailing institutional forms of state power including political institutions (Hewison, Rodan, and Robison 1993, 4–5).[12]

Importantly, as Jessop (2008, 44) observes, the precise form that these institutions take influences which particular interests are advanced or harmed through the exercise of state power. Institutions are *strategically selective* in that they are more open to certain actors, rather than actors in general, in pursing particular strategies. Although this process broadly favors capitalist class interests, dynamics in the political economy can generate "conjunctural opportunities" for other forces in a given historical period. This has implications for strategic political calculations of contending and aligning forces within and beyond the state. This includes calculations by different elements of the capitalist classes competing with each other over the exercise of state powers, as well as calculations by social and political forces seeking to exploit intra-elite friction for their own ends. State powers—"inscribed in particular institutions and agencies" (Jessop 2008, 37)— are thus always "activated through the agency of definite political forces in specific conjunctures" (37). That agency can involve elite strategies of political management of conflict through institutions of participation and related ideologies of representation.

Jessop's theorization of the state offers a broader framework through which Schattschneider's (1975) important insight about the significance of institutional forms for the scope and nature of permissible political conflict can be further developed. Schattschneider was particularly concerned with key roles afforded to a plurality of pressure groups in the United States at the expense of broad-based political parties and the mobilization of majorities. The consequence was the privileging of some conflicts over others, with especially deleterious effects for the representation of the weak and poor. Schattschneider observed that any political system attempting to exploit all community tensions "would be blown to bits" (64). However, the selection that transpires reflects "the dominance of some conflicts and the subordination of others" (64–65). Indeed, the way that institutions shape the exploitation, use, and suppression of specific conflicts is fundamental to political strategy: "He who determines what politics is about runs the country, because the definition of the alternatives is the choice of conflicts, and the choice of conflicts allocates power" (66).[13]

The struggle over the permissible bounds of political conflict, though, has ideological and institutional dimensions. With particular reference to the institutionalization of dominant ideologies, Gramsci (1971) emphasized the artificial distinction between state and civil society under capitalism, attempting to highlight how patterned power differentials between different social classes were reinforced across these seemingly separate spheres. Gramsci clearly recognized that ideological positions were not simply determined by social class. Civil society constituted a realm within which ideas could be fiercely contended, the results of which were fundamental to political rule. Yet class structures fundamentally shape the conflicts and limits around which prospective coalitions between groups form in this battle of ideas. As Gramsci observed (12), ideologies have profound implications for whether or not persistent unequal social, political, and economic relationships are subject to scrutiny and potential political mobilization.

None of the above diminishes the significance of political institutions for shaping political behavior, but it attributes analytical primacy to the coalitions of power underpinning the emergence of institutions and shaping the way they operate in practice.[14] Furthermore, this approach incorporates a particular political economy perspective within which the structural power relations and social conflicts and contradictions of capitalist development are central to understanding these coalitional dynamics. As Hadiz and Robison (2013, 41) contend, the core political economy task "is to explain the forces and interests that are historically thrown up in the evolution of capitalism and how conflicts between these shape economic and political life and the institutions in which they operate."[15]

A strength of this approach is that its focus on the inherently dynamic and conflict-ridden nature of capitalist development enables it to explain the pressures for political—including institutional—change. The uneven social, material, and environmental effects of capitalist development generate potential opportunities for challenges to the existing social and political order. However, prevailing structural relations of power also enhance and constrain different groups and interests in contests over the shape of institutions in any address of these pressures. Institutions are best understood, then, as sites of conflict over whether changes to the prevailing social and political order are accommodated, deflected, or obstructed. Crucially, institutional change can be pivotal to each of these three scenarios, but the dominance of the transition paradigm has thus far limited the exploration of which option prevails and why.

Importantly, there are significant variations in both the stages of capitalist development across countries and in the precise organizational form capitalism takes. In Southeast Asia, for example, industrial capitalist transformations are more advanced in Singapore and Malaysia than in Burma or Cambodia. Among earlier industrializers, contrasting forms of and rationales for state capitalism in Singapore and Malaysia have accompanied the embrace of private global capitalism. Elsewhere, in the Philippines and Indonesia, by contrast, private oligarchic capitalism has been more pronounced than state capitalism.

These and other variations necessarily affect, and reflect, the complexion of the social forces, the nature of social conflicts, and hence the coalitions seeking to influence how state power is exercised, including through political institutions. In all cases, though, institutions are specific sites of conflict—and the attempted containment thereof—in wider struggles between sociopolitical coalitions with competing interests in how political participation and representation are structured and ideologically rationalized. Yet the general historical context of capitalist development in Southeast Asia also has profound significance for the patterns of struggle over state power and political institutions in the region.

Capitalist industrialization in late developing countries has occurred in a context of advanced economic globalization, quite unlike the conditions associated with earlier industrialization in established liberal democracies. Complex divisions of labor have altered the relative structural power of capital and labor, greatly reducing labor's capacity for effective collective organization. Crucially, the precise way that these factors play out is mediated by the specific configuration of interests—especially class interests—in any given context.

Robison (1986) broke new theoretical ground in applying this insight in *Indonesia: The Rise of Capital* to contradict democratic optimism about the impact of capitalist development in Southeast Asia. Coalitions of interest between politico-bureaucrats, entrepreneurial generals, and ethnic-Chinese crony capitalists, he explained, served to constrain both liberal economics and democratic politics during Suharto's reign. A similar approach by Robison and Hadiz (2004) revealed how prevailing oligarchs' interests were reconstituted through new economic and political institutions in postauthoritarian Indonesia.

Bellin (2000, 178) amplified this insight in a broader comparative analysis, arguing that "the peculiar conditions of late development often make capital and labor much more ambivalent about democratization than was the case for their counterparts among earlier industrializers." They are "contingent democrats," precisely because they are "consistent defenders of their material interests," and regime preferences by these class forces are mediated accordingly (179).

Under late development, Bellin argued that both capital and labor have become more dependent on the state. For the former, this is to contain or block more expansive popular notions and expectations of democracy than pertained during earlier democratizations in Europe. For the latter, amidst greater global capital mobility, the state's potential importance to realizing or protecting interests has intensified (179). Yet, as her examinations of Korea, Indonesia, Mexico, Saudi Arabia, Egypt, Tunisia, Brazil, and Zambia revealed, the specific material interests of capital and/or labor were being progressed through democratic regimes in some cases, while in other instances authoritarian regimes were calculated to be more useful.

The historical context of late development also includes the impacts of the Cold War. In Southeast Asia—as in other parts of the Global South—independent trade unions and civil society organizations (CSOs) more generally were the targets of concerted state suppression and worse during the Cold War, not least in Western-supported authoritarian regimes charting capitalist paths in Indonesia, Malaysia, Singapore, the Philippines, and Thailand (Shalom 1986; Munro-Kua 1996, 100–104; Hutchison and Brown 2001; La Botz 2001, 168–69; Easter 2005; Deyo 2006; Lau 2012; Gills and Gray 2013, 109). Meanwhile, in the postcolonial context, independent organizations on the other side of this ideological war, such as in Vietnam and Cambodia, were also brutally crushed or obstructed (Kiernan and Boua 1982; Edwards and Phan 2008, 199–202).

This has left an enduring political legacy. Independent intermediary political organizations in general, and independent labor organizations in particular, never recovered or developed in Southeast Asia to anything remotely comparable to what characterized the experience of industrialization and social democracy in Western Europe (Rodan and Jayasuriya 2009). As Luebbert (1991) observes of Western Europe, "The institutions of the modern state, of the economy, and of the party system were the projects of mass movements; they were institutions that reflected the balance of interests those movements contained" (314; also see Eley 2002). By contrast, political institutions in Southeast Asia have emerged, and are refined and contested, in a structural context unfavorable to independent—especially class-based—intermediary organizations seeking to represent social forces challenging elite power, interests, and ideologies (Hewison and Rodan 1994, 2012; Törnquist 2009). Generally, where independent civil society organizations have emerged in Southeast Asia, they do not articulate with formal political institutions such as political parties (Tomsa and Ufen 2013).

In the chapters to follow, the importance of this legacy for political regime directions in Southeast Asia is explained and demonstrated. The focus is on a mix of postauthoritarian and authoritarian regimes in the Philippines, Singapore, and Malaysia.

The Philippines is the oldest procedural democracy in Southeast Asia where—despite the interlude of authoritarian rule under Ferdinand Marcos between 1972 and 1981 and what many analysts regard as incomplete democratization—opposition parties and presidential candidates have been able to win office. By contrast, systemic constraints on political competition in Singapore and Malaysia have helped the same core ruling parties to continually control power. Yet technocratic authoritarian rule in Singapore operates differently than in Malaysia, where ideologies of race are central to the exercise and rationalization of power.

The case studies will examine the emergence, conflicts over, and regime implications of a range of parliamentary and extraparliamentary institutions. There are differences to the complexions and interests of elites across the three regimes and related contrasts in how capitalism is organized and controlled. Yet in all cases social conflicts and transformations ensuing from capitalist development have manifested in new pressures and challenges for established elites seeking to reproduce the existing social and political order.

As will be shown, a striking theme in elite political management of these pressures has been the attempt to exploit and consolidate the paucity of strong independent intermediary organizations. Political institutions and ideologies of participation and representation are at the heart of these strategies, the aim being to expand political space but in ways that fragment social forces and contain the scope and nature of conflict permitted.

However, the framework for conducting that enquiry requires further elaboration. A case has been made immediately above for a distinctive social foundations/social conflict understanding of political institutions. Without this we cannot adequately explain the emergence of any particular institution or modification thereof. We now need to resolve the question only partially addressed in the earlier part of this chapter, namely, what are the best conceptual tools to progress a more open enquiry into the nature and significance of those institutions? The answer lies in conceiving political regimes, and struggles within them, through the lenses of modes of political participation: the focus of the next chapter.

IDEOLOGIES OF POLITICAL REPRESENTATION AND THE MODE OF PARTICIPATION FRAMEWORK

This chapter provides a detailed outline and explanation of how ideologies of representation are conceptualized and employed within the modes of participation (MOP) theoretical framework adopted in this book. This includes concrete illustrations of how these concepts help explain which MOPs are ascendant in Southeast Asia and why they may converge or diverge from one regime to another as capitalism develops.

Struggles over who can participate, how, and why involve contests of forces with different interests in either containing or expanding the limits of institutionalized political conflict. Ideologies of participation and representation are a critical part of the attempt to rationalize institutional arrangements functional for particular interests and social forces.

The MOP framework identifies four ideologies of political representation. Two are established concepts in the literature—democracy and populism. The others—consultative and particularist—are original contributions that capture distinctive ideologies, the conceptualization and theorization of which are vital to a better understanding of struggles over formal and informal political institutions.

Another crucial component of the MOP framework is acknowledgment and conceptualization of the different *sites* through which institutional and ideological struggles over political participation and representation are conducted. Sites may be state-based, involve the articulation with the state of societal forces based outside the state, or be entirely civil society–based and operate autonomously from the state. They may also accommodate or block participation for collective organizations and/or individuals. As is explained below, these different modes of participation—within and across sites—and the ideologies employed to rationalize them—matter for the nature and scope of permissible political conflict and for which interests benefit most from participation or representation.

Democratic and Nondemocratic Ideologies of Political Representation

It was with the aim of transcending the constraints of the authoritarianism-democracy dualism pervading the hybrid regime literature, and of analyzing political regimes on their own terms, that Jayasuriya and Rodan (2007) introduced their initial MOP framework. It conceptualized complex contemporary realities of political participation in Southeast Asia, hitherto obscured by the dominant state-society conceptual divide informed by liberal pluralist theoretical assumptions. Thus, included in the framework are not only both parliamentary and extraparliamentary modes of participation but also sites of extraparliamentary political participation *within* the state (780).[1] In effect, this framework confirms that "institutions matter,"[2] but this is fundamentally because of how they permit, contain, or block particular forms of conflict via different modes of political participation (773–74). Crucially, this is as much about who should be involved and why as it is about how.

Accordingly, Jayasuriya and Rodan argued that, implicitly or explicitly, ideologies of representation provide rationales for privileging, marginalizing, or excluding particular interests or conflicts from political processes. Significantly, this includes alternatives to democratic representative government (780–81). Yet this important observation was not accompanied by any sustained attempt to elaborate, specify, or theorize the relationship between forms of participation and representation ideologies. Therefore, the framework and study here go further, identifying and distinguishing democratic and nondemocratic ideologies of representation, and evaluating their appeal and utility for different social forces—elites and non-elites—struggling over the forms and bounds of institutionalized political conflict. Indeed, this is the basis for one of this book's most distinctive contributions, since nondemocratic ideologies—similarly to nondemocratic institutional forms and practices—have been beyond the general purview of the transition paradigm. A fuller examination below of different MOPs will benefit, then, from first distinguishing between democratic and nondemocratic ideologies of representation.

While the complete range of ideological perspectives is a matter of empirical investigation, the conceptual categories guiding this enquiry distinguish between *democratic, populist, consultative,* and *particularist* ideologies of representation (Rodan 2012). These four categories are not all strictly mutually exclusive but nevertheless have major differences of emphasis in the respective rationales for, and means of implementing, representation.

In *democratic* ideologies of representation, the principal emphasis is on actors— whether elected or appointed to represent people, sectors, ideas, or interests— being either directly or indirectly accountable to fellow citizens. Thus, the authority of those being represented has to be able to be exercised in some way. It is this accountability that gives these actors political authority as representatives (Pitkin 1967). Moreover, representation is a mechanism through which political conflict and competition is conducted, intrinsic to which are intermediary groups from civil society, including political parties, trade unions, and interest groups. The precise mix and complexion of electoral and non-electoral collective organizations through which representation is conducted may change, but it must still involve authorization from, and accountability to, those being represented (see Chandhoke 2009; Collier and Handlin 2009; Törnquist 2009; Houtzager and Lavalle 2010).[3]

Emphasis here on authorization and accountability does not disregard long-standing differences among theorists over how democratic representation is understood and what its purpose is (see Brito Vieiria and Runciman 2008).[4] Also taken into account are more recent perspectives grappling with the significance of societal transformations under advanced capitalism and economic globalization for democratic representation. In this vein, Urbinati (2000, 2002) makes the case for "representation as advocacy" without direct authorization of those—often politically marginalized—communities whose interests activists claim to promote (see also Mansbridge 2004; Warren and Castiglione 2004). Dryzek and Niemeyer (2008), particularly cognizant of the growing international context of decision making, also champion "discursive representation" whereby democracy "can entail the representation of discourses as well as persons or groups" to foster broader deliberative processes (481; see also Dryzek 2015).

The concept of democratic ideology adopted here acknowledges that multiple forms of representation are essential to maximizing the indirect participation of citizens in the political process (Kuper 2004; Brown 2006; Runciman 2007; Mansbridge 2009). However, it also insists that these different forms of representation and participation must not constitute alternatives to, but instead serve as supplements for, democratic authorization and accountability in representation.[5]

Moreover, the democratic significance of deliberative and consultative processes rests on the extent to which they ideologically and structurally facilitate challenges to existing inequalities of power. In the absence of this they may serve more to sustain and reproduce a hierarchical social and political order instead of facilitating political competition. This is why struggles over representation are often conducted between opponents of authoritarianism, and not just between supporters and opponents of authoritarianism. Some reformers, for example, look to democratic institutions to progress social redistribution and egalitarian goals, while others seek to promote a market-functional meritocracy that may be less threatening to the existing social and political order.

Populist ideologies of representation, by contrast with democratic ideologies, emphasize direct links between "the people" and the leadership of political movements, often in claims of direct democracy. The interests of ordinary people are characteristically juxtaposed against those of elites in general (Laclau 2007). Consequently, intermediary bodies linking citizens with government and political institutions more generally are viewed with skepticism and preferably bypassed (Mouzelis 1985; Hawkins 2010; Gill 2013). Indeed, the objective of populist mobilizations is usually to widen the scope of popular political participation in order to challenge prevailing political institutions and those who control them. This is generally threatening for established elites, but can also be harnessed in intra-elite power struggles, such as those involving President Joseph Estrada in the Philippines (1998–2001) and Prime Minister Thaksin Shinawatra (2001–2006) in Thailand in the Southeast Asian context (Pasuk and Baker 2004; Thompson 2010).

Significantly, in the context of increasingly unequal distributional outcomes of capitalist development, both left wing and right wing variants of populism have emerged in recent decades across a range of political regimes globally. The precise political reform agendas attached to populist ideologies of representation and associated mobilizations vary considerably (Aram 2004; Arnson and Perales 2007; Roberts 2007; Mizuno and Pasuk 2009; Remmer 2012; de la Torre 2013; Weyland 2013), depending on the specific nature of the conflicts precipitating these movements and their social bases (Ionescu and Gellner 1969). While this includes progressive possibilities, bypassing or dismantling intermediary organizations increases the potential for the curtailment of political pluralism and tendencies toward authoritarianism.

In contrast to the above two categories, *consultative* ideologies of representation emphasize the problem-solving utility of incorporating stakeholders, interests, and/or expertise into public policy processes to ensure the most effective functioning of economic, social, or political governance. These ideologies privilege such problem solving over political competition, thereby limiting the political space for contending normative positions over the fundamental objectives of public policy through new spaces of technocratic governance. Importantly, wide consultation of experts and other groups and individuals under consultative representation does not infer or involve collective or equal power in decision making, nor does it mean those consulted have any democratic authority to represent others.

Consultative ideologies promote depoliticization but they do so, as Burnham (2001, 128) argues, through a "process of placing at one remove the political character of decision-making" to enhance political control. This involves both forms of "arena shifting" at the expense of representative institutions of democracy, but also processes that more broadly project the exercise of state power as disinterested and legitimate, rather than intrinsically political and class biased (Burnham 2014, 196). In other words, depoliticization is guided by the notion that power relations in state and civil society are completely separate, and consultative representation involves historically specific attempts to reinforce that notion through new spaces of governance.

Under consultative ideologies, processes of extraparliamentary deliberation and consultation are generally promoted as an alternative avenue to political contestation in parliamentary institutions and lay the basis for claims by elites that the public interest is represented in policy formulation. Such processes may incorporate individuals or groups into state-based or state-sponsored avenues of political participation—in either case affording prevailing political and bureaucratic elites greater control over who participates, on what, and how. Crucially, those projected as, or claiming to be, representatives do not necessarily have any authority to act on behalf of others, nor be subject to any disciplining or accountability by them. Indeed, it is precisely the potential of consultative ideologies to rationalize a marginalization of democratic representative politics that makes them so attractive to many established elites. Importantly, these ideologies are also not without their appeal to some civil society actors, who either lack organizational or social bases through which authorization and accountability could be conducted, or who eschew political parties.

While consultative representation almost always takes place outside the formal political system, it can also work to subvert the idea of democratic authorization of representatives from within. This is the case with Singapore's scheme of nominated members of parliament (NMPs), whose introduction has provided new spaces to promote technocratic governance incorporating unelected members of parliament.

Ideological appeals to consultation, and the projection of these processes as indicative of consensus politics, are of course not new. They have been integral to various forms of corporatist representation of functional interests, most of which under modern capitalism are historically associated with attempts by elites to preempt or contain industrial conflict and popular protest (Malloy 1977; Schmitter and Lembruch 1979). They are common to ethnic, religious, regional, and other ideologies of consociationalism (Lijphart 1968, 1977; Nordlinger 1972; McRae 1974). However, consultative ideologies are understood here as a historically specific set of rationales for establishing new spaces of technocratic governance in opposition to democratically authorized political representation. It is no coincidence that these ideologies have proliferated in the context of heightened social pressures and conflicts associated with the maturation of market capitalism in general and the impacts of neoliberal policies and globalization in particular.

Importantly, the salience of consultative ideologies is evident within established democracies where mass-based political parties and social democratic movements have been in sustained decline (Katz and Mair 1995; Tormey 2015). Trends toward depoliticization and the containment of political contestation have been observed in the UK and Western Europe, for example (see Hay 2007; Flinders and Wood 2014), often in conjunction with new forms of participation and ideologies that this framework highlights—especially technocratic ideologies of consultative representation.

In the particular context of contemporary Southeast Asia, amidst rapid economic and social change, a lack of well-organized and clearly defined independent functional and interest groups has posed new challenges and opportunities in the political management of capitalism. Thus, to varying degrees elites have sought to develop structures and ideological rationales for containing conflicts and absorbing new social forces into state-sponsored or state-controlled institutions. In this context, professional expertise and technical knowledge have become much more significant in rationales for consultative ideologies of representation.

The final category of representation ideologies in this framework is *particularist* ideologies. These ideologies variously emphasize the rights to representation of discrete communities and identities based on ethnicity, race, religion, geography, gender, and culture. Such ideologies can be deployed to assert and justify both claims to representation by politically dominant and marginalized groups. Naturally the significance of each variant of particularism differs across territories, as does the extent to which these different ideologies remain separate or may be mutually reinforcing in the way they are harnessed in attempts to shape political institutions.

In Malaysia, for example, ideological rationales for ethnic Malay political dominance are core to the political regime and are reflected in institutional aspects of parliamentary and extraparliamentary representation. This dominance is ideologically reinforced by arguments about the need for Islamic religious representation in various state and state-linked bodies. At the same time, this creates an ideological basis from which minority ethnic and religious groups attempt to advance counter claims for representation (Brown 2000). Elsewhere, such as in the Philippines, claims for an autonomous Bangsamoro region in Mindanao are embedded in rationales about Islamic religious and cultural identities warranting special political representation in a Christian-dominant society. Muslims in Mindanao argue that, since they were never subjugated by Spain during colonization, they are not "Filipinos" (Rodis 2015). Ethnic Malay Muslim minorities in southern Thailand mount comparable arguments and seek similar recognition through representation (see McCargo 2011).

Particularist ideologies of representation can have complex historical roots, though dubious or inflated claims to historical roots can also be made. The attraction for elites in promoting and institutionalizing particularist ideologies of representation is their utility for preempting the formation of class-based or cohesive cross-class and/or multiethnic reformist movements. As this book will demonstrate, these ideologies have assumed growing importance in the way conflicts over the social contradictions of capitalism are politically managed or contested.

To reiterate, these four ideologies are not all strictly mutually exclusive. However, the emphases of each ideology significantly differ, with major implications for who can participate in politics, how, and on what issues. It matters profoundly whether these different ideologies—either individually or in articulation with each other—open up the scope and nature of political contestation, or help to insulate existing power relations from effective scrutiny and challenge.

Modes of Participation in Southeast Asia

The essence of the MOP framework is to subject institutions of political participation in any regime to scrutiny over the nature and extent of contestation permitted or blocked through them. That scrutiny must be equipped with adequate conceptual tools to detect and understand ideologies of representation competing or dominating to shape institutions of participation, hence the discussion immediately above. But these conceptual tools are only relevant in relation to the structural forms of participation giving those ideologies concrete expression. These interrelationships are examined below to highlight different ways that political space has expanded in Southeast Asia in recent decades. The framework enables us to understand why, paradoxically, more participation has often gone hand in hand with less political contestation.

Rather than analyzing institutions per se, the MOP framework distinguishes between different *sites* of participation: some are state based or state/trans-state sponsored while others are more autonomous from the state, with contrasting levels of *inclusion* in political participation through those sites; some entail individual participation while others admit collective organizations. The point is not that a sharp state-civil society divide either does or can exist, but that these sites differ in

TABLE 2.1 Modes of participation

LEVEL OF INCLUSION	SITES OF PARTICIPATION	
	STATE AND TRANS-STATE SPONSORED	AUTONOMOUS FROM THE STATE
Individual	**Administrative Incorporation** Public grievance processes (Law on Complaints & Denunciations, Vietnam) Public feedback mechanisms (REACH, Singapore Pemandu, Malaysia)	**Individualized Political** **Expression** Bloggers Talkback radio Political cartoons Petitions
Collective	**Societal Incorporation** Nominated members of parliament (Singapore) Economic Consultative Councils (Malaysia) Participatory budgeting (Philippines)	**Civil Society Expression** Political parties Labor unions Social movements Business organizations Ethnic organizations Student organizations Cultural organizations

the way that political conflict is managed. On this basis, four different MOPs are delineated in table 2.1: *individualized political expression*; *civil society expression*; *societal incorporation*; and *administrative incorporation*.

These modes are another layer to the MOP framework, allowing for a fuller understanding of the complex interrelationships mediating the institutional and tactical contexts within which actors variously employ democratic, consultative, and particularist ideologies of representation. The following explains the underlying processes shaping the nature and extent of conflict permissible through each mode. The case study chapters will subsequently demonstrate in more detail the utility of these categories, and the complexity and importance of their links with ideologies of representation.

Individualized political expression is relatively autonomous from the state and refers to attempts by individuals to directly or indirectly influence public policy and governance, or political debate thereof. It can articulate with parliamentary politics, such as through an individual meeting with a local member of parliament. Extraparliamentary expressions are generally more diverse and range from letters to newspapers, calls to talkback radio, petition signing, political cartoons, and consumer choices, for example to avoid products linked to abusive labor practices. However, the most expansive individualized expressions in recent decades involve internet media, blogs, and other online activities (Jayasuriya and Rodan 2007, 789).

To be sure, the scope to exploit these technologies varies. In some parts of Southeast Asia bloggers face the risk and reality of harsh repression, not least in Thailand, where draconian lèse-majesté laws bar any debate about the monarchy, and in Vietnam, where authorities have also imprisoned bloggers for "anti-state" activities (Greenslade 2014; Human Rights Watch 2014). Yet, precisely because of the constraints on collective independent political activity in authoritarian regimes, attempts to exploit the internet and other social media for individual expression have been integral to increased political space in much of the region.

The distinction between individualized expression and social activism involving the internet can be blurred, and is a critical political consideration. In Singapore, for example, the last decade has witnessed a proliferation of individual blog sites (J. Gomez 2006, 2008; Mydans 2011; Nur Asyiqin 2015; Ortmann 2015), but no commensurate progress toward independent collective organizational capacity through civil society. By contrast, in Malaysia, many prominent bloggers have formal or informal links with opposition parties or nongovernmental organizations (NGOs) and their individual expressions take on a different significance (see Rodan 2013, 27–28; Weiss 2014b). Individual expression by an atomized political actor is one thing, but it is something else when that expression inspires or helps coordinate the mobilization of civil society forces. Authorities in authoritarian regimes in Southeast Asia and elsewhere understand this distinction and target and regulate accordingly (see Rodan 2003; King, Pan, and Roberts 2013). Furthermore, citizens can use individual expression not just to promote varying democratic ideologies of representation, but also nondemocratic ideologies of representation, such as through religious particularist criticisms against the state.

Civil society expression constitutes a separate mode of participation involving independently created forms of collective action. The boundaries of this political space are to varying degrees flexible and determined by activists themselves. As the most independent, collective MOP, civil society expression poses the greatest potential threat to state political control and related elite interests. The forms this can take vary, including political parties and a wide range of organizations that may or may not act in concert with such formal political entities. This encompasses specialist interest and pressure groups, trade unions, business organizations, through to mass social movements which, in most extreme form, may have revolutionary objectives and modus operandi.

Various analysts of established liberal democracies in early capitalist developing countries have noted the decline in recent decades of traditional forms of civil society expression through parties and trade unions in particular (Katz and Mair 1995; Hay 2007). Others have emphasized the emergence and potential of new forms of collective action (Tormey 2015). This includes the Occupy Wall Street protests in the United States in response to class-biased policy from policymakers and regulators following the 2007–2008 subprime mortgage credit crunch and related global financial crisis (see Van Gelder 2011; Graeber 2013). Occupy Wall

Street activists attacked income and wealth inequalities. They claimed the movement represented 99 percent of the population in trying to redress the concentration of power and privilege accorded the 1 percent whose interests were well served by policymakers.

Civil society expression in late developing countries has in some cases taken radical and even revolutionary directions in recent times—not least through the Arab Spring starting in late 2010. The causes and forms of collective action varied in the different countries of the Middle East and northern Africa involved. However, public rallies and labor strikes were thematic, as was popular disenchantment with extreme material, social, and political inequalities accompanying capitalist development.

Civil society expression is generally suppressed under authoritarian regimes in Southeast Asia, such as in Cambodia, Singapore, Burma, and Vietnam, although struggles continue in each country to try to open up independent political space. Such collective expression is, to varying degrees, more prevalent elsewhere in the region. However, Cold War legacies and the historical context of capitalist development have meant that even in postauthoritarian regimes civil society expressions have rarely involved powerful class-based organizations or radical mass movements. The recent exception to this has been the various forms of campaigning and mobilizing of social and political forces in support of parties linked to Thaksin Shinawatra in Thailand with redistributive reform agendas.

More commonly, social forces in postauthoritarian societies, most notably the Philippines and Indonesia, have organized around discrete issues, including privatization, environmentalism, governance reform, consumer rights, and social justice, that have emerged or expanded with accelerated capitalist development. These issues have been taken up by NGOs that may or may not have a popular membership base. Various embryonic civil society groups seeking to expand their independent space under authoritarian regimes in the region appear to be headed down a similar path.

Sometimes such collective actions cohere to form a significant movement, recent examples of which include Bersih (Gabungan Philihantaya Bersih dan Adil, Coalition for Clean and Fair Elections) in Malaysia and the Coalition Against Corruption in the Philippines. Expressions of this sort can reflect demands for democratic ideologies of representation, but this is also an MOP through which diverse reform agendas and nondemocratic ideologies of representation can be advanced. Theoretically, these particular MOPs can thus lead to democratic reform, but the framework of this study emphasizes how such outcomes are contingent on the *strategic selectivity* of such institutions and the related balance of forces competing to harness any mode to particular reform ends.

Civil society expression may also manifest in spontaneous mobilizations by groups that are especially disconnected from formal representative institutions, such as the urban poor. Accelerated urbanization and underemployment in the formal sector of the economy in many parts of Southeast Asia and elsewhere in the global south have given rise to informal settlements and economies at the margins of urban centers, and a host of related conflicts over access to basic services such as water and electricity. Periodic, albeit short-lived, collective action around these and other protests—symptomatic of acute social and material inequalities—occur in spite, and because of, the dearth of mediating structures linking such groups to formal political institutions (Jayasuriya and Rodan 2007, 785–87).

This can be concerning for established elites, but even more so when mobilizations are occasionally intended to influence intra-elite struggles over formal political power. Such was the case in 2001 in the Philippines when the urban poor protested over the arrest of President Estrada, who espoused pro-poor rhetoric (Hutchison 2007). This episode illustrated the potential dangers for entrenched interests posed by populist ideologies of representation and related forms of political participation. Popular protests by the middle class to protect their privileges amidst reform pressures from the marginalized are another important recent phenomenon emerging in Southeast Asia and Latin America—including in Thailand, the Philippines, Brazil, and Venezuela (see Surowiecki 2013; Hewison 2014; Mena 2014; Saxer 2014).

Such potential helps explain why, as social and economic transformations in Southeast Asia present new challenges for the political management of conflict over capitalist development, many elites have sought to incorporate more social forces into creative new forms of state-controlled or state-sponsored MOPs: societal incorporation and administrative accountability. Crucially, state control over who can participate—and on what issues and how—offers the possibility of expanding political space while narrowing the substantive issues open to contest.

Societal incorporation encompasses some established state corporatist institutions but also a range of new institutions through which state strategic control can be exerted over the sorts of conflicts open to scrutiny and how. To varying degrees, these institutions provide channels through which participants may influence public policy and debate thereof, but not on terms set by the participants themselves—in contrast to civil society and individual expressions. On the contrary, state actors determine which groups are appropriate to represent communities in public policy consultations (Jayasuriya and Rodan 2007, 783), guided by consultative ideologies of representation emphasizing the utility of participants for solving state-defined problems of economic, social, or political governance.

Under this mode, select civil society groups and new state-conceived categories of social groups are incorporated principally to contribute to the refinement
of the delivery of public goods and services rather than to engage in an open-ended
debate over policy and reform options. Thus, when civil society groups enter into
this mode, they operate under different circumstances from other forms of participation described above. Initiatives in societal incorporation span authoritarian and postauthoritarian regimes and involve domestic states in their own right
and trans-state partnerships with multilateral agencies in promoting the participation of NGOs and other social groups.

Direct incorporation of NGOs or other social groups into state-based or
government-initiated bodies includes their incorporation into public procurement
bodies and a wide range of citizens' advisory committees on specific aspects of
public policy.[6] In some cases these articulate with formal political institutions, such
as through Local Development Councils required under the Local Government
Code in the Philippines and Musyawarah Perencanaan Pembangunan (Musren-
bang, Development Planning Consultations) in Indonesia. More radically,
nominated members of parliament in Singapore are appointed by a parliamentary
committee controlled by the ruling People's Action Party (PAP). In effect, this
amounts to a site within a site. This scheme incorporates individuals considered
to have specialist policy-relevant expertise and are notional representatives of
discrete interests such as domestic business, labor, women, and ethnic organizations. Both categories of NMPs are explicitly and principally rationalized on
the basis of consultative ideologies of representation, although particularist ideologies often add to the rationale for some appointments.

Trans-state initiatives in societal incorporation have increased considerably as
multilateral and international aid agencies partner with domestic governments
in strategies to shape the governance regimes and social outcomes of capitalist
development. Aid funding for governance reform, capacity building programs,
and poverty alleviation in particular has instigated or supported direct incorporation of NGOs into various new modes of political participation. Large-scale
World Bank poverty alleviation projects in Thailand, Indonesia, and the Philippines, for instance, have involved varying forms of community-level participation but few spaces for combative collective organizations. With particular reform
objectives in mind, participants are targeted accordingly and often administra-
tively defined (Jayasuriya and Rodan 2007, 784). Crucially, the predominant rationale for this "community empowerment" is that involving "stakeholders" best
ensures effective governance for sustainable market systems (Carroll 2010). Thus,
again, consultative ideologies of representation exert a pervasive influence.

Notwithstanding variations in the forms and nature of societal incorporation,
they share technocratic or managerial rationales for incorporating state-defined

groups into consultation around largely state-defined public policy agendas. Con-flicts over structural inequalities and other contentious issues are largely filtered out or contained, as indeed are social forces and interests seeking to engage around them, such as independent trade unions. Nevertheless, this mode is in many con-texts attractive for NGOs with specialized public policy concerns, including those hoping to harness these new political spaces for more ambitious, including demo-cratic, political ends and wider conflict than their elite architects intended.

Membership-based civil society organizations—including trade unions, political parties and business organizations—may also be incorporated into state-controlled and/or initiated sites for particular policy feedback or consulta-tions, where state authorities and independent activists both see potential gains. At this point, though, activists have temporarily entered a different site where they have less control over how they participate, and on what, than they experi-ence through civil society expression.

The final mode of participation, *administrative incorporation*, channels in-dividual participation down state-controlled paths that narrow and depoliticize public policy. Through public grievance, consultation, and feedback mechanisms, individuals have been increasingly availed of opportunities for direct engage-ment with state bureaucracies. At one level this constitutes enhanced bureau-cratic accountability, opening up new political space for questioning how state power is exercised and for demanding more information and transparency in public administration. However, instead of these mechanisms enshrining citizens' democratic rights to discipline elites, conflicts over public policy are translated into administrative issues about the implementation and refinement of policy. These mechanisms are promoted as an alternative, rather than a complement, to collective forms of competitive representative politics.

The emergence of initiatives in administrative incorporation in Vietnam is in-structive, coinciding with the shift from a command to a market economy and new social forces and conflicts being generated by this transition. This has included tensions over rising material inequalities and disputes among competing elites over private versus state-based commercial interests. In this context, public grievance mechanisms were introduced in 1998 and thereafter developed through the Law on Complaints and Denunciations. Of the hundreds of thousands of annual com-plaints, approximately 80 percent relate to land management disputes. Complaints about the implementation of social policies and policies on the environment are also prominent (Asia Foundation 2009; *Viet Nam News* 2010).

Two points warrant emphasis about this mechanism. First, complaints must be confined to issues about the *process* of policy implementation—whether corrupt or wrongful administration of the law has occurred. Second, the law does not allow collective attempts to participate in the process. Citizens must individually craft and submit their administrative petitions and letters of complaint to authorities. Indeed, the purpose of the law is to preempt the mobilization of collective interests and identities—whether by legal or political means. Through administrative processes, then, conflicts over the effects of Vietnam's social and economic transformation are framed as fundamentally procedural rather than substantive, and open to individual but not collective forms of political participation.

Singapore provides examples of more diverse forms of administrative incorporation. In particular, in 1985, the Feedback Unit was established, and renamed Reaching Everyone for Active Citizenry @ Home (REACH) in 2006. Currently based in a department of the Ministry of Communications and Information, REACH provides avenues for both complaints and suggestions about the refinement of public policy, as well as for information gathering and dissemination on topics and issues of interest to authorities. The bulk of these activities involve individuals communicating with REACH, mostly online, and REACH ensuring complaints and suggestions are directed to the relevant government department or ministry. There are also select opportunities for collective participation in public policy consultations with groups handpicked or constructed by state authorities, at which point participation becomes societal rather than administrative incorporation.

Administrative incorporation thus embraces and institutionalizes a technocratic conception of politics involving processes of bureaucratic rationality. This promotes a focus on issues of administrative delivery and efficiency in public policy ahead of more substantive conflict about the nature of that policy (Jayasuriya and Rodan 2007, 788). Crucially, it also atomizes political actors and compartmentalizes their concerns, working against the formation of groups and coalitions of shared broader reform goals. Indeed, in that respect it presents as an alternative to political representation, which is bypassed entirely. Yet the technocratic notion of politics embedded in administrative incorporation also has powerful ideological resonances with consultative representation: emphasizing a noncompetitive, problem-solving approach to managing political conflict.

Importantly, while societal and administrative incorporation give principal emphasis to technocratic ideologies, particularist ideologies can also be advanced through them—either in articulation with technocratic ideologies or as a supplement to them. This is especially evident in Singapore through the NMP scheme and REACH, where notional representatives of different ethnic groups are part of the government's strategy to reinforce political fragmentation and depoliticization.

What then explains why a regime adopts particular modes of participation, which ideological rationales are institutionalized through them, and what political outcomes result?

The transformative nature of capitalist development periodically generates new and heightened forms of social and economic inequalities, with the potential for other societal cleavages over ethnicity, religion, and race, in particular, to intensify. This generally increases the possibility of new coalitions of social and political forces seeking to challenge or consolidate the institutional avenues and dimensions of political conflict. However, which MOPs are attractive to what social forces, and precisely how those MOPs operate in practice necessarily plays out differently in each country. The intensity and nature of struggles over MOPs vary because the interests, conflicts, and contradictions specific to how capitalism is organized differ from one country to another. This affects both elite strategies and preferences for MOPs and those of social and political forces in general.

It is no coincidence, for example, that ideologies and institutions of consultative representation involving societal and administrative incorporation are most extensively promoted by elites in Singapore. Technocratic conceptions of, and solutions to, conflict reflect the worldviews of politico-bureaucrats and rationalize their acute concentration of power under a specific model of state capitalism.

In sharp contrast, technocratic ideologies of consultation are rightly understood by elites in Malaysia as potentially destabilizing for state patronage relationships integral to a different model of capitalism and associated interests. These ideologies have thus been less systematically adopted and proved much more problematic in strategies to contain political conflict. By contrast, particularist ideologies are pivotal to the justification for ethnic Malay political supremacy and the cultivation of an ethnic Malay bourgeoisie in Malaysia. Consequently, elites in Malaysia have predominantly channeled political participation through parliamentary institutions that are strategically selective in design, thereby limiting the potential of opponents to take power and recast the permissible bounds of political conflict—either by institutionalizing consultative or democratic ideologies of representation.

The complexion of popular forces and their respective interests in either reforming or maintaining existing state power relations also differ across capitalist societies. This reflects in forces of varying organizational strength and ideological commitment to both democratic and nondemocratic institutions and ideologies of representation. Among the three countries of this study, and indeed Southeast Asia more generally, the Philippines has the most extensive range and volume of NGOs and CSOs engaged in civil society expression. However, there are differences among these forces over the causes and responses to social and economic inequality accompanying capitalist development, and over the precise organizational means for progressing reform. Consequently, some social forces are, for example, more likely to accommodate themselves to state initiatives in societal incorporation than others. And forces entering into societal incorporation vary in the extent to which they seek to open up the bounds of permissible political conflict.

As the case studies to follow demonstrate, in all three countries examined, different elites contending with contrasting mixes of social forces and interests seek to contain conflict through MOPs. Yet nowhere are elites able to instrumentally adopt and adjust political institutions simply as they please. Even in Singapore, where state capitalism and authoritarianism have combined to most effectively limit both civil society and individual expression, elite projects to foster preferred MOPs face challenges.

Nevertheless, in all cases the outcomes of struggles over MOPs are shaped by Cold War political legacies compounded by the historical context of late capitalist development. This conjuncture has generally militated against powerful coalitions of popular forces oriented toward MOPs that ideologically and structurally facilitate challenges to existing inequalities of power. To differing degrees and in varying ways, new and old MOPs have expanded political representation. However, the strategic selectivity of these institutions has placed serious limits on the scope for political contestation and helped to reinforce political fragmentation among non-elite social and political forces.

The theoretical and conceptual framework outlined in this and the previous chapter lays the basis for an open examination of institutions of political representation, encompassing consideration of nondemocratic and democratic representation as well as extraparliamentary and parliamentary representation. In this MOP framework, the primary importance of political institutions is that they define the permissible bounds of conflict relating to the organization and control of social and economic power. These bounds shape whose interests are protected, advanced, or challenged through the forms and ideologies of representation promoted or blocked under any given political institution.

Thus, what matters most about institutions is not whether they "work" in some technical sense, but who can be represented through them, how, on what, and why. This profoundly matters for whether conflicts over land ownership, inequalities in wealth and income, the environmental impacts of development, language policy, corruption, and other fundamental governance and distributional conflicts are accommodated, marginalized, or excluded altogether from representation in political institutions.

In seeking to understand why these conflicts reach a point that warrants institutional and ideological responses from elites, the framework gives particular emphasis to the dynamic and contradictory nature of capitalist development and the varying ways this manifests in different political economies. Struggles over political institutions are situated within the wider, historically specific struggle over state power and the coalitions of interests served or threatened by how that power is exercised. Indeed, it is only by understanding the nature of those coalitions of interest that we can understand either the significance of challenges elites face in their political management of capitalism, or the strategies of political management adopted by them.

In particular, different coalitions of interests around how capitalism is organized and controlled lay different social foundations for institutional strategies open to elites and other social and political forces in attempts to contain or expand the permissible bounds of political conflict. As the next chapter explains, tensions and contradictions inherent to capitalist development present growing challenges for the way that political elites in Singapore, the Philippines, and Malaysia reproduce their power. However, because the interests and conflicts associated with capitalism vary, so too do the strategies different elites adopt to defend and/or modify existing modes of political participation and ideologies of representation.

3

HISTORY, CAPITALISM, AND CONFLICT

There are significant convergences and divergences among Southeast Asia's political regimes. Neither can be adequately explained without examining the historical and social foundations of these regimes. In particular, legacies of the Cold War and economic globalization have generally militated against strong and cohesive independent civil societies in the region. By virtue of its dynamic and contradictory character, capitalist development also lays bases for potential challenges to existing limits on the permissible bounds of political conflict. Yet precisely how this plays out varies in Singapore, the Philippines, and Malaysia—and elsewhere—owing to the different interests embedded in the specific ways that capitalism and state power are organized in each case.

Authorities in Singapore, the Philippines, and Malaysia contained politics by various means well before the advent of the Cold War. It was the Cold War, though, that sparked a systematic and intensified clampdown on independent civil society organizations and political parties challenging the status quo. A major casualty of this was independent labor movements aligned with reformist political parties (Iriye 1974), as had been emblematic of earlier successful democratizations in western Europe (Luebbert 1991; Eley 2002). Under economic globalization and related neoliberal domestic reforms, impediments to such movements were subsequently compounded by the enhanced mobility and power of capital (Deyo 1981). To the extent that independent mass-based organizations survived, they tended to involve ethnic and religious organizations (Tomsa and Ufen 2013). Small issue-specific nongovernmental organizations (NGOs) have often emerged to fill the political vacuum—some enjoying organic links to those they claim to represent or advocate for, but many not.

The challenge for elites seeking to reproduce such fragmentation has grown as capitalist accumulation strategies have generated new social forces, tensions, and contradictions. Yet this challenge, and elite responses to it, necessarily vary in Singapore, the Philippines, and Malaysia. This is because the precise interests underlying, and affected by, the dynamics of capitalism differ in all three political economies.

Singapore

It is no coincidence that institutions of administrative and societal incorporation, and explicit official ideologies of consultative representation, have been most extensively developed in Singapore. Alongside the city-state's incorporation into global markets, authoritarianism and state capitalism have combined under the People's Action Party (PAP) in a distinct way since the 1960s. This has entailed the emergence and consolidation of a virtual class of technocratic politico-bureaucrats—an ideologically cohesive social group, imbued with technocratic and elitist worldviews rationalizing their extensive powers over the economy, society, and polity. As the PAP sees it, the social and political order must reflect a "meritocracy" and be guided by one.[1]

Consequently, as social conflicts arising from, or compounded by, the city-state's spectacular capitalist development have emerged, the PAP has looked to contain the possibility of challenges to the interests of Singapore's ruling class. Hence its introduction of new institutions of participation has been skewed toward a noncompetitive, technocratic conception of politics. Social and political forces in Singapore have not uniformly embraced these modes of participation (MOPs), some seeking instead to have the space for more competitive civil society (including parliamentary civil society) and individual expression expanded. However, the relative strength of the ruling elite vis-à-vis the forcibly disorganized and politically weak popular forces, coupled with the technocratic mode of governance favoring this particular elite's interests, has been fundamental to outcomes in the accommodation in Singapore between different forces struggling over MOPs.

The remarkable elite cohesion and the technocratic nature of authoritarian rule in Singapore are interconnected with a particular form of state capitalism. This state capitalism was born out of conflict between contending factions of the PAP that came to power at the 1959 elections for self-government.

Throughout the 1950s, independent trade union, student, cultural, and ethnic organizations were active, often in defiance of colonial authorities attempting to moderate the extent and nature of political mobilization. The labor movement became particularly strong and militant, the radical Middle Road Group controlling complete sectors of industry and public services (Clutterbuck 1973, 100). Colonial authorities were increasingly anxious in this context about the suspected influence of the outlawed Malayan Communist Party through front organizations (Turnbull 1982, 247–48). Ironically, it was British concern about communism, and, indeed, socialism, that resulted in the incorporation of leftists within a formidable PAP electoral coalition in the approach to self-government in 1959.

The PAP was formed in 1954 as an alliance between largely Chinese-language-educated popular forces and the English-educated middle class nationalists, led by Lee Kuan Yew. The former provided the necessary mass organizational bases for effective electoral politics otherwise unavailable to Lee and his colleagues, while the attraction of the latter for leftists was the projection of respectability and political moderation in British eyes (Josey 1974). Significantly, the domestic bourgeoisie's close interdependence with colonial capitalism curbed its enthusiasm for a self-governing Singapore, leaving it without much influence over politics once it arrived.

It was not long after the PAP came to office that this coalition imploded. Consequently, the PAP splintered in July 1961 with the formation of a separate party, the Barisan Sosialis (BS, Socialist Front), depriving the PAP of extensive grassroots organizational structures. Authorities responded by harassing and intimidating PAP political opponents and critics, to undermine their social and organizational bases in civil society—especially organized labor (Deyo 1981). The BS's leadership was decimated when, in February 1963, 115 people were arrested under Operation Cold Store ordered by the Internal Security Council (*Far Eastern Economic Review* 1963), with a further twelve arrested the next month (Clutterbuck 1973, 160).

Such were the constraints on critics and opponents of the PAP that by October 1966 all BS members of the Legislative Assembly had resigned in protest (H. C. Chan 1971, 23). According to BS leader Lee Siew Choh, party members would instead "take our struggles into the streets" (quoted in Fong 1980). However, there would be no more opportunities outside parliament as inside it to contest the PAP's power and ideas. Consequently, not only did the BS promptly cease to be a political force, but no other organization would emerge to fill the vacuum. In the ensuing years, the PAP extended and refined the techniques for both denying political oxygen to civil society and isolating opposition parties from links with social forces.

The amended Societies Act 1968 was emblematic of the PAP's strategy to sever such party-political-civil society links, rendering any political expression from within organizations other than political parties potentially vulnerable to prosecution. Authorities were especially sensitive to entries into public political debate they considered supportive of policies or positions advanced by the PAP's party-political opponents, or involving social activists with suspected opposition links. Indeed, such sensitivity led to twenty-two arrests under the Internal Security Act (ISA) in 1987 under the spurious claim of a "Marxist conspiracy" by predominantly Catholic lay youth workers (Barr 2010; W. P. Tan 2012).

Meanwhile, opposition politicians that persisted in attempts to engage the public would have to contend with a constantly expanding array of regulations covering licenses and permits for public gatherings and disseminating political materials. Invariably authorities exercised these regulations to stymie or greatly complicate such endeavors. Defamation suits also became a favored means by which critics and opponents were tamed or politically persecuted—especially after the 1987 ISA arrests aroused such widespread international criticism (Lydgate 2003; Rajah 2012).

PAP leaders understood, however, that repression alone would not be adequate if it were to retain elections and succeed through them. What it needed was its own power base. A key element of this was to substitute independent labor organizations with PAP-affiliated ones, giving birth to the National Trades Union Congress (NTUC). The more general and profound strategy, though, involved a merger of state and party, recasting the political economy of Singapore. It was this political project that generated a powerful new class of politico-bureaucrats, with vital roles in social and economic infrastructure investments (H. C. Chan 1975). However, the PAP brand of state capitalism evolved to render Singaporeans directly or indirectly reliant on the state for economic and social resources, including housing, employment, business contracts, and access to personal savings (Tremewan 1994; Chua 1997; Rodan 2008). Citizens' vulnerability to political co-option and intimidation was greatly facilitated by this structural relationship.

As Singapore's economy progressed, so too did state capitalism, with vast sums of capital generated by government-linked companies (GLCs) and held by sovereign wealth funds bolstering the economic and political power of the PAP state and the politico-bureaucratic class.[2] This has shaped the domestic bourgeoisie's opportunities, favoring dependence on, or complementarity with, state capitalism ahead of competition with it. Opportunities for the middle class have been no less conditioned by state capitalism—whether directly through employment within the state in one or another of the government departments, statutory bodies, or GLCs, or indirectly through the provision of professional, legal, commercial, or other services (Rodan 2004).

Despite all the authoritarian controls in place in Singapore and their reinforcement through structural relationships embedded in the domestic political

economy, dramatic capitalist development manifested in new political challenges for the PAP by the early 1980s. At the 1984 polls there was a 12.9 percent
swing to the opposition, although this translated into just two opposition seats
under Singapore's first-past-the-post voting system. Disquiet about industrial
restructuring in response to competitive global pressures and rising living costs
had already resulted in a 1981 by-election victory to the Workers' Party in the
working-class seat of Anson—the first opposition seat in parliament since the
1960s. Subsequently, Lee Kuan Yew's 1983 pronouncements on eugenics particularly irritated many educated women (Rodan 1989, 184–85), whose ranks had
swelled as a result of Singapore's economic development. The PAP's 1984 election postmortem pointed to a broader dynamic—a rapidly expanding younger,
middle-class constituency—educated women being one component (Chua
1994, 659). The PAP's vote share fell again in the 1988 and 1991 general elections, by which time there were four elected opposition members of parliament.

Indeed, rapid and sustained capitalist development—not the lack of it—has
generated most of the PAP's new political challenges. Singapore's high growth
model has depended on a continuing influx of foreigners at both the most and
least skilled ends of the economy, respectively commanding the lowest and highest salaries. To contain costs and meet demand in manufacturing, construction,
and hospitality, guest workers from South Asia and China increased significantly
from 2000. Meanwhile, the progress of financial services, biotechnology, and other
higher value-added sectors necessitated global recruitment strategies. Foreign labor
expanded to such an extent that it accounted for one-third of Singapore's total
workforce by 2010, and related immigration also helped to boost the city-state's
population by around 32 percent in the decade from 2000 (Chun 2013b).

Significantly, after the initial phase of capitalist development under the PAP,
characterized by high levels of upward social mobility and broadly distributed material benefits, income inequality did not improve after the 1980s and rapidly
deteriorated from the 1990s. Indeed, Singapore's Gini coefficient increased
from 0.442 in 2000 to 0.478 in 2012 (Chun 2013a).[3] Absolute poverty levels were
also estimated at around 10–12 percent in 2011 (Chun 2013b). Yet Singapore's
gross domestic product (GDP) grew by an average 7.8 percent in the 1980s,
7.3 percent in the 1990s, and by as much as 5.7 percent for 2000–2014, despite
the economy by then having a substantially higher base (Singapore Department
of Statistics 2015).

PAP reluctance to moderate market pressures through either minimum wages
or adequate levels of social redistribution intensified inequalities inherent to Singapore's capitalist model. Meanwhile, beginning in the 1990s, various public utilities were corporatized, ensuring that market principles and profit seeking guided
their operations more fundamentally (Saxena 2011, 82–83). To some degree, the

ideological notion of meritocracy internalized by technocratic PAP elites limited their appreciation of, and empathy toward, those who had not prospered. Fundamentally, though, Singapore's authoritarian elites remained wary of citizenship-rights claims on government as a basis for social redistribution—hence their hostility to so-called western welfarism.

While increased inequality was especially felt by Singapore's lowest socio-economic groups, the inflationary costs of housing, transport, and health generated by immigration and high professional and executive salaries have also had significant impacts on the middle class. Indeed, much of Singapore's social and physical infrastructure—including the hitherto (justifiably) acclaimed mass rapid transport system—was under growing strain from the late 2000s. Public concerns would also surface about the implications for social cohesion of ever increasing numbers of foreign workers and the environmental sustainability of the prevailing growth model (Shibani 2013).

Crucially, the PAP understood how the emergence of new social forces and conflicts accompanying rapid capitalist development exposed limitations to established institutional mechanisms of political co-option, notably the NTUC and Citizens' Consultative Committees (Seah 1973). The nature of social conflict and social groups was evolving, which reflected in the emergence during the 1980s and 1990s of a group of small independent middle-class NGOs working in areas of the environment, consumer issues, women's rights, migrant workers, and human rights. Although these were politically moderate groups that operated within the strict official constraints imposed on civil society organizations, the PAP embarked on creative institutional measures to further ensure that the emerging NGOs remained moderate and constrained.

These measures emphasized administrative and societal incorporation, the purpose of which was to steer social conflicts as much as possible through institutions controlled by the politico-bureaucratic class. In the process, consultative ideologies of representation emphasizing the technical problem-solving rationale of political engagement would also be more fully developed and elaborated.[4] This direction represented a new and more sophisticated phase in the attempt to reproduce authoritarian rule—one that was more attuned to the challenges posed for it in a dynamic and advanced capitalist society. It reflected what was by now the absolute dominance within the PAP of technocrats, following the progressive replacement of so-called old guard with second-generation leaders that began in 1976—a process reinforced by the increasing importance of technocrats to Singapore's evolving state capitalism (Rodan 2008, 238–39).

Modest opposition seat gains therefore precipitated modifications to, and new initiatives in, political institutions by the PAP. This included the introduction in August 1984 of non-constituency members of parliament (NCMPs), allowing for a minimum of three seats with limited voting rights for the strongest opposition losers in general elections. At one level, the PAP wanted to appear tolerant of opposition.[5] However, Lee Kuan Yew's parliamentary speech on behalf of the reform ridiculed parliamentary democracies where oppositions played a prominent role.[6] By providing for NCMPs in a PAP controlled environment, Lee expected to be able to demonstrate the futility of opposition (Rodan 1989, 171). However, opposition parties did not immediately or generally embrace this mechanism.[7]

Another PAP strategy to contain electoral opposition appeal involved the introduction in 1988 of group representation constituencies (GRCs), comprising teams of three to six candidates and requiring at least one member from a racial minority community—be it Malay, Indian, or another minority. The official PAP rationale for this was to safeguard multiculturalism by ensuring minority group representation and averting the threat of ethnic-based voting patterns and parties. Yet, paradoxically, GRCs institutionalized and encouraged racial and ethnic political identities and forms of organization ahead of class-based perspectives and organization (Chua 2007). Such particularist ideologies of representation were reinforced through public housing allocations. Manipulation of electoral boundaries further helped to limit the scope for working-class Malay communities in particular to maximize their voting power (MARUAH 2013; N. Tan 2013).[8]

The strategy to increase the avenues for political and public policy participation included government parliamentary committees, periodic large-scale public inquiries, and the establishment of a public policy think tank—the Institute of Public Policy. These in part were meant to address a contradiction between the elitist PAP ideology of meritocracy and limited opportunities for university-educated middle class Singaporeans to influence public policy. However, there was also a deeper problem of how to direct the concerns of other social forces down institutional paths favoring technocratic approaches and solutions to social conflict.

One of the centerpieces of the PAP strategy to foster alternatives to competitive party politics was the establishment of the Feedback Unit (FU) within the Ministry of Community Development in 1985—renamed Reaching Everyone for Active Citizenry @ Home (REACH) in 2006. This was to facilitate individual and group feedback on public policy, as well as disseminate information about government policies. Over time it has developed a diverse array of electronic and in-person mechanisms to engage the public, mostly as individuals but also in select forms of group consultations. In essence, this institution steers public engagement toward government departments and agencies considered relevant to the submitted suggestion—or grievance—on a policy issue or process.

Another centerpiece institution has been the nominated members of parliament (NMPs), introduced in 1990 as an explicit alternative to democratic representation. NMPs are publicly nominated to a PAP-dominated parliamentary select committee that makes recommendations on who should be appointed. Appointed NMPs have comparable voting rights to NCMPs. Significantly, while this scheme initially placed much emphasis on the individual expertise and professional qualifications of appointees, in keeping with the elitist ideologies of the PAP, this was increasingly accompanied and guided by attempts to absorb new social forces and contain conflicts emerging from, or exacerbated by, capitalist development. This was reflected in the state-conceived social categories under which nominations were invited, as well as in the state-aligned and independent social groups whose members were incorporated into parliament as NMPs. This included business, labor, women, environmental, and ethnic organizations.

In their different ways, REACH and NMPs have been designed to foster a compartmentalization of public policy issues and a political fragmentation of those engaged in it. Official rationales for these institutions exude technocratic ideologies about the nature and purpose of political engagement, in contradistinction from competitive and democratic representation. Some Singaporeans have embraced these rationales, while others participate through them for lack of better options, and with different ideological rationales in mind from those of technocratic elites. In the face of continuing challenges in the political management of capitalist development, the PAP has looked to refine and supplement such institutions of administrative and societal incorporation.

It was in the context of mounting social contradictions associated with Singapore's capitalist model that the PAP's share of total votes dropped a combined 15 percent in the 2006 and 2011 elections. Support for the PAP was at its lowest since independence in 1965. The PAP still commanded 60.1 percent support in 2011 and, with the help of Singapore's first-past-the post voting system and an electoral gerrymander, it held all but six of the eighty-seven seats in parliament. Nevertheless, four of the Workers' Party's six seats inflicted the first PAP defeat in a multiseat GRC. The extent and nature of public criticism and questioning of PAP policies and ideologies had also risen substantially, with individual bloggers as well as opposition parties using the internet to increased effect (Mydans 2011). Significantly, the PAP's ideology of meritocracy was a repeated target in cyberspace.

The 2011 election results in particular rang loud alarm bells within the PAP. The creative energy invested in institutions of administrative and societal incorporation was meant to discourage support for elected opposition and limit the bounds of permissible political conflict. However, while the intensification of tensions inherent to Singapore's model of capitalist development was producing more challenging conditions for this political strategy, the PAP had no intentions of abandoning it.

On the contrary, the government promptly looked to shore up the strategy through a yearlong series of consultations under Our Singapore Conversation (OSC), launched in the second half of 2012. Chaired by Education Minister Heng Swee Keat, the OSC involved a twenty-six-member committee including members from business, academia, media, the legal profession, and community groups. The exercise entailed varying forms of consultations with over 47,000 Singaporeans (REACH 2013, 3). PAP leaders portrayed feedback from OSC as instrumental in subsequent policy adjustments, with a view to again discrediting competitive politics as the best modus operandi for addressing conflict. This theme was especially prominent during the subsequent campaign by the PAP for the 2015 general election.

Meanwhile, increased social spending by the government followed Prime Minister Lee Hsien Loong's declaration that his government would "play a bigger role to build a fair and just society" (quoted in R. Chan 2013a). How far this would go remained to be seen, as did the extent to which this could be reconciled with profitable accumulation strategies under the existing development model. Furthermore, PAP leaders were not conceding any ideological ground to concepts of citizenship rights or social justice. Instead, it was a "compassionate meritocracy" that was now purportedly in train (C. T. Goh 2013).

Importantly, tensions inherent to Singapore's capitalist development model stimulated more conflict over how the city-state was governed, resulting in greater preparedness among Singaporeans to support opposition parties and express their views outside PAP-controlled institutions—most notably through social media. However, the greatest threat to Singapore's techno-political class of elites would be if new organizational bases for, or greater cohesion between, the PAP's politically fragmented party-political and limited civil society opponents were to emerge. Toward keeping any such threat at bay, institutions of societal and administrative incorporation, and related ideologies of consultative representation, would remain crucial, although more as a complement than an alternative to existing authoritarian controls. The 9.8 percent swing back to the PAP at the 2015 general election helped reinforce the ruling party's confidence in this formula.

The Philippines

In sharp contrast with Singapore's mix of state capitalism and economic globalization under the dominance of technocratic elites, the apparatus of the state in the Philippines has generally been exercised to foster acute concentrations of private wealth, power, and coercion (Sidel 1999). Precisely because of these concentrations, the interests of oligarchs have been well served through electoral democracy before and after the period of authoritarian rule under Ferdinand Marcos.[9] This political dominance and form of state power has facilitated highly profitable capital accumulation strategies compatible with entrenched poverty and official corruption. Neither diversification of oligarchic economic interests nor recent accelerated economic growth has changed this. Consequently, struggles for more effective popular participation by moderate and radical forces continue. However, differences in substantive reform agendas and, hence, political strategies of these forces reflect in the institutions and ideologies of representation they have sought to promote or embrace.

In these struggles over institutions and ideologies of representation the form that oligarchic power takes in the Philippines assumes considerable importance. Winters (2012, 53) generally observes that oligarchic power "is distinct because it is materially based." Sometimes this can involve a blending of material power with other resources, including high political office, so that oligarchs and political elites overlap. In the Philippines case, we can go so far as to refer to a "capitalist oligarchy" that structurally shapes such material and political interrelationships. This is especially reflected in the way that politicians are often linked either to powerful capitalist families or to how members of those families may be directly involved in politics.[10] In both cases, though, capital accumulation strategies are reinforced through political rule.

The historical roots of oligarchic state power in the Philippines run deep. Both Spanish and American colonial powers contributed to the power consolidation of local clans and, in turn, a landowning class engaged in commercial agriculture (Teehankee 2013, 188). Therefore, when elections and political parties were introduced early during American colonial rule, networks of state political patronage favoring landed oligarchs simply became more institutionalized through limited intra-elite competition.[11] Despite policy and structure limitations, these parties could marshal extensive private and state resources to electoral advantage, not least for intimidation (Hedman and Sidel 2000, 39–40).

How colonial rule embedded the interests of local oligarchs was crucial and would have long-term implications. Indeed, as Sidel (1999, 19) explains, "a distinctive pattern of state formation shaped the processes of twentieth-century capital accumulation in the Philippines." Specifically, this state formation "facilitated the emergence and entrenchment of small-town bosses, provincial 'war-lords,' and authoritarian presidents by providing mechanisms for private monopolization of the resources and prerogatives of the state" (ibid.). Private power concentrations were aided by the state, which facilitated the capacity of oligarchs to resource political candidates and, in some instances, to intimidate or eliminate others.

From this perspective, the absence of highly centralized administrative and regulatory apparatuses is not a sign of a "weak" state vulnerable to particularistic demands and patronage politics (Hutchison 2001, 44). Instead, the state's institutions and capacities are well suited to serving specific class (oligarchic) interests. This means arresting the power of oligarchs is not a matter of strengthening the state but of transforming state power relations so that different class interests benefit. By definition this would require changes in the nature, purpose, and effect of state institutions—with implications for institutions of political participation and representation, and the scope of conflict permitted through them.

The reproduction of oligarchic economic and political power, though, has necessarily involved dynamic interrelationships between state power and class interests. Hutchcroft's (1998) concept of "booty capitalism" and associated analysis of how oligarchs diversified into industrialization from the 1950s capture such a process. He demonstrates how capitalist development in the Philippines came to rely on, and reinforce, patron-client relations facilitated by privileged access to state power. These interrelationships proved important in subsequent diversifications by oligarchs into finance, real estate, and construction. They were especially conspicuous in the 1990s privatization of utility, infrastructure, and energy sectors, through which, as Heydarian (2015) observes, "well-connected, family-dominated conglomerates came to relish an unprecedented era of oligopolistic profits in strategic sectors of the economy."

Thus, oligarchic interests continue to be profitably served by capital accumulation strategies involving low-paying and low-productivity activities in agriculture and other sectors, despite diversification (see also Diola 2014). A sad irony in this is that such accumulation strategies have forced a huge number of skilled and unskilled Filipinos to go overseas for work, creating new oligarchic business opportunities as a result of domestic consumption driven by remittances from overseas Filipino workers. This source amounted to one-tenth of the Philippines' GDP in 2013, providing a stimulus for shopping mall and other property investments by oligarchs (Nye 2011, 10; Raquiza 2014).

Reformist attempts to reduce poverty and inequality through formal political institutions have been severely constrained by the acute class bias in the exercise of state power in the Philippines. Local level private power concentrations have also facilitated repression and intimidation particularly targeting militant worker and peasant organizations, as well as local journalists reporting on oligarchic practices and interests. Not surprisingly, neither strong social democratic movements involving cross-class alliances nor sustainable, powerful, class-based alternatives have emerged. Meanwhile, there has instead been a fragmentation of social and political forces opposed to oligarchic rule and the periodic rise of radical movements.

Both under colonial rule and during the Cold War, the most organized opposition political forces involved leftist and nationalist-led mass peasant and worker movements whose focus was not principally electoral politics. These included the unsuccessful armed Huk Rebellion (1946–1954) against the Philippine government, demanding major land reforms to limit peasant exploitation.[12] The Communist Party of the Philippines (CPP), founded in 1968, withdrew from electoral politics altogether shortly thereafter in favor of revolutionary armed struggle (Quimpo 2008, 55).

However, as the Cold War intensified, so did the opportunity for elites to generally suppress their opponents and critics on the pretext of combating communism. Under Marcos's rule this process was ramped up, especially following his declaration of martial law in 1972. Apart from the Catholic Church, civil society organizations were broadly harassed, with working class and peasant organizations subjected to greatest repression (Hilhorst 2003, 235).[13] Executive control over the military and police was bolstered and politicized, while anti-communist vigilantism also increased (Hedman and Sidel 2000, 4).

Marcos retained enterprise unionism but also sought to politically co-opt and control a disparate labor leadership via the establishment of a single peak union, the Trade Union Congress of the Philippines (TUCP). However, he did not formally shut down the labor federations that failed to join, nor was he able to contain communist-led extraparliamentary opposition. Consequently, under his authoritarian rule the labor movement became more polarized ideologically (Hutchison 2015, 68–73). The CPP-linked Kilusang Mayo Uno (KMU, May First Movement) was formed in 1980, following which the American Federation of Labor and Congress of Industrial Organizations supported Marcos's labor strategy. Indeed, the latter provided more money to the TUCP to compete with the KMU than it gave to any other labor movement in the world (Scipes 2011, 36).[14]

Intra-elite friction was also inherent to authoritarian rule under Marcos. Indeed, this regime potentially threatened what B. Anderson (1988) labeled post-War "cacique democracy," under which oligarchy faced no serious challenges.[15] Not only did Marcos move to centralize control over resource patronage,[16] he also generally favored cronies beyond the traditional elite through granting preferential access to state licenses, monopolies, and loans (McCoy 2009). It was, however, the 1983 assassination of Benigno Aquino II, a senator of traditional elite pedigree intending to contest for power, that united and activated oligarchic elements in opposition to Marcos (Winters 2012, 61). Thus, these elements combined with liberal and conservative business and Catholic Church critics of Marcos, alongside popular forces with more reformist and radical agendas, to mobilize against him (Thompson 1995; Hutchcroft and Rocamora 2012).

Following the "People Power" overthrow of Marcos in 1986, there were competing attempts to shape the institutional and ideological forms of democracy (Boudreau 2009), affecting the scope and nature of political conflict permissible under this regime. According to the 1987 Constitution, the rights of "marginalized sectors"—including workers, farmers, women, the urban poor, and the elderly—were to be represented in local governments. Hence it was mandated in the 1991 Local Government Code that one quarter of seats be reserved in all municipal, city, and provincial legislative assemblies for NGO representation of various social sectors. Owing to resistance from traditional political elites, though, Congress never enacted the proposed enabling law (Cuarteros 2005, 48).

Before long, it became apparent that electoral institutions restored under President Corazon Aquino (1986–1992) simply resulted in the resumption of elite democracy (Bello and Gershman 1990). This pattern would further consolidate, as established and new political dynasties dominated electoral politics (Rivera 2011, 59–73; Rood 2013). The significance of this went beyond the recurrence of particular families and personalities in Philippine politics, or even the influence of individual presidents. The consolidation of the structural power of oligarchic capitalism underlay these tendencies in political institutions. Certainly, continued capitalist expansion and diversification made the emergence of new entrants into the economic and political elite possible (Pinches 1996; Hedman 2012). Nevertheless, under post-Marcos liberal democracy, the nexus between economic and political power remained strong.

Yet this nexus did not entirely obviate the need for political concessions to opponents of traditional elite politics and/or oligarchic capitalism. The emphatic reassertion of traditional elite power through elections aroused widespread disquiet among civil society forces that needed to be contained, lest it provide a stimulus for more radical popular alternatives. What transpired was the emergence of new formal and informal political institutions of participation and representation. However, these tended to reinforce or compound the structural weaknesses and fragmentation of the opponents of traditional politics and oligarchic capitalism (Boudreau 2009).

It was precisely amidst mounting popular disenchantment with the reassertion of elite-dominated electoral democracy that the 1987 Constitution was modified to guarantee seats in the House of Representatives for hitherto underrepresented groups. Through the 1995 Party-List Act, up to 20 percent of the House of Representatives seats could be elected on the basis of proportional representation, enabling traditionally marginalized sectors, organizations, and parties to hold up to three seats each. The rationale was to strengthen the party system and make Philippine politics more "issue oriented." In practice, though, the party-list system has facilitated a political pluralism characterized by a continued disaggregation of interests and policy issues among challengers to traditional political parties (Wurfel 1997). Paradoxically, the system confers validation for

NGOs as stand-alone entities, which many embrace in preference to broader alliance building with other civil society forces.

Class-based organizations also made few gains following the collapse of authoritarian rule. By 2011, just 4.4 percent of the labor force—or 8.7 percent of all wage and salary earners—were members of a union. More tellingly, less than 1.0 percent of the total workforce and only one in eight union members were sufficiently well organized to be able to collectively bargain over wages and conditions (Hutchison 2015, 66). Economic globalization contributed to this, not least through the decline of the garments industry arising from the end of preferential market access under the Multi Fibre Agreement, as well as the growth in service employment in business call centers where unions have struggled to get a foothold (Ofreneo 2009, 546, 548). The 1993 split of the KMU into blocs reaffirming or rejecting the CPP's armed struggle for state power added to the inability of labor to act as a cohesive political force (Hutchison 2015, 75). The lure of better-paid overseas employment for skilled and educated workers has also had a negative impact on the pool of possible labor leaders (E. S. Cruz 2014).

There has nevertheless been a proliferation of a wide and diverse range of other organizations to fill some of this political vacuum (Yu-Jose 2011). In particular, middle-class–led NGOs have increased significantly to prosecute many causes and issues of concern to the poor and marginalized. Many such organizations, though, are dependent on multilateral aid funding, which can constrain or influence the nature and extent of their activism—especially as it relates to the developmental strategies promoted by elites.

This has been especially evident since the late 1990s with the advent of pro-market governance reform aid programs, including NGO watchdog roles to promote greater accountability and transparency (Rodan and Hughes 2012). Whereas some activists embrace such neoliberal reform agendas, others attempt to modify them by engaging with aid agencies and government, or eschew them altogether to pursue more expansive reform agendas by other political means. This has contributed much to what Hilhorst (2003, 14) observes as civil society's increasing fragmentation "into multiple communities and non-communities."

The absence of any cohesive social or political movement to effectively represent the interests of the most economically and socially marginalized creates conditions for the periodic appeal of populist ideologies of representation. The charismatic Joseph Estrada was thus elected president in the wake of the 1997–1998 Asian financial crisis espousing pro-poor and anti-oligarchy rhetoric. He was removed in 2001, though, by extra-constitutional means following corruption allegations and a related People Power II mobilization against him.

However, class factors underlay the coalition of forces seeking Estrada's removal. Estrada and his cronies were a threat to particular established oligarchic interests by seeking a bigger share of the economic pie under the aegis of apparent market liberalization. The direct representation he offered the poor was also presented as an alternative to intermediary organizations claiming that role. This included middle-class–led NGOs whose reform priorities often favored "clean," liberal governance ahead of major redistributive and structural changes. A subsequent and unsuccessful People Power III mobilization to have Estrada reinstated was almost exclusively supported by working class and poor Filipinos (Hutchison 2006).

It was no coincidence that new state-sponsored forms of political participation and representation emerged thereafter, with poverty alleviation strategies adopting community-driven development (CDD) projects especially prominent. This would see institutions and ideologies of local "empowerment" targeting the poorest communities through the joint initiatives of the Philippines government and multilateral aid agencies.

The Kapit-Bisig Laban sa Kahirapan (Linking Arms Against Poverty)-Comprehensive and Integrated Delivery of Social Services (Kalahi-CIDSS) project has been central to this CDD strategy. Jointly funded by the Philippines government and the World Bank, it was first implemented in 2003 by the National Anti-Poverty Commission (NAPC) in conjunction with the Department of Social Welfare and Development (DSWD). Under Kalahi-CIDSS's expansion during the following decade, competitive participatory processes to determine service delivery and development fund allocations were institutionalized, including through public meetings, elections, and other mechanisms to generate feedback and preferences on project priorities. It is a core assumption of Kalahi-CIDSS that arresting "elite capture" of development projects and reducing poverty depends on developing local capacities to design, implement, and manage development activities (World Bank 2011, 7).

However, instead of CDD-related political participation serving to activate more cohesive civil societies, it has tended to operate as an alternative to them. First, individuals incorporated into the political process do not do so as representatives of collective organizations but as individuals in small village-level communities. This is often reinforced though multiple separate barangay (village)-level consultations and representations. Second, the decision making that representatives participate in has a heavy technical or administrative orientation. While this creates opportunities for some NGOs to assist with local capacity in project selection and implementation, these processes are not designed to accommodate wider debate or contestation over how best to combat poverty. On the contrary, they are premised on the notion that market-supportive mechanisms are pivotal to solving poverty (Reid 2005, 2008).

A new phase in this strategy of societal incorporation was entered when President Benigno Aquino III (also popularly referred to as "Noynoy" Aquino) came to office in 2010, pledging to reduce corruption and poverty through strengthening local participation, campaigning on the slogan *"Kung walang corrupt, walang mahirap"* (If there is no corruption, there would be no poverty) (BBC News 2011). In early 2012 his administration introduced bottom-up budgeting (BUB) and related mechanisms to further increase local input to state-defined poverty alleviation projects. President Aquino implored NGOs to partner the government in this and other CDD initiatives (Burgonio 2012a).[17]

This initiative reflected the influence within Aquino's administration of a broad coalition of technocrats, including those with NGO backgrounds, for whom technical capacity building and the marginalization of corruption at the local level were critical to combating poverty (Dressel 2012). Others within this coalition were less ideologically committed to consultative representation, but through constructive engagement in societal incorporation sought to push the boundaries of legitimate conflict over the causes of poverty and corruption and appropriate policy responses.

The significance of these ideological differences among reformist forces became more conspicuous as impressive increases in economic growth rates under Aquino—which some linked to a harder official line against corruption—were accompanied by the consolidation of inequality and poverty. Despite a 6.4 percent increase in GDP in 2012, much of it fuelled by overseas Filipino workers' remittances, the Philippines' poverty incidence of 27.9 percent remained among the highest in Southeast Asia (Burgonio 2013).[18] It was meanwhile reported in *Forbes Asia* that forty Filipino billionaires increased their wealth by 38 percent, from US$13 billion in 2011 to US$47.4 billion in 2012 (Abinales 2013, 228).

Thus, on the eve of the president's July 2013 State of the Nation address, the Catholic Bishops' Conference of the Philippines demanded that the government demonstrate how the poor and the jobless would benefit from economic growth (Doronila 2013). Then, as Aquino delivered his speech in Congress, leftist Bagong Alyansang Makabayan (Bayan, New Patriotic Alliance) and allied organization activists clashed with police amidst protests for more action on inequality and poverty (Padua 2013). Inside Congress, Aquino pronounced that "inclusive growth" would now be his government's thematic objective.

To be sure, Aquino's goal resonated strongly with the concerns of all civil society forces opposed to poverty and inequality. The question that would continue to generate contention among and between elites and civil society forces was just what institutions and ideologies of representation were needed to realize this goal. This was not principally a struggle over the quality of institutions but about the extent and nature of conflict over the structural power of oligarchic interests permitted through them.

While this struggle was playing out, though, the ineffectiveness of established institutions or new MOPs to adequately address popular concerns once again made it possible for the election of another populist president. In May 2016, Rodrigo Duterte, mayor of Davao City who formed the small Hugpong sa Tawong Lungsod (People of the Towns Party) in 2011, was elected president. Duterte's anti-oligarchic rhetoric and law and order agenda to address social problems trumped the campaigns by his liberal and conservative opponents. Significantly, his support base extended beyond the poor to include upwardly mobile middle-class elements anxious about rising crime and preserving their own social and material gains. Duterte's moral politics portended not structural reform to address inequality but discipline and punishment of behavioral practices among the poor who threatened social order (Curato 2016; Thompson 2016).

Malaysia

In contrast with Singapore and the Philippines, in Malaysia technocratic consultative ideologies and institutions of representation have exerted little influence. They pose a potential threat to a political regime founded on the premise of ethnic Malay political supremacy, and around which extensive systems of patronage are built. Instead, particularist ideologies of ethnicity, race, and religion have been central to rationalizing the interests of a state-promoted ethnic Malay bourgeoisie and the related powers of a politico-bureaucratic elite. They also guide public policies meant to ensure socially equitable outcomes of capitalist growth. However, the political management of capitalism under the ruling Barisan Nasional (BN, National Front) faces periodic challenges due to intra-elite tensions inherent to Malaysian state capitalism and, increasingly, contradictions between official particularist ideologies of race, ethnicity, and religion and concrete outcomes of growth.

Consequently, despite authoritarian controls, significant oppositional civil society and individual expressions have at times surfaced outside the parameters of the dominant BN-controlled MOPs. Indeed, since the mid-2000s, this has involved unprecedented mobilizations to reform the very electoral institutions that have hitherto been so effective in incorporating diverse interests while controlling the limits of permissible political conflict. Yet organizational limits rooted in colonial and Cold War legacies and internal tensions to these movements have made it difficult to forge sustainable and shared alternative ideological visions for new MOPs.

History has significantly shaped the social foundations of contemporary particularism in Malaysia. Under colonial capitalism, the numerically ascendant indigenous ethnic Malays as well as immigrant ethnic Chinese and Indian communities were predominantly incorporated into distinct labor and capital market roles (Puthucheary 1960; Sundaram 1988). As Khoo Boo Teik explains, Malaysia's political economy was "Janus-like: its *ethnic* aspect constantly exposed while its *class* aspect was hidden. Thus, the structures of political economy and the inequalities they bore were susceptible to political mobilization that seized upon real and 'perceived' ethnic differences [italics in original]" (B. T. Khoo 2005, 1).

Ethnic ideological and political lenses were reinforced by the way that colonial authorities engaged and fostered ethnic elites and their organizations. This approach was pivotal to the brokering of a compromise deal among ethnic elites that led to the Federation of Malaysia in 1948 and Malayan independence in 1957. Importantly, this deal was also premised on anticipated ethnic affirmative action. Under the 1957 Constitution, ethnic Malays and the indigenous people of Sabah and Sarawak—collectively referred to as the Bumiputeras ("sons of the soil") and composing approximately 50 percent of the population—were accorded "special positions." The Constitution prescribed "reserve quotas" for Bumiputeras in the civil service, scholarships and training opportunities, university places, and permits and licenses for trade and business regulated by federal law. It also accorded Islam the status of Malaysia's official religion.

Colonial authorities' promotion of ethnic politics was accompanied by their sensitivity toward class-based notions of solidarity and organizations through which the interests of peasants and workers could be represented (Nonini 2015, 36–39). The Malayan Communist Party—and the Pan-Malayan Federation of Trade Unions, among which it had some influence—were eventually banned in 1948. A declaration of a state of emergency in 1948 also precipitated a general period of intimidation directed at organizations with any suspected communist elements or sympathies. Consequently, left-wing–oriented organizations were almost entirely banned by the end of the 1940s (Mohamad 2009, 121). The communist bogey would continue during the 1950s and 1960s to provide authorities with a rationale for dismantling union and opposition party leaderships under the Internal Security Act and other repressive laws (Munro-Kua 1996, 40–57).

Another part of the earlier British anti-communist strategy involved local elections, to steer activism away from radical action. This created limited opportunities, particularly in towns and cities, for social democratic and socialist political parties still seeking to transcend communal politics. However, success in local elections by such parties led to the indefinite suspension of these elections in the mid-1960s. When the Labour Party was also deregistered in 1972, the foundations for viable class-based or cross-class alternatives to ethnic politics were dealt a further and decisive blow.[19]

A political framework of ethnic representation and interethnic power sharing was adopted under Prime Minister Abdul Rahman and the Alliance coalition of parties that ruled from 1957 until 1969. This coalition comprised the United Malays National Organization (UMNO), the Malayan Chinese Association (MCA), and the Malayan Indian Congress (MIC) (von Vorys 1975).[20] However, the Alliance largely included conservative interests with a common stake in the preservation of the same capitalist order that had presided over widespread social inequality and poverty (Sundaram 1988, 247).

Consequently, the Alliance coalition failed to meet the expectations of impoverished ethnic Malays or lay foundations for social harmony.[21] In the May 1969 general elections, the Alliance secured just 48.5 percent of the popular vote in peninsula Malaysia, where substantial opposition seat gains were made by the predominantly ethnic-Chinese Democratic Action Party (DAP) and Gerakan Rakyat Malaysia (Malaysian People's Movement), as well as the ethnic-Malay Parti Islam Se-Malaysia (PAS, Pan-Malaysian Islamic Party) (Wong and Othman 2009, 12). At this point, polls were suspended for the rest of Malaysia, race riots broke out, and a state of emergency was declared, which would last until 1971.

As Sundaram (1988, 254) observed, "In the absence of strongly influential, class-oriented ideologies and organizations capable of forging a multiracial, class-based solidarity, the opposition towards some of the felt consequences of postcolonial development surfaced in interracial antagonism." What followed, though, was the ideological and institutional elevation of ethnicity in elite strategies to politically manage capitalist development, reinforced by increased authoritarian controls over ruling coalition opponents and critics. The centerpiece of public policy, announced in 1970, was the New Economic Policy (NEP).[22]

The NEP constituted a distinctive interventionist strategy of state capitalism, emphasizing the promotion of an ethnic Malay bourgeoisie and accompanied by assorted distributional policies favoring ethnic Malays in general (E. T. Gomez 2002; Pepinsky 2009; E. T. Gomez and Saravanamuttu 2013). Crucially, state patronage to develop a Malay business class was not dispensed randomly but in ways that strengthened UMNO's power base.[23] Such a system was conducive to corruption and periodic conflicts over patronage between contending coalitions of party-political, bureaucratic, and business interests (Searle 1999; E. T. Gomez 2002).

This new phase of Malaysian capitalism was accompanied by a strategy of incorporating a wider range of parties into the federal ruling coalition. For lack of better options to influence public policy, many hitherto opposition parties responded positively to government rhetoric about "power sharing."[24] Under the ruling coalition, now called the BN, which parties contested what seats was strategically guided by the ethnic composition of constituencies.[25] Yet power sharing was fundamentally premised on ethnic Malay political dominance. Hence, by the mid-1970s, UMNO leaders had come to monopolize virtually every key post in Cabinet (B. T. Khoo 2005, 15).

Importantly, this strategy differed from consultative representation, despite its goal and effect of reducing political competition. Foremost, those incorporated were elected rather than appointed. Moreover, rather than working to depoliti-cize coalition decision making by emphasizing technocratic problem solving, this strategy reinforced particularism as the foundational ideological basis of politi-cal representation. Appeals by non-UMNO parties to technocratic consultative ideologies occurred for a brief period under Prime Minister Abdul Razak Hus-sein in the early 1970s and intermittently thereafter, but without being taken up by UMNO leaders with sustained collective conviction.

However, as tensions and contradictions inherent to Malaysian state capital-ism manifested, BN strategies for containing the permissible bounds of political conflict faced challenges—from supporters as well as opponents of particularism. The NEP helped raise the political confidence and material expectations of Malays in general (Milne and Mauzy 1999, 81–82), including those seeking to advance religious particularism. For some, this extended to Sharia law and even the eventual goal of an Islamic state, which was at odds with BN policy and would account for PAS's departure from the BN coalition as early as 1997. At various points, the BN would see the need to co-opt, repress, and attempt to accommo-date social forces advocating religious particularism (Mohamad 2010).

Among the tensions associated with Malaysian state capitalism, none is more important than intra-elite struggles over patronage during economic crises and restructuring. These tensions create motivations and opportunities for greater crit-ical scrutiny of BN ruling elites and their institutions. This is precisely what hap-pened when Mahathir Mohamad, who became prime minister in 1981, pushed through liberalizing reforms in the mid-1980s to expedite Malaysia's industrial transformation and maximize economic growth.

Under Mahathir, increased civil society and individual expression critical of ruling elites and their institutions were routinely met with repression, rarely ac-companied by creative new MOPs as in authoritarian Singapore. Thus, more than a hundred people were detained under the Internal Security Act (ISA) in Operasi Lalang (Weeding Operation), beginning in October 1987 and targeting a range of Mahathir's party-political and civil society critics and opponents (Weiss 2003, 36). Some detainees wanted particularism harnessed to different interests and val-ues from Mahathir; others sought more liberal and/or democratic institutions to enforce greater elite accountability.

Mahathir subsequently pursued his reform agenda through the New Develop-ment Plan, introduced in 1990. This fostered new conglomerates through extensive privatizations of state assets, availing various select, politically trusted business figures of privileged monopolies or oligopolies (B. T. Khoo 2006, 184). However, the 1997–1998 Asian financial crisis found many new conglomerates overexposed to loans, sparking UMNO factional competition. A pledge in 1997 by Deputy Prime Minister Anwar Ibrahim that there would be no bailing out of politically connected conglomerates was overruled, resulting in a string of scandals and controversies over corporate rescues by the state from early 1998 (E. T. Gomez 2002, 101–7; Pepinsky 2009, 136–42).

Economic crisis morphed into political crisis following Anwar's expulsion from UMNO and imprisonment in September 1998,[26] resulting in the formation in 1999 of the Parti Keadilan Nasional (National Justice Party).[27] This party drew significant ethnic Malay support away from UMNO and helped ignite the broader *reformasi* (reformation) movement characterized by unprecedented cooperation among BN party-political opponents and between these parties and civil society activists. Social forces who variously embraced democratization, liberal notions of good governance, and/or Islamic religious morality found common cause against state corruption and power abuses (Rodan and Hughes 2014, 60–75), although differing on the root causes of, and solutions to, such state practices. Included in this was an expansion of middle class NGOs, who were predominantly ethnic Chinese, but nevertheless espoused non-ethnic politics. Despite massive public demonstrations over several years and some opposition electoral gains in 1999, though, the *reformasi* movement soon collapsed. Infighting over religious and ethnic sensitivities resulted in a retreat back to segmented forms of political organization around single issues (Weiss 2006, 127–61).

Significantly, amidst the tumult of the 1980s and 1990s, the BN explored state-based societal incorporation involving consultative representation in a bid to contain conflict, notably with the establishment of the National Economic Consultative Council (NECC). The NECC incorporated party-political, NGO, and other notional representatives for major policy recommendations. It convened in 1989–1991 with a view to smoothing the transition from the NEP to the New Development Plan, and in 1999–2000 to advise on the next development plan— the National Vision Policy (2000–2010). However, the NECC failed to exert influence or gain broad acceptance within government. Its recommendations on reducing and eliminating social, economic, and regional inequalities, and on how to balance economic growth with such goals, were at odds with the interests of powerful senior bureaucrats and BN leaders. This failed experiment made it more likely that disaffected citizens would increasingly look to other MOPs, notably independent organizations and parties outside the BN coalition seeking reform (H. H. Lim 2005).

This likelihood was further fuelled in the approach to the 2008 general elections as expanded growth was accompanied by new social and material inequalities. In the most recent phase of Malaysian capitalism, inequalities became more significant within ethnic groups, between regions, and between urban and rural communities (E. T. Gomez and Saravanamuttu 2013; Sundaram and Wee 2014; UNDP 2014). Conflicts over these inequalities could no longer be as effectively contained through the existing BN frameworks of ethnic representation. Support for coalitions within the BN began to strain, and more concerted cross-ethnic mobilizations in opposition to the BN became possible. Anwar's release from prison in 2004 gave this mobilization a fillip.

Importantly, increased inequalities were linked in part to accumulation strategies of BN-linked conglomerates that raised utilities and services costs affecting lower middle and working classes in particular (B. T. Khoo 2010, 19; Mohamad 2013). This included oligopolistic charges by highway concessionaires, operators of urban light rail, electrical power producers, and urban waste disposal providers (B. T. Khoo 2010, 19). Meanwhile, Malaysia's wealthiest enjoyed a rapidly growing share of the country's GDP (UNDP 2014, 48–49).

Signs that the BN framework of ethnic political representation was faltering were dramatically evidenced in November 2007 when approximately 30,000 Indians, aligned with a new Hindu Rights Action Front (HINDRAF) NGO, protested against social and economic marginalization. Religious and ethnic discrimination were core HINDRAF grievances, but Indians were also disproportionately concentrated in the lowest paid and unsafe employment and among the most adversely affected by rising costs of, and reduced access to, services due to privatization (B. T. Khoo 2010, 23). The mere establishment of HINDRAF was a major rebuff for the Malaysian Indian Congress (MIC) and the ruling coalition's framework of political representation controlled through the mode of party and parliamentary politics.

A more concerted threat to that framework emerged in November 2007 through Bersih (Gabungan Pilihanraya Bersih dan Adil, Coalition for Free and Fair Elections)—whose 40,000 multiethnic supporters assembled in central Kuala Lumpur demanding electoral reform. Cleaning up electoral processes was now a strategic priority to address material, social, and religious inequalities and state power abuses through a change of government. More and larger Bersih demonstrations in defiance of authorities would occur in subsequent years. Bersih reflected deep structural changes in the post-Mahathir political economy that built on sociological and demographic impacts of earlier capitalist development (B. T. Khoo 2012).

The approach to, and results of, the 2008 general elections seemed to signify enhanced cooperation among BN's varied opponents. This included a new opposition coalition—Pakatan Rakyat (PR, People's Alliance)—comprising Parti Keadilan Rakyat (PKR, People's Justice Party), DAP, and PAS and led by Anwar Ibrahim.

Anwar denounced the BN's ethnic politics and the core related proposition that Malay political supremacy was pivotal to distributional justice in Malaysia. Highlighting that most people living in poverty were ethnic Malay, Anwar asked: "What type of supremacy is this? We should instead abolish the question of ethnicity and solve the problem of poverty" (quoted in Asrul 2010).

The BN retained government in 2008, but its vote share fell to just over 50 percent. The BN vote share dropped further at the 2013 elections, and only extreme electoral malapportionment saved it from defeat (H. G. Lee 2015). By this time, middle-class support for PR across ethnic categories had consolidated in major cities and towns—especially in peninsula Malaysia where ethnic Malays had been core to preelection rallies and demonstrations (Welsh 2013a).

Yet the 2013 election results also highlighted uneven transformations in ethnic political identity and the complexity and importance of class and geography as mediating factors in this process. Increased BN appeals to communalism prompted record opposition votes by ethnic Chinese, disproportionately middle class and located in cities and towns. However, the BN's pitch and targeted handouts to working-class and rural ethnic Malay voters in west and, particularly, east Malaysia proved decisive in securing government (Welsh 2013b). Critically, UMNO emerged even more politically ascendant, now accounting for two-thirds of all BN seats. The corollary, though, was heightened political polarization in Malaysia.

Political expectations and demands of Islamic religious particularists and extremist Malay nationalists heightened after the 2013 election. Such was the atmosphere that in November 2014 Prime Minister Najib Razak not only abandoned a 2012 vow to repeal the Sedition Act, apparently meant to win back support from ethnic minorities and young urban voters, but committed to reinforcing it with new provisions "to protect the sanctity of Islam and other religions" (Fuller 2014). This act would be used extensively to curb antigovernment criticism and dissent, especially following the public reaction to a February 2015 Federal Court ruling that found Anwar guilty of sodomy and sentenced him to five years in jail (Grant 2015).

Yet UMNO's enhanced political ascendancy was also accompanied by possibly the party's biggest official scandal ever, giving further cause for contestation over prevailing governance and political institutions. In July 2015, the *Wall Street Journal* and the *Sarawak Report* website reported that US$700 million, allegedly originating from Malaysia's heavily indebted sovereign wealth fund One Malaysia Development Bank (1MDB), were deposited in Najib's private bank accounts.

These allegations escalated factional efforts within UMNO to defend or remove Najib (Lee and Chew 2015; Wright and Clark 2015), including criticism from Mahathir and the sacking of five ministers. The controversy precipitated more public demonstrations, under the fourth Bersih rally, in September 2015. In this context, a National Security Council Bill was introduced, with sweeping new powers concentrated in the prime minister. This greatly enhanced Najib's ability not just to suppress peaceful assembly but also to intimidate and neutralize challengers to his power within UMNO and beyond (Ramzy 2015).

However, it was not just the BN that was struggling to maintain its coalitions after the 2013 elections but also PR. Following PAS's poor showing at those elections, its Islamic agenda became more vigorously reasserted, accompanied by a clean sweep of senior leadership posts by conservative clerics in June 2015, wiping out the progressive pro-PR professionals' faction. This brought to a head simmering intra-PR differences over whether local government elections should be reintroduced in states where PR had won office, and contention over *hudud*—the Islamic criminal code allowing for punishments such as amputation and whipping. The two issues were not unrelated. The DAP in particular saw local elections as an opportunity for the opposition to dominate urban centers, whereas PAS conservatives in rural states like Kelantan did not want the implementation of *hudud* complicated by majority Chinese populations resisting such policies (*Straits Times* 2015). The underlying ideologies of political representation informing these parties' rationales for local participation differed considerably.

The PR alliance officially ended in July 2015, although this did not mean a complete end to cooperation—including the continuance of the PR government in highly urbanized Selangor (*Malaysiakini* 2015d). The opposition coalition also partially reformed in September 2015 minus PAS, in the context of the mounting controversy over 1MDB (Reuters 2015). However, ethnic Chinese overly dominated the fourth Bersih rally in the absence of PAS's involvement.

Capitalist transformations had helped close the gap in the sociocultural experiences of Malays and non-Malays (B. T. Khoo 2012), but this was an uneven and incomplete process. Ethnic and religious particularist ideologies remained a powerful force outside, as well as inside, the ruling coalition. Yet as the contradictions of Malaysia's distinctive model of state capitalism intensified, the BN framework of ethnic representation through the parliamentary MOP could no longer contain political conflict as effectively as before. Indeed, cognizant of this, the regime's most extreme supporters increasingly also took to the streets in late 2015 to demonstrate as a counter to Bersih.

Such growing political polarization and extraparliamentary activism reflects the difficulty of material and ideological interests embedded in Malaysia's model of state capitalism being reproduced through as wide a range of MOPs as in either Singapore or the Philippines.

In essence, four broad points can be distilled from the above, providing a basis for proceeding in subsequent chapters to embark on more detailed examinations of contemporary initiatives in, and struggles over, institutions of political representation in Singapore, the Philippines, and Malaysia.

First, notwithstanding important variations in the nature of colonial rule, transitions to independence, and Cold War politics in all three countries, these processes have uniformly worked against strong and cohesive class-based or cross-class independent collective organizations to compete with, or arrest, elite power. This has profoundly shaped struggles over political representation, wherein elites have generally sought to reproduce or build on this legacy to ensure continued political fragmentation among their opponents and critics.

Second, the transformative and contradictory nature of capitalist development nevertheless creates potential for new social forces and coalitions seeking to exert influence over institutions and ideologies of representation. Yet this potential and how elites go about trying to contain it necessarily vary. Capitalism is organized around particular coalitions of interest that shape the possibilities of, and limits to, elite strategies of capital accumulation and the political management of conflict arising from such accumulation.

This is why, for example, the forms and degrees that neoliberal policy directions have taken are not identical in each of these countries. It is also why consultative ideologies and institutions feature to varying degrees in Singapore and the Philippines but are inconsequential in Malaysia. As we have seen above, capitalism in Malaysia is so closely tied to the interests of an emerging ethnic Malay business class reliant upon UMNO, and vice versa, that state power cannot be easily accommodated to technocratic ideologies and institutions of political representation.

Third, even where similar MOPs are adopted across regimes, the motivations behind institutional strategies and nature of the coalitions of interest underpinning them may differ significantly, with important political implications. This is quite clear in the contrast between the respective pushes for consultative institutions in Singapore and the Philippines. In the former, the introduction of the FU/REACH was intended by elites to incorporate individuals and groups into state-controlled forms of political participation in order to demobilize their critics and opponents. By contrast, at least some of the architects of BUB in the Philippines envisaged this institution as a way of creating a new class of engaged and mobilized citizens to bring about governance and/or social and political reform.

This reflected in the precise mix of experts and other social forces that elites were inclined, or resigned, to incorporate into consultative institutions within Singapore and the Philippines. The coalition behind the BUB in the Philippines comprised both liberal technocratic and radical leftist reformers, united in their opposition to corrupt oligarchic rule. In contrast, the driving rationale behind Singapore's extensive forays into consultative representation has been to defend and extend the interests of technocratic authoritarian rule.

Fourth, the underlying assumption of this chapter is not that all social conflict can be traced to capitalist development or that there is any simple cause-and-effect relationship between capitalism and the ideologies and institutions of political representation. The point is, however, that capitalist dynamics fundamentally shape the structural context within which new and existing social conflicts may be ideologically or institutionally accommodated, repressed, or contained—either inside or outside the formal political system.

Building on the above three points, the following chapters attempt more focused examinations of contemporary elite strategies of, and wider struggles over, ideologies and institutions of political representation with a view to casting much more detailed light on the core research questions of this study—namely, what forms and ideologies of political participation take root, why, and to what effect.

NOMINATED MEMBERS OF PARLIAMENT IN SINGAPORE

Jennifer Gandhi (2008, xxiv) has observed that the presence of legislatures and parties within authoritarian regimes offers "little in the way of representation and accountability to participants and ordinary citizens." In keeping with this observation, Levitsky and Way (2002, 54) have depicted Singapore under the ruling People's Action Party (PAP) as having a "façade electoral regime" where "electoral institutions exist but yield no meaningful contestation for power." If Geddes (2006, 161) is right that relatively few authoritarian regimes "have hit upon a formula for successful and stable inclusionary authoritarianism," then Singapore certainly seems to be in this select camp. This is possible, though, because the PAP has developed creative new modes of participation (MOPs) through nondemocratic institutions in response to dynamic social conflicts and forces. To be sure, some of these forces seek to exploit these institutions for democratic ends. However, the effectiveness of such strategies is constrained by the way that these new MOPs generally help consolidate and reinforce the disorganized and politically fragmented nature of civil society.

The introduction in 1990 of nominated members of parliament (NMPs) has been the most explicit and significant nondemocratic institution of political representation under the PAP. This institution hovers on the conceptual border between administrative and societal incorporation, fostering avenues for political participation by individuals in their own right, and as members of state-conceived and independent social groups. The NMP scheme is also significant in operating within an established political institution: the parliament. This highlights the complex layering that can involve new MOPs, sometimes superimposed on an existing mode of participation, with implications for how the latter functions.

Crucially, the PAP's rationale for the NMP category of parliamentarians officially embodies a consultative ideology of representation as an alternative to democratic representation. This ideology emphasizes the problem-solving utility of incorporating stakeholders' interests, opinions, and/or expertise into public policy processes and deliberations thereof. In this technocratic or managerial view of politics, conflict and competition give way to rational debate and ideas functional for improved economic, social, or political governance. What matters in this ideology is not a citizen's democratic right to discipline representatives, but that there are deliberations and consultations which can represent the public interest by availing ruling elites of useful information and perspectives. Such engagement lays the basis for elite claims to consensus politics, though not its substance, since the PAP controls the scope and nature of contending interests and views represented.

However, in contrast with the general preoccupation of transition theory in analyzing political institutions in so-called hybrid regimes, the point of this chapter is not to dismiss NMPs on the basis that they are intended as an alternative to, rather than an adjunct of, democratic representation. The purpose is instead to gain insight into the nature of the PAP's ideologies of representation by explaining why this particular institutional innovation emerged and what its significance is for political regime directions in Singapore.

The NMP scheme is part of a wider PAP response to the growing social complexity and emerging conflicts generated by capitalist development evident from the early 1980s. In essence, the PAP embarked on state-sponsored institutional innovations in an attempt to politically manage these pressures by undercutting the foundations for more potent, collectively organized competition with PAP interests and ideas. In particular, new structures and ideologies of representation promote political participation in such a way as to bypass or attempt to control intermediary organizations.

Indeed, as this chapter will demonstrate, the NMP scheme helps to reproduce political fragmentation, providing functional representation of discrete interests, including domestic business, labor, women, and ethnic organizations. This fosters a compartmentalization of policy issues and communities, successfully drawing attention away from underlying thematic structural factors and related power relationships. A consultative ideology of representation is dominant here, but often in articulation with particularist ideologies, especially of ethnic identity. Political engagement through the NMP scheme thus presents itself—to individuals and groups—as an alternative to the cultivation of political coalitions around broader or systemic issues that might lay the basis for an independent reform movement. Moreover, various activist groups and individuals—including those with environmental, feminist, and assorted liberal or democratic reform goals—have either embraced the NMP scheme or tactically accommodated themselves to it. In the process, nondemocratic ideologies of representation have been institutionally shored up, although not universally internalized by NMPs.

The NMP scheme's significance and durability owes much to the dynamic complexion of NMP appointments. Conflicts have changed in nature and emphasis as a result of social and economic transformations of capitalism. Appointments meant to contain conflict have thus shifted accordingly. However, against the backdrop of parliamentary gains at the 2011 polls by Singapore's elected opposition, critics of the scheme questioned its continued relevance. For the ruling party, though, NMPs became all the more important to arresting growing party-political polarization over the social and political management of capitalist development's impacts in Singapore. More broadly, the NMP scheme remains integral to PAP strategies to consolidate political fragmentation, both at the ideological and organizational levels, so that any opposition electoral gains are not accompanied by broad reformist coalitions to strengthen and widen the political challenge to the PAP.

Origins of the Nominated Members of Parliament Scheme
A Technocratic Solution to Capitalist Problems

The NMP scheme, among other new MOPs developed by the Singapore government,[1] was in response to declining PAP electoral support amidst rising social discontent accompanying the city-state's capitalist transformation. Competitive global pressures facing Singapore's export-oriented industrialization strategy resulted in disruptive restructuring policies beginning in the late 1970s. General cost of living pressures on lower-income Singaporeans, most notably in healthcare, transportation, and housing, had also started to emerge, suggesting that the initial phase of comparatively egalitarian material and social outcomes of this strategy might be difficult to replicate without additional redistributive mechanisms (Rodan 1989, 182–86). Popular concern over these changes was reflected in the 1984 election results, including loss of two PAP seats to the opposition in (largely) working-class areas. The PAP-controlled National Trades Union Congress (NTUC), and other grassroots parapolitical institutions (Pang 1971; Seah 1973), appeared to be less effective than previously in mobilizing working-class support for the ruling party.

Concurrently, for the rising middle class, the city-state's social transformation under capitalism was producing a more educated and socially differentiated population, laying the basis for a new range of separate identities, interest groups, and even collective organizational structures outside the direct control of the PAP. Indeed, in 1985, the feminist Association of Women for Action and Research (AWARE) was established, and other small organizations dominated by middle class professionals soon emerged or became more active, including over environmental issues.

There was also a growing disjuncture between official claims that Singapore was a meritocratic society that placed a premium on talent and formal credentials (Worthington 2003; Barr 2006, 2014), on the one hand, and the dearth of opportunities for so many middle-class professionals to play a policy/political role, on the other. This appeared to assume all the more importance as demographic trends and class transformations combined. Just over 50 percent of the 1.5 million eligible voters at the 1984 election were under thirty-five years of age (Rodan 1993, 86). In the PAP's electoral postmortem, this suggested a need to politically reach out to the fast-growing, better-educated, and younger middle class, to preempt any broader electoral drift or emergence of new independent collective political capacity to contest PAP ideas and interests.

Developments elsewhere in Asia during the 1980s gave PAP leaders additional cause for reviewing the adequacy of existing strategies for reproducing authoritarian rule in Singapore. Authoritarian regimes fell in Taiwan and South Korea, which had both, like Singapore, experienced rapid export-oriented industrialization under capitalism and expanded middle classes. The removal of Marcos and return to democracy in the Philippines, a landslide electoral victory for the National League for Democracy in Burma, and the student uprising in Tiananmen Square in China also served in different ways to underline the complex and dynamic challenges for authoritarianism in the region.

Importantly, it was also during the 1980s that the first generation of PAP leaders were progressively replaced by a group with less diverse social backgrounds and lacking comparable political skills in oratory, organization, and mobilization that earlier leaders possessed. These new leaders had risen to power boasting technical or managerial skills functional to the economic interests of the party-state (Mauzy and Milne 2002, 45; Rodan 2008, 238–40). This leadership shift was symptomatic of the heightened structural importance of statutory bodies and government-linked companies to Singapore's domestic political economy (Rodan 2008, 244–46). In this context, the interests of Singapore's professional middle class became more dependent on the state, compared with its counterparts in Taiwan or South Korea.

Crucially, as state capitalism flourished alongside the deepening of Singapore's incorporation into global capitalist markets, the ideological hegemony of technocratic elites consolidated and extended within the party-state. This hegemony greatly accentuated and helped to synthesize views of politics as a technical problem solving—rather than fundamentally normative—exercise, with the importance of people with expert knowledge and skills having decisive control over public policy decisions.[2] Both ideological impulses would be central to the NMP scheme's emergence in 1990, and the ideology of consultation that underlay it.

Cementing NMPs in Consensus Politics

In the wake of the 1984 election, the then Deputy Prime Minister Goh Chok Tong, subsequently prime minister between 1990 and 2004, asserted that: "What a plural society like ours needs is a tradition of government which emphasizes consensus instead of division, that includes rather than excludes, and that tries to maximize the participation of the population in the national effort, instead of minimizing it" (C. T. Goh 1986, 7). Importantly, this sort of consultation was seen as functional for elite rule, enabling the gathering of intelligence helpful to the effective refinement, implementation, and political management of public policy.

This was a point that Lee Hsien Loong (1999), deputy prime minister at the time, was even more explicit about later: "In a rapidly changing environment, much of the valuable up-to-date information is held by people at the frontline. Policy makers must draw on this knowledge to understand realities on the ground, and reach better solutions." He reiterated this perspective on the eve of his ascension as prime minister in 2004, endorsing more civic political participation on the basis that: "The overriding objective is to reach the correct conclusions on the best way forward" (H. L. Lee 2004).

In explaining the need for NMPs, Goh Chok Tong sought to address what he saw as a public misconception that the PAP was closed to alternative points of view on policy. Yet it was clear that he did not consider the views advanced through opposition political parties as valuable to policy deliberations. NMPs were therefore intended to be nonpartisan and "concentrate on the substance of the debate rather than form and rhetoric" (C. T. Goh 1989, col. 700). The legislation altering the Constitution referred to "independent and non-partisan views" in the selection criteria for NMPs (Republic of Singapore 1990, sec. 3.2). Deputy Prime Minister Lee Hsien Loong also expressed the hope that NMPs would help arrest the increasing support for opposition candidates (*STWOE* 1989, 6). Significantly, though, Goh made mention not only of the value of incorporating talented people with special expertise in the professions, commerce, industry, social services, and cultural domains but also of sections of society currently underrepresented in parliament, including women (C. T. Goh 1989, col. 697).

From the outset, then, the rationale for NMPs straddled a couple of arguments. One was the elitist and technocratic argument that the parliament needed apolitical experts who could steer debate towards constructive public policy contributions, elevating exchanges beyond combative engagement.[3] This conformed in some ways with Edmund Burke's (1968) emphasis on the substantive virtue and expert knowledge of representatives as trustees of the public. However, the scheme was also an admission, in effect, that various social interests and segments of society were underrepresented and needed to be more effectively incorporated into parliament to preempt their drift to oppositional politics. Indeed, as the scheme evolved, expert knowledge increasingly came to be viewed by the Select Committee to include a "good feel" for views and aspirations among different sections of the population.

Implementing the NMP Scheme

By the standards of Singapore's parliament, the NMP bill aroused exceptional controversy. Not surprisingly, opposition parties saw the scheme as an attempt by the ruling party to further marginalize it by stacking parliament with pro-PAP NMP "stooges." Many PAP backbenchers were also concerned that this initiative would erode their own status as representatives, with almost one-third of PAP members of parliament (MPs) expressing opposition to the scheme when the bill was first introduced into parliament in November 1989. Up until this time, a standard PAP response to critics about the lack of accountability in Singapore was to emphasize how all MPs had to face the electorate's judgment. Notwithstanding the constraints to electoral competition, PAP MPs generally took the relationship with constituents seriously, and the most popular ones were those who did. The PAP backbench reaction to the NMP idea was thus understandable.

There was no more concerted PAP critic of the NMP proposal than Tan Cheng Bock. Tan was chairman of the Feedback Unit from 1985 to 1999, so he was a strong supporter of new MOPs. However, he voted against the NMP scheme in every parliament until he retired in 2006, principally on the basis that NMPs were not accountable to any constituency. Meanwhile, Tan's PAP colleagues quickly came to accept the NMP scheme as part of the wider set of institutional innovations meant to protect the PAP from a transition toward a more competitive party system. More importantly, enough individuals and organizations not aligned to the PAP found the NMP scheme attractive, or at least worth trying to harness to some limited political ends.

NMPs are appointed for terms of up to 2.5 years by the president, on the advice of a Special Select Committee appointed by parliament, chaired by the speaker and invariably dominated by PAP MPs.[4] Nominations from the Select Committee include candidates considered to have undertaken distinguished public service or brought honor to Singapore (Republic of Singapore 1990, sec. 3.2). The Committee also invites candidate proposals from social, community, sectoral, and professional organizations for consideration. In contrast with elected MPs, NMPs cannot vote on money bills, bills to alter the Constitution, or motions of no confidence in the government. However, they can speak on these issues, and vote and speak on any other bills and motions. In order to allay concerns within its own ranks, the government required that each new parliament would have to approve the continuation of the NMP scheme. Yet not only was that approval secured without exception thereafter, but in 2009 the Constitution was also amended to permanently enshrine NMPs. In 1997, the number of NMPs allowed for was increased too, from the original maximum of six to up to nine.

The numerical significance of this seemingly modest permanent NMP presence was especially highlighted following the 2011 election results, which saw the share of valid votes by the opposition rise to 40 percent. Due to Singapore's first-past-the-post voting system and electoral gerrymandering, this translated into just six opposition seats by the Workers' Party (N. Tan 2013),[5] equivalent to two-thirds of the NMPs that were appointed to the Twelfth Parliament. Even if we take account of the three non-constituency members of parliament (NCMPs) appointed, the number of NMPs was still comparable to the PAP's party-political opponents in parliament. As is explained below, though, while members of the PAP establishment, if not overt supporters of the PAP, have tended to dominate NMP appointments, there has also been selective incorporation of political progressives with reform aspirations of some kind. Thus, however inconsequential the NMP scheme may have been for policy reform, it has nevertheless been important to keeping the PAP's critics and opponents politically fragmented.

Absorbing and Fragmenting Social Interests

Since the first two appointments of NMPs to the Seventh Parliament in 1990, the scheme has expanded significantly to involve seventy-four different people and a total of ninety-four appointments by the Twelfth Parliament in 2014, with some NMPs serving more than one term of appointment. The complexion of appointments suggests they have been intended to both supplement existing mechanisms of political co-option and provide a new avenue for political participation by Singapore's expanded middle class. Significantly, it has not just been conservative but also some progressive elements of this class that have been attracted to the NMP scheme. Indeed, Singapore's fledgling civil society organizations have been targeted in an apparent PAP strategy to discourage their maturation as independent organizations and to limit their potential to form broad reform coalitions, either among themselves or with opposition parties.

Table 4.1 identifies the chief characteristics and dynamics of the various NMP appointments on the basis of functional groups or social sectors. The categories adopted here approximate, but do not passively replicate, those used by the parliamentary Select Committee, in an attempt to more sharply distill the essence of the different social forces and interests absorbed into the scheme. The categories used are thus: NTUC; academia, professional; business; women; societal; ethnicity; and youth. Official categories of functional groups have not only changed over time, to keep societal incorporation abreast of emerging or potential conflicts, but they have also been part of the strategy to compartmentalize and depoliticize public policy engagement.[6] Official categories such as "social and community service organizations," "media, arts, and sports organizations," and "civic and people sector organizations," for instance, obscure the distinction between civil and civic society organizations.

Notwithstanding variations in the degree of specialization on issues NMPs have focused on, NMPs can generally be depicted as principally belonging to one sector. Some also straddle categories, which appears to be a strategy by the parliamentary Select Committee responsible for the appointments to simultaneously incorporate or address different target interest groups and sectors.[7] Table 4.1 takes this into account. In the subsections below, we will further explore how these categorizations have been used to government ends.

Professionals and Academia

One striking theme to NMP appointments has been heavy inclusion of people from the professions and academia, with medical and legal professionals especially prominent. Academics and professionals account for 24.9 percent and 27.2 percent of all NMP appointments. In addition to being appointed in their own right, academics and professionals have often been appointed as notional representatives of women, ethnic minorities, or as champions of environmentalism or social welfare. In this way, the link between formal educational credentials and public policy expertise is reinforced at the same time as functional groups are politically incorporated. This reflects and reinforces elitist and functional premises of the PAP's technocratic worldview.

TABLE 4.1 Single and multiple categorizations of NMPs by sector

PARLIAMENT		NTUC	ACADEMIA	PROFESSIONAL	BUSINESS	WOMEN	SOCIETAL	ETHNICITY	YOUTH
13th	2016–...	1 (0)*	2 (0)	0 (1)	4 (1)	0 (2)	1 (0)	1 (3)	0 (0)
12th	2011–2016	2 (0)	3 (1)	1 (2)	7 (1)	0 (4)	3 (0)	1 (2)	1 (1)
11th	2006–2011	2 (0)	3 (1)	1 (1)	5 (2)	0 (4)	3 (2)	1 (2)	3 (3)
10th	2002–2006	2 (0)	2 (2)	3 (2)	7 (3)	0 (8)	2 (3)	0 (3)	2 (2)
9th	1997–2001	3 (0)	4 (0)	5 (3)	10 (2)	0 (6)	3 (0)	1 (5)	0 (0)
8th	1992–1996	2 (0)	3 (0)	1 (5)	3 (2)	2 (1)	0 (2)	1 (3)	0 (0)
7th	1989–1991	0 (0)	0 (0)	1 (0)	1 (1)	0 (0)	0 (0)	0 (0)	0 (0)
Sub-totals		12 (0)	17 (4)	12 (14)	37 (12)	2 (25)	12 (7)	5 (18)	6 (6)
		11.65%	16.50%	11.65%	35.92%	1.94%	11.65%	4.85%	5.83%
Total		12	21	26	49	27	19	23	12
		6.35%	11.11%	13.76%	25.93%	14.29%	10.05%	12.17%	6.35%

*Figures in parentheses refer to the number of NMPs who primarily belong to another category but who overlap with this secondary category. Note also that some NMPs have been appointed in more than one parliament, so they are counted for each parliament.

Business and Labor

The most heavily represented single category of NMPs has involved the business sector, accounting for 35.9 percent of the single and 25.9 percent of the multiple categorizations. What is especially significant in these appointments is the repeated incorporation of senior past or present figures from within peak employer and business bodies.[8] Historically, the PAP has been apprehensive about the domestic private sector constituting an independent political base that might be exploited by political opponents (Rodan 1989, 98; see also Trocki 2006; Visscher 2007). State capitalism may have subsequently eroded that potential capacity, but Singapore's increasing exposure to economic globalization has brought continuing challenges for the domestic private sector and its political management by the ruling party.

Not least of these challenges has been reconciling a growing business dependence on skilled and unskilled foreign workers with the government's ambitions to continually upgrade the economy.[9] The transition to higher productivity has proved especially difficult for many of Singapore's small-to-medium enterprises. The costs of government levies on foreign worker visas, and their use to enforce greater productivity, have thus been a periodic source of tension. Consolidation and expansion of government-linked companies (GLCs) have also raised local private business concerns about "crowding out" within domestic markets and the limits to their articulation with GLCs' offshore activities (Low 2001, 2006).

Extensive appointments of business sector NMPs bolster the presence of pro-PAP forces in parliament while acknowledging competing interests and conflicts among these forces over precisely how capitalism develops in Singapore. Such appointments signal the government's interest in gathering information about these concerns. While some of these conflicts cannot be fully resolved, the information can inform better political management of them.

The starkest use of NMP appointments in implicit admission that existing institutions of political co-option are no longer sufficient involves state-controlled trade unions. Since the Eighth Parliament, there have been twelve separate NMP appointments—involving eleven different people—of (almost all) senior officials from the PAP-affiliated NTUC. These NMPs traverse public and private sector unions covering utilities, petroleum, chemical, insurance, and manufacturing industries.

The PAP's more vigorous embrace of economic globalization in recent decades certainly fueled rapid economic growth. However, for most of this period, market impacts of low-cost foreign workers on domestic wages were combined with an increasing aversion by ruling technocratic elites to social redistribution. Consequently, Singapore's income gap, as measured by the Gini coefficient, steadily rose (Chun 2013a). Meanwhile, costs in housing, transport, and health increased, due to dramatic population growth and high professional and executive salaries. Exorbitant ministerial and senior civil servant salaries, justified in elitist terms, compounded resentment within the working class about rising inequalities.

With the inability of NTUC officials to forcefully represent workers' interests to the government exposed (see Rodan 2006b, 156–57), generous representation of the NTUC in NMP appointments has served as a symbolic gesture to counteract the idea of NTUC impotence. Yet contributions of these NMPs to parliamentary debate, compared with almost all other NMPs, have been limited and rarely distinctive in nature from those of government MPs. On issues of social and material inequalities, as we will see below, some NMPs from other sectors have submitted more forthright and original arguments. Consequently, the attempt to boost working-class support for the PAP through this MOP essentially failed.

This was particularly reflected in the electoral gains by the Workers' Party (WP) as the myriad social contradictions associated with Singapore capitalist development increasingly manifested. The results of the 2011 election finally underlined this, and contributed to the establishment of the Our Singapore Conversation (OSC) public consultation exercise, through which there was direct engagement with the working class. It took such an electoral shock for the PAP to fully comprehend that appearing to understand and respond to the material grievances of the working class was its biggest political challenge. In the meantime, the PAP's creative efforts through the NMP scheme continued to be directed at trying to politically absorb and contain the diverse ranks of the professional middle class.

Civil Society Organizations

Among the most significant NMP appointments are those in the three categories in table 4.1 of women, societal, and ethnicity, since these have involved independent civil society organizations (CSOs). The number of appointments principally under these categories has not been substantial but strategic. Moreover, when we take into account crossovers with other appointments, it becomes clear that the Select Committee has been keen to project the idea that the concerns and interests of these groups can be accommodated through the NMP scheme. For the PAP, this is preferable to such organizations evolving into more overtly politically independent advocacy groups and/or forging links with opposition parties and each other.

The appointment to the Eighth Parliament of orthopedic surgeon and founding AWARE president Kanwaljit Soin, for example, was a conspicuous attempt to steer AWARE activists toward direct engagement within a PAP-controlled institution. AWARE's focus included issues, such as domestic violence and discrimination against women in the civil service, that opposition parties had not yet seriously pursued. The articulate Soin did much to give the NMP scheme a degree of credibility, dominating parliamentary question time and occasionally shaping public debate, as in 1995 when she introduced a private member's bill, the Family Violence Bill. Although this was defeated, the government made amendments to the Women's Charter that, according to Soin (1999), "incorporated many of the principles and concepts of the aborted Family Violence Bill."

Significantly, Soin (1999) reasoned that, "in Singapore's achievement-oriented society," being a surgeon "added a little more weight to what I had to say." Moreover, she not only endorsed the NMP scheme in view of the prevailing limits to political space at the time, but also declared that "even if a bipartisan system should eventually evolve here, there will still be a role for non-partisan NMPs to add another perspective to issues."

Another president of AWARE, Braema Mathiaparanam, was also appointed as an NMP to the Ninth and Tenth Parliaments after basing her AWARE-supported application around foreign domestic labor advocacy. She was foundation president of the Transient Workers Count Too, an organization that was officially registered in 2004. Its initial focus on the plight of foreign domestic workers subsequently broadened to issues facing migrant workers generally, with bans on joining unions and minimal legal or other institutionalized rights leaving migrant workers especially vulnerable. These constraints on migrant workers are integral to the material inequalities inherent in the Singapore model of capitalism.

Foreign workers' rights have never been a priority for opposition parties. The Select Committee seemed to appreciate, however, that this was an area of potential conflict whose political management might nevertheless be aided by an NMP appointment. A strike by Chinese bus drivers in November 2012 and a riot in Singapore's Little India district in December 2013 involving approximately 300 foreign workers from Tamil Nadu and Bangladesh later confirmed that potential (Chun 2013c; Chun and Fung 2013), but also the inadequacy of token NMP representation to address it.

The NMP scheme has also incorporated representation of activists from the environmental group the Nature Society of Singapore (NSS). The NSS became active from the late 1980s and early 1990s on a range of land-zoning issues affecting wetlands and bird habitats (Rodan 1996a, 107). It was against this background that the NSS's first female president and ophthalmologist, Geh Min, was appointed an NMP in Singapore's Tenth Parliament.[10] Another NSS activist, Faizah Jamal, was also appointed to the Twelfth Parliament, by which time zoning issues had been joined by wider contention over the broader environmental sustainability of economic and population growth in the city-state.

At one level, Jamal's emphasis on "holistic environmentalism"—linking education and health to environmentalism—took her more out of the political mainstream, even more so than Geh Min. Yet, Jamal had a background in law, including working for the government's law firm, which she speculated gave the Select Committee reason to assume that she was "not so strange that she's a renegade, you know, like one of those human rights guys."[11]

Jamal's term coincided with the parliamentary debate over the controversial Population White Paper, and she was one of three NMPs that voted against it. This debate highlighted for Jamal the opportunity availed by the NMP scheme, giving her a prime opportunity in front of Singapore's policymakers to "question all the [economic] fundamentals from an environmental perspective."[12] Her general message of "no environment, no economy" was accompanied by concrete environmental impact assessment advocacy, notably regarding projected mass rapid transport plans to cope with population expansion (Jamal 2013).

The most recent significant societal incorporation of middle-class groups into the NMP scheme involves the arts community, whose nominees Audrey Wong and Janice Koh were respectively appointed in the Eleventh and Twelfth Parliaments. In 2000, the Singapore government initiated its Renaissance City Plan to promote the arts as a new plank of the economy. The advent of the global financial crisis later that decade led to even further official emphasis on this direction and related infrastructure investments. Yet a range of professionals in this sector felt the PAP's instrumental view of the arts, and its various laws constraining free expression, were in tension. As Audrey Wong (2011, 3) put it: "Ironically, despite the Renaissance City plan and all the state investment in the arts, there has been a growing sense among artists of being disempowered."

Significantly, Wong's nomination was the outcome of a broadly supported and concerted effort from the arts community to have NMP representation. This was, according to Wong, indicative of "the arts scene maturing to a stage where people actually felt that we need to have a voice in policy."[13] At the time of her appointment in 2009 she signaled that she would be reflecting people's views on such issues as internet freedom, political films, and education (Loh and Ong 2009). While she did this to some extent, her main focus was more pragmatic, namely, "improvement of conditions for freelancers in the arts and creative sector, as, after all, these are Singaporean workers in an industrial sector."[14]

Wong and colleagues in the arts community understood the Select Committee's decision to appoint her as guided by the PAP plan for the arts to become one of the "future drivers of the economy." Yet Wong also thought she was a comparatively unthreatening candidate, despite her background with the Substation theater company, which had a history of controversial productions testing the limits of censorship laws. "I think they knew that I was a safe choice," she explained, adding, "I tend to be rather quiet and much more a negotiating kind of personality than somebody who goes to the media." At the same time, she also sensed that the Select Committee wanted to "indicate that the space is opening up for artists."

To be sure, neither Wong nor her successor arts NMP, Janice Koh, were under any doubts about the limits to that space. Yet, as Koh explained, "we have come to realize that it is quite critical to have a voice because a lot of the issues raised in parliament tend to focus on bread-and-butter issues,"[15] such as costs of housing, transport, and wage levels. According to Koh, she entered parliament somewhat neutral about the NMP scheme, but she now felt "that it is necessary, especially in the short term, because the NMPs raise issues and topics that right now, with a small opposition, will not be taken up by opposition MPs."[16]

The NMP scheme has also played a role in managing ethnic politics. Officially sponsored conceptions of ethnic and racial identity and consciousness have been important to the PAP's political strategies and state structures of political co-option. Singaporean identity cards, for example, categorize citizens according to whether they are Chinese, Malay, Indian, or "Other." Public policies further reinforce and institutionalize the idea that such identities are a natural way to represent interests and view the world. This includes through state-supplemented self-help welfare groups organized around racial categories, and immigration policies to retain the prevailing proportional dominance of the ethnic Chinese majority (Rahim 2001). However, in 1999, out of frustration with Mendaki—the officially sanctioned council representing ethnic Malays and controlled by Malay PAP MPs—the independent Association of Muslim Professionals (AMP) was established. Many Malays saw Mendaki as inadequately representing the interests of the Malay community, with other ethnic groups enjoying greater benefits from Singapore's economic and social transformation (ibid.).

Subsequently, AMP Chairman Imram bin Mohamed was among the 1994 NMP appointments. PAP tolerance of AMP independence is in part a function of ruling party preference for problems of socioeconomic disadvantage being viewed through ideological lenses of ethnic particularism rather than of social class (Rodan 2009, 451). But the AMP's attempts to test this tolerance have been instructive. In 2000, the AMP proposed replacing Mendaki's monopoly of official Malay representation with a "collective leadership" comprising "independent non-political" Malays. The AMP claimed this would be consistent with the spirit of "active citizenship" being promoted by then prime minister Goh (Venudran 2000). However, the idea got short shrift, with Goh warning the AMP not to stray into the political arena, and it promptly retreated (Ahmad 2000). Amidst growing public concerns about inequalities, though, another AMP director, Ismail Hussein, was appointed as an NMP to the Twelfth Parliament in 2014.

Other explicit appointments of ethnic minority representation have included lawyer and author Shriniwas Rai to the Ninth Parliament, and corporate strategy consultant and current affairs television host Viswa Sadasivan, who was a past vice president and secretary of the Singapore Indian Development Association (SINDA) executive committee. Rai assisted the Singapore North Indian Hindu Association in 1988 in preparing materials relating to the debate over a PAP-proposed national ideology, which subsequently translated into the government's Shared Values legislation. In addition, through various other appointments the Select Committee has included ethnic Indians, Malays, and Eurasians to project inclusive, non–party-political space for minority ethnic communities.

Sadasivan's NMP experience further highlighted how championing progressive causes did not result in strategic alliances with opposition MPs. In his maiden speech in July 2009, he put forth a motion calling on the House to reaffirm support for the multiracial values embodied in the Singapore National Pledge. The Pledge referred to "one united people, regardless of race, language or religion," which Sadasivan contrasted with the government's institutional promotion of separate racial identities, not least through racially based self-help groups such as SINDA established to address social and material inequalities. In response to this implicit challenge to the particularist ideology of race, Lee Kuan Yew attacked Sadasivan's ideas as based on "false and flawed" arguments, asserting that the Pledge was not an "ideology" but an aspiration that may take centuries to be realized. Yet, instead of receiving support from the opposition party MPs, Sadasivan recounted in an interview how he was instead castigated by some of them for wrongly "deconstructing the Pledge."[17] Reflecting on the three motions he put forth in parliament—the greatest number of any non-PAP MP thus far—Sadasivan observed about the opposition that "when I filed them, the opposition MPs failed to give me tacit support for my efforts in raising issues."

Sadasivan's controversial motion may demonstrate that there are political risks for the PAP in trying to incorporate some critical and/or progressive voices into parliament through the NMP scheme. We should not lose sight, though, of the fact that the PAP's dominance of parliament enables it to contain and even utilize such challenges. Sadasivan signaled during his earlier NMP Select Committee interview that he was interested in issues such as multiculturalism, media control, and social inequality. But not only was he personally known by members of Cabinet and not expected to do anything "wacko," he also suspected the Select Committee may have anticipated that his views were not a serious threat "as long as we demolish them with our counter arguments. And we've got the firepower. So it's a win-win. . . . We've demonstrated that we are open enough to have someone like him, coming in as an NMP. The system is open."

In any case, PAP control over appointments allows adjustments to be made to pull back from more ambitious or critical voices than the ruling party feels comfortable with. This appears to have been what happened with the appointments in mid-2014, following increased levels of questioning of the PAP's policies and parliamentary processes by some progressively minded NMPs, including Eugene Tan, Janice Koh, and Faizah Jamal. The 2014 appointments would be the last before the next general election and contained no noteworthy CSO activists or individuals known for questioning core PAP values or policies. Meanwhile, Eugene Tan's attempt to secure a second appointment was unsuccessful. He had been a prolific contributor to parliamentary debate, his 194 entries in Hansard dwarfing those of almost every other NMP. Possibly his reappointment cause was not aided by, among other contributions, having exposed how little time many of the PAP's highly paid MPs actually spent in parliament.

Youth

The category loosely referred to in table 4.1 as "youth" further illustrates how changing PAP perceptions of its own political challenges affects NMP appointments. At the 2006 general election, around 40 percent of eligible voters were born after Singapore became an independent nation in 1965 (Mydans 2006). The PAP therefore sought to guard against future erosion of its vote from so-called Generation X (born between 1965 and 1982) and Generation Y (born between 1983 and 1994). Eunice Olsen, a television show host, volunteer youth worker, part-time musician, and 2000 beauty queen, had already been NMP-appointed in 2004 to become the youngest ever member of the Singapore parliament. Following the 2006 election, Olsen was not only reappointed but was joined by Patricia Soh-Khim Ong, a PhD in mechanical engineering and recipient of the 2004 Singapore Youth Award for Science and Technology. Thirty-one-year-old lawyer and political blogger Siew Kum Hong also entered the Tenth Parliament as an NMP in 2006.[18] Each coming from a different social milieu, collectively these NMPs gave expression to the rapidly changing age demographic of the Singapore electorate.

Siew's appointment was a conspicuous initiative toward young internet-savvy progressives channeling their political energies through a PAP-controlled institution. His experience was instructive at various levels. In the 2007 debate over the Penal Code (Amendment) Bill, Siew presented a petition to parliament to decriminalize homosexuality, section 377A. Singapore Progressive Party leader Chiam See Tong spoke briefly on the bill but made no comment about section 377A, while Workers' Party leader Low Thia Khiang failed to speak at all. Prime Minister Lee noted Low's failure to enter the debate, using it to bolster his argument that "Chinese-speaking Singaporeans are not strongly engaged, either for removing section 377A or against removing section 377A" (H. L. Lee 2007, col. 2401). It served the PAP well that the opposition did not embrace this issue. This was then another illustration of how political fragmentation among PAP critics can be reinforced, if not created, through the NMP scheme. It also highlighted, importantly, how the scheme can provide selective space for an airing of progressive political aspirations. Indeed, the NMP scheme has at times provided a platform for ideological competition with the PAP. However, the political risks of this translating into any prospect of commensurate reform have been well calculated by the PAP as slim.

Expanding Space, Containing Coalitions

In summary, the Select Committee has sought to ensure broad cross-sectional representation of social forces as part of a strategy of politically managing dynamic conflicts, often generated or amplified by capitalist development in Singapore. This extends to select incorporation of moderate reformers, notably ones with middle class and professional backgrounds and perceived as adopting nonconfrontational approaches to politics. Yet this strategic incorporation of a wide range of social forces into parliament involves an increasingly detailed set of official categories of functional representation conducive to advocacy of a multitude of seemingly discrete issues. This can stunt political imagination. Some NMPs are aware of this and seek to transcend such a constraint. As former NMP Sadasivan observed, "If you keep people sufficiently occupied with day-to-day municipal issues they wouldn't have the time or inclination to think about raising other issues. This is where more enlightened NMPs can add significant value—by raising larger, more fundamental issues into the parliamentary debate."[19]

More fundamentally, a recurring theme in interviews of reform-minded NMPs was the view that the scheme enabled issues to be raised that are not taken up with seriousness, if at all, by political parties. Ironically, the technocratic approach to politics fostered by the PAP through NMPs affords these issues legitimacy not readily available through the existing parties, even if that legitimacy has not translated into significant policy reform.

Significantly, then, advocacy of progressive causes in parliament by some NMPs has not paved the way for strategic alliances with opposition parties. Regardless of the substance of that advocacy, opposition parties remained reticent to team up with NMPs. As the Workers' Party chairperson, Sylvia Lim, explained, "Actively pursuing or endorsing any formal collaborations is sort of giving credence to the scheme which we don't think is something that we want to do."[20]

To be sure, other factors contribute to the distance between opposition parties and progressive civil society activists. Reluctance of opposition parties to alienate either nationalist or socially conservative elements of their social bases, such as on issues of foreign workers' or women's rights, is certainly important. The effect of the NMP scheme is to reinforce and compound these points of departure. Meanwhile, by providing conditional space in parliament for these progressive NMPs, the PAP can appear to be comparatively sympathetic to certain contentious issues.

Representation Ideologies of Nominated Members of Parliament

Although Gandhi (2008) found little evidence of representation emanating from inclusive authoritarianism in her comprehensive study, there has been a definite attempt through the NMP scheme in Singapore to compete with or supplant the sorts of democratic parliamentary representation that Gandhi was searching for. The authority to represent under the NMP scheme is not principally derived from any demonstrated endorsement of a represented constituency. Instead, the ability, as perceived by the Select Committee, to conduct nonconfrontational debate and/or contribute expertise and information functional for addressing and politically managing public policy problems takes priority. But how widely has this consultative ideology of representation been reflected in individual NMPs' understandings of their political roles and practices?

Interviews with NMPs offer some insights, even though they could only capture a sample of the seventy-nine NMPs thus far.[21] Many felt that the Select Committee was, as one interviewee put it, "clearly sounding people out as de facto representatives or at least people who could be projected as such."[22] However, where NMPs did regard themselves as representatives, what this meant varied.

The most concerted attempt to harness the NMP scheme to some approximation of democratic representation has involved the arts community, with both Koh and Wong claiming themselves as representatives of an arts "constituency." The process of candidate recommendation to the functional group coordinator, usually the head of the Arts Council, starts with a town hall meeting open to members of the arts community at which potential candidates may speak. A vote or a petition process to collect signatures in support of a candidate then follows.[23]

Once appointed, within resource constraints, Koh tried to replicate how elected MPs operated, but "instead of a ward I had a constituent sector." For example, Koh conducted a dialogue session for each of her first twelve months with educators in the arts. Koh's claim to be a representative, though, was more expansive than acting on behalf of arts constituents: "On top of that, I also feel that I represent a point of view, so the people who are interested in the success of the arts in society also tend to be from a certain point of view which I also feel I need to represent."

Asked what characterized that point of view, Koh explained: "it is probably more liberal, certainly more left leaning and progressive, which already makes it distinct from the dominant party perspective." This had resonances with Dryzek and Niemeyer's (2008) concept of "discursive representation," in which democratic representation does not rest on authorization of, or accountability to, those being represented but on the value of broadening the range of ideas entering public debate (also see Dryzek 2010).[24]

While not on a par with the arts community in terms of how nominations were determined, other respondents also made claims to representing constituents that were backed by significant engagement with civil society elements. This included Edwin Khew, who saw himself representing local business and had a clear idea of his constituents: members of the manufacturing and business community. The Singapore Manufacturers' Federation (SMF), of which Khew was president, and the Singapore Business Federation (SBF) jointly proposed his application. Moreover, he established groups of major business leaders within the SMF and the SBF who chaired committees, to receive and review input from the business community. According to Khew, at that time people within the SMF in particular were of the view that "the interests of manufacturing weren't well represented in parliament."[25] Interestingly, the problem appeared to be attributed in part to the fact that not since Robert Chua, an NMP in the Eighth Parliament who was chairman of the Singapore Manufacturers' Association, as it was then known, had there been any direct representation of the manufacturing sector. This suggested that, within this sector, NMP appointments were viewed as politically strategic.

A theme evident in other NMP responses was a claim not so much to representing a clearly defined constituency with whom some sort of structured or even unstructured engagement occurred, but to representing views and interests neglected by the political parties. Some of these claims implicitly appealed to the notion of discursive representation to a far greater extent than Koh did. Whereas Koh conceived of her role as trying to represent constituents of a "certain point of view," others emphasized the advantage of not being constrained by the prevailing party politics of constituent representation.

Geh Min, for example, asserted that she represented "environmental issues and interests" and other issues neglected by the parties.[26] She was president of the NSS and regularly received solicited and unsolicited feedback from members and her own network, but there was no routine process of consultation with groups or individuals. Yet for Geh, the inability to seriously claim representation of identifiable constituents brought advantages and disadvantages. "NMPs don't have any ground to stand on if they take a confrontational stance," observed Geh, since they were not voted in by an electorate. By the same token, "the luxury of being an NMP is bringing up issues that are relevant but won't win many votes, such as issues of interest to the NSS, which enjoys niche support."

Goh Chong Chia, a professional architect who was also an NMP in the Ninth Parliament, echoed this perspective. He was nominated by a professional body and saw himself "representing views not readily expressed in parliament by either the PAP or the opposition," emphasizing how, because "NMPs are not beholden to anyone and are not seeking reelection from a constituency, they are at liberty to pursue those interests."[27] Goh saw himself, much like Geh, as having networks and experiences that could not be conceived of as constituencies, but which availed him of perspectives and information useful to parliament.[28] It was Goh's hope that the scheme will prove "a transitional institution, not an alternative to a civil society."

Two NMPs in the Eleventh Parliament located in table 4.1 under "youth," Siew and Olsen, had even less structured avenues for consulting any supposed constituents. In an interview Siew stated that he saw himself as "representing a specific segment of the population: young, late twenties, English-educated, western in outlook, fairly liberal, internet savvy."[29] Although philosophically opposed to the NMP scheme because he considered it undemocratic, Siew added that "on a conceptual level I can see the value of the scheme, if it is able to bridge that gap—that is always inherent in partisan politics."[30] Olsen conceded that technically she could not represent anybody, but she nevertheless "would like to represent the thoughts of the youth" in particular.[31] She maintained that her role in the media and her music afforded informal opportunities to gauge youth issues. In practice, she spoke on a surprisingly diverse range of topics, including on government-linked companies' accountability.

One of the clearest articulations about the distinctiveness of the NMP role as "representative" came from academic lawyer Thio Li-Ann. According to her, NMPs provide "indirect representation," and she saw herself as representing issues rather than people as constituents. Nominated by the president of the National University of Singapore, she came to parliament to expressly advance issues about constitutionality and human rights. However, Thio believed that she should not be confined to the areas identified in her application and could exercise "a roving commission."[32] Thio made no claim to consulting anyone on the matters she raised in parliament.

This is admittedly a limited sample of NMP respondents on the extent and nature of their roles as representatives. Nevertheless, it does demonstrate some important points. Despite the absence of adequate mechanisms for consultation with, or disciplining of, NMPs by the public, there are other respects in which NMPs have laid claim to being "representatives." This includes raising issues lacking advocacy, from government or opposition parties, and transcending the divide between partisan politics that constrains parliamentary debate. It is especially significant that these views can be found among middle-class progressives. Thus, while many of these NMPs are at one level critical of the way the scheme departs from democratic ideologies of representation, they have also accommodated themselves to it in an attempt to broaden the range of ideas presented in parliamentary debate. This apparent pragmatic embrace of discursive representation by the NMPs increases political pluralism in Singapore, which some might equate with improved democratic quality. However, it also fits neatly with elite interests, as it seems to forestall coalition building—linking different elements of civil society—and thus the likelihood of effective challenges to existing inequalities of power.

At the same time, select middle-class progressives have voluntarily organized their own representative mechanisms within their organizations, injecting a degree of "democratic" selection of NMP candidates and a modicum of accountability to those purportedly represented. This demonstrates how some NMPs can and do depart from the PAP's script. Yet even if this practice were more developed and widely adopted, could such arrangements ideologically and structurally facilitate challenges to existing power distributions? This is the real test of the veracity of democratic representation. Clearly not even the most "representative" NMP can do that, nor has any such attempt been made by any of them. This is because the forcible dismantling and fragmentation of popular forces that shaped authoritarian rule under the PAP places continuing limits on the capacity of even the most resourceful and democratically inspired NMP to link with wider social forces and build powerful coalitions.

The absence of democratic transition in Singapore has led many theorists to highlight political continuity in the city-state. However, there have been important institutional changes in recent decades to accommodate new social forces and contain conflicts and discontent associated with Singapore's particular path of capitalist development. New institutions of political participation have been introduced to contain contestation with the PAP and shore up authoritarian rule. The NMP scheme has been central to this, ushering in new structures of political representation ideologically rationalized as a corrective against adversarial politics. Wider incorporation of social forces into rational approaches to solving problems of policy and governance would supposedly bolster political consensus.

At one level, the political significance of the NMP scheme appears to be remarkably modest. Notwithstanding assorted government policy refinements over the years due to NMP advocacy, just one piece of legislation initiated by an NMP—Walter Woon's Maintenance of Parents Bill in 1994, which resonated with PAP ideas of filial piety—has become law. At another level, though, a range of pro-PAP forces from business, labor, and medical and commercial professions has embraced the NMP scheme, viewing it as an avenue for airing concerns. More importantly, the scheme has proved attractive for middle-class activists within emerging CSOs advocating socially progressive causes. Incorporation of these social forces into parliament has helped reinforce the separation between opposition parties and CSOs. The nature of that incorporation has also encouraged each CSO to work away on their respective specific agendas, militating against wider reform coalitions among CSOs.

The political fragmentation of social and political forces outside the PAP state is rooted in the earlier establishment of the authoritarian regime during the Cold War and the subsequent consolidation of the PAP state through state capitalism. Authorities' use of the Internal Security Act in the late 1980s against lay Catholic social justice activists who sought to work with an opposition party dramatically highlighted the PAP's preference for political parties and social activists to keep their operations separate (Barr 2010). Opponents and critics of the PAP still have to contend with formidable constraints in their political engagement.

Understandably, then, various progressives have participated in the NMP scheme despite some misgivings about its nondemocratic rationale. However, for many such NMPs, their experiences in parliament have reconfirmed in their minds the limitations of political parties in general—and the opposition in particular—on the issues that matter to them. Equally understandably, elected opposition MPs can hardly align with NMPs without undermining their own status as democratic representatives and helping to legitimate the PAP's strategy to refurbish the authoritarian regime.

Indeed, it is precisely the contribution of the NMP scheme to obviating the formation of alliances among independent organizations and/or with opposition parties that renders it most significant to the PAP's project of authoritarian renewal. Ironically, a greater plurality of worldviews, and an associated discursive representation ideology embraced by progressives, can be accommodated by this project. This is a price the government is apparently willing to pay in order to maintain control over how and when these progressive views can be aired.

Consequently, the importance of the NMP scheme for the PAP in particular is not likely to recede because of seat gains by the elected opposition or increased online debate, as some have argued or speculated (R. Chan 2014; Tham 2014). On the contrary, state-controlled media have sought to disabuse the public of any such expectation. A *Straits Times* (2014) editorial argued, for example, that the scheme's rationale "assumes even greater importance in this milieu—especially when account must be taken of the partisanship and political wrangling during parliamentary debates."

Yet the credibility of the NMP scheme also necessitates that the PAP's strategic control over appointments is balanced by sufficient space for voices that occasionally challenge some PAP orthodoxies. Given the PAP's authoritarian re-flexes, striking this balance remains a challenge for the ruling party. The record shows, however, that even critical NMP voices have generally failed to exploit the opportunity through parliamentary motions to set agendas for debate and con-sciousness raising. When such rare occasions have arisen, notably Sadasivan's challenge over particularist ideologies of race, this has afforded the PAP an op-portunity through its overwhelming numbers in parliament, and senior leaders in particular, to counter competing ideas before they get serious political traction.

In the context of the growing questioning and challenging of core PAP ideas through social media, the PAP has every interest in getting the balance right in its NMP appointments. This will ensure that its parliamentary dominance can be fully exploited in the battle of ideas. It can also help retain interest in the scheme among progressives, which has thus far diverted them from exercises in wider co-alition building to challenge PAP ideas and institutions. However, the NMP scheme is not without its limitations as a mechanism to absorb societal discontent. After all, prior to the 2015 general election there was a sustained electoral drift away from the PAP toward the opposition from the working class in particular. Dif-ferences among constituencies and postelection survey data also suggest that it was the working class that remained most solid in aligning with the PAP's opponents in 2015 (Chong 2015b). It would appear, therefore, that those con-stituencies most frustrated with the PAP continue to be those who have been least successfully co-opted through the NMP scheme. The PAP's careful strategies to limit the risks of serious political contestation to technocratic authoritarian rule through consultative representation have not been without trade-offs.

PUBLIC FEEDBACK IN SINGAPORE'S CONSULTATIVE AUTHORITARIANISM

Public feedback through state-sponsored and controlled institutions has been integral to the strategy of Singapore's People's Action Party (PAP) of expanding political space to shape the extent and nature of permissible conflict. Indeed, the first major institutional initiative in this strategy was the Feedback Unit (FU) established in 1985, which was renamed Reaching Everyone for Active Citizenry @ Home (REACH) in 2006. Alongside the extensive mechanisms this has provided for citizen engagement in policy discussion and debate, public consultation has also become a growing feature of periodic government-led committees of enquiry. This reached a high point with Our Singapore Conversation (OSC), involving 12 months of deliberations starting in August 2012, engaging 47,000 Singaporeans. These intricate and dynamic new modes of participation (MOPs) reflect the exceptional depth and cohesion of control over the PAP party-state by technocrats and the political logic thereof.

The logic behind such processes is at one level no different from that which inspired nominated members of parliament (NMPs): providing alternative channels of political participation to opposition political parties and civil society activism in response to mounting social contradictions associated with capitalist development. However, much of this feedback and consultation is conducted through public administrative institutions affording more intricate structures for influencing who can participate, how, and on what. This amplifies the opportunities for authorities to promote the atomization of citizens as political actors and the compartmentalization of their concerns. It also enables technocratic ideologies—portraying politics as a noncompetitive technical exercise of solving problems—and improving government policy effectiveness to be mutually reinforced through diverse forms of engagement with one or another arm of the state.

Yet, as we shall see, struggles over Singapore's different modes of participation and representation, within which such feedback mechanisms are located, are also dynamic. They are mediated by social conflicts linked to the PAP's political management of capitalist development and their articulation with new media technologies.

The greater the momentum of Singapore's capitalist growth, the more income, wealth, and related social inequalities have opened up. In this context, the inadequacy of existing social redistribution to alleviate market outcomes has become increasingly contentious, and the PAP's ideological championing of self-reliance ahead of welfarism less resonant with the public. Rapid economic growth has also compounded dependence on foreign workers and immigrants, straining social and physical infrastructure and testing social cohesion. The environmental sustainability of such development in the city-state has also come under question.

Such contradictions manifested in new or intensified conflicts over a range of government policies, including housing, transport, health, education, pensions, welfare, wages, and immigration. Implicitly and explicitly, these conflicts have given rise to new levels of scrutiny of core PAP ideologies justifying the political regime—not least the proposition that Singapore is currently ruled by a meritocracy and its future prosperity depends on this continuing. Moreover, this scrutiny has increasingly taken place through social media, expanding the scope for individual expression and select attempts by political parties and small civil society groups to politically harness these media. In response to such trends, the PAP has looked to new MOP initiatives to shore up consultative ideologies of representation that would disincline Singaporeans to support oppositional politics.

This chapter first analyzes the establishment of the FU, its evolution, and eventual revamping and renaming as REACH. It explains how mechanisms of societal and administrative incorporation of this institution have been integral to the PAP strategy of promoting new MOPs and why they have had to be adaptive and creative in the context of Singapore's dynamic political economy. Indeed, it was in an attempt to more effectively containing the trend toward more combative and oppositional politics in this context that the OSC, the latest and arguably most "successful" new MOP, was born.

Feedback Unit

When it was established in 1985, the FU was officially portrayed as having four objectives: to take suggestions from the public on national policies and problems;

to collect feedback on existing or pending policies; to ensure rapid responses by government departments to complaints by the public; and to help educate and inform the public about national policies and problems. Notwithstanding the government's intention to deploy the FU to promote its own policies, opportunities for Singaporeans to submit policy views and ideas were real, and proliferated over time.

However, since the FU was housed within a government ministry—originally the Ministry of Community Development, but later in equivalents thereof—engagement with the FU, and later REACH, has involved entering a sphere of state administrative power and potential control over the forms of political conflict accommodated. This has not only pertained to the forms and structures of engagement, but also their ideological purpose. Engagement has been promoted on the basis of the need for rational suggestions and debate to solve or avoid problems, rather than citizens' rights to shape policies of concern to them.

In essence, the FU was conceived as a facilitator of engagements between government departments on the one hand and the public on the other. This role was formalized and elevated in 2004 through changes to the Instruction Manual of the Civil Service, requiring a paragraph in all policy proposal memoranda to cabinet to outline related prior public consultations (H. L. Lee 2004). The government not only wanted to be seen as attaching importance to public ideas on policy. It also understood how such feedback could enable policymakers to better anticipate public reactions when projecting and defending proposed government policy.

However, who could be involved in consultations, why, how, and on what matters was subject to various administrative controls and political judgments. At the formal level, directions set by supervisory panels of the FU (and later REACH) offer broad guidance on these questions. The relevant minister, invariably a serving PAP member of parliament (MP), chairs this panel. The remaining members usually comprise a mix of other government MPs and assorted elements of PAP-affiliated organizations, and government-linked companies (GLCs) including media organizations. Over time this composition has been supplemented by elements of the private sector that might nevertheless be considered part of the PAP social and political establishment.

Opposition politicians are conspicuously absent from the supervisory panel, as are independent civil society activists. This is consistent with the government's aim of fostering a "consensual" rather than competitive conception of, and framework for, political engagement. As one FU chairman, Wang Kai Yun, explained when asked about the feasibility of a civil society organization instead assuming the FU's role, "For the Unit to function well, we need to build trust between the Unit and the rest of Government. The issue does not arise now because the Feedback Unit is part of the Government" (quoted in *Straits Times* 2005).

To be more precise, the FU was part of a de facto one-party state. The point of the FU for the PAP was to develop new spaces of political participation within that state. The modes of participation adopted toward this end have included various forms of administrative and societal incorporation. Mechanisms for incorporating individuals have been particularly extensive, in effect providing direct engagement alternatives to political representation of any sort. There is also engagement through notional representation of groups and social categories that are either constructed by authorities or involve select existing groups that enjoy the trust of authorities.

As is elaborated below, these processes of engagement foster an acute compartmentalization of political issues, and work against social cleavages cutting across those issues—particularly class issues—being comprehensively examined or mobilized around. Such mechanisms could only be conceived and implemented on such a scale, and with such coherence, where technocratic rationality and controls across state and party were deeply embedded and institutionalized.

Individual Participation

In sharp contrast with less technocratic forms of authoritarian rule, the embrace of new electronic technologies has been a feature of state strategies in Singapore to promote preferred forms of political participation. Online channels of consultation and engagement were crucial to the FU's promotion of new modes of individual political participation. Email in particular was integral to incorporation of Singaporeans into FU processes, accounting for 90 percent of all feedback by 2004 (Feedback Unit 2004, 51). Some of this feedback was solicited from among a People's Forum database of 7,000 registrants, guided by demographic considerations of interest to FU or a government department or agency.

One of the most direct attempts to link individual participation to public administration processes has been through e-consultation papers (eCPs) published by government departments and agencies on national issues and policies. Although some of these eCPs particularly invite comment from target audiences, such as the business sector, mostly they seek general individual comment through email or SMS.[1] Discussion forums also provided online individual consultation under the FU, via the FU's own website. In contrast to eCPs, topics for discussion were also more open-ended. Yet discussions could also be generated by the FU calling for reactions to a particular fact or issue, which implicitly defined the nature of the problem to be debated.

It was through the general feedback channel that individuals were most at liberty to submit comments and views beyond prescribed categories or topics. Significantly, though, these contributions were not publicized on the FU website.

Instead, the FU would direct them to specific government departments or agencies for a private reply to the individual. Consequently, there would be no public debate of these individual criticisms, complaints, or suggestions, or any prospect of them being incorporated into analysis of wider political issues or themes.

Clearly, the various forms of individual participation provided for under these mechanisms sought to tap into issues of wide public concern, but in a way that afforded the state a range of means by which to frame and contain debate over these concerns. This entailed a combination of attempted agenda setting and more defensive responses to popular sentiments.

Collective Participation

Live meetings for feedback and consultation were less extensive under the FU, but often resulted in more demonstrable policy influence as well as being more suited to group participation and implicit or explicit forms of political representation. This took the form of Dialogue Sessions, Tea Sessions, and Policy Feedback Groups.

Dialogue Sessions and Tea Sessions are usually small-scale informal consultations on policy topics determined by ministers or the FU (Feedback Unit 2004, 35). Two supervisory panel members generally chair these meetings, including a government MP. FU Dialogue Sessions were in principle open to the general public, but tended to be organized through select invitations to members of the People's Forum and to "strategic partners," such as the PAP-affiliated National Trades Union Congress (NTUC) (35–37).

Tea Sessions are not so policy focused and provide greater opportunity for participants to raise their own concerns and submit ideas. However, the FU conceived the social sectors around which these discussions would be organized, including professionals, students, youth, ethnic communities, women, small and medium enterprise operators, and so-called heartlanders that might otherwise be thought of as working class Singaporeans with the least prospect of upward social mobility. Tea Sessions, then, were not conducive to cross-group interaction.

The creation of these different social categories fosters such political fragmentation of social forces as to preempt coalitions that define the causes and solutions to conflict in different terms. Such categories also act as conduits through which various particularist ideologies may be bolstered and exploited to the same end, including by promoting discrete identities of ethnicity, gender, youth, and religion.

The FU's Policy Feedback Groups, introduced in 1997 by then prime minister Goh Chok Tong, were best able to demonstrate policy influence. Feedback Groups were chaired by people from either the private or social sectors and would undertake in-depth policy studies of their own choosing, culminating in policy proposal submissions to government at annual conferences. Feedback Groups could consult as far and wide as they saw fit in the process of developing their proposals.

In a 2005 publication entitled *Closing the Loop and Shaping Our Home: Turning Ideas into Reality*, the FU detailed and celebrated twenty instances of feedback from these groups that it claimed were instrumental in changing policy (Feedback Unit 2005). Most persuasive links between feedback and policy outcomes involved proposals from the Health Feedback Group, such as those on the need for portable medical benefits.[2] This was to address the growing trend of workers changing employers in a context of a dynamic and increasingly competitive globalized economy.

In stark contrast, the 2002 recommendations of the political-matters-and-media Feedback Group on Best Practices in Political Governance for Singapore fell on deaf ears. It called for an independent electoral commission to level the political playing field; transparency and accountability for government-linked companies; measures to ensure legal and judicial impartiality; and reforms to foster freedom of association and greater access to the media for opposition parties. This group was exceptional in the preparedness of its chairman, private media entrepreneur and journalist Viswa Sadasivan,[3] to incorporate the views of independent party political and civil society activists into consultations (see Rodan and Jayasuriya 2007, 803–4). Unsurprisingly, none of these propositions were taken up by the PAP.

This set of policy proposals highlighted an element of political risk for the PAP by open invitations for serious policy suggestions from experts. Not all of Singapore's policy experts were in state bureaucracies, nor necessarily shared the PAP worldview. It also demonstrated, though, that discretion over what would be taken seriously emphatically resided with the PAP. Underlying the appearance of a technical process of policy engagement was a fundamental political consideration: the consolidation of power in the hands of a politico-bureaucratic elite in a de facto one-party state.

Through the various FU mechanisms of individual and collective political participation, then, state-based MOPs are specifically designed to define and depoliticize the nature and limits of permissible conflict over public policy. Yet while at one level this has involved processes of wide inclusivity, this has also been tempered by the systematic avoidance of opposition political parties and a heavy reliance on social and community organizations aligned with the PAP rather than critical of it. As such, the FU cultivated forms of engagement that were strategically selective in even more acute ways than the NMP scheme, with little incorporation of existing civil society organizations in an attempt to co-opt them. The idea was to maximize state control over what conflicts were structured in and out of permissible political participation. This did not mean issues that independent civil society organizations and political parties focused on were to be ignored, but that the aim was to reframe and disaggregate them through a different institutional site affording even more control than the PAP-dominated parliament.

Capitalist Challenges and the FU's Refinement

The PAP was returned at the May 2006 polls with all but two of the eighty-four seats under Singapore's first-past-the-post system. However, despite a booming economy (*Economist* 2006), as well as extensive authoritarian controls and meager opposition party resources, one-third of the total valid votes went to PAP opponents. Rising living costs and inequalities had much to do with this, especially among working-class voters. Around 108,000 new jobs were created in 2005, but only 30,000 went to locals. Competition in manufacturing from lower-cost sites in China, India, and Vietnam was also reducing employment opportunities for around 500,000 Singaporean workers with below secondary-educational levels in an economy restructuring toward more skilled jobs (Rodan 2006a).

To address some of these issues, an election-eve budget included a S$2.6 billion (~US$1.9 billion) Progress Package with some benefits to low-income Singaporeans, notably through a workfare scheme providing one-off wage bonuses to workers of forty years or older on especially low incomes. However, the most successful opposition party at the 2006 polls, the Workers' Party (WP), called for more substantive changes.

The WP manifesto, *You Have a Choice*, proposed a minimum wage and an "unconditional needs-based safety net to ensure that no one who needs help is left stranded" (quoted in Rodan 2006a, 12). It also advocated abolishing three institutions integral to the reproduction of the PAP state: grassroots organizations such as resident committees; the elected president; and ethnic quotas for housing estates. These proposals were variously described as "time bombs" and "poisons" by PAP leaders (ibid.). The WP manifesto proposed too that government ministers be barred from holding office in trade unions, almost all of which were affiliated with the PAP.[4]

PAP structures of societal incorporation were being directly targeted in WP reform ideas. These were conflicts over distributional and power relations of the sort that FU generally avoided or marginalized through the strategic selectivity of participatory institutions. Yet electoral gains by the WP suggested that they resonated with popular concerns. New media proved crucial in this.

While the PAP government appreciates the economic potential of promoting new information technologies and has invested accordingly, the PAP is also anxious about the possibility of this technology facilitating greater scrutiny of, and political competition with, the ruling party's governance practices, policies, and ideologies. It has therefore regulated internet usage through new laws and the enforcement of existing ones within cyberspace, including defamation and sedition laws (see *Economist* 2013; Weiss 2014a). Both individual and civil society expressions were targeted in these laws.

From 2004, though, internet blogs grew in significance as a space for social and political commentary and information. By the time of the May 2006 general election, there were an estimated fifty political or semipolitical websites and online forums. Authorities' strategies to contain online political content were also less effective than at previous elections, so that assorted videos, rally photographs, and citizen journalist reports were available to voters. There was significant defiance of 2001 regulations barring podcasts and videocasts with "explicit political content" by individuals or political parties (J. Gomez 2006, 24–25).

Uneven social and material outcomes of capitalist development in Singapore were thus creating conditions conducive to greater support for competing policies and ideological perspectives to the PAP on welfare and social distribution. A further worry for the PAP was that this was the first election since Singapore's 1965 independence in which citizens born after 1965 constituted more than half the electorate. Structural economic, demographic, and technological trends thus combined to pose new challenges for the PAP's goal to limit competitive politics through strategies of societal and administrative incorporation, such as the FU. These strategies needed refinement if rising conflicts over costs of living and social and material inequalities were to be contained, so that consultative representation could arrest the appeal of competitive politics and democratic representation.

Reaching Everyone for Active Citizenry @ Home
The FU in New Clothing

It was toward such refinement that in September 2006 the FU underwent a major review leading to its renaming as REACH the next month. REACH's head, PAP MP Amy Khor (2006), explained that the institution "needs to move beyond gathering feedback to helping Singaporeans feel engaged and that they can make a difference." This required the FU's existing roles "to be enhanced, its reach widened and its channels of communication strengthened" (ibid.), so that "we [can] engage [Singaporeans] in playing a more active role in formulating new policies or refining existing ones" (REACH 2007, 5). As mechanisms of engagement expanded and diversified, though, the capacity of REACH in helping to arrest the appeal of democratic representation would be further tested due to intensified social contradictions associated with Singapore's capitalist development.

While most existing FU channels of communication were continued under REACH, a range of new channels was introduced to more fully exploit electronic media and reach new, especially younger, audiences, and in response to increasingly heightened public concerns about government policies. This included policies on immigration and foreign workers, public health, public transport, pensions, employment, and income distribution. The PAP had a strong interest in limiting how these conflicts were defined and addressed, given the many entailed ideological or material interests inherent to Singapore's particular model of state capitalism—including over welfare responsibilities and the profitability of GLCs (Rodan 2016). Total feedback volumes from both new media and traditional formats grew sharply, up 68 percent from 26,900 inputs in 2009 to 45,232 in 2014 (Khor 2015, 4).

Intensified targeting of younger tech-savvy Singaporeans included REACH opening a Facebook account in 2009; a Twitter account in 2010; an Instagram account in 2014; and the staging of a Q&A on Facebook in 2015. REACH also introduced a program called Youth Ambassador, enabling young Singaporeans to organize feedback sessions themselves. In 2007, REACH introduced e-Townhall webchats, generally chaired by the REACH head or other government MPs, providing opportunities to engage citizens following major policy announcements. The first e-Townhall webchat was held in February 2007 and sought public reactions to the 2007 national budget speech, discussed in real time online with Minister of State for Finance and Transport Lim Hwee Hua and REACH head Amy Khor. This platform would thereafter expand considerably to involve a wide range of ministers and issues as determined by REACH.[5]

Meanwhile, in-person platforms included the introduction in mid-2014 of the Listening Point concept, whereby booths were located in accessible public locations to disseminate information about national policies and receive policy suggestions. From mid-2014 to mid-2015, Listening Points covered, for example, policies on medical insurance, retirement income, and on various policies referred to in National Day Rally and budget speeches.

By 2013, REACH had also created a new target social category for consultations: professionals, managers, executives, and technicians (PMETs). As Khor (2013, 2) explained, "We recognize that PMETs currently form more than half of Singapore's workforce, and this is expected to rise to some two-thirds of the total workforce by 2030." This dynamic was a function of the restructuring of Singapore's globalized and increasingly knowledge-based economy, bringing with it anxieties about the need to adapt to technological change, reemployment of older workers, and shortages of local employees.

In other modifications, Policy Study Workshops (PSWs) were launched in 2008 to replace Policy Feedback Groups. PSWs were less bureaucratic and routine, involved no national conference, had a finite life, and would make recommendations directly to the government. As per Feedback Groups, though, PSWs comprised expert professionals, who had the power to determine which groups to seek out as representative in their consultations, and continued past practices of generally involving groups that would not be viewed by the PAP as political.[6]

PSWs were created on issues of aging, health, education, employment opportunities, environment, social integration, and manpower, among others. However, PSWs appeared to have little policy impact on, or public relations utility for, the government. These PSWs reflected the highly bureaucratic mentality and institutional inclinations of the PAP, as it struggled to come to terms with the pace and nature of change in political engagement amidst increasing social contradictions associated with Singapore's capitalist development. Politico-bureaucrats were now seriously focused on harnessing new electronic media technologies to state-controlled MOPs, but it was a learning-by-doing exercise. The rapidly accelerating growth and scale of contention over a range of policy issues necessitated this quick tactical reorientation.

Thus, other platforms with more immediate capacity to engage the public became more important in the lead-up to the 2011 election in the attempt to counter the rising impact of independent cyberspace commentary and criticism of government policies. In particular, space for critical interactive commentary and topic nomination within a dedicated online discussion forum increased.

Yet what was posted remained ultimately under government control. This capacity was bolstered with the introduction in December 2013 of a registration requirement and Facebook login for the discussion forum. The change was explained by REACH as a guard "against abuse and hate mongering" (Khor 2015, 3), and followed Prime Minister Lee's declaration that "we must fight back against trolling, and provide a safe, responsible online environment which promotes constructive participation" (H. L. Lee 2013b). Lee's critics in cyberspace saw the move differently, though, including by charging that the PAP was active in trolling to contain critical debate on more independent sites: "And since they are so concerned with alternative media sites like the *Real Singapore*, *Singapore Alternative Blogspot*, *TR Emeritus* (formerly *Temasek Review Emeritus*), and others, they actually bother to create FB [Facebook] pages attacking these sites" (*Real Singapore* 2013).[7]

Renewed Challenges of Capitalist Development

It was, however, the results of the May 2011 election that gave the PAP cause to reexamine its overall strategy to reinforce consultative representation, which would go beyond the continuing refinement of REACH. The ruling party's vote share slipped further to 60.1 percent—its worst performance since independence in 1965. In the process, the opposition WP picked up six seats, including by inflicting the PAP's first loss of a multiseat group representation constituency (GRC).[8] Voter concerns again centered on problems linked to the PAP's growth strategy.

The consequence of accelerated growth under the PAP's capitalist model was that income distribution in Singapore by 2011 was among the most unequal in the developed world (Low and Vadaketh 2014, ix), accompanied by estimated absolute poverty levels of 10–12 percent and relative poverty levels twice that figure (R. Chan 2013b; Chun 2013a). Meanwhile, inflationary costs of housing, transport, and health ensuing from population growth and high professional and executive salaries adversely affected many middle-class Singaporeans too. Pressure on public infrastructure—especially congestion on public transport[9]— also manifested in growing disquiet about guest workers and immigration levels (see E. Tan 2011).

Collectively, these problems created a climate conducive to an unprecedented questioning of several core ideological propositions expounded by the PAP, including that Singapore was, and had to remain, ruled by a meritocracy, and that consensus politics through consultative representation rather than competitive politics was the best route to policy reform. Moreover, social media would once more assume significance in bypassing the limitations of government-controlled media—and, indeed, REACH and NMPs—to question and criticize government policy, as well as submit independent policy and ideological prescriptions. The advent of Facebook subsequent to the 2006 election had significantly increased the scope for information and ideas sharing thereafter (George 2011).[10]

To be sure, despite advances in social interaction, new media did not fundamentally transform the small and fragmented nature of civil society. It principally boosted individual expression as a political modus operandi. The manner of this expression, though, reflected a qualitative shift in Singapore's political culture away from unquestioning deference to authority—including sharp anti-PAP rhetoric and parody. Indeed, political polarization was more discernible than increased political deliberation; George (2011, 159) observed nevertheless how the "cyberopposition showed that it could out-shout the government."

Although social media was yet to be harnessed by a coherent democratic movement, the outcome of the 2011 election and the shift in political culture were both unqualified threats to the PAP's consultative ideology of representation. Thus, while recognizing the electoral necessity of policy responses to contain if not resolve social inequities inherent to the existing model of capitalist development, the PAP also moved after the election to try and strengthen consultative representation and the related notion of consensus politics. It wanted to demonstrate not only that the government was serious about policy reform, but also that its content would be guided by public feedback suited to the task. This meant supplementing REACH with a new mechanism for political participation.

It was difficult to know whether, in the absence of the societal and administrative incorporation of REACH and the NMPs, the electoral drift toward the opposition might have been greater still. In any case, the PAP understood that it was in growing danger of permanently surrendering its hitherto ideological hegemony if it could not demonstrate that pressure from political opposition was unnecessary for a government responsive to the needs of Singaporeans. Thus the refinement in technocratic MOPs would take another turn.

Our Singapore Conversation

To allay public concerns about rising inequality, the first postelection budget was labeled by the government "the inclusive budget" and contained more social spending. Prime Minister Lee Hsien Loong depicted this in his 2012 National Day Rally speech as the beginning of a "new strategic direction for Singapore" that would involve striking a "new balance in our social compact" (H. L. Lee 2012). In the same speech, another aspect of the PAP's response to its electoral decline was announced: a "national conversation on Our Singapore to define what sort of country we want and how we can achieve it," to be led by Education Minister Heng Swee Keat. The result was Our Singapore Conversation (OSC), a twelve-month inquiry encompassing extensive public feedback starting in October 2012.

Government-led committees of enquiry incorporating public participation and views on policy problems, directions, and vision statements were not new. Previous such exercises included the Economic Committee (1986), the Next Lap (1991), Singapore 21 (1998), Remaking Singapore (2002), and the Economic Restructuring Committee (2002). However, OSC was different in the scale, forms, and methodology of public consultation. This included by affording some initial space for normative dialogue by participants. The PAP was not abandoning the notion of public policy as principally a technical problem-solving exercise. However, social conflict, aided by the advent of social media, now threatened to open up the ideological parameters of debate over those policies and processes. According to Prime Minister Lee, the PAP now needed to "accept more of the untidiness and the to-ing and fro-ing, which is part of normal politics" (quoted in Weymouth 2013). A new approach to public engagement was a necessary precondition for reasserting politics as problem solving.

In the course of OSC, an estimated 47,000 people participated in over 660 Dialogue Sessions involving forty organizations (OSC Committee 2013, 2). This unprecedented scale of feedback reflected how important it had become for the PAP to project itself as genuinely interested in a diverse range of views and concerns among Singaporeans. Channels of engagement were extended and modified accordingly and included those centrally organized by the government; organized by grassroots organizations and unions linked to the government; and organized by select interest groups, civic and civil society organizations, and companies.

OSC Process and Findings

In contrast with earlier more focused government-led public enquiries, the OSC started with greater exploration into the nature of public policy challenges. Deliberations also involved more flexible and less formalized organizational processes, including greater opportunities for participating organizations to shape the format and decide the setting of consultations. The 660 dialogues, organized by the OSC committee, government agencies, and community organizations, were conducted in 75 different locations, including small groups in coffee shops. Additional feedback was received through 1,331 email threads, 4,050 Facebook wall posts, 211 Facebook private messages, and 73 YouTube videos (OSC Committee 2013, 3). A media engagement strategy to promote widespread exposure of, and interest in, the OSC was also integral to the process.[11]

The initial phase of the OSC, which ran for just over six months, was loosely structured around questions of Singapore's overall direction, as, according to Heng, "some general consensus around where we would like Singapore to go" was a necessary basis for detailed policy discussion (quoted in Wong and Sim 2012). Heng invited honest and forthright participation, declaring there would be no "OB [out of bounds] markers or sacred cows" (ibid.).[12] However, he also tried to temper participants' expectations, stating that OSC was not a "culling exercise" of sacred cows but will seek instead to "reaffirm, recalibrate and refresh" national values and policies (quoted in Chang 2012). Similarly, while Prime Minister Lee pronounced that "we leave no stone unturned," he also said, "Some stones, after we look at them, the original place was quite nice and we put them back" (ibid.).

The upshot of phase one was the identification of twelve perspectives, distilled by the OSC committee as thematic among the multitude of views encountered or observed through Dialogue Sessions as well as emails and Facebook messages. These perspectives served as a guide for the more policy-focused second OSC phase (Chang 2013). The specific policy areas that this phase concentrated on were health care, housing, education, and old age (Toh 2013), although the scale and foci of these deliberations ranged widely.

The resulting final document—*Reflections of Our Singapore Conversation: What Future Do We Want? How Do We Get There?*—identified five "core aspirations that citizens feel should guide our society," which the OSC committee had apparently deemed thematic to the feedback received: "opportunity" for all; communities with "purpose"; "assurance" of basic needs; "spirit" for a compassionate society; and "trust" in engagement with policy makers (OSC Committee 2013, 4). Implicitly, these core aspirations embodied some sort of consensus, which left the government a separate task of working out how to give them effect.

Importantly, the aspirations identified through OSC were not startling revelations. Conflicts over inequalities, elitism, and materialism, for example, had been rising over the last decade in reaction to the PAP's political management of capitalist development. Indeed, opposition parties had submitted a range of specific policy solutions to address some of these public concerns.

The overwhelming tenor of the report was one of celebration of the inclusive nature of the process and the diversity of views unearthed and recorded. This included views departing from pivotal values and policies of the PAP, such as widespread questioning and criticism of the PAP's heavy emphasis on Housing Development Board flats as assets to be drawn on to support old age, and challenges to traditional notions of marriage and family. It was also acknowledged that the concept of meritocracy had come under scrutiny, especially in education. Here, though, OSC participants were portrayed as calling for a "recalibration of the way we practice meritocracy" (ibid., 27), inferring something well short of a fundamental challenge to the ideology of meritocracy.

Public servants involved in, or close to, the OSC exercise have portrayed the OSC as constituting a major qualitative shift in government-public engagement, inclusivity being but one aspect. Indeed, Kuah and Seok (n.d., 13)[13] argue that what set the OSC apart was the adoption of "open dialogues with broad agendas, structured (or 'unstructured') to allow for divergences, detours, digressions, and disagreement."

According to Kuah and Seok (2014), the distinctiveness of the OSC approach to engagement was a function of Singapore's postmodern condition, the city-state's plurality and diversity now rendering a single grand political narrative implausible.

However, the core issues of contestation that gave rise to the OSC and dominated the agenda were intimately related to specific contradictions and tensions of Singapore's model of capitalist development—not just to general processes of social and ideational diversity and complexity attendant to advanced capitalism everywhere. Furthermore, the OSC processes through which different perspectives of Singaporeans were engaged was not as open as officials claimed. The OSC path entailed political risks for the PAP, but there were also accompanying strategies to render those risks manageable.

Controlling Who Influences the OSC

According to Minister Heng, leader of the OSC committee, OSC committee members had been drawn from all walks of life to reflect the diversity of society, the committee's role being to "catalyse the conversation" so that it was as "inclusive as possible" (Aw 2012; Channel News Asia 2012). However, government and establishment people dominated the OSC committee, suggesting that this shift in how state-based MOPs were conceived was not quite as dramatic as asserted by Heng.

In addition to Heng, another six PAP MPs with either ministerial or high-level government responsibilities were members, as well as the assistant secretary-general of the PAP-affiliated NTUC, and the deputy editor of the Chinese-language daily newspaper *Lianhe Zaobao*, owned by Singapore Press Holdings—a GLC. Other members comprised a mix of public and private sector professionals from government ministries, tertiary institutions, and legal, artistic, and media firms. The bulk of these members were also part of the social or economic elite, although several boasted records of voluntary service with sporting, charitable, or nonprofit welfare organizations. A taxi driver and polytechnic student completed the committee.

Opposition politicians, civil society actors, and leading bloggers critical of the PAP were conspicuously absent from the OSC committee, raising serious concerns in those quarters about the consultative exercise's purpose. Chee Soon Juan of the Singapore Democratic Party contended that a "conversation is only as strong as the participants: If the participants are selected from those inclined to agree, little policy development will result" (quoted in Ng 2012). Chee's party colleague Wong Wee Nam (2012) argued that the need for OSC could be obviated by "a more open society, a free press, a respect for alternative opinions." Reform Party leader Kenneth Jayaretnam was most emphatic in his dismissal of OSC, labeling it a "national monologue" and a "stage play in which all the parts had been chosen" (quoted in Phua 2012).

In his efforts to counter these apprehensions and criticisms, Heng declared that OSC "is not a partisan exercise . . . every Singaporean is welcome to provide their views, including members of the Opposition" (quoted in *Real Singapore* 2012).[14] Another OSC committee member and PAP MP, Indranee Rajah, asserted that the conversation was "apolitical" (quoted in Phua 2012). OSC committee member and academic Kenneth Tan later conceded, though, that the committee could have been more inclusive by incorporating people "who were a little further from the mainstream" (quoted in Toh 2013). Yet he also explained that he came to understand why this was not the case: "While you want a diversity of views, you might also want a reasonable amount of consensus so the process can start" (ibid.).

Importantly, however, the PAP's priority was not to incorporate political opponents but to avail those that might be influenced by them of alternative, state-sponsored modes of political participation and engagement with the government. As Tan observed from his time on the committee, the "OSC's idea of 'inclusiveness' was actually tied to its efforts to engage with Singapore's 'silent majority'" (quoted in OSC Committee 2013). The objective was to ensure that as many of the "silent majority" as possible could be persuaded that these state-controlled feedback mechanisms offered a direct and effective avenue for engagement with the government by citizens. The more this could be achieved, the less likely that such Singaporeans would feel the need to vote for the opposition. The OSC presented as a nondemocratic alternative MOP to combative parliamentary politics. It was imbued with ideological presuppositions about how shared understanding and direct participation was superior in solving real problems to political competition and independent collective organizations.

OSC, and hence its report, then, were guided by a committee unrepresentative of Singapore's political diversity. Consequently, many opposition and civil society activists steered clear of participation in OSC forums. This limited not just the spectrum of views presented, but also the extent to which those participating belonged to independent collective organizations. Thus while the process invited critical engagement, and this materialized to some degree, there was no potential for concerted collective challenges to fundamental PAP ideological or policy positions. It generally favored individualized political expression over civil society expression, even though it involved roles for a range of different social and community organizations as well as those linked to the PAP facilitating the incorporation of societal forces into new MOPs.

Not surprisingly, government departments and agencies were active organizers of OSC dialogues on issues of immediate policy relevance to them. However, grassroots organizations and unions linked to the government also played a key role in initiating and supporting Dialogue Sessions. None were more important than the parapolitical People's Associations and the NTUC, which collectively command the most extensive national and local networks of any non-state organizations. Their reach into working-class communities rendered them strategic in ensuring political participation from socioeconomic groups most adversely affected by, and anxious over, the rising inequalities and foreign labor accompanying Singapore's particular capitalist development model. It was, after all, the working class that provided the strongest electoral support for the PAP's opponents.

The *Reflections* report indicates that forty different organizations, outside government, initiated or led dialogues (OSC Committee 2013, 45).[15] Melissa Khoo, director of the OSC program office responsible for coordinating the national conversation, explained that many dialogues "were ground up initiatives—we were prepared to partner with interested parties, in the spirit of having an inclusive national conversation."[16] However, the organizations that presented had a civic rather than civil society complexion. Khoo explained: "In particular, we wanted to reach out to the less advantaged in a setting they were comfortable with, hence Salvation Army, ISCOS (ex-offenders), Lions befrienders (elderly), AWWA [Asian Women's Welfare Association] were among examples of voluntary welfare organizations and interest groups that stepped forward to host the conversations with their beneficiaries, and we welcomed their support."[17]

Among the forty organizations hosting dialogues, there were others that had more overtly political significance—although not as conspicuously as in the case of the NTUC. In addition to GLC media organizations Berita Harian and Lianhe Zaobao, this included the Chinese Development Assistance Council (CDAC) and the Singapore Indian Development Association (SINDA) Youth Club. CDAC and SINDA were established in the early 1990s in direct response to the PAP's decision to promote approaches to social welfare through ethnic-based self-help organizations. Such organizations were part of the PAP's strategy to discourage class-informed conceptions of the root causes of poverty and disadvantage in favor of particularist identities and related forms of political representation (Rahim 1994; Chua 2007).

An exception to the above pattern was a dialogue session initiated by NMP Janice Koh for members of the creative sector, including media, heritage, and design—many of whom were politically progressive and critical of the PAP.[18] A key organizer of that dialogue session, Kok Heng Leun, artistic director of Singapore theatre company Drama Box, came out of the process with no more conviction that the government was interested in core artistic concerns, such as censorship, contained in the report on that dialogue session submitted to the OSC. The single-paragraph distillation of that report in *Reflections* made no mention of censorship (OSC Committee 2013, 13). Kok observed: "while we were talking about arts, we were also talking about politics and I think we were really questioning some of the fundamentals . . . you know I don't think that feeds into the real agenda of the OSC."[19]

Despite the organizations involved in OSC being skewed heavily toward PAP-linked and civic society organizations, this neither undermined its utility for the government nor tempered claims by it about the exercise's fundamental political significance as an inclusive process. In particular, the PAP would link OSC processes to major policy reforms in the lead-up to, during, and following the 2015 election. The general absence of any organized political opposition and other civil society from OSC participation was more a help than a hindrance for the PAP's strategy. It afforded greater control by the PAP over how feedback was conducted, recorded, and, most importantly, interpreted in its impact on government policy.

Controlling How OSC Linked to Policy

Significantly, the final forty-eight-page report arising from the yearlong engagements—*Reflections of Our Singapore Conversation: What Future Do We Want? How Do We Get There?*—did not lead to policy recommendations. This report, it was emphasized, was "NOT a policy document that outlines government responses to Singaporeans' contributions to OSC. Government agencies will use the views from OSC as an important source of inputs for policy reviews" (OSC Committee 2013, 2).

Crucially, then, the absence of policy recommendations in the report afforded the government maximum discretion in linking its policies with the OSC process. On this basis, it could assert the influence citizens can have by working with the PAP and its feedback institutions, rather than the more independent, competitive alternatives. The underlying ideological basis to the MOPs involved in the OSC was the notion that shared information, including about people's normative views, was functional for technocratic elites to ultimately craft effective solutions to the problems of Singaporeans.

At one level, OSC appeared to significantly depart from the PAP's ideological notion of politics as a problem-solving exercise. At another level, though, OSC introduced a division of labor that achieved the same result: the PAP retained strategic control over how feedback translated into policy. Singaporeans could thus still be projected as part of a collective, apolitical problem-solving exercise. This was a more sophisticated form of consultative representation ideology than previously practiced.

However, the PAP's strategy of positively linking OSC to policy reform started badly. In January 2013 the government released its white paper on population, prior to the issue being fully debated and reported on through OSC. The white paper provided for an increase in Singapore's population to 6.9 million by 2030, with Singaporeans comprising just 55 percent of the population by then. Such was the public outcry that on February 16 approximately 4,000 people gathered to protest at inner city Hong Lim Park—the biggest demonstration since 2000, when such events became legal. Opposition condemnation of the PAP's strategy of generating economic growth through such high levels of immigration as socially and environmentally unsustainable resonated with protesters (Adam 2013). For critics of OSC, this policy projection confirmed their suspicions the exercise was not sincere. Even for some OSC committee members, the white paper appeared to preempt discussions (Toh 2013).

Thereafter, there were concerted attempts by the government to demonstrate OSC's influence on policy formation. In Finance Minister Tharman Shanmugaratnam's 2013/14 budget speech, in March 2013, he emphasized how inputs from different ministries sourced from OSC informed a range of policies.[20] Then, in his August 2013 National Day Rally speech, Prime Minister Lee declared that the government "must intervene more to keep ours a fair and just society" (H. L. Lee 2013a), projecting significant policy refinements and initiatives in health care for the aged, public housing affordability, and education and income supplements for disadvantaged families. Lee and other senior government leaders explicitly linked the OSC to the government's philosophical shift toward greater social redistribution—described as "compassionate meritocracy" (see Law 2013; A. Ong 2014a)[21]—and specific policies through which this was enacted (Fernandez 2013; C. T. Goh 2013; L. Lim 2013).

Tony Tan (2014) also invoked OSC in his presidential address in May 2014, not just declaring that the government would give substance to the many voices of OSC, but also emphasizing the need to uphold the "constructive politics that puts our nation and our people first." This concept of "constructive politics" was elaborated on by Prime Minister Lee to include "developing effective policies for Singaporeans, which means solving problems, creating opportunities and making difficult trade-offs to improve lives . . . putting forward good people to lead and maintaining high standards of integrity and honesty" (quoted in Saad 2014). The next month—in defense of "constructive politics"—PAP MP Indranee condemned the WP for its attempt to claim credit for enhancements to public health insurance it had advocated. These were, Indranee insisted, the sum of the efforts of the Singaporeans who took part in the OSC, civil servants, and the review committee (A. Ong 2014b).

The battle lines were between constructive politics and the ideology of consultative representation, on the one hand, and a more competitive politics of democratic parliamentary representation on the other. PAP leaders still employed the rhetoric of "democracy," but envisaged a regime continually finding ways to bypass combative politics and, with it, any prospect of an end to PAP rule. As Culture, Community and Youth Minister Lawrence Wong explained, "Opposition for the sake of opposition will not promote or strengthen our democracy. . . . How does this sort of discourse help us in solving the real and vital problems affecting our nation?" (quoted in Y. L. Lim 2014). The solution, for Wong, lay beyond partisan politics: "a democracy of deeds, made up of active citizenry who get involved in developing solutions for a better society" (ibid.). Such active citizenship would be conducted through PAP-controlled institutions shaping the forms of conflict permissible over Singapore's problems and the solutions to address them.

Impact of New MOPs on the 2015 Polls

The tussle between competing ideologies of political representation was central to the 2015 election campaigns. By this time, the PAP government had ushered in substantial spending boosts to redistributive social welfare targeting the aged and needy, laid out major investments in public transport and housing, and slowed the rate of growth in foreign workers. The question was: Why? And, since both the PAP and opposition parties argued more reform was needed, what was the best way of ensuring it?

WP leader Low Thia Khiang attributed the government policy direction to increased support for political opposition: "Before 2011, the ruling party cruised along with policies that led to escalating cost of living, employment and retirement insecurity, and strained infrastructure due to runaway immigration" (quoted in Kor 2015). After the shocking 2011 loss of a GRC in particular, though, Singaporeans witnessed "a more responsive government that is sensitive to the needs and struggles of the people" (Low quoted in Zakir 2015). Voters, Low contended, saw how balancing against PAP dominance resulted in PAP "policy U-turns" (Chang 2015a). "Without co-drivers, Singaporeans keep getting taken for a ride," Low explained (quoted in L. Lim 2015); but voters could now entrench their empowerment by further boosting opposition numbers "to supervise the Government" (Low quoted in Z. L. Chong 2015a).

Emeritus Senior Minister Goh Chok Tong compared Low's claims about opposition policy influence over the PAP to the fable of the rooster boasting that its crowing was responsible for the sun rising (Chow 2015). According to Goh, the integrity of PAP MPs, not "this seductive line of check and balance," is what mattered. "You don't need the opposition to check on the Government, you need the PAP to check the PAP," Goh asserted (quoted in Chang 2015b). Prime Minister Lee supplemented this position, proclaiming that "good policies are a result of the people working directly with the PAP—no need for intermediaries or co-drivers" (quoted in Chang 2015c). OSC was the latest such working relationship largely bypassing independent intermediaries.

The September 11 polls delivered the PAP an emphatic victory with 69.9 percent of the vote, up by 9.8 percent on 2011, delivering 83 of the total parliamentary 89 seats. The WP lost the seat of Punggol East, while the five-seat Aljunied GRC was narrowly retained, and the single seat of Hougang held with a reduced margin. Rather than progress toward the critical mass of twenty seats sought by Low (Ng 2015), the PAP had arrested and reversed the last decade's opposition gains.

Clearly, nondemocratic MOP institutions matter to real political outcomes, regardless of how short they fall against liberal democratic benchmarks emphasized by hybrid regime theorists. Policy adjustments to address voter concerns over the impacts of Singapore's model of capitalist development were crucial to the election results. However, these policies gained added legitimacy and maximum political impact through the PAP linking these reforms to OSC. OSC helped reduce the perception that PAP technocratic elites were aloof and uncaring about those left behind in Singapore's "economic miracle." The government appeared to have recovered some ground in reasserting the idea that government responsiveness to public concerns was not reliant on competitive politics and democratic MOPs, but could be achieved through state-sponsored and controlled MOPs guided by ideologies of consultative representation. In the process, the OSC availed PAP leaders of a deeper appreciation of the different perspectives and anxieties of the electorate, enabling it to fine-tune rhetoric and choice of candidates, and more generally improve its strategic thinking.

Not surprisingly, then, following the election, PAP leaders projected a ramping up of societal incorporation, not least by Minister Heng, who headed OSC. According to Heng, support for and confidence in the PAP meant the ruling party needed to "engage even more extensively and even more deeply" (quoted in Sim 2015a). The SGfuture series of dialogues, consequently, was launched in late November 2015 to engage one hundred young Singaporeans over such issues as security, the environment, and "how to build an empathetic society." Led by the minister for culture, community, and youth, Grace Fu, and minister in the prime minister's office, Chan Chun Sing, the SGfuture public engagements ran until mid-2016. Their purpose, according to Chan, was to "build consensus about the future they [young Singaporeans] wish to have, and to commit their aspirations to action" (quoted in Sim 2015a). Fu added that, through SGfuture, "we want Singaporeans to step forward to put the values that they envisioned in the OSC into action" (quoted in Sim 2015b).

More public forums and Dialogue Sessions on specific issues were also anticipated. Indeed, REACH chief Amy Khor declared that the opposition was welcome to participate in the increased and diverse dialogues and social media sessions: "We are open to hearing from everyone, as long as they enrich the discussion and address the *issues at hand* [italics added]" (quoted in C. Yong 2015). Deputy Prime Minister Tharman also portended that "everyone will be included in the way we go forward, and everyone must feel included in the way we go forward" (quoted in C. Yang 2015). This extended to political opposition as well as to online and social media, "which play an important role in shaping opinion, and should continue to do so *as constructively as possible* [italics added]" (ibid.).

Meanwhile, straying from the "issues at hand" and not acting as constructively as possible remained risky for PAP critics owing to a range of laws. Those risks had not abated since the advent of the OSC. As Human Rights Watch deputy Asia director Phil Robertson observed, "In 2015, bloggers and online news portals increasingly faced punitive action for any criticism of the government" (quoted in Han 2016b).[22] According to Robertson, "Singapore's crackdown on bloggers and others asserting their free speech rights shows the government's determination to place controls over freedom" (ibid.). In August 2016, the Administration of Justice (Protection) Bill was also passed, lowering the threshold for contempt of court to further reinforce constraints on attempts by bloggers and other civil society actors seeking to scrutinize public authorities and the way justice is administered in Singapore (Han 2016a; Choo 2016).

Crucially, the likelihood is that the institutions through which more extensive and deeper engagement is promoted will continue to afford the PAP strategic—if not total—control over the definition of the "issues at hand" and "constructive" politics.

Since the mid-1980s, the PAP has developed and refined institutions for public consultation and feedback to fortifying the authoritarian regime. However, as the results of the 2006 and 2011 elections demonstrated, the effectiveness of refinements to societal and administrative incorporation is mediated by the interaction of material and ideological forces. In the absence of policies to address the concrete problems of electors, neither the FU nor REACH could adequately stem the growing support for elected political opposition or criticism and scrutiny of PAP policies and ideologies in cyberspace. It was in this context that OSC was born, marking a new level of sophistication in modes of participation developed by the PAP to incorporate public feedback into policy formation.

OSC combined state-sponsored political spaces for both normative and policy dialogue, designed to incorporate an unprecedented scale and range of participants through diverse and often loosely structured engagements. It recognized the need to concede some measure of control over deliberations in order to ensure the widest participation. This was not a risk-free exercise by the PAP; potentially it opened it up to unpredictable ideological contestation and policy scrutiny. Nevertheless, because the process deliberately avoided specific policy recommendations, the PAP government retained total discretion in the translation of feedback into policy. This also enabled reforms to be depicted as the outcome of a direct engagement between government and the people—an argument that was central to the PAP's successful campaign strategy at the 2015 polls.

Whatever the specific paths of public feedback exercises in societal and administrative incorporation ahead, the social impacts of Singapore's capitalist development will continue to present challenges for PAP leaders in struggles over political representation. As Prime Minister Lee observed on the especially thorny issue of foreigners and immigration, "there are no easy choices—and every option carries a downside and some pain" (quoted in *Economic Times* 2015). Similarly, it remains to be seen whether the PAP's compassionate meritocracy, which it distinguishes from welfarism (see Rodan 2016), adequately contains social and political conflict over inequalities into the future.

The 2011 election results serve also as a further reminder that increased critical noise in the blogosphere by PAP critics does not necessarily portend a more coherent and potent democratic reform movement. This requires the building of collective independent organizations and coalitions thereof, something that individual expression may complement but not replace in struggles over political representation. Authoritarian controls and related political economy relationships continue to make this a difficult path to forge. It will be all the more difficult if the PAP's project of absorbing more diverse social forces into the orbit of societal and administrative incorporation through more creative feedback mechanisms succeeds.

THE PHILIPPINES' PARTY-LIST SYSTEM, REFORMERS, AND OLIGARCHS

Although the overthrow of Marcos in 1986 ending authoritarian rule in the Philippines enjoyed broad cross-class support, the precise institutional arrangements of the democratic regime to replace it proved contentious. Some sought to restore traditional elite political rule favoring capitalist oligarchic interests but others wanted a transfer of power away from such elite dominance. Consequently, various demands for electoral and related reforms that surfaced during the Constitutional Commission did not make it into the 1987 Constitution. Of those that did, many required implementing laws that never materialized. One reform that did eventually pass both hurdles was Reform Act 7941—the Party-List System (PLS) Act of 1995, first elections for which were held in 1998.

Through a form of proportional representation, the PLS set aside 20 percent of seats in the House of Representatives, ostensibly to facilitate some change in who could be represented in Congress. Hopes were raised too that the PLS would lay foundations for more programmatic-based political parties rather than those based on personalities and patronage. Underlying such aspirations were reformist goals of addressing fundamental cleavages in Philippines society, especially over poverty and inequality born out of oligarchic capitalism. This potentially posed a challenge for the privileged access to state power so crucial to the capital accumulation strategies and related interests of oligarchs.

Differences over the root causes and solutions to such cleavages among reformers notwithstanding, arresting the power of traditional politicians, pejoratively referred to as *trapos*, was a shared objective of many reformers and a popular sentiment elites could not tactically ignore. The charge of being a *trapo* was applied to politicians—especially those who were linked to powerful capitalist families—variously engaging in corruption, fraud, terrorism, or patronage for their capitalist backers (Quimpo 2008, 4). The attraction of political office for *trapos* was not just power over how their interests were regulated, but the ability to bilk the state—including through discretionary control over public funds available to legislators, or "pork barrel,"[1] and other access to state agency budgets (Abinales and Amoroso 2005, 240).

In contrast with new modes of participation (MOPs) in the authoritarian regime in Singapore, which are initiated and tightly controlled by the state, the PLS was originally a "civil society expression" MOP, driven by reformers and "leftists."[2] This has resulted in more political contestation over the intent and design of this MOP, but, significantly, has ultimately not stopped the PLS from becoming an important tool for the Philippine elite for containing threats to its dominance and the preservation of oligarchic capitalism. Indeed, much of this contestation has been *between* reformist elements, adding to the elite's ability to use the PLS to contain and fragment civil society.

Entangled in this new MOP is a political struggle between reformist elements over whether the fundamental purpose of the PLS is to enhance electoral representation of the marginalized and underrepresented, or to more generally facilitate political pluralism. At its core, this struggle centers on competing ideological notions of democratic representation. For some reformist forces, democratic representation requires modes of participation permitting effective challenges to existing inequalities of power, as democratic ideologies of representation are defined in this study. For others, the yardstick is less exacting and instead emphasizes liberal values of political pluralism and competition—these are necessary but not sufficient conditions for democratic representation as understood in this book.

Such ideological differences have manifested both in contending positions on how the PLS should operate among different social and political forces and in contrasting, sometimes contradictory, interpretations and judgments by authorities on this matter—especially by the Commission on Elections (Comelec) and the Supreme Court. This is a struggle over the strategic selectivity of the PLS affecting which actors and conflicts are advantaged or not by this particular MOP. The PLS is, therefore, not simply an institution impaired by ambiguous legislation that can be overcome by legal clarification. It is one site in a continuing struggle over how social, economic, and political power is organized in the Philippines. Indeed, all state institutions must be viewed in relationship to wider social conflicts and power structures from which they cannot be disentangled or rise above (see Sangmpam 2007). While much has been written concerning the "technical" deficiencies of the PLS, analysis of the PLS via this perspective offers fresh understanding of the inherent limitations of institutional reform in a contested environment.

The central argument in this chapter is that entrenched elite privilege in the Philippines has continually triumphed over reform elements in the struggle over democratic representation via a PLS, principally by promoting particularist ideologies of representation and institutionalizing political fragmentation. Under the PLS there has been a flowering of single-issue groups and a promotion and/or reinforcement of particularist ideologies, including those of gender, ethnicity, indigeneity, and geography. Intra-left ideological struggles and contested refinements to the PLS model since its inception have had the effect of intensifying, rather than ameliorating, a lack of collective organizational strength and cohesion among reformist forces across civil society. Moreover, whatever the intention behind these refinements, they have resulted in more elite representation in Congress—often under the pretense of representing peasants and workers by exploiting anti-*trapo* rhetoric. These strategies have helped shore up traditional parties and political dynasties and promote specific emerging business interests through a presence in Congress. Consequently, while capital accumulation strategies have evolved and diversified since the "booty capitalism" of the 1950s (Hutchcroft 1998)—notably through privatization of state assets and services—this has done little to increase economic competition and much to bolster the profits of established oligarchs.

The chapter starts with an account of the competing interests and objectives inherent to the establishment of the PLS, which laid the foundations for dynamic struggle thereafter. Focus then shifts to key turning points in the struggles and strategies of contending forces participating in the PLS. This will highlight how elites have used their privileged status to both foment, and then capitalize on, fragmentation within the PLS across the years. Actions by Comelec and rulings by the Supreme Court over how to interpret and implement the act feature in all turning points. The impacts of these rulings have been mediated, though, by wider power relations within and beyond the state to generally contain the political space to progressive forces through the PLS.

Foundations of Party-List System Conflict
PLS Origins: Competing Democratic Ideologies

In the aftermath of the popular mass uprising against Marcos, President Corazon Aquino established a Constitutional Commission (ConCom) to enshrine guiding beliefs and institutions for a democratic Philippines. Although commissioners debated a wide range of contentious issues, ultimately the Constitution gestured toward, but made few firm commitments about, substantive shifts in social, economic, and political power (Lane 1990, 24; Abinales and Amoroso 2005, 234–35). One concrete change to the political system the ConCom and the Constitution did prescribe was the introduction of "a party-list system of registered national, regional, and sectoral parties or organizations or coalitions thereof" to constitute 20 percent of the representatives in the House of Representatives (Republic of the Philippines 1995, sec. 2).

Commissioners supporting a PLS did so via contrasting logics and with varying political objectives in mind. For reformers, ideological differences over democratic representation saw disagreement over whether the PLS should focus on giving priority to sectoral or pluralist forms of representation (ConCom 1986, 256).

Sectoral representation was by now an established concept, having initially been introduced under Marcos to incorporate functional groups into Congress.[3] Although the nature of Marcos's appointments discredited that experiment (Wurfel 1997, 21), such an initiative in co-option acknowledged the existence and potential threat of mass organizations seeking to represent the interests of the disadvantaged and poor. Crucially, it also reinforced the status of discrete identities across the basic sectors, with the potential to foster assorted particularist ideologies unhelpful for building cohesive social movements capable of challenging elite power and/or holding elected representatives to account. While ConCom reformers' advocacy of sectoral-based representation was more genuine than that of Marcos, nevertheless the concept of sectors as independent units of formal political representation was being championed.

Certainly, support for sectoral representation of the disadvantaged was strong enough among delegates to result in a proposal for exclusive and permanently reserved seats for such representatives in Congress.[4] This view emphasized the right of the sectors to be represented (ConCom 1986, 578), and the systemic constraints on representatives from marginalized groups in open electoral competition with powerful *trapos* and elite-backed parties and candidates (255, 565). As argued by ConCom commissioner Joaquin Bernas (2007), "The idea of giving meaningful representation, particularly to the farmers and the workers, would be our Commission's humble gesture of extending protection to the interests of these groups which are not adequately attended to in normal legislative deliberations."

Other delegates were not convinced that this was the best way for opening up representation in Congress. Some reformers placed emphasis on a more general need for political pluralism not principally limited to basic sectors and/or the need for limited PLS seat reservation for the sectors. These reformers envisioned the

PLS as allowing space not only for marginalized sectoral groups, but also for underrepresented political parties and groups, such as environmental parties (ConCom 1986, 258).

During these debates over democratic ideologies of representation with a PLS, conservatives were not silent. Indeed, traditional elites arguably held the balance of power in the ConCom, so it would be their voices (and votes) that would determine the nature of the PLS. While President Aquino emphasized the need for the ConCom to be broadly inclusive, there was also a remarkable degree of social and political homogeneity among commissioners, who generally shared backgrounds of high educational and/or professional achievement and privileged family status, linking them as "a group of influence and privilege in Philippine national life" (Rush, quoted in Franco 2001). Some moderate reformers inspired by liberalism and social democracy were included, but representatives from left-wing mass organizations with either radical socialist or revolutionary communist ideologies were largely absent.[5] The boycott of elections by the Communist Party of the Philippines (CPP) in 1978, in favor of armed struggle, had helped conservatives rationalize such selectivity.

By supporting a PLS MOP, elites could present themselves as being responsive to public demands for a more inclusive democracy. Alongside this, though, some delegates were attracted to a PLS for its potential to contain the communist-inspired insurgency and secession movements, by redirecting them away from armed resistance and toward electoral politics (ConCom 1986). Congress was an arena where, arguably, elites could more easily control reformist aspirations.

The pluralist interpretation of the PLS—which allowed for a broader interpretation of who should be allowed to vie for a PLS seat (including elites themselves)—best suited elite interests, and thus this was the form encouraged. Arguments by sectoral representation reformers about structurally based power advantages to traditional elites and *trapos* were downplayed by elites, with several commissioners contending that only an initial period of reservation was needed to allow marginalized sectoral groups to become strong enough to compete in open PLS elections. As a former minister in the Marcos administration, Blas Ople (quoted in ConCom 1986, 568), asserted, "I see no reason why after having occupied seats in the House of Representatives . . . representatives may not be able to combine their forces in order to form their own political parties or become powerful adjuncts to existing political parties."

Consequently, the proposal for permanent exclusive sectoral representation was defeated, twenty-two votes to nineteen (ConCom 1986, 584), with a provision instead for temporary, initial reservation for the sectors in the PLS (see Republic of the Philippines 1987, sec. 5.2). The PLS, then, after this initial reservation, would open to include national and regional non-sectoral groups as well.

This vote did not mark the end of contestation between reformers over exactly how the PLS would enable broader political representation, and was just the beginning of elite manipulation of the PLS. The debates did, however, help to reinforce the legitimacy of sectoral political representation, although there would be a continuing struggle hereafter over how much of it was appropriate and who had the credentials to provide it. These debates about the strategic selectivity of representation would be mediated by both competing interests and ideologies over the scope of permissible political conflict through the PLS.

PLS Elections Begin: Institutionalizing Political Fragmentation

Strategies and tactical judgments by reformers of all complexions were necessarily affected by the prompt reassertion of oligarchic power in Congress (Coronel et al. 2004). This reassertion had the potential to contain even moderate changes to the regulation and distributive effects of resources under capitalist development in the Philippines. Thus, aspirations for a ban on political dynasties in the PLS, while a priority for many progressives, including pluralists, met with intense elite resistance. Extensive lobbying efforts by radical and moderate reform groups translated into bills in both the Senate and the House of Representative for a PLS. The former bill called for a ban on the five biggest parties in the first three PLS elections, whereas the latter sought no such restrictions. Reflecting the oligarchic dominance of Congress, these proposals were merged in a compromise specifying a ban only for the first election (Quimpo 2008, 215).

Crucially, despite assertions in the act that the PLS "shall promote proportional representation" (Republic of the Philippines 1995, sec. 2), the *trapo*-dominated Tenth Congress inserted a provision that placed a three-seat limit on the top PLS group vote getters. This was a far cry from the ten-seat cap that pluralist Con-Com delegate Christian Monsod had advocated earlier, thereby fundamentally limiting the potential of the PLS to facilitate the emergence of cohesive political parties as alternatives to well-established ones. It was instead a recipe for political fragmentation among, and containment of, those forces seeking to challenge elite electoral, and wider societal, dominance. The possibility of such a challenge is what renders political competition meaningful for many reformists and what most distinguishes a genuinely democratic ideology of political representation. From this perspective, the authority and capacity to effectively represent popular interests is linked to the extent and nature of collective organizations.

When inaugural PLS elections were held in 1998, a total of 123 accredited groups contested, 14 of which attracted the 2 percent or more of votes required to take up seats in Congress. Rodriguez (2009, 167) observed that "the party-list representatives of the Eleventh Congress were dominated by civil society groups and thus there were high hopes that they would bring to Congress the concerns of the marginalized sectors and perhaps their development needs." Victors included radicals from Akbayan and from Sanlakas, a multisectoral group with links to organized labor. Various other successful groups broadened representation in Congress, including Abanse! Pinay, representing women; the National Federation of Small Coconut Farmers; Alyansang Bayanihan ng mga Magsasaka, Manggagawang Bukid at Mangingisda, representing farmers, fisherfolk, and peasants; Butil, representing small farmers; Alagad and Adhikain at Kilusan ng Ordinaryong Tao, both representing the urban poor; and the National Confederation of Cooperatives (Coop-NATCO).

Yet fragmentation of groups was also evident, and it would need to be addressed for the PLS to facilitate more formidable collective representation within—let alone across—sectors. For example, thirteen trade union–based parties ran, but none passed the requisite 2 percent vote threshold. Similarly, there were nine competing groups from the peasant sector (Wurfel 1997, 27; Añonuevo 2000; Eaton 2003, 479). This fragmentation was exacerbated by the three-seat limit.

The PLS seat limit could not have been more at odds with the aspirations of the leftist radical reformers who formally established Akbayan, the Citizens' Action Party multisectoral political party in January 1998. They advocated proportional representation for electing the entire legislature, not just the PLS, aligning them with more pluralist interpretations of the PLS. Ideally, they wanted a parliamentary rather than presidential system. Proportional representation, they reasoned, could nevertheless depersonalize campaigns and foster greater focus on parties and their programs (see Quimpo 2008, 223). Akbayan and other progressive forces would persevere with the PLS, looking to it as an avenue for contesting, if not transforming, *trapo* political domination.

The far-left, revolutionary, multisectoral Bayan Muna (Nation First) party, formed in 1999 in the wake of the first party-list elections, was less convinced of the use of the PLS as a tool for proportional representation. Despite an extraordinary debut of 1.7 million votes in 2001, it only earned the maximum three seats. This would prove the catalyst for Bayan Muna's subsequent fragmentation into separate sectoral-based parties.[6] The total number of votes Bayan Muna garnered in 2001 was thrice that of the lead party in 1998, the Association of Philippine Electric Cooperatives (APEC), and almost equivalent to the combined votes of the top five place getters that year (Santuario 2001).

To some extent this came at the cost of Akbayan, which won only one seat in 2001, and other reformist groups that suffered such significant vote declines that they could not secure any seats, notably Sanlakas and Abanse! Pinay. Signaling early tension in the competition among leftists for votes of the marginalized,

Akbayan also alleged harassment of some of its candidates by the CPP's New People's Army (Llamas 2001), often linked to Bayan Muna. Importantly, this friction was in part another legacy of the 1995 three-seat restrictions, imposing representation limits even when popular forces *do* organize themselves in broad-based parties.

Elite Reaction to Progressive Gains
Ruling in Favor of Exclusive Sectoral Representation

Candidate participation increased at the 2001 party-list polls to 162 groups, but principally because of escalating attempts by traditional political forces to exploit the system. Deep political fissures surrounding the impeachment of President Joseph Estrada and Gloria Macapagal Arroyo's ascension to the presidency in January 2001 elevated the importance attached to the party-list. In particular, according to Llamas (2001), the "highly charged and acute polarization compelled elite factions to use every available means to win the elections," including the party-list. Access to the Priority Development Assistance Fund (PDAF), available to all members of Congress for their pet projects, added to the appeal of PLS participation.

Despite their differences, Akbayan, Bayan Muna, and other reformers were united in their outrage over a raft of PLS candidates linked to traditional political parties and powerful and wealthy interests inside and outside the state. This included Mamamayan Ayaw sa Droga (Citizens Against Drugs), a semigovernmental body with ties to ousted president Estrada, which secured 1.5 million votes to join Bayan Muna as the only other group taking the maximum three seats. Other extremely contentious groups included elite political parties Lakas National Union of Christian Democrats and the Nationalist People's Coalition, as well as Citizens Battle Against Corruption (CIBAC) and Buhay Hayaan Yumabong (BUHAY, Let Life Prosper), fronted by people of immense personal wealth and with strong links to religious organizations (Teehankee 2002, 183–84).

Such was the consternation over whether these groups should be eligible to compete that Comelec's proclamation of seat winners was delayed, pending a Supreme Court ruling in the *Ang Bagong Bayani vs. Comelec* case in June 2001. The court's landmark ruling endorsed the earlier defeated sectoral-based position at the Con-Com that the exclusive purpose of the PLS was representation of the "marginalized and underrepresented." Chief Justice Artemio Panganiban was influential in this turnabout, emphasizing the PLS as a tool for "social justice" that should not be "open to all" (Supreme Court 2001, "Epilogue").

The 2001 ruling did not bar major political parties from contesting, but it was now incumbent on them to demonstrate that they represented the interests of the marginalized and underrepresented. Parties and organizations could not be "an adjunct of, or a project organized or an entity funded or assisted by, the government" either (Supreme Court 2001, "Fourth Issue"). Religious organizations did not constitute a marginalized or underrepresented sector, so they were not eligible, but individual religious leaders seeking to advance the interests of marginalized and underrepresented sectors were. Subsequently, 14 seats were proclaimed and, in a protracted process, all but 46 of the 162 contestants were disqualified, including all major traditional parties.

Comelec's new guidelines for the 2004 party-list election reflected the Supreme Court's 2001 rulings and resulted in accredited groups dropping sharply to sixty-six. Yet many of those approved appeared to contravene the guidelines, including some revamped versions of groups and parties previously disqualified, and others that arguably should have been. APEC, BUHAY, CIBAC, Alagad (Disciple), Veterans Freedom Party, and Coop-NATCO were among the twenty-four party-list groups to gain seats for the Thirteenth Congress, whose claims to be representing the marginalized were widely regarded as spurious. The same groups were largely responsible for why half the new entrants to Congress were millionaires (Manalansan 2007, 62).

Accusations of corruption and political partisanship within Comelec had periodically surfaced (Llamas 2001; Hedman 2006; Kawanaka and Asaba 2011), but they escalated following these and other contentious accreditations. Soon allegations extended to vote rigging at the 2004 polls, including the party-list, following broadcasting on radio and television in June 2005 of an earlier telephone conversation between President Arroyo and Comelec Commissioner Virgilio "Garci" Garcilliano (Tuazon 2007, 136; Verzola 2010, 7). Subsequent appointments by the president to Comelec were also criticized for boosting the prospects of further fraud and corruption, not least through regional posts for many of the officials implicated in the "Hello Garci" telephone scandal (PCIJ 2006).

Intrastate elements conspiring to counter the intent of the 2001 ruling extended widely, including through sustained attacks against far leftist groups. Immediately following the 2004 polls, Bayan Muna denounced a "state-directed, military managed fraud and terrorism" campaign against them (Corpuz 2004). Violence by the Armed Forces of the Philippines (AFP) and associated militia against leftists accused of belonging to communist front organizations was not new (Holden 2009). Now, however, it was claimed that the AFP and Comelec were intimately colluding to undermine left-wing party-list groups and transfer votes to pro-military and pro-Arroyo parties (Corpuz 2004; Holden 2009, 384–85). Subsequently, an even more incriminating leaked document to the president from the

Office of External Affairs inside the president's office referred to Arroyo electoral campaign objectives, including to "provide full support to several Comelec accredited party-list groups that are ascertained to be pro-administration" and to "contribute in the overall campaign to substantially lower the number of votes of leftist and left-leaning party organizations" (Office of External Affairs 2006).

A wide range of elites understood not just how limiting such forces in Congress could contain reform debate, but also how useful party-list seats and Arroyo's administration were for the patronage politics benefitting oligarchic capitalism. For Arroyo, as pressure for her impeachment mounted following the "Hello Garci" scandal, maximizing use of the party-list was integral to her political survival. The scale and nature of apparent contraventions of the 2001 Supreme Court ruling had only increased from one election to the next since then. Consequently, renewed attempts by reformers to defend the interests of the marginalized and underrepresented soon followed.

Opening the Floodgates to Regional Elites

Despite elite ability to circumvent the 2001 Supreme Court ruling, both Bayan Muna and Akbayan continued to push for structural changes to the PLS, with a focus on the three-seat limit (Visto 1999; Esguerra 2007; Supreme Court 2009, "Allocation of Seats for Party-List Representatives"). Abolishing the seat limit would enable the growth of strong alternative parties and reduce the need for larger party-list groups to fragment, as happened with Bayan Muna from 2004. It would also help ensure that the number of seats in Congress allocated to the PLS came closer to the 20 percent provided for under the PLS Act. With these goals in mind, Bayan Muna petitioned the Supreme Court following the 2007 election (Supreme Court 2009).

Meanwhile, the court was also petitioned by the Arroyo-linked Barangay Association for National Advancement and Transparency party-list group to expand the number of PLS groups in Congress, not through increasing the seat limit, but instead by abolishing the 2 percent threshold. For Bayan Muna and Akbayan, contrastingly, maintenance of a 2 percent vote threshold was as important as raising the seat limit, since this threshold ensured promotion of parties with substantial support bases to counter leftist fragmentation. These petitions were set against a background of protracted legal challenges concerning the mathematical formula by which seats were allocated (see Muga 2007; O. F. B. Tan 2007, 2008). The Supreme Court consolidated the two petitions and ruled in April 2009 with major ramifications (Supreme Court 2009).

Associate Justice Antonio Carpio, who penned the 2009 court ruling, agreed that the PLS seats needed, constitutionally, to increase to 20 percent of all the seats filled in the House of Representatives, but the court did this via removing the 2 percent threshold rather than increasing the three-seat limit. This seat cap ensured the continued constraint against the formation of broad-based coalition parties. Meanwhile, much smaller groups than hitherto would be able to gain congressional seats, owing to the dispensing of the vote threshold. Indeed, as later elections would demonstrate, this was a recipe for increased disproportionality.[7]

The immediate effect of this ruling, however, was an increase in the number of party-list seats from twenty-three to fifty-five in the Fourteenth Congress by revisiting the 2007 results.[8] This included increasing the representation of Akbayan and Bayan Muna in Congress, with each picking up an additional seat. To the dismay of progressives, though, expanded representation had opened the door of Congress to an assortment of groups and candidates unrelated or even hostile to social, economic, and governance reform. Most controversial of these was retired AFP major general Jovito Palparan, the first nominee of Bantay (Sentinels) party-list group, purportedly representing victims of communist rebels, the Civilian Armed Forces Geographical Unit, former rebels, and security guards. Human rights activists had earlier branded him a "butcher" for his role in campaigns against alleged communist insurgents (Porcalla 2009).

Thus, far from the bolstering of party-list seats for representatives of the marginalized, the 2009 ruling by Associate Justice Carpio had simply heightened existing tensions over the gulf between the 2001 Supreme Court ruling and the actual seat winners. In effect, the 2009 Carpio ruling had lowered the entry bar for those seeking to represent quite different interests.

To be sure, any Supreme Court decisions can be the outcome of complex and incompletely understood influences. This is partly because this powerful institution has long shrouded itself in secrecy, limiting public scrutiny and accountability. Nevertheless, allegations of judicial corruption and blatant political appointments to the Court have been widespread (Vitug 2010, 2012; E. S. Cruz 2013), and they mounted during President Arroyo's nine-year term, during which her appointment of twenty-one justices allowed her to "pack the court," according to Vitug (2011, 2014). This may well help explain the shift in Court sympathies on the PLS controversy. Yet neither should we underestimate the ideological appeal of political pluralism as the primary indicator of democracy among many genuinely independently minded liberal members of integrity within the judiciary.

In any case, what followed was an explosion of interest in party-list candidacy at the 2010 elections. From 250 groups seeking accreditation, Comelec admitted a record 187 entrants, up from 93 in 2007. Electoral watchdog Kontra Daya publicly identified forty-nine of these as bogus groups (see Umil 2010). The results of the election substantially consolidated elite domination of the party-list.

Tuazon (2011, 152–55) calculated that 79 percent of the party-list seats in the Fifteenth Congress went to *trapos* linked to traditional politicians, big business, and religious groups. This helped explain why forty-seven of the fifty-six party-list representative seats were now held by millionaires, the average net worth of representatives nearly doubling between the Fourteenth and Fifteenth Congresses (Cayabyab and Flores 2012, 35).

The 2010 party-list campaigns mattered to the political fortunes of the increasingly unpopular ruling administration, whose aims by this time included securing the speakership for Arroyo in the next Congress. What the 2009 ruling had precipitated, though, was greater exploitation of the regional power bases of local business and political clans to win seats, predominantly in articulation with traditional political parties. Increased regional-based elite strategies often involved tactical appeals to particularist ideologies of representation to secure seats.

In the 2010 election, nineteen seats were won by groups that were new to Congress, with eleven of these not even attempting to run in the previous PLS election.[9] Significantly, only two of these party-list groups—Ako Bicol and 1st Consumers' Alliance for Rural Energy (1-CARE)—would have met the previously required 2 percent vote threshold. Moreover, the three wealthiest party-list seat winners in 2010 came from this batch of nineteen, namely, nominees from the Association of Laborers and Employees, Ang Galing Pinoy, and Ako Bicol. All three groups involved regional political or business clans and had evident or alleged links to the Arroyo administration. Among other blatant attempts by Arroyo associates to exploit particularist ideologies in 2010 was party-list group Abante Tribung Makabansa's claim to represent indigenous people. Its first nominee was Army Col. Allen A. Capuyan, who was linked to the "Hello Garci" controversy.

Ako Bicol's emergence as the leading vote getter in 2010 was spectacular; it captured 1.5 million or 5.2 percent of the total votes, as a regional party representing Bicol. Ako Bicol's board chairman was business contractor Zaldy Co, a close friend of the Arroyos (Diaz 2010), while his wealthy lawyer brother Christopher was its first nominee. Despite no significant organizational structures, Ako Bicol could draw on the considerable resources and networks of the Bicol-based Co business clan. This was harnessed in a massive media campaign pitched around particularist ideologies of geo-ethnic regionalism appealing to the cultural pride of Bicolanos (Tuazon 2011, 153). As promoted on the Ako Bicol Facebook page, "Ako Bicol endeavors to . . . foster patriotism among Bicolanos through the promotion of Bicol history, arts and culture, appreciation of the role of Bicolano heroes, national figures and other role models in the historical and cultural development of the region" (AKB 2010). Consequently, Ako Bicol won over 60 percent of all the votes in the largest provinces in the Bicol region (Bueza 2013).

Newly seated party-list groups involving powerful regional clans were not confined to ones serving as a front for Arroyo. Congressional seats had potential utility for clan interests under any political administration, and after this election there would be a new president. Many sought to capitalize on the 2009 Carpio ruling. This included Ang Asosasyon sang Mangunguma nga Bisaya-Owa (AAMBIS-Owa, Association of Bisaya Farmers), closely connected to the Garin clan based in Iloilo. Claiming to represent coconut farmers nationally, it snared a seat with 1.22 percent of votes. Its first nominee and representative in Congress was multimillionaire Sharon Garin, while another clan member, Jimmy Garin, was the third nominee. As much as 61 percent of this party's votes were drawn from the Iloilo region (Cayabyab and Flores 2012, 70). It was not the desire to represent workers nationally that was the real basis of this party-list group's ideological appeal, but the exploitation of the particularist ideology of regionalism.

Similarly, Abante Mindanao (ABAMIN), which was registered to represent marginalized Mindanao groups and had picked up a seat with 1.29 percent of votes, was linked to the powerful Rodriguez family in that region. All three party nominees were members of the Rodriguez family, and when Maximo Rodriguez Jr. took up the party-list seat, he joined multimillionaire brother and Cagayan de Oro district representative Rufus in Congress. Similar to Ako Bicol, ABAMIN appealed directly to the Mindanao identity to gain votes in the region: "Be true Mindanao-non!! Act and think for Mindanao!! Make a difference for Mindanao. Let your voice be heard! Join ABAMIN!" (ABAMIN n.d.).

Regional party-list groups used appeals to particularist ideologies to facilitate elite dominance through the PLS MOP. These ideologies combined with promises of PDAF for local projects and/or established patronage networks to substantially boost seats by elites at the 2010 elections. This, consequently, dealt a blow to the formation of strong, national, programmatic-based parties in the PLS and Congress. The demonstrated ability of powerful clans to capitalize on the vote threshold abolition would only further raise the stakes in the next elections in 2013. This would be against the backdrop of three years in office of new president Benigno Aquino III and his Liberal Party–led coalition government. As a member of a wealthy political dynasty, Aquino epitomized elite politics. However, eradicating state corruption was the centerpiece of his stated liberal reform agenda, raising the possibility of greater professionalism by Comelec and reform of the PLS.

Pluralism Reaffirmed under a New Liberal Government

The advent of the Aquino government brought changes to personnel within key state institutions. In January 2011, experienced electoral lawyer Sixto Brillantes was appointed chairman of Comelec, followed in April 2013 by electoral reform enthusiast Luie Guia's appointment as a commissioner (Legaspi 2013). Meanwhile, Aquino and allies successfully pursued the impeachment of Chief Justice Renato Corona, a controversial "midnight" Arroyo appointment accused of politically biased decisions. Describing Corona's impeachment as a process that "brightened the essence of our democracy," Aquino appointed Justice Maria Lourdes Sereno as the new chief justice of the Supreme Court in August 2012 (quoted in Bordadora 2012).

However, it was not so much the democratization of the state as liberal reformism that Aquino sought to usher in (see Rodan and Hughes 2014, 161–65). His chief objective was to contain corruption and professionalize the exercise of state power. This had the potential to neutralize some of his political adversaries, who were well networked within the state, but also carried possible implications for how the PLS Act was interpreted and implemented by Comelec. Yet Comelec decisions could be reinforced or overturned through the Supreme Court, so whether these institutions walked in step over who should be represented through the party-list was no less important.

Progressive reformist forces redoubled their efforts to contain elite exploitation of the party-list at the midterm polls scheduled for May 13, 2013. By September 2012, though, 209 party-list groups had sought accreditation, 165 of which were new. Election watchdog Kontra Daya filed a petition with Comelec seeking extensive disqualifications (Silverio 2012a). The signs from Brillantes around this time were encouraging. He described the PLS as a "joke," acknowledging that many groups were organized by the wealthy capitalists whose handpicked nominees were either members of powerful political clans or former government officials. Accordingly, a Comelec resolution authorized a review of groups to disqualify those not genuinely representing marginalized and underrepresented sectors (Uy 2012).

Subsequently, on October 10, 2012, Brillantes announced that the biggest winner in 2010, Ako Bicol, and at least twelve other groups were barred from contesting in 2013 (Esmaquel 2012). In the following months, Comelec blocked many more groups as the scale of disqualifications reached unprecedented levels. However, no less than ninety-five petitions went to the Supreme Court challenging disqualifications. Consequently, when Comelec officially pronounced 123 eligible groups in late January 2013, this included 39 previously registered groups and 13 new applicants that had secured status quo ante orders from the court against their disqualifications (*Sun Star* 2013a). There would be more contention and uncertainty over candidate eligibility before and after the May 13 elections.

What the disqualifications indicated about Comelec under Brillantes was open to interpretation. Kontra Daya drew attention to major inconsistencies in the Comelec purge, leaving numerous party-list groups on the ballot that were not genuine representatives of the marginalized or underrepresented. The likelihood was that select commissioners whose tenures predated Brillantes's chairmanship continued to smooth the way for questionable groups. As one congressman remarked, "It was common knowledge among the political class that there was still room for negotiation in Comelec with regard to party-list accreditation."[10] According to Akbayan's Ibarra "Barry" Gutierrez, "the main reason why Comelec was so hell-bent on reviewing the qualifications of all party-list organizations was because of a management consideration, which is, they wanted as few parties as possible to appear on the ballot."[11] Whatever was driving the disqualifications, Comelec's actions precipitated an opportunity for the Supreme Court to reenter the PLS dispute.

The Supreme Court's intervention was indeed a major turning point, but not the one hoped for by sectoral representation supporters. On April 2, 2013, the court voted ten-to-two to overturn the 2001 ruling that deemed the party-list the preserve of the marginalized and underrepresented, and to instead open the system up to national political parties and other parties and organizations representing a wide range of special interests and concerns.[12]

The court remanded all existing petitions to Comelec, issuing it new eligibility guidelines that ultimately meant nearly all previously disqualified groups now qualified (see, for example, *Sun Star* 2013b; Zurbano 2013). Finally, in early August 2013, all fifty-eight seat winners were pronounced. Not surprisingly, dynastic political families and other established elites again took the lion's share of party-list seats, including ones that Kontra Daya repeatedly sought to have disqualified. Only nine of the fifty-eight seats went to reformist parties of the (Bayan Muna-led) Makabayan (Patriotic Coalition of the People) coalition and Akbayan.

The opening up of the party-list to national parties came with the caveat that this would be via their independent sectoral wings, a majority of whose members needed to be either "marginalized and underrepresented" or lacking in "well-defined political constituencies." Past rulings that sought to completely bar any such alignment in favor of sectoral-based organizations and parties were characterized by Associate Justice Antonio Carpio, who penned the decision, as judicially legislated "socio-political engineering" in violation of the Constitution and the law (Supreme Court 2013, "The Party-List System").

What explains this profoundly important decision by the Supreme Court? One view is that the retirement of Chief Justice Reynato Puno, a strong advocate of the PLS as a social justice tool, was decisive (see Panganiban 2013). However, if Puno's advocacy was so crucial, then it only highlighted how vulnerable the social justice argument had become over time. Appointments under Arroyo would likely have contributed to this, and by this time Aquino had the opportunity to make just four new appointments. Significantly, though, these appointments adopted varying positions in the 2013 ruling. Dissenting voices included new chief justice Lourdes Sereno, who criticized the ruling because it "fails to appreciate that the party-list system is not about mere political plurality, but plurality with a heart for the poor and disadvantaged organizations" (quoted in de Quiros 2013). Bienvenido Reyes concurred, arguing that the PLS "is not simply a mechanism for electoral reform" (quoted in N. H. Cruz 2013). Meanwhile, two other Aquino appointments, Estella Perla-Bernabe and Marvic Leonen, voted with the majority.

A more professional Supreme Court less prone to corruption was thus not necessarily uniformly more receptive to arguments favorable to the building up of stronger organizational bases to contest elite power. Instead, consciously or unconsciously, liberal ideological emphasis on political pluralism as the preferred measure of democratic representation is an important influence among judges of integrity, and not just something to be cynically exploited as it had by other judges whose integrity had been questioned. The implication is that competing ideologies of democratic representation are likely to continue to manifest in legal interpretations of how the PLS should operate.

Moreover, wider reactions demonstrated that this ruling could not give legal finality to a fundamentally political struggle. Kontra Daya and the Makabayan coalition led criticism of the court's ruling. Kontra Daya's co-convenor, Fr Joe Dizon, predicted the "SC [Supreme Court] guidelines on party-list will open floodgates to non-marginalized groups, posing as regional parties" (quoted in *ABS-CBN News* 2013) and described the decision as "the final nail on the coffin of the party-list system as a social justice tool" (quoted in Kontra Daya 2013). Makabayan held a protest outside Comelec's office, urging it to defend its disqualifications and calling on the Supreme Court to reconsider. The ruling, it contended, "only exacerbates the elitist and oligarchic control of our political system and allows the rich to further dominate the already measly 20 percent of the seats in Congress allotted to the party-list system under the guise of political 'pluralism'" (quoted in Punay 2013). The Alliance of Concerned Teachers (ACT Teachers) party-list representative Antonio Tinio portrayed the ruling as going beyond facilitating a backdoor entry to Congress by traditional political families. "In fact, the backdoor is now another main entrance," according to Tinio (quoted in Alvarez 2013), opening up a "free-for-all for the rich and powerful to fully exploit, without anymore bothering to feign representation of the people they oppress" (quoted in Salamat 2013).

However, the Supreme Court ruling was precisely about who participants need to "feign" to represent and how. Indeed, the point is that different Court decisions have fundamentally shaped the strategic selectivity of the PLS as a MOP, making it easier or harder for certain actors and interests to gain representation. These decisions, and the wider struggles over the permissible bounds of political conflict they are connected to, are mediated in significant part by competing ideologies of who should be represented, why, and how. In particular, the ideological notion that democratic representation should facilitate the capacity to challenge elite power structures is pitted against a notion that political pluralism ought to be the principal goal of democratic representation. Meanwhile, capitalist oligarchs and those with interests aligned with them exploit these differences, including through appeal to particularist ideologies also consistent with liberal ideological emphasis on political pluralism.

Not surprisingly, support for the Court's ruling flowed in from many controversial groups Comelec had initially disqualified. Ako Bicol's representative Rodel Batocabe, for example, lauded the decision, dismissing fears of elite domination because "of the safety nets put in place" and argued that the desire to serve the marginalized and underrepresented could not be some sort of "political franchise" for left-leaning groups (quoted in Requejo 2013). You Against Corruption's representative, Carol Jayne Lopez, whose net worth according to Kontra Daya (2012) made her one of the wealthiest members of Congress, also saw the intervention by the Supreme Court as "the beauty of judicial review" (quoted in Panti 2013a).

Fragmented Attempts to Reform Congress
Fragmenting the Left

Significantly, Akbayan's response to the 2013 Supreme Court ruling was different from that of other leftists. It welcomed the Court's rejection of the idea that the PLS was the preserve of sectors, in favor of a more inclusive, pluralistic set of groups competing for seats on the basis of proportional representation. However, it was concerned that the ruling did not address serious imperfections in proportional representation because it constrained the development of sizable alternative national parties. Akbayan party-list representative Barry Gutierrez thus again advocated reintroducing the 2 percent vote threshold to deter smaller party sizes. He called for the abolition of the three-seat ceiling, or at least increasing the limit to six, in order to encourage party growth. According to Gutierrez, what needs changing is instead the "ill-advised formulation by the Supreme Court in its latest decision, which actually results in a disincentive for parties to become bigger."[13]

The contrast here with the Makabayan position was not really over the need for enhanced proportional representation. Bayan Muna had previously mounted petitions toward the same end (Supreme Court 2009, "Issues"). It was rather over who should be able to compete on the basis of proportional representation. Tensions between Akbayan and Bayan Muna—and more recently the broader Makabayan coalition—have grown with the PLS. These tensions are in part a function of the way the PLS promotes political competition and thus fragmentation through the absence of genuine proportional representation, but are also reflective of the different capacities, interests, and strategies of Akbayan and Bayan Muna in trying to harness the PLS to their reform goals.

Bayan Muna responded to the seat limit by setting up a range of affiliated sectoral parties. Thus it had formed the Makabayan coalition of party-list groups in April 2009, which grew to comprise Bayan Muna, Anakpawis, Gabriela, Kabataan, Courage, Piston, Migrante, ACT Teachers, Katribu, Akap Bata, Kalikasan, and Aking Bikolnon.[14] This strategy plays to the more extensive grassroots organizational bases it enjoys compared with Akbayan. Meanwhile, Akbayan persevered in "maintaining this one party and using it as a platform to actually expand, professionalize the party, in terms of coming up with platform-based politics and making it a grassroots-based party with a mass membership with a real program. But we actually engage with mainstream politics in the Philippines."[15] That engagement has always been a point of departure from Bayan Muna, but Akbayan's incorporation into the Aquino administration in 2012 further sharpened differences over the PLS.

Akbayan supported Aquino as the Liberal Party's presidential candidate in 2010 and was later incorporated into his administration. Against this background, in October 2012 the youth groups aligned to Bagong Alyansang Makabayan (New Patriotic Alliance) commonly known as Bayan, led by Anakbayan, petitioned Comelec to disqualify Akbayan.[16] The petition contended that Akbayan was "well entrenched" within the Aquino government, thus its nominees were not marginalized or underrepresented (Anakbayan 2012). Bayan's secretary-general Renato Reyes argued that "Akbayan is already a party in power. It has significant influence in government and has undue advantages over others, given the position of their high officials." Reflecting his disdain for Akbayan's particular engagement with mainstream politics, Reyes added: "Akbayan is a supporter of a reactionary, anti-people, and anti-nationalist Aquino regime" (quoted in Silverio 2012b).

Akbayan chairperson Risa Hontiveros responded that "we believe that the marginalized deserve better than token representation. We believe the people must have full representation. To say otherwise is to argue for perpetual marginalization of the people" (quoted in Salaverria 2012). It was precisely because the interests of marginalized sectors were not uppermost on the agendas of government institutions, Hontiveros continued, that more people were needed within government to push their case. Akbayan's Gutierrez, at the time deputy presidential advisor on political affairs, said critics confused representation of the marginalized with marginalization of the organization.

Moreover, there is awareness and concern within Bayan Muna that winning party-list seats through sectoral groups can militate against a strong multisectoral national party. Bayan Muna's votes declined progressively, from 1.7 million in 2001 to 750,000 in 2010. Meanwhile, sectoral party votes for Gabriela and Kabataan, for example, generally headed in the opposite direction, rising as Bayan Muna's votes fell. Bayan Muna's party-list representative at the time, Neri Colmenares, acknowledges the challenge this poses for harnessing Makabayan support toward a vision of "comprehensive social reform": "Our [Bayan Muna's] problem electorally is, because we go into different issues, people don't remember what we represent. 'What do you fight for again?' It's human rights, peasants, workers. . . ." Given the prevalence of a "sectoralized perception," Colmenares projects that Bayan Muna may need to be more selective in future campaigns: "We will try to focus on at least three or four issues that we think people will also remember us by."[17]

Fundamentally, then, it is not that Bayan Muna is less concerned than Akbayan about the blocking of more meaningful proportional representation, but these parties differ over the extent and nature of political pluralism appropriate to the PLS, and over strategies of engagement with the elite. This is reflected in the Genuine Party-List Group and Nominee Act introduced to Congress by Makabayan representatives seeking to reverse the Supreme Court's 2013 ruling (Republic of the Philippines 2013b). Stricter nominee criteria under the Act are directed not just at rich and powerful elites, but also Akbayan's engagement strategy. The act would bar anyone who was appointed and served office in government in the last five years from the position of bureau chief up to any cabinet position (sec. 5). To Gutierrez, this reform emphasis is antithetical to Akbayan's desire to "normalize and mainstream the idea of a political party that has broad coalitions."[18]

Amidst intensified divisions between the two key reform groups in the Philippines, one sympathetic but apparently exasperated columnist, Randy David (2012), declared: "The ruling class of this country must feel amused to see Akbayan and Anakbayan, who represent two strands of the Philippine left, fight over crumbs that have fallen from the dinner table of the powerful—instead of joining forces to attack the shameless way in which the latter cling to power."

Bayan's Reyes defended participation in the party-list on the basis that "our participation was because we wanted a venue where the mass movement can also air its position and a venue that can help strengthen the mass movement, exposing the rotten nature of the current political system. So, we have no hang-ups as far as the 'crumbs' are concerned."[19] Meanwhile, Akbayan pointed to the party being among the principal sponsors of significant legislation,[20] along with having support roles in ousting ombudsman Merceditas Gutierrez and former chief justice Corona and in defending the conditional cash transfer antipoverty welfare program, as examples of progressive gains through Akbayan's participation in the PLS (Panti 2013b). Thus, while the progressives saw their roles in promoting democratic reforms differently, they were nonetheless united in their belief in the PLS as a valuable MOP.

Entrenched Oligarchic Dominance

Following whistleblower allegations in July 2013 of widespread scamming of the PDAF involving dynastic political families and other political elites, public support for the liberal Aquino government waned. Mass demonstrations, including a Million People March in Manila's Rizal Park during August, were followed by a Supreme Court ruling in late 2013 that the PDAF was unconstitutional. Significantly, rather than being a MOP capable of helping to address such public concerns, the PLS had served more to exacerbate elite privilege. This increased the potential for populist alternatives to gain traction amidst escalating concerns about elite corruption alongside persistent inequalities and poverty. It was against this background that populist Rodrigo Duterte was elected president at the 2016 elections, ending the liberal reformist administration.

In general, though, the 2016 PLS votes for candidates with oligarchic backgrounds or links remained high, including regional group Ako Bicol as the only party to secure three seats (see Adel 2016 for election results). A new party-list group, 1Pacman, was the third highest vote getter, riding on the back of the popularity of Filipino boxer and now senator Manny "Pacman" Pacquiao (Della 2016), who claims his own childhood poverty as grounds for representing the poor, even though Pacquiao is now one of the richest members in the Senate (*Daily Mail* 2016). Votes for Akbayan and Bayan Muna dropped, both parties securing less than 2 percent of the vote. For Bayan Muna, this was part of an ongoing trend of fragmentation, with its Gabriela counterpart picking up proportionally more votes and landing the second highest vote count. For Akbayan, its partnership with the Aquino government appeared to have taken a toll. The party's vote share dropped from 827,405 votes in 2013 to 608,449 votes in 2016 (Adel 2016; *Rappler* 2016), and one of its leading PLS representatives, Walden Bello, resigned from Akbayan in 2015 and subsequently stood as an independent senate candidate in 2016.[21]

In line with President Duterte's populist rhetoric, shortly after the 2016 election he signaled his support for the abolition of the PLS, calling it a "mockery of the law" which is abused by "the rich" (quoted in Nilles 2016). He also contended that some party-list groups have Communist Party connections and channel their funds to the New People's Army (Luci 2016). Meanwhile, despite their poor electoral showings, and the dominance of elites in the 2016 PLS election, Akbayan and Bayan Muna have both continued to argue for the PLS as a means of reform (Diaz 2016b; *Update. PH* 2016). As maintained by Bayan Muna's Neri Colmenares, "Genuine pro-people party-list groups have considerably contributed to checking abuse and corruption in government. . . . What should be done is not to abolish the party-list system, but to jettison its proliferation as a tool of the economic-political elite, major political parties and other groups and regional aggrupation which do not have any claim to marginalization" (quoted in Diaz 2016a).

However, with the increasing fragmentation of the left and the continued dominance of political dynasties in parliament—the latter unlikely to change under a new populist president—it is improbable that these reformers would bring about fundamental changes. Indeed, it has become increasingly evident that whatever can be achieved through the PLS remains fundamentally circumscribed by power structures thus far insulated from reform.

The problem for radical and revolutionary reformers alike has not fundamentally changed since the 1987 Constitution's projected social, economic, and political reforms were ratified under the presidency of Corazon Aquino. Oligarchic dominance serving particular capitalist interests remains entrenched, and attempts by reformers to progress anti-dynasty bills continue to meet with resistance in parliament. Bayan Muna's Colmenares (among others), for example, introduced the Anti-Political Dynasty Act in November 2013, to finally enable law to give effect to the 1987 Constitution's declaration on this matter (Republic of the Philippines 2013a, "Explanatory Note"), but by the end of the Aquino government this bill had not progressed. New anti-dynasty bills have again been promoted since the 2016 election (Diaz 2016a), but, due to the continued dominance of oligarchic interests in Congress, these bills are destined to the same fate and/or will be "declawed" so as to not affect substantial change.[22] The congressional dominance of dynastic families remains, then, a safeguard against many of the egalitarian social and economic reform gestures in the Constitution being progressed via mass participation through formal political institutions such as the PLS.

The PLS has been constantly embroiled in controversy over its purpose and institutional form. At the outset, the PLS appealed to many elites as a way of dissuading reformist forces from armed struggle and revolutionary agendas. Such was elite dominance that opening up selective space for "alternative" representatives did not appear to risk any substantial loss of political control. The appeal of the PLS to other social and political forces rested, by contrast, on the aspiration that such an opening could provide a basis for building stronger organizational and ideological challenges to elite rule over time.

As the PLS evolved, though, it became more an avenue for enhanced representation of elite actors and interests than for hitherto marginalized or underrepresented interests and actors. Yet this has not been a passive evolution. On the contrary, the struggle to determine who can be represented through the PLS continued to be conducted through legal and other state institutions, as well as occasional civil society protest action, and reflected competing ideologies of political representation. At its core, this is both a tussle over the extent and nature of conflict the PLS is meant to accommodate, and who is entitled to be engaged in that conflict. The divisions here are not simply between elites and reformers, since the scale and nature of reform envisaged by the latter vary. This reflects in the contrasting ideological importance these forces attach to political pluralism and the building of collective organizational capacities to more fully realizing democratic representation.

Significantly, the PLS has also unfolded in such a way that it has compounded political fragmentation among leftist reformist forces in particular. This is in part a by-product of the emasculation by elites of genuine proportional representation. More broadly, limits on PLS seats by any one party have also been conducive to the promotion and tactical exploitation by elites of particularist ideologies of representation that further fuel political fragmentation. Structural and ideological factors thus combine to reinforce fragmentation.

In the ensuing struggle over the PLS, though, intra-elite dynamics are not without significance. The abolition of the PDAF under the Aquino government, for instance, has the potential to affect some calculations about the extent, sources, and modus operandi of political patronage secured through obtaining PLS seats in future elections. Yet such are the entrenched privileges of elites that this does not fundamentally change their electoral advantages or underlying motivations for winning PLS seats. As was apparent in the 2013 and 2016 elections, for example, massive media campaigns and vote buying remain options in competing against the most organized reformist groups.[23] PDAF has never been the sole basis of the attraction of PLS seats for elites, nor their ability to constrain alternative parties. It also remains to be seen whether populist president Duterte has the ability or desire to eliminate elite abuse of this MOP—through its abolition or otherwise. His priority upon taking office was a brutal "war on drugs" that, by mid-2017, had involved extrajudicial killings by police and vigilantes estimated to have exceeded three thousand suspected drug users or dealers (ABC 2017).

Despite the serious limitations to the PLS as an institution for reformist politics, progressives are currently committed to persevering with it, albeit with a view to rendering it more effective in opening up democratic space. However, much reformist energy and imagination has already been expended on legal and technical debates toward such an end. What that history shows is a site of conflict between contending interests and ideologies. Thus, neither the persuasiveness of argument nor the perfecting of the "right" design will simply determine the direction of such MOPs.

However, with the ascension to power of populist president Rodrigo Duterte in 2017, supporters of the PLS have to confront a new problem. To be sure, abolishing the PLS would require constitutional change and be no simple exercise. Significantly, though, Duterte also signaled his desire for constitutional changes facilitating a "strong president," citing the need for greater powers to shape foreign policy, declare war, and exercise police powers. These powers were "intended to keep the integrity of the country intact" and steer the Philippines toward progress and justice, according to Duterte (Luci 2016; *Philippine Star* 2016). It is thus not new MOPs to which Duterte looks to transform politics.

PARTICIPATORY BUDGETING IN THE PHILIPPINES

Following the fall of Marcos in 1986, the 1987 Constitution provided for various forms of political representation and participation—not just national parliamentary initiatives, such as the Party-List System (PLS), but also the inclusion of marginalized social sectors at local and municipal government levels. Although this appeared to indicate that oligarchs and their political allies in the Philippines were responsive to popular economic, social, and political demands emanating from civil society, these provisions on local participation have been largely under-realized (Cuarteros 2005).[1] Over the years, government departments have paraded their support for community participation in a wide range of governance reform programs, but—similarly to the PLS—in ways enabling oligarchs to generally protect and advance their power and interests.

However, with the advent of Benigno Aquino III's predominantly liberal administration in 2010, government rhetoric about popular participation intensified markedly and was aligned with anti-corruption strategies. In his first State of the Nation address, the president depicted such participation as crucial to the *daang matuwid* or "straight path" of governance essential to improving people's welfare (Aquino 2010). Nowhere did this rhetoric more directly translate into reform strategy than through linking participatory budgeting with poverty alleviation. Thus, in early 2012, the government introduced bottom-up budgeting (BUB) as part of its Empowerment of the Poor program.[2]

BUB initially involved 595 of the Philippines' poorest municipalities, but by late 2013 all of the country's 1,634 cities and municipalities were invited to participate in the BUB for the 2015 budget. This led to the Philippines becoming the first country in the world to implement participatory budgeting on a national scale. Funding for this reform started with an outlay of P8.4 billion (~US$0.18 billion) in 2013, but by 2014 the figure was P20 billion (~US$0.42 billion) and a further P24.7 billion (~US$0.52 billion) was projected for 2016 (Burgonio 2012b; DBM 2015, 24).

BUB's underlying rationale was that by incorporating civil society actors into all aspects of the budget cycle—project selection, implementation, and monitoring—the impact of corruption and patronage politics could be reduced in favor of projects reflecting local needs. Linking popular participation to poverty alleviation in this way, and on such a scale, was unprecedented. This innovative new societal incorporation mode of participation (MOP) was intended to alter the operation of state power to get around some of the electoral dominance and local government networks of capitalist oligarchs and/or *trapos*, or traditional politicians, engaged in patronage and corruption. BUB thus raised reform expectations and attracted significant support, and opposition, among different social and political forces.

According to Björn Dressel (2012), new policy emphasis on political participation in public finance in the Philippines reflected the emergence of an influential coalition, pivotal within which were technocratic civil society actors and policy brokers, including so-called crossovers: political actors with substantial civil society background.[3] Dressel's account, adopting an advocacy coalition framework,[4] illuminates crucial aspects of this coalition's historical specificity, shared governance values, and points of strategic convergence. Yet the same framework is limited for precisely the emphasis it places on advocacy coalitions as a "group of actors that share fundamental norms and values as well as perceptions about distribution of resources and political authority" (Sabatier and Jenkins-Smith quoted in Dressel 2012).

The coalition that emerged to emphasize participatory budgeting in the Philippines, alternatively, contained a variety of interests and ideologies, providing the potential for intra-coalition tensions to arise over the nature and extent of reform.[5] Coalition differences over the nature and purpose of changes to state power became more manifest—through competing attempts to shape the institutional form and practice of the BUB—than was evident in the initial national budget-planning exercise that Dressel centered his attention on.

Studies of earlier participatory budgeting in Latin America acknowledge the importance of struggles over the design of such informal political institutions for political regime directions (see Goldfrank and Schneider 2006). Reflecting on participatory budgeting in Brazil, Wampler (2007, 281) observes that when governments and civil society organizations not only work together but do so while allowing these organizations "to actively contest the claims of government, we see the best conditions for advancing the deepening of democracy." More fundamentally, Pateman (2012) distinguishes between participatory and deliberative democracy in evaluating the political potential of participatory budgeting. The latter, she cautions, "still leaves intact the conventional institutional structures and political meaning of 'democracy'" (10). By contrast, the former necessarily entails reforming undemocratic authority structures in order to transform rather than supplement existing institutions (10–11).

This chapter will show that even *within* BUB reform coalitions both the meaning and the importance attached to "democratic deepening" varied. For leftist reformers in the Philippines, the inclusion of combative mass-based organizations is central to democratic empowerment and is pivotal, in Pateman's terms, to ensuring that the reform of undemocratic structures transforms rather than supplements existing political institutions. Their commitment to BUB was based on the potential contribution this MOP could make—ideologically and structurally— to widening the scope for political conflict over existing inequalities of power. Moderate reformers, by contrast, placed greater emphasis on problem solving and promoting efficiency in public policy, both of which require institutional capacity building but not necessarily strong, membership-based collective civil society organizations. Consultative ideologies of representation combined with liberal notions of democratic competition as important influences among moderate reformers.

These ideological differences were reflected in intra-coalition tensions over the dispensing of resources and roles to different state agencies and civil society organizations (CSOs). Two of the most contested such issues within the BUB coalition, during its implementation (2012–2016), are the focus of this chapter: the relative roles of the Department of Interior and Local Government (DILG) and the National Anti-Poverty Commission (NAPC) in overseeing participatory budgeting reform; and the incorporation into BUB of the World Bank–inspired Kalahi-CIDSS[6] model of community driven development.

Importantly, BUB had political economy foundations in a historically specific form of oligarchic capitalism and related conflicts over the causes of, and remedies to, acute poverty and corruption. These foundations and conflicts are integral to explaining the establishment in 2012 and termination in 2017 of BUB, the particular configuration of contending interests and ideologies within the BUB coalition, and how these link to a wider set of struggles over political regime directions in the Philippines. They are also an essential part of explaining the boundaries of what is politically possible through such a MOP, as reform measures to regulate corruption and patronage grapple with the embedded social and economic power serving oligarchic and related interests.

Civil Society Divisions in the Philippines

The BUB initiative in participatory budgeting needs to be seen in the context of a dynamic postauthoritarian struggle over the relationship between democracy and capitalism in the Philippines. Integral to this struggle are competing ideas within civil society about the form and purpose of political representation of the poor and marginalized. This has been a complex process as many activists have reassessed their positions and strategies. In distilling the essential strands in this tussle, though, we can broadly distinguish between moderate reformers, radical reformers, and revolutionaries. These groups have differing positions on poverty alleviation and political empowerment, leading to ideological and tactical conflicts. Crucially, these conflicts reflect differing ideas about MOPs.

Moderate reformers have emerged over time to exert a contested ideological ascendency within Philippine civil society. This strand of contemporary civil society activism has historical roots in the Cold War and reaction to communist influence among the poor and marginalized in particular. Among the counters to communism were ideological appeals to social justice, egalitarianism, and social solidarity, often accompanied by calls for socioeconomic reform and redistribution. Religious, notably Jesuit, activists were especially important in this period, developing farmers' and workers' organizations. They were at the forefront of activists identified as social democrats (socdems), seeking to temper capitalism rather than replace it.[7]

Under Marcos, church-based CSOs dominated by socdems provided cover for a diversity of progressive civil society forces with reform agendas, ranging from radical redistribution to more liberal goals of political freedoms and human rights. Thus, with the collapse of authoritarian rule in 1986, socdems had significant organizational credentials and potential to play a role in shaping the direction of civil society (Tolosa 2012). However, in the post-Marcos proliferation of aid programs, organizational work declined among socdems, while small, cause-oriented NGOs multiplied, providing a new avenue for moderate reformers (Lane 1990, 37–38). Typically, these NGOs were professional, middle class–led, and highly dependent on funding from international aid agencies and, to a lesser extent, government and corporate sources.[8] Meanwhile, placing champions in government and strategic state institutions became more important to moderate reformers. Indeed, the vast majority of crossovers emerged from the moderate reform camp.

Established in 1990 as a confederation of the ten largest NGO networks in the Philippines, the Caucus of Development Non-Governmental Organizations (CODE-NGO) became a core institutional base for moderate reformers, not least for key crossovers within the Liberal Party. By 2013, CODE-NGO boasted 1,600 affiliated organizations. Notwithstanding some ideological and organizational variations among these affiliates, moderate activists have long dominated CODE-NGO's center of power, rather than those aligned with mass organizations and radical reform agendas. Indeed, much CODE-NGO activism is channeled through aid and government agency-funded projects premised on removing obstacles to effective capitalist markets, and related institutions, as the principal way to address poverty (Reid 2008).

In sharp contrast to the moderate reformers, revolutionary elements of Philippine civil society continue to place a premium on class-based organizations and mass mobilization, with the ultimate aim of replacing capitalism with socialism. They view poverty and inequality as structural problems inherent to global capitalism and the subordination of national interests to neocolonialism or neo-imperialism, including patterns of land ownership and lack of employment in non-service and nonagricultural sectors. Thus, they eschew NGO projects and programs founded on notions of improving access to, or efficiency of, markets.

Indeed, they more generally see ideological work with, and organizing of, peasants, workers, national minorities, and other oppressed people through people's organizations (POs) as the basis for a "national democratic revolution" in opposition to the existing state and its institutions (Africa 2013, 53). Although Philippine POs vary in size, they include some significant mass membership–based organizations and coalitions. Spearheaded by the Communist Party of the Philippines (CPP), this national democratic (natdem or ND) movement comprises a network of thousands of organizations grouped under the Bagong Alyansang Makabayan (Bayan, New Patriotic Alliance) (Quimpo 2008, 58; Törnquist 2013). However, these networks lack cohesion—a problem compounded in the post-Marcos period under neoliberal globalization—and operate in isolation from other reformist forces (Hutchison 2015). Consequently, the greatest political impact of the mobilization of these revolutionary forces is through involvement in the Party-List System, which affords no significant influence over state power.

Finally, radical civil society reformist ideas and strategies have their origins in elements that broke with the CPP and ND in the late 1980s. While substantively retaining the understanding of poverty and inequality as structurally rooted in the power relations of capitalism, they seek to transform these relations through gradual empowerment of popular forces operating both outside and inside state institutions. Radicals particularly emphasize the importance of developing and respecting the integrity and autonomy of CSOs, vis-à-vis political parties and the state, for raising democratic political consciousness and capacity, something they see lacking in the ND movement (Quimpo 2008, 87). For radicals, subverting elite democracy requires the cultivation and support of a genuine participatory democracy.

Among the most influential of radical reformist elements are those within or linked to the Akbayan Citizens' Action Party, formed in 1998 by leftists who abandoned the ND and assorted ex-socdems, Christian socialists, and nonaligned activists. Activists from the Movement of Popular Democracy (popular democrats or popdems) who withdrew from the CPP were especially significant in Akbayan's formation and ideological direction. By Akbayan's (2010) account, this represented a new stage in the prosecution of the core popdem ideas on empowerment: "Social movement groups wanted to be part of the formal processes of government. Akbayan was thus conceived as an effort to institutionalize people power and thereby deepen Philippine democracy." Alongside Akbayan, a range of radical left-oriented parties and CSOs have, in the past decade and a half, variously proclaimed and sought to advance a new politics grounded in similar ideologies of democracy and strategies of political engagement with the state and related institutions (see Quimpo 2008, 90).

Radicals share with revolutionaries the emphasis on the importance of mass-based organizations to political struggle, but differ in seeking to harness them in efforts to modify existing elite-dominated institutions (Africa 2013). With similar aims in mind, radicals also share with moderates their emphasis on the strategic importance of trying to develop champions in government (Quimpo 2008, 170). As Nathan Quimpo perceptively cautioned some years ago, though, it is not the forging of alliances with other reformers in government that is the greatest challenge. Rather, it is ensuring that this does not draw radical reformers into "a milieu (local politics) in which the revisionist neoliberal perspective has a much stronger influence than the radical democratic perspective" (197).

Reflecting the differences described above, while radical and moderate reformers have joined forces to contest local patronage networks of power through institutions such as the BUB, revolutionaries see such a project as too accommodating to existing state power relationships. However, it would transpire that there were also important differences between moderates and radicals over the political space within the BUB for contesting the hegemony of neoliberal solutions to poverty.

Building the Participatory Budgeting Coalition

Establishing the Coalition—Dominance of Liberal Crossovers

Although Benigno Aquino III was not the first president to enter office promising to arrest corruption, his reputation as a "clean" politician raised many Filipinos' hopes. During his various terms as a member of the House of Representatives and later the Senate, though, there was no foreshadowing of substantive ideas

and strategies portending BUB. These emanated instead from within a reform coalition encompassing crossovers and elements of business, state bureaucracies, the
World Bank, and CSOs. Access to and influence over Aquino varied within the
coalition, as did the nature of interests in, and rationales for, participatory budgeting. This generally favored moderates, but also presented radicals with possible reform opportunities.

As far back as 1988, moderate and radical civil society activists had called for
some form of popular involvement in budget processes (for an example see Brillantes 2007, 56). However, mounting accusations of corruption under President
Arroyo (2001–2010) precipitated broader and more strategic alliances, laying foundations for concrete policy reform. On July 8, 2005, at the height of the "Hello
Garci" scandal—alleging President Arroyo's involvement in vote-rigging the 2004
national election[9]—seven cabinet members and three bureau heads resigned from
her administration (*Philippine Daily Inquirer* 2009). This so-called Hyatt 10 group
of predominantly liberal technocrats helped prepare the ground for a post-Arroyo
reform agenda, linking public finance with civil society empowerment (Dressel
2012, 73s–74s).[10]

Thus, in 2008 the Hyatt 10 established the International Center for Innovation,
Transformation and Excellence in Governance (INCITEGov). It was to "steward
initiatives that would address the transition periods in which future engagements in governance can be established and democratic practices in governance
can be restored" (INCITEGov 2008, 29). INCITEGov's ideas broadly mirrored
the good governance agenda of multilateral aid agencies, and the World Bank in
particular, especially its emphasis on institutions of transparency and accountability as the basis of improving market performance and reducing poverty.

This emphasis resonated with many in civil society, including developmental
NGOs, and those in the Makati Business Club, seeking curbs on political patronage, and graft-blocking competitive contract tendering and investment opportunities. Radical reformers also embraced the good governance rhetoric, but with a
view not so much to restoring democracy as expanding it, through forms of accountability that enhance the political authority of membership-based collective
organizations, such as POs, to influence reform agendas (Rodan and Hughes 2014,
123–32).

The coalescing of this coalition entered a new phase with the advent of Benigno Aquino's presidential candidature. Aquino's campaign manager was Liberal Party colleague Florencio "Butch" Abad, one of the Hyatt 10 and a seasoned
crossover with deep roots among moderate CSOs. Civil society mobilization
behind Aquino's candidature was significant. Akbayan, for example, aligned with
the Liberal Party in 2010 in support of Aquino's candidacy.[11] Against this background, Aquino appointed a number of crossovers to his cabinet, including Abad

as secretary of the Department of Budget and Management (DBM); another Hyatt 10 member and former CODE-NGO national secretary, Corazon "Dinky" Soliman, as secretary of the Department of Social Welfare and Development (DSWD); and Akbayan's Joel Rocamora as secretary of the NAPC.

Non-crossover cabinet appointments were also significant, although for different reasons. Jesse Robredo as secretary of DILG was well received by CSOs in view of his pro-poor policies, including pioneering initiatives incorporating representatives of POs (and others) into local government deliberations while he was mayor of Naga City. Thus, at the time BUB was introduced, Abad, Soliman, Robredo, and Rocamora headed, respectively, the three departments and single agency responsible for BUB: DBM, DSWD, DILG, and NAPC. Crucially, the appointment of Cesar Purisima as secretary of the Department of Finance meant that, alongside co–Hyatt 10 member Abad, the two key public finance positions rested with liberal technocrats (Dressel 2012, 76s).

Of all the players in the participatory budgeting reform coalition, though, Abad was most influential. He was pivotal in drawing on and articulating with different circles of power inside and outside the Liberal Party, rendering him especially valued by Aquino, and influential within cabinet.[12] Abad's liberal economic reform agenda was premised on a key market facilitative role for public policy and related governance institutions. As he explained, "through good governance, we can truly enable the private sector to perform its rightful role as the engine of economic growth . . . through a fair, stable and predictable policy, regulatory, physical and political environment." Yet Abad also underlined the need to build a reform coalition because it "can provide strong, widespread and sustained political support and demand reforms, such that reversal of reforms in the future becomes politically and economically costly" (Abad 2013, n.p.).

Critics from the revolutionary ND movement viewed this perspective less as far-sighted reformism and more as political opportunism. Antonio Tinio, elected representative of the Bayan-linked party-list group ACT Teachers, asserted: "Let's face it. The Liberals do not have a political mass base. . . . President Aquino and the Liberal Party are promoting a new brand of political patronage by tapping the civil society networks that are very close to the Palace, such as the Social Democrats, CODE-NGO and Akbayan" (quoted in *Manila Standard* 2012).

However, even within the participatory budgeting coalition, let alone the wider CSO community that needed to be engaged through BUB, there was contention over economic and social reform priorities to address poverty. While Abad was quite clear about the public policy problems and solutions for economic and social transformation, he saw that these must be married with a political strategy to galvanize support and neutralize the backlash from powerful forces whose interests were threatened by such policies. The political challenge for the liberal technocrats was therefore to both inspire civil society mobilization around reform and also to contain its parameters. This implicitly acknowledged the extensive influence over state power, and local government in particular, directly and indirectly exerted by capitalist oligarchs, *trapos*, and related networks of interest. Abad therefore attached importance to not exacerbating friction with these powerful interests over the scale of conflict that would be institutionalized through this new MOP.

President Aquino spoke explicitly to this theme about the need for disciplined and moderate activism in support of BUB. Addressing CODE-NGO, he thanked the organization for supporting his "straight path" agenda, especially in partnering with the government in implementing the BUB: "You're our eyes against anomalies; ears for our country's problems, and the voice of our marginalized sectors. In fact, some government officials came from your sector." Yet he added: "When you engage in dialogue let's make sure we're contributing sensible points, instead of making brownie points like other people. We can't keep criticizing, yet keep our mouth shut when it comes to solving problems" (quoted in Burgonio 2012a, n.p.).

In a similar vein, the World Bank (2009, 25) had earlier declared that the challenge for Philippine NGOs lay in "developing the necessary technical capacities to actively participate in key functions of government such as national budget scrutiny . . . and moving beyond the significant historical experience of being part of the political opposition movement." Indeed, growing synergies between the World Bank and liberal reformers in the Aquino administration, concerning their stance on civil society involvement, extended to varying degrees of subscription to consultative ideologies of representation, which also underlay intra-coalition tensions.

Containing Civil Society with Consultation

Consultative ideologies of representation emphasize the problem-solving utility of incorporating stakeholders, interests, and/or expertise in public policy processes for effective functioning of economic, social, or political governance. It is an underlying assumption of consultative ideologies that conflict can be avoided or substantially contained by rational dialogue and deliberation applied to public policy problems in cooperative state–civil society alliances.

These ideologies can be compatible with democratic ideologies of representation embracing limited notions of political competition over elite-defined public policy problems. However, they are incompatible with democratic ideologies of representation inspired by the aim of usurping elite control over how public policy problems and solutions are defined. Indeed, this is precisely the friction inherent in the participatory budgeting coalition, with the ascendant liberal technocrats preferring forms of representation and accountability most likely to facilitate a market-oriented approach to addressing poverty and corruption in the Philippines.

Aware of the risks of political co-option, radical reformer and NAPC head Rocamora nevertheless saw working cooperatively on local participatory budgeting with moderate reformers and state institutions as presenting progressive possibilities. As he explained, "Instead of shouting 'the sharpest line' from outside government, I have chosen to work within the 'belly of the beast,' longing for just enough power to make a difference, hoping not to get consumed in the gastric juices of the beast" (Rocamora 2013, 2). His priorities through BUB related to aspirations about transforming undemocratic authority structures, consistent with Pateman's (2012) concept of participatory democracy. The first was to help strengthen organizations of the poor and the poor's capacity for collective action, and heighten political consciousness. The second was to "break the existing circuit of patronage running from national to regional to municipal bureaucratic and other political players" (Rocamora 2011, 4).

However, the existing limitations of organizations of the poor, and their lack of links with technocrats, also helped account for why Rocamora's radical reform prescriptions lacked relative force alongside moderates in Cabinet. Moreover, there was an element of apprehension among moderates about the implications of powerful collective civil society organizations for disciplining reform directions. After all, any attempt to dismantle or impair such extensive "circuits of patronage" would invariably meet with resistance and was no minor tactical challenge. Control and/or influence over decisions of local government legislatures and assorted subcommittees, as well as various local state agencies, was not something that oligarchs and *trapos* would surrender lightly. As was demonstrated in the previous chapter in the context of the PLS, these elites can harness considerable financial and other resources to consolidate and defend their interests from the prospect of threatening changes to political representation.

Clearly liberal technocrats enjoyed strategic advantages within the participatory budget coalition, and this would have implications for the upcoming struggle for political representation. Nevertheless, without CSO support, the implementation of BUB would be difficult, and cultivating the constituencies to embed reform unlikely, especially in areas where only POs are present (or where there are few or no collective organizations at all). Moreover, despite its strong links with CODE-NGO, the government could not expect passive acceptance on all aspects of its plans for BUB, either within or beyond this civil society community.

In contrast with consultative MOPs in Singapore, conceived by established elites as a way of blunting challenges to their power, reformist forces in the Philippines sought to arrest some of the ways that powerful oligarchic elites secured their interests through state power. Rather than seeking to demobilize reformist forces, the objective in the Philippines was to mobilize them. Yet the creation of BUB was thus not without political risks for the different elements of the coalition responsible for its introduction. Radicals had in mind a long game that BUB was linked to, building up the capacity of independent organizations to ultimately mount more substantial challenges to both oligarchic power and market power. Moderates had more immediate and pragmatic priorities. Both radicals and moderates understood that their priorities were at risk, depending on who was mobilized through BUB and how.

Intra-state Struggle over BUB Implementation

The ushering in of civil society "empowerment" under BUB entailed a highly bureaucratic process administered by the state. Each annual budget round was guided by a detailed Operations Manual and a Joint Memorandum Circular—cosigned by DILG, DSWD, DBM, and NAPC—spelling out not just the extent and roles of local CSO involvement in project selection and implementation, but also the particular roles and powers of the signatories in facilitating and overseeing this process. Moderates and radicals alike rightly understand that *where* a function rests has implications for *how* different interests within the reform coalition might be advanced through CSO representation. Nowhere was this clearer than in the tension around bureaucratic control over the processing of project proposals and the organizing of local CSO participation regarding the role and departmental location of the Project Management Office, as explored below.

BUB was designed to link local government development plans more directly to the budgets of national agencies, but in such a way as to more effectively incorporate the poor and those depicted as their representatives into decision making about project priorities in those plans. The nine-stage process for the BUB outlined in the Joint Memorandum Circular started with the annual convening of a general assembly of all CSOs at the city or municipal level, at which CSO representatives for a Local Poverty Reduction Action Team (LPRAT) were determined. The LPRAT was charged with leading the formulation of a Local Poverty Reduction Action Plan (LPRAP). This involved identification of priority poverty reduction projects within the eligible list for funding, and monitoring their implementation.

In its initial form, the LPRAT comprised equal numbers of government and nongovernment representatives, with detailed prescriptions regarding the complexion of CSO representation, which included leaders from both NGOs and POs.[13] Elected officials of the Local Government Unit (LGU), their immediate relatives, and LGU employees were ineligible as CSO representatives.[14] Furthermore, three CSO representatives' signatures were required for a Local Poverty Reduction Action Plan, and the associated list of priority projects, to be valid. These provisions, and the Joint Memorandum Circular's inclusive definition of CSOs,[15] appeared to promote a breadth and extent of engagement consistent with official rhetoric about the empowerment of the poor. It thus appeared that the BUB was intended to ensure genuine representation of the poor through a diverse range of CSOs, even if the leaders of different CSOs were not necessarily democratically elected to office within their own organizations.

However, the way that prescriptions on CSO representation and roles translated into practice was not just mediated by the strategies of entrenched oligarchic and *trapo* interests intended to compromise or bypass BUB processes. The respective agendas and influences of different pro-BUB key actors within state bureaucracies implementing it were also critical. Consequently, moderates and radicals were engaged in struggles over bureaucratic divisions of labor shaping BUB's implementation, particularly around responsibility for the Project Management Office (PMO).

Initially this office rested with NAPC. Of all the state-based bodies involved in BUB, NAPC was the one with the longest-standing and most explicit interest in advancing collective democratic representation. It was established in 1998 with a legal mandate for selecting official representatives of the fourteen "basic sectors."[16] This gave NAPC representatives and its council official status in negotiating with government agencies and provided a venue for organized encounters between sectors and government. NAPC has remained one of the smallest state agencies, with a limited budget. Its opportunities for influence thus rest principally on its relationships with other actors inside and outside the state. NAPC's creation was effectively an admission that formal political processes had failed to incorporate adequate representation of those most affected by persistent poverty. At the same time, different presidents have also sought to cultivate civil society allies within and through NAPC to either harness or neutralize CSOs (Reid 2004).

The original phase of BUB, with NAPC at the helm of the PMO, looked promising for radical reformers. The appointment of Joel Rocamora to NAPC suggested Aquino's appreciation of the need to supplement existing administration links to CODE-NGO with reach into broader CSO communities. Moreover, with Jesse Robredo also at the helm of DILG, the basis appeared to be in place for strong complementarities between DILG and NAPC roles in BUB.[17] After all, it was a shared strategic view within the BUB coalition that direct links needed to be constructed between reformist-held national-level institutions and the new BUB structures insulated from local *trapos*.

With NAPC assigned the PMO role, LPRAPs from participating municipalities went directly to NAPC for processing, bypassing regional DILG offices. As Rocamora explained, "the region was iced out, which was deliberate on our part. We wanted to break the circuit of patronage."[18] There were, he elaborated, "no long term regional staff with whom congressmen and governors could work out patronage relations" (Rocamora 2013, 7). NAPC's role also extended to organizing civil society participation, which included commissioning CSOs with a presence in the provinces to identify local organizations at the municipal level to implement the BUB. For Rocamora, though, this role had to be viewed as broadly contributing to the political enhancement of CSOs in helping to set reform agendas: "To empower the poor, they have to be assisted in organizing themselves for meaningful, and effective participation in shaping anti-poverty programs and projects. Apart from participating in 'invited spaces,' the poor should develop the capacity for 'collective action' in support of asset reform" (4). Unless civil society groups could engage in both cooperation *and* contention then BUB would simply amount to co-option of civil society forces (Rocamora 2012).

However, when Jesse Robredo died in a plane crash on August 18, 2012, and Liberal Party senator Mar Roxas—a liberal technocrat—became the head of the DILG, departmental roles were reassigned, as other moderates in the administration sought enhanced roles in BUB at NAPC's expense. Regional bureaucracies were reintroduced into the local budget process: DILG regional directors were now heading the Regional Poverty Reduction Action Teams (RPRATs) and responsible for processing and approving LPRAPs. Tellingly, the PMO was also moved from NAPC to DILG (Rocamora 2013, 7–8).

Budget Secretary Abad tried to portray these changes as ones meant to preserve the distinct role of NAPC rather than trying to marginalize it: "NAPC is a council, so therefore it is not an operating structure. And we want to keep it as a council. The idea of having a NAPC is that the poor have a very strong voice in the cabinet."[19] By contrast, DILG had an administrative presence from the center of government right down to the municipal level and was ideally suited to the task of implementing BUB, according to Abad.

This was, though, more than an administrative adjustment in the BUB's implementation. It amounted to a consolidating of specific sites of state power under the control of moderate reformers. With an eye to the 2016 presidential elections, Abad and other key liberal reformers were especially keen to get material results on the ground to build a political constituency for another reformist administration, without being overwhelmed by civil society requests (Jiao 2011). From this perspective, DILG's established capacities in local planning processes and the networks between DILG and moderate CSOs were attractive assets to increase the technical efficiency and political discipline of BUB processes. Middle class–dominated professionalized NGOs that already had extensive links with state bureaucracies, business, and the Liberal Party would certainly not be disadvantaged by this relocating of the PMO.

By contrast, organizations that have tended to focus on contentious issues—including asset reform, agrarian reform, fisheries reform, and related collective activities—lack access to the same state networks. They were confined to NAPC, or, in the case of many ND organizations, not even that. Therein lay the appeal of BUB and the importance of NAPC housing the PMO for Rocamora: the opportunity to foster a greater diversity of CSOs into public policy processes within the state and especially those prepared to raise contentious issues—in effect, seeking to expand the permissible bounds of institutionalized political conflict. This included the hope that some ND revolutionary elements could be enticed into the process.[20]

The appointment of Roxas as DILG head was not helpful for this. Bayan leader Renato Reyes attacked this appointment as the "ultimate 'trapo' maneuver courtesy of Mr. Aquino," pointing out that Roxas came from a wealthy traditional political family and was now in a position to influence local government units for party political purposes (quoted in *GMA News* 2012). By contrast, Reyes had praised Robredo for championing some contentious issues at odds with Aquino and others in his administration, notably on urban resettlement.

To be sure, incorporating a broad range of CSOs, and ensuring entrenched local elites abide by BUB provisions, had already proven challenging under NAPC's PMO stewardship, reflecting the deeply embedded social conflict mediating outcomes of this MOP. Predictably, given entrenched corruption and other problems, there was a tendency of many mayors to arbitrarily replace projects without proper consultation with CSO representatives in the LPRATs. However, NAPC undersecretary Maria Labajo observed, in the 2013 BUB round after Roxas's appointment, that now this often involved interventions by municipal level functionaries of DILG "in circumventing the process to make it more acceptable to the local chief executives/mayors."[21] Independent studies confirmed such practices in a range of municipalities, including a report by the Ateneo de Manila University's Institute of Philippine Culture (2013).

In an online article with social media news network *Rappler*, CODE-NGO executive director Sixto Macasaet (2013) also conveyed reports of some LPRAT CSO leaders refusing to sign documents that had deviated from the expressed wishes of CSOs, while many felt pressured and signed. To illustrate the significance of the problem, in the municipality of Dolores in East Samar, the final draft proposal submitted to the Regional Poverty Reduction Action Team's technical review panel allocated more than half the municipal budget to farm-to-market roads that were not in the original draft. In this case, although the revised draft included three signatures from CSOs selected by the LPRAT, according to Dolores RPRAT representative Ian Mosquisa, the proposal should have been returned, discussed, and endorsed by the LPRAT composed of all CSO representatives and the LGU participants. Mosquisa points out that the DILG-chaired RPRAT made the changes at the regional level (*Rappler* 2013).

Therefore, the move for greater control of BUB processes by the—now liberal technocrat-leaning—DILG was not just an internal struggle between radical and moderate elements within BUB over the meaning and significance of democratic political representation. There was resistance to BUB from powerful vested interests that operated within, and in articulation with, different apparatuses of the state. The political tensions and strategies of the BUB coalition thus had to be viewed as part of a *broader* set of struggles about how state power is used in the Philippines, not least by *trapos*.

Having NAPC's endorsement of CSOs as one of the key criteria for accreditation for the 2015 BUB round gave some encouragement to radicals that it was still worth trying to work "in the belly of the beast," but the withdrawal of the PMO from NAPC was a setback that seriously tested radicals' (such as Rocamora's) commitment to work with liberal technocrats on BUB.

Harmonizing Kalahi-CIDSS and BUB

In January 2013, changes were enacted to the Joint Memorandum Circular (for the 2015 budget round) toward integrating and harmonizing BUB with Kalahi-CIDSS, a decade-old antipoverty empowerment strategy adopting a particular community-driven development (CDD) approach. Despite its poor record for promoting CSOs, Kalahi-CIDSS enjoyed strong support among liberal technocrats for increasing *barangay* (village)-level community participation in service delivery and reducing elite corruption and collusion within LGUs. For radicals, though, this integration posed another challenge in trying to ensure spaces for collective organizations—and contentious politics—through the representative processes of participatory budgeting.

Kalahi-CIDSS and Technocratic Ideologies

A plethora of CDD programs have emerged in the Philippines, many of which were inspired or financially supported by the World Bank and, to a lesser extent, other multilateral agencies. Kalahi-CIDSS is the lead such program, first implemented by DSWD in 2003 in partnership with local government units and funded by loans from the World Bank. Liberal crossover Corazon Soliman was DSWD secretary at the time Kalahi-CIDSS was introduced, a position she resumed under the government led by Benigno Aquino III. DSWD became the lead agency responsible for overseeing the harmonization of Kalahi-CIDSS and BUB in the 2015 budget cycle.

The perceived need for greater cohesion between BUB and Kalahi-CIDSS arose in the context of massive and increasing outlays on the conditional cash transfer (CCT) programs, also financially supported by World Bank loans,[22] upon which the Aquino administration had vested much of its political capital prior to the 2016 elections. Put simply, and although this was never officially declared, the ideal scenario from the government's point of view would be for community choices in participatory budgeting to positively articulate with other development programs, not least with CCT social investments in health and education. It was also in this context that Kalahi-CIDSS was earmarked for significant expansion (Ronda 2014).

Kalahi-CIDSS was premised on the notion that acute poverty in certain localities was principally linked to shortfalls in basic skills, infrastructure, and market access (Reid 2005, 42). It was also an earlier attempt, prior to BUB, to compensate for some of the inadequate implementation of the Local Government Code of 1991. As with that code, Kalahi-CIDSS also targets poor municipalities with the aim of empowering communities to participate in more inclusive LGU planning and budgeting. However, Kalahi-CIDSS is also very process driven and incorporates various technical and rational data evaluation aspects, guided by a detailed Community Empowerment and Activity Cycle (CEAC) that initially comprised sixteen stages (later reduced to four). Importantly, in contrast with BUB, which involved municipal-wide participation, the focus of Kalahi-CIDSS is on *barangay*-level participation, and significantly, inter-*barangay* competition, in project selection.[23]

Even more significantly, by way of contrast with BUB, Kalahi-CIDSS has never involved concerted attempts to promote CSOs. It was conceded in the 2013 National Community-Driven Development Program Final Aide Memoire that "experiences with engaging CSOs under Kalahi to date have been less promising than hoped" (World Bank 2013, 11). An earlier World Bank review (2011, 23) also noted a correlation between areas where Kalahi-CIDSS operated and "a decrease in the proportion of households that participate in collective action activities." The same report stated that "despite gains observed in *barangay*-level governance, results from the qualitative evaluation indicate that the project did not achieve similar successes at the municipal level" (24). Therefore, while representation under Kalahi-CIDSS appears to be more democratic than under BUB— Kalahi-CIDSS representatives are community volunteers chosen at *barangay* assemblies by their peers—the process has decreased the collective democratic potential of the people in these areas.

The inherently technical nature of the process has been a contributing factor in this pattern, especially before the original sixteen-stage CEAC process for organizing participation was abbreviated. Many of the Kalahi-CIDSS processes entailed powers and functions by state bureaucrats that effectively usurped or subordinated the roles open to CSOs. For example, the team of seven area coordinators deployed in the municipality to help implement Kalahi-CIDSS on the ground was comprised entirely of contracted DSWD staff.[24] Despite Secretary Soliman having a CSO background, neither she nor others who presided over DSWD and Kalahi-CIDSS had effectively promoted roles for collective organizations.

Yet, while this disappointed NAPC and civil society activists, support for Kalahi-CIDSS from liberal technocrats has remained strong. Liberal technocrats draw positive conclusions from the Kalahi-CIDSS experience, heralding the transformative role of individual leaders in community participation and highlighting the way the program has helped build social capital, including trust in the political process, in poor communities. Underlying this evaluation is an ideological predisposition among liberal technocrats toward consultative ideologies of representation emphasizing cooperative problem solving within largely state-defined reform agendas. As the MOP framework explains, strategic selectivity that actively promotes individual participation over roles for collective organizations in processes of political representation can be a powerful structural force toward this ideological end.

The World Bank's (2011, 8) Kalahi-CIDSS review lauded the program for instigating a qualitative shift in the perception of villagers toward *barangay* assemblies "as mechanisms for participation, transparency and accountability." Greater participation in assemblies, it explains, has resulted in more knowledge of the *barangay*'s income and expenses, outcomes attributed principally to "a new pool of leaders from community volunteers, especially women, that can effectively engage elected *barangay* officials."

These leaders "are considered to be more service-oriented and committed than previous *barangay* leaders and, in some cases, they have been elected to a *barangay* office" (ibid.). The Asian Development Bank similarly emphasized the roles of community volunteers who "are perceived as a new type of community leader for whom residents have different expectations" (ADB 2012, viii). Consequently, "Individuals in Kalahi-CIDSS municipalities are now more likely to trust both fellow community members and strangers than they would have in the absence of the project" (World Bank 2011, 22). The World Bank also observed that communities possessing more developed social capital assets are more likely to secure funding. Furthermore, according to the World Bank (7), Kalahi-CIDSS "was designed to minimize the risk of elite capture and it appears to have been successful in doing so," a conclusion with which the Asian Development Bank (2012, ix) concurred.

Yet this had been achieved without fostering roles for collective organizations on any significant scale and especially without opening up political spaces for CSOs principally concerned with more expansive structural reform agendas to address poverty. Paradoxically, then, owing to the competitive nature of the project selection process between *barangays*, Kalahi-CIDSS has done at least as much to contain debate about the causes of and solutions to poverty as it has done to promote it.

Importantly, for radicals (and revolutionaries), the problem of poverty is not simply one of corruption and "elite capture" that can be combatted by more virtuous community-oriented leaders and individuals. Poverty has its roots in power relations that afford dominance to elite interests in general, and not just the dominance of individually corrupt elites. Whereas moderates seek principally to build "trust," in and through prevailing institutions, with the help of CDD programs,[25] radicals aim to transform these institutions in ways that would ultimately and fundamentally erode elite dominance of them.

Alternatively, from the liberal technocrats' perspective, the ability of Kalahi-CIDSS to bypass existing networks between CSOs and local government is appealing, and is something that they do not consider to have been happening fast enough under BUB. This view is partly informed by a concern about *trapo* networks of patronage and corruption but also by a particular ideological understanding of "community."

According to Budget Secretary Abad, "The good thing about the Kalahi-CIDSS is it always seeks to enable the community to drive the projects, not the municipal council or the government, but the community. And I think, for me, that is the real key."[26] Assistant Secretary of DSWD Camilo Gudmalin also explained that his department's analysis of the BUB had shown that LPRAPs had contained virtually the same projects identified by local government and CSO representatives therein, whereas "the projects that were identified using the Kalahi-CIDSS process are more or less the ones that are being identified with the communities, meaning they are more responsive to the needs of the communities."[27]

To be sure, as was dramatically highlighted in the 2013 exposé of the alleged Janet Napoles pork barrel scam and in subsequent other similar cases, bogus CSOs can be established as vehicles for the diversion of public funds for private gain (Matsuzawa 2015). For this and other reasons it is always important to scrutinize the representative credentials of any CSO. However, these views within the administration were also characterized by an ideological emphasis on individual participation as the conduit through which authoritative expressions of community were arrived at. This was consistent with a tradition among some strands of liberalism to treat collective organizations with a degree of suspicion, as potential groupings of vested interests that often need to be circumnavigated by policymakers to deliver good policy. Yet while equating the community to a mass of individuals—bypassing mayors and CSOs—may be functional for efficiency and problem solving from liberal policymakers' perspectives, this also poses a challenge to the status of democratic representation through collective organizations.

Consequences of the "Harmonization"

It was far from clear that Kalahi-CIDSS elicited any more genuine an expression of community through the new breed of leaders the World Bank and the Asian Development Bank highlighted in their reviews of Kalahi-CIDSS than what radicals were advocating for under their vision for BUB but which had yet to materialize. Consequently, the incorporation of Kalahi-CIDSS into BUB constituted another tension within the participatory budget coalition over preferred forms of, and rationales for, political representation. Would it lead to greater strategic selectivity in participation, working against collective organizations to contain the permissible bounds of conflict within BUB? Radicals feared so.

Indeed, Rocamora worried about a possible colonizing of the BUB under the CDD approach: "The CDD approach is not to work with civil society organizations; the CDD approach is for the government to create invited spaces for 'the people' to participate. . . . [S]ure, you can get people to participate, because they get projects out of this, but you're not developing their capacity for collective, political action, including the possibility of entering the treacherous spaces of contentious politics." This meant there were "still open questions on what's going to happen to the role of organized groups, and how are they going to relate to the participation generated at the *barangay*-level through this alternative approach."[28] Indeed, as of 2014, those municipalities engaged in the harmonization of the BUB and Kalahi-CIDSS would be required to have a new composition to the LPRAT, one that reduced the role and power of the CSOs. Where originally the team was composed of an equal number of government and CSO representatives, under the harmonized system the places reserved for nongovernment members were now divided between CSO and Kalahi-CIDSS–nominated (individual) village representatives (DBM-DILG-DSWD-NAPC 2013, 4). And, importantly, the inter-*barangay* competition for project selection would continue.

NAPC's undersecretary Labajo reinforced the seriousness of concern within this agency about the harmonization of BUB and Kalahi-CIDSS. She highlighted how the scale of participation and representation through Kalahi-CIDSS is antithetical to the sort of collective organizational representation most functional for addressing the problems of the poor: "You will not be able to capture the agenda of the organized, basic sectors through the Kalahi-CIDSS . . . because in the Kalahi-CIDSS it's always like the *barangays* competing. . . . And the locus of planning is a *barangay*, and whatever will be funded, they need to compete among themselves. For the basic sectors, many of the things, many of the reforms, many of the projects that they want, cut across *barangays* . . . for example, problems about municipal waters or small fisher folk."[29] According to a NAPC official involved in women's organizations, there had been no real change in the way Kalahi-CIDSS operated with the advent of harmonization with BUB in the 2015 round.[30] Priority projects already determined at the *barangay* level under Kalahi-CIDSS were incorporated into the regular BUB process for funding. Consequently, the inherent bias against collective organization at the *barangay* level continued and would likely not change with the termination of BUB in 2017.

This is not to suggest that the only obstacles to harnessing participatory budgeting to representative organizational structures for widening the scope of political contestation are limited to the problems of how Kalahi-CIDSS fosters the geographic and social fragmentation of representation. POs are in many cases virtually the only CSOs present in a municipality, and some are more independent than others. In some instances, government departments have heavily shaped the development of such organizations—calling on them to assist in the implementation of policies rather than to submit independent input into, let alone scrutiny of, government policies.[31] This problem is reinforced or compounded by some LGUs and other authorities only accrediting preferred POs or NGOs.[32]

In many municipalities, the only CSOs that exist are also very small scale, with no official accreditation or funds, and rely exclusively on volunteers. These are often religiously inspired self-help groups, most frequently involving social action centers of the Catholic Church.[33] Meanwhile, vast areas of the rural Philippines are lacking CSOs of any significant size, in a local political economy context where oligarchic powers are most in need of arrest to improve the social and economic conditions of poor Filipinos. Here control over the institutions and funding meant to facilitate political participation by the marginalized becomes all the more important in mediating the relative influence of moderate and radical visions of participatory budgeting. Different models of participatory budgeting privilege different forms of representation through the organizations promoted—either by building capacity to assist policymakers in problem solving, or by building the political capacity to more effectively define the problems to be solved.

The above analysis of the new MOP through BUB introduced under the Benigno Aquino III government is not an attempt to ascertain whether or not it was ever "working," or likely to. It instead explains this institutional initiative as a dynamic struggle over the permissible bounds of conflict through political representation. That struggle has been both between reformers and powerful established interests benefiting from patronage and corruption, as well as among reformers with differing ideas on the nature of political representation required to alleviate poverty. At its essence, this was a struggle over whether BUB contained or facilitated *substantial* changes to the operations of state power.

The emergence of the participatory budget coalition was an unequivocal reaction against how the exercise of state power had aided, rather than arrested, oligarchic interests and persistent poverty. This was not a new problem, nor was the idea of popular participation as a strategy to address the problem entirely novel. On the contrary, BUB came about because previously legislated prescriptions to ensure better local government representation of the economically and socially marginalized had been effectively blocked in practice.

However, the preferred forms of political representation of moderates and radicals through BUB reflected different substantive reform agendas and related margins for institutionalized political conflict. For moderates, and especially liberal technocrats, this political participation and representation was largely viewed as a means to more effectively unleash market forces to both arrest corruption and political patronage on the one hand and to lay the foundations for social and economic transformations to eradicate poverty on the other. Moreover, moderates looked to civil society actors to support this agenda. This meant helping to get demonstrated results for the poor in a timely way and mobilizing party political support in the hope of consolidating the liberal technocrat-led reform agenda during and beyond the life of the Aquino administration.

By contrast, while radicals were also attracted to participatory budgeting to restrain patronage politics, it was not market power in which they invested most hope of eradicating poverty. It was instead the power of collective organization to strengthen the independent voices of the poor, both inside and outside the state to temper market forces. This, of course, was a long-term goal, and radicals had to be accordingly realistic in assessing the political utility of participatory budgeting. Nevertheless, remaining in the participatory budgeting reform coalition required some progress, or prospect thereof, toward expanded political space for collective organizations inclined to question as well as support government priorities in addressing poverty. Intra-coalition tension necessarily centered around who should be mobilized through BUB and how.

The future of such state-sponsored MOPs is problematic in the Philippines, however. In comparison with Singapore, the coalitions that sought to embed such MOPs in the Philippines never enjoyed comparable control over how state power was exercised. Local project determination under BUB had been alarming enough for entrenched interests to meet with various forms of elite resistance to, and defiance of, BUB processes. This again underscored the deep and pervasive networks of power at the disposal of capitalist oligarchs and *trapos* in the Philippines. Yet there were other critics of oligarchic power, corruption, and administrative inefficiencies who viewed MOP initiatives—such as the BUB—as contributing to, rather than helping to solve, these problems. This was emphatically demonstrated through the election of populist leader Rodrigo Duterte as president in 2016.

Although unaligned to any major political party, Duterte resoundingly defeated the liberal technocratic candidate, the Liberal Party's Mar Roxas, and outflanked all opponents. He did so by attracting substantial cross-class support with both anti-oligarchy and pro–"law and order" rhetoric and reform prescriptions. The head of Duterte's media team also alleged in the campaign that Roxas used BUB to cultivate support from local executives (Frialde 2016). The abolition of BUB was subsequently among the first initiatives of Duterte's administration; Budget Secretary Benjamin Diokno described BUB as a "political tool" and "waste of funds" when announcing the decision (Alvarez 2016).

Consequently, the 2017 budget ceased funding for the BUB, replacing it with the Assistance to Disadvantaged Municipalities confined to select municipalities. Moreover, under this change, the identification of projects is conducted by the mayor and one accredited CSO representative of the mayor's choosing (Soliman 2016). Doikno also declared that each member of Congress could propose P80 million (~US$1.6 million) worth of projects for their respective districts. He contended that the latter did not amount to a revival of the Priority Development Assistance Fund (PDAF)—or "pork barrel"—deemed unconstitutional by the Supreme Court in 2013. Identified projects would have to be channeled through the budgets of relevant government departments and agencies prior to the president signing off (Remitio 2016). However, it remains to be seen whether this does not afford a degree of maneuver for politicians that enjoy powerful networks of influence within the state.

The nature and extent of the translation of Duterte's anti-elite rhetoric into concrete policies is yet to fully play out. This will determine whether the complex, cross-class coalitions inside and outside Congress initially supporting Duterte's presidency will endure. His record as the mayor of Davao clearly suggests, though, that he is much more likely to progress change without new institutions and ideologies of representation, state-sponsored or otherwise. Duterte presents himself as the direct personal representative of "the people"—reviving a populist ideology of representation in the Philippines.

Ironically, populist ideologies of representation transcend the fragmentation of multiple political identities encouraged through various models of consultative and particularist representation. Here instead it is the collective identity of the people juxtaposed against an entrenched and self-interested elite. What is downplayed, though, are the roles of independent collective organizations, especially class-based organizations.

MALAYSIA'S FAILED CONSULTATIVE REPRESENTATION EXPERIMENTS

Colonial capitalism laid extensive social foundations for the dominance of particularist ideologies of representation in Malaysia. It fostered largely distinct roles in labor and capital markets for indigenous and immigrant ethnic Chinese and Indian communities. Colonial authorities also promoted ethnic-based political identities and organizations, a direction embraced by domestic elites and fundamental to political processes leading to Malayan independence in 1957. The resulting constitution was also premised on racial and ethnic affirmative action for the Bumiputera or "sons of the soil," including ethnic Malays and indigenous groups. This was a political project that would reinforce and elevate particularist ideologies of representation.

Particularist ideologies were generally elevated with the introduction in 1972 of the New Economic Policy (NEP). This followed the failure of the Alliance coalition government to satisfy reform expectations of impoverished Malays, resulting in riots. The NEP's declared aims were a social transformation to dismantle entrenched links between racial identification on the one hand and economic function and poverty on the other. Affirmative action to realize these aims, though, placed strategic emphasis on rapidly developing an ethnic Malay business class. This portended a distinctive model of state capitalism, under which the United Malays National Organization (UMNO), the dominant party of the newly formed Barisan Nasional (BN, National Front) ruling coalition, would foster a Malay capitalist elite directly dependent on state patronage. Hence the term UMNOputera, "sons of UMNO," emerged as a popular unofficial characterization of this relationship.

The roles and powers of ethnic Malay state bureaucrats also expanded—both in support of select, politically favored Malay business elites and also through the administering of various socially redistributive policies generally targeting Bumiputeras. NEP policies therefore generated a broad sociopolitical coalition of UMNO support bases. Crucially, though, particularist ideologies of political representation offered a rationalization of UMNO's strategic control over the exercise of state power and the associated interests of Malay political, business, and bureaucratic elites.

To be sure, in conjunction with the NEP, UMNO leaders rhetorically championed notions of power sharing and adopted coalition electoral pacts with assorted political parties. Indeed, the BN was at one stage comprised of as many as fourteen different parties, including various ethnic Chinese and ethnic Indian coalition partners (Mauzy and Barter 2008, 214). UMNO's intention was to render the parliamentary mode of participation more effective in managing political conflict. Yet this also further institutionalized particularist ideologies of race, ethnicity, and religion as the basis of political representation. So-called power sharing was premised on political supremacy by Malay elites.[1] State institutions, not least the Election Commission (EC), were also controlled to foster strategic selectivity favoring racial and ethnic-based representation to UMNO's and the ruling coalition's advantage.

The focus of this chapter is on how, why, and with what political consequences new MOPs emerged alongside UMNO's strategy for formally reproducing power via electoral institutions. Major societal incorporation initiatives in consultative representation through the 1989–1990 National Economic Consultative Council, and its 1999–2000 successor institution, are particularly subjected to scrutiny against these questions.

As the NEP approached its official end in 1990, anxieties increased among social and political forces inside and outside the ruling coalition, who variously sought to defend, modify, or abandon existing affirmative action and related policies. The gulf between UMNO rhetoric and reality about coalition power sharing thus became more problematic and the potential increased for defiance of authoritarian controls through more independent civil society expression. Critically, by this time Malay business interests produced by the NEP had diversified, which helps explain why Prime Minister Mahathir was willing to experiment with consultative representation through the establishment of the 1989–1990 National Economic Consultative Council (NECC I).

The NECC I was designed to both permit and contain conflict over post-NEP public policy directions, incorporating parliamentary and extraparliamentary representatives and expertise into what was depicted as a policy problem-solving exercise. Societal incorporation and consultative representation were thus introduced to supplement, and articulate with, the party political and parliamentary MOP. UMNO never intended to discard particularist ideologies justifying its rule. Rather, extraparliamentary consultation was explored for its potential utility to help limit NEP-related social anxieties and resolve intra-elite differences over what capital accumulation strategies should be emphasized in the next phase of capitalist development.

Yet even this mild flirtation with consultative representation generated proposals unacceptable to UMNO's leaders and support base, resulting in moves to contain the NECC I and to introduce a more controlled and restricted NECC II, with only selective adoption of NECC recommendations. The interests that prevailed were those of the UMNOputera, which could benefit from specific and limited market reforms and which could align with strategies to maintain Malay electoral support. Hence, despite the novelty of the NECC as a MOP, in practice, structural forces fundamentally shaped what could be achieved through it. The appeal of such consultative mechanisms beyond elites was therefore short-lived, as was their centrality to elite strategies for containing the permissible limits of political conflict through new forms of participation.

Extraparliamentary consultative and related bodies to contain conflict would not entirely disappear from Malaysian politics. However, they would predominantly involve high-level, closed-door deliberations among business and bureaucratic elites to advise Cabinet, or small expert economic advisory committees to government. Where popular participation was incorporated, this would involve even more effective and sophisticated controls than was true of the NECCs. This is demonstrated below through examination of initiatives in administrative incorporation under Prime Minister Najib Razak that accompanied his strategy to push Malaysia toward a high-income economy by 2020. Crucially, as with the NECC experiments, these new MOPs did more to increase than contain tensions over possible reforms to Malaysian capitalism and its governance.

NECC I and II: Experiments in Consultation

Just as in Singapore and the Philippines, Malaysia's elite explored new MOPs as a way of containing conflict, notably consultative representation through two NECCs. Although inclusive of a plurality of social and political forces, the way these forces were represented, and the reform suggestions that could be accommodated, were mediated by interrelated structural and ideological factors that were more restrictive than in either Singapore or in the Philippines. While some intra-elite conflicts could be addressed through these consultative mechanisms, reform suggestions that could impinge on discretionary state powers to dispense and control state patronage posed a threat to the political regime and the ideologies meant to justify it. This is demonstrated below, first by examining how and why NECC I both raised and disappointed popular reform expectations and, second, by examining how NECC II confirmed that consultative representation in Malaysia had quickly evolved into a limited elite political project.

NECC I Rationale and Composition

The approach to the official expiry of the NEP in 1990 was one of generally heightened tension and apprehension over Malaysia's future development strategy, including among Malaysia's political and economic elites. With the advent of the 1985 recession, intra-elite friction escalated within UMNO, and between UMNO and its BN partners. Meanwhile, contention involving party political and civil society critics and opponents—some advocates of particularist institutions of representation, others seeking more liberal and/or democratic institutions—led authorities to invoke the Internal Security Act (ISA) to detain over a hundred people in late 1987 (Weiss 2006, 119). This effectively closed down public debate over the NEP, but it did not resolve the conflict over the extent or nature of transition from it.

A significant institutional experiment in consultative representation was thus subsequently introduced to try and politically manage this conflict: the 150-member extraparliamentary NECC I. This was projected as a new inclusive forum for developing a post-NEP economic policy. Although the NECC I lacked independent policy-making powers, Deputy Prime Minister Ghafar Baba emphasized that the government would implement proposals arrived at by consensus (Ho 1992, 212–13).

It was Ling Leong Sik, president of the Malaysian Chinese Association (MCA), who put the idea of the NECC to Ghafar. The MCA, a leading party within the BN, had found it necessary to suggest a new MOP precisely because of its waning influence over government policy. Since the advent of the NEP, the MCA had lost key portfolios within government and been adversely affected by the redrawing of electoral boundaries bolstering the weighting of ethnic Malay votes. The alienation of ethnic Chinese business and middle classes also escalated dramatically from the mid-1980s (Heng 1997, 283).

Against this background, the MCA produced a report in 1988 expressing concerns that non-Malays were the sole bearers of the pressures to restructure Malaysian society. The next year, the Institute for Strategic Analysis and Policy Research (INSAP)—an MCA think tank comprising business leaders, management consultants, lawyers, academics, and professional economists—was established. INSAP proposed measures to monitor "deviations" in the NEP's implementation, alluding to the unchecked use of state power for political patronage. Moreover, INSAP's Malaysia Unity Plan recommended that "policies of state intervention and restructuring have to be replaced by new policies that reward risk, hard work and enterprise, irrespective of race" (quoted in Heng 1997).

According to Mauzy (1995, 78), Ling's NECC proposal to Ghafar was for a "small inter-ethnic group formed to standardize data and work out compromises, but did not request a large, unwieldy, official, widely-publicized council that would raise expectations." Prime Minister Mahathir instead proceeded with a larger body, with wider inclusion of social and political forces. This maximized the government's potential to project policy consultation as encompassing diverse national interests in a sincere attempt to develop good policy (Ho 1992, 222–23).

Importantly, Mahathir had already begun charting his own course of economic liberalization. However, this was intended to rationalize—not to abolish—state patronage systems favoring more competitive but politically aligned business conglomerates and interests. Others within UMNO were even less enthusiastic about dispensing with existing interventionist policies. Who would be represented in the NECC I and, critically, *how*, was meant to strike a balance between different political objectives and struggles within the BN. This was not just over the extent and nature of the rationalization of patronage among ethnic Malay business interests, but also the role of ethnic Chinese capital and its significance for any such rationalization.

The composition of the NECC I was carefully calibrated to project inclusivity, both in terms of party political and civil society representatives. Thus, there was equal weighting for the MCA and UMNO, each accounting for ten out of the forty ruling BN representatives. This was a significant concession to the MCA in particular and to coalition partners more generally. A further twelve representatives came from opposition parties, five of which were from the Democratic Action Party (DAP).

The remainder of the representatives included people from a range of employer federations, chambers of commerce, professional organizations, trade unions, academia, private companies, and religious and cultural organizations. There were also individuals—especially from business, the professions, and academia—who had loose or no connections with collective organizations. These inclusions particularly enhanced the appearance of the government facilitating a more technocratic, problem-solving approach to policy consistent with consultative representation.[2]

The overall composition of the NECC I thus comprised a mixture of democratically authorized representatives (from political parties) and others who were variously appointed under the pretext of providing representation to specific interests or precisely because they could be projected as apolitical. This hybrid form of consultative representation—compared with Singapore, where opposition parties were deliberately bypassed—reflected two factors. First, the MCA had been the chief instigator of the NECC. Second, UMNO leaders did not share a deep ideological commitment to technocratic representation but saw the tactical political potential of such an institution to contain conflict at this time.

Crucially, for UMNO leaders the NECC was meant to complement rather than replace particularist ideologies of representation as the NEP formally drew to an end. Much emphasis was therefore placed on how equal numbers of Bumiputeras and non-Bumiputeras were represented on the NECC I. Many organizations, particularly the respective racially based chambers of commerce and industry, were self-evidently identifiable in these terms (Chinese, Malay, and Indian). Official documents also identified the racial or ethnic status of individuals not notionally representing any organization.

Significantly, the meager representation of two from the Malaysian Trades Union Congress reflected its modest membership and organizational base. This was a legacy of the repression of the labor movement during the Cold War (Munro-Kua 1996, 40–57). Indeed, the weakness of civil society organizations necessitated the incorporation of various individuals in implicit concessions to assorted progressive causes. This included, for example, Martin Khor, research director of the Consumers' Association of Penang; Paul Tan of the Catholic Research Centre, who had a record of public advocacy on social justice issues; and F. R. Bhupalan, especially renowned for championing women's rights.

The resources at the disposal of these representatives were extremely modest, though, compared with business representatives of civil society. Political plurality did not mean equally effective representation of different interests. Indeed, according to one of the BN coalition representatives on the NECC I, Toh Kin Woon of the Parti Gerakan Rakyat Malaysia (Gerakan, Malaysian People's Movement Party), although the NECC I was "pretty inclusive," "the groups representing the upper strata of Malaysian society were better represented . . . there was a class bias."[3] Notwithstanding some representation of the "lower strata," these people had little impact, according to Toh. Instead, the principal "arena of contestation was actually among the elites, between the different ethnic groups and even within ethnic groups." Thus, NECC I was certainly not a wholesale departure from particularist representation.

Nevertheless, it was widely viewed by participants as a genuine opportunity to influence public policy. According to Toh, "they thought that [Prime Minister] Mahathir might be genuine enough to want to seek our opinions on what sort of economic direction we should pursue after the end of the NEP." In particular,

the chambers of commerce invested heavily in consultants to help prepare detailed reports modeling the economic impacts of changes to procurement policies
and pro-market reforms.

Introducing Change with NECC I

Notwithstanding the class bias underlying the seemingly inclusive NECC I, representation was sufficiently diverse to ensure that defenders of existing affirmative
action policies would have to contend with liberal arguments about market efficiency and meritocracy, as well as a push for a needs-based approach to poverty
eradication. Indeed, UMNO leaders would be surprised and alarmed at some of
the policy recommendations in the NECC I's interim report, prompting significant changes to how the NECC operated.

The substantive issues that mattered to UMNO's BN coalition partners were
well known in advance of the NECC I. These included quotas restricting non-
Malay access to procurements in public infrastructure contracts, state-funded
tertiary education places, public sector employment, land ownership, and land
settlement schemes (Heng 1997, 287). Aspects of this agenda were not inconsis-
tent with Mahathir's evolving program of selective deregulation, privatization, and
liberalization to foster opportunities for more competitive ethnic Malay business
elements. They were a threat, though, to other ethnic Malay, and to some extent
petit bourgeois ethnic Chinese, business interests that feared the rise of conglomerates. Assorted individual representatives concerned with social justice issues
were also opposed to "trickle down" economics as the basis of future development.

Most detailed NECC I debates took place through five working groups, the most
important of which was the group tasked with restructuring of society. The other
four groups focused on data standardization; poverty elimination; the national
economy in the context of the international environment; and the development
of human resources. Engagement across these groups also took place at plenary
sessions. Importantly, the NECC I provided new political space for contending
ideas on efficiency and merit- versus race-based state intervention. Within this
context, ideas of transparency, accountability, and social justice were all given
expression.

The dynamics of NECC I deliberations generated both a degree of fluidity of
positions among some participants and a hardening of positions among others. According to Toh, fluidity occurred over the principles underlying state intervention
within the all-important restructuring working group. In particular, whereas the
MCA had initially aimed for increased admissions to universities and access to
government and other contracts for ethnic Chinese, it became more receptive

over time to the idea of linking reform to need-based affirmative action coming from other groups and individuals.

Yet, this reinforced anxiety within UMNO and other ethnic Malay groups. Arguments that Malays would be among the biggest beneficiaries of a needs-based approach had least impact on those concerned about the dominance of Chinese capital.[4] More generally, the preparedness of some Malay nationalists to engage around such issues was open to question. According to NECC I representative and academic Lim Teck Ghee, who was also a member of the report drafting committee, some "made their speeches, had their glory, and were never seen again."[5]

Despite such polarization on the restructuring issue, on August 9, 1990, the NECC I Steering Committee circulated a 270-page draft report. Priority policy recommendations included the elimination of rentier elements, power abuse, corruption, waste, discrimination, and other policy deviations (Sundaram 1994, 38). Accordingly, this report also contained recommendations for greater public access to official data and, crucially, the establishment of an independent monitoring agency to oversee the implementation of the new development program. Such an institutionalized accountability mechanism was clearly in conflict with prevailing practices of state political patronage. It would also reduce the capacity of the state to conceal from non-Bumiputeras the full extent of restructuring that had occurred in order to shore up the continued case for NEP policies. According to MCA representative Michael Yeoh, "All of us thought that this was the single most important recommendation that we put together."[6]

A conjuncture of factors made such recommendations possible: the doggedness of those genuinely seeking such reforms; the presence of a sufficient number of liberal-minded Malays from outside UMNO affecting the dynamics of negotiation; and a degree of complacency by the most sectarian custodians of the status quo who, according to Lim Teck Ghee, "knew that the government would cherry-pick."[7] Moreover, the party rather than Mahathir and his government had selected UMNO's NECC I representatives. Consequently, various members of the so-called Team B, which lost out in the 1987 UMNO leadership challenge, were selected—including the prominent Abdullah Badawi. As NECC I participant and University of Malaya economist Jomo Kwame Sundaram observed, "He wasn't going to whip them [UMNO representatives] into accepting a particular line."[8] According to business leader and MCA representative on the NECC I Yong Poh Kon, "[Abdullah] Badawi was more open to discuss alternative approaches as he was not in government."[9]

UMNO leaders in government certainly did not anticipate the report's critical focus on the integrity of state institutions and other reform proposals. This focus implicitly contained a liberal ideological conception of the state as a facilitator of free and fair economic and political competition. Selective aspects of this ideology had appeal, or tactical political utility for, advancing the respective reform priorities of elements of business, professional, and civil society with representation on the NECC I.

Yet there would be no compromising of the discretionary powers of state officials, nor any official diluting of particularist ideologies justifying these powers. Thus, as Mauzy (1995, 85) observed, it appeared that within the Cabinet, or the Economic Planning Unit (EPU) of the Prime Minister's Office, it was quickly concluded that UMNO members on the NECC I Steering Committee had conceded too much (Mauzy 1995, 85). Thereafter, previously established NECC procedures were abandoned—notably that no report recommendations could be overturned without support by a two-thirds vote.

Although there had been little attempt hitherto by UMNO leaders within the NECC I to enforce a tight party line, pressure from leaders outside the NECC I appeared to have changed that. These leaders within the NECC I now argued that there would need to be report changes to guard against Cabinet dismissing it, while new members were also added to the NECC I Steering Committee. According to the media, the report would now be delayed to accommodate new views. In late August, Mahathir publicly pronounced that because the NECC I was now unable to reach a consensus the government was not bound by its recommendations, precipitating the resignation of five DAP members from the NECC I who denounced the exercise as farcical (Sundaram 1994, 49; Mauzy 1995, 85).

Containment of NECC I's "Consensus"

Work on a revised report continued, and the final version was submitted in February 1990, written in Malay and entitled *Dasar Ekonomi Untuk Pembangunan Negara* (*DEPAN*, Economic Policy for National Development). To be sure, *DEPAN* contained significant divergences from the NEP, including a shift in emphasis toward greater reliance on economic growth to accompany distributional policies as a basis for development, as well as the need for policy responses to redress intra-ethnic, intra-sectoral, and intra-regional imbalances and other inequalities. Measures recommended to equalize opportunity included considering ethnicity, need, and merit, but eliminating the ethnic approach once imbalances are removed; and extending a need-based approach to areas other than poverty eradication irrespective of ethnicity (Sundaram 1994, 31, 40).

Precisely how much influence the *DEPAN* had on the Second Outline Perspective Plan (OPP2)—which led to the National Development Policy, 1991–2000—is uncertain. OPP2 was well advanced when *DEPAN* was announced (Sundaram 1994, 49). There were overlaps and departures between them.

DEPAN contained selective pro-market reforms designed to manage intra-elite conflict and mutual interest among different fractions of the capitalist class, a process of which the NECC I was a part. As Heng Pek Koon observed, *DEPAN*'s "emphasis on the development of a more resilient Malay private sector, to trim public sector involvement in the economy and to promote policies of growth over policies of income redistribution, reflected the thinking of a new NEP-created class of highly successful and self-confident Malay professionals and entrepreneurs" (Heng 1997, 289). Various concessions to the MCA reform agenda signaled earlier in its Malaysian Unity Plan were functional for the UMNOputera, who were the biggest beneficiaries of state privatization under the NEP. "These entrepreneurs had become the allies of Chinese business interests and it was the shared interests of the new Sino-Malay entrepreneurial class in Malaysia that the new policy sought to address," according to Heng (1997, 289). This fitted with Searle's (1999, 248) broader argument that, during the 1990s, the capital of Chinese business groups became increasingly integrated with, and dependent on, Bumiputera capital.

To be sure, Yong Poh Kon, MCA representative and chairman of the MCA-aligned INSAP, exerted a significant influence over the NECC I deliberations and as a co-drafter of the NECC I report's recommendations. Academic economist Jomo Kwame Sundaram described Yong as having the most explicitly liberal economic view on the NECC I.[10] Importantly, though, the NECC I also incorporated various Malay and Chinese professionals who could reinforce neoclassical economic arguments favoring a shift toward greater emphasis on growth and competition to further development (Heng 1997, 287). They included banker Malek Merican; Kamal Salih, head of the Malaysian Institute of Economic Research; Mohamed Noordin Sopiee, director-general of the Institute of Strategic and International Studies; and University of Malaya economist Fong Chan Ong, who subsequently became vice-president of the MCA and also an MCA parliamentarian and government minister. The material interests and worldviews of these actors, none of whom were hardcore economic libertarians, could be accommodated within, and harnessed to, the economic upgrading Mahathir sought to facilitate in the new development plan.

Others who participated in the NECC I, and who championed politically liberal ideology and/or nonracial social redistribution agendas, had less to cheer about. Sundaram (1994, 49–50) lamented the government's failure to accept what he saw as the NECC I's most important recommendations: "to ensure transparency, accountability and justice." Gerakan's Toh also argued that the "key thrust" of the NECC I report had been ignored—that the state should intervene on the basis on needs to "close the gap between the different income classes irrespective of race."[11] This was unsurprising, as it fundamentally conflicted with the material and ideological interests of UMNO's leaders and socioeconomic base.

Although *DEPAN* retained the earlier controversial NECC I call for an independent, nonpartisan commissioner to monitor the implementation of the new development plan, this never saw the light of day either. UMNO leaders well understood the threat posed by such a "paradigmatic break" from the NEP, as one NECC I participant described this proposal (Ho 1992, 216). What was at stake with this recommendation was nothing less than discretionary strategic control by UMNO over the exercise of state power. This control was integral to the political and economic logic of Malaysia's brand of state capitalism and the elite interests served by it and rationalized through particularist ideologies of political representation. Consequently, government officials made no public mention of this proposal following *DEPAN*'s submission.

The 1989–1990 NECC helped to contain and manage intra-elite conflict over the extent and purpose of state intervention, but it also highlighted tensions between particularist and consultative ideologies and institutions of representation in Malaysia. The greater the political polarization in society, the more inclusive participation needed to be for it to be effective. Yet this also risked less control over the limits of political conflict through policy consultation. In any future such consultative body, therefore, UMNO representatives might need to be chosen more carefully and their strategies of engagement adjusted accordingly.

For many outside the BN who participated in the NECC I, or had hopes for it, the experience was deeply disappointing. UMNO interventions in the NECC I's processes following the committee's draft report had been instructive. Moreover, subsequent resistance, despite recommendations in *DEPAN*, to either a meaningful shift toward a needs-based approach to development or reforms to the administration of state institutions educated these forces about the limits to what might be possible through such consultative representation.

NECC II

NECC I had been disappointing for Malaysians hoping for different and more significant reforms to the political regime and related political economy relationships than it could deliver. Yet a decade later there would be another attempt at consultative representation through a second NECC amidst rising sociopolitical conflict again linked to the dynamic tensions associated with Malaysia's variant of state capitalism. However, NECC II would prove even less successful than its predecessor as a government-controlled MOP for channeling popular participation down paths most conducive to the existing regime. Instead, the very disappointment of NECC I had contributed to more Malaysians looking to independent civil society expression rather than such societal incorporation for their political participation.

The advent of the 1997–1998 Asian financial crisis unleashed a new round of tensions within and beyond the ruling coalition over the exercise of state power. Indeed, economic and political crises precipitated a *reformasi* (reformation) movement comprising diverse ethnic, social, and political elements. Its modus operandi included street demonstrations and civil disobedience—despite harsh police measures to suppress public protests—and new links between independent civil society forces and parties opposed to, or critical of, the BN.

It was in this context that BN leaders launched another NECC in August 1999, a few months before general elections in November that year. The government's failure to implement the very checks and balances NECC I had advocated to arrest state power abuses and political patronage was pivotal to the increased civil society expression with which it was now contending. Yet NECC II would confirm that any opportunity by elites to contain this conflict through incorporation in a state-controlled MOP had largely passed.

The New Development Plan that followed NECC I facilitated new opportunities for politically favored conglomerates, particularly through the privatization of state assets (B. T. Khoo 2006, 184). However, the 1997–1998 Asian financial crisis revealed the heavy loan exposure of these same conglomerates, while foreign investment sharply declined and multilateral institutions called for governance reforms in Malaysia (Hilley 2001, 72–77). In the intra-UMNO factional struggle over state patronage that ensued, deputy prime minister and finance minister Anwar Ibrahim sought unsuccessfully to block state bailouts of select conglomerate interests. Such was the intensity of this struggle that by September 1998 Anwar was expelled from UMNO and imprisoned (Khalid and Abidin 2014, 401).

Anwar's political persecution alienated many Malays from UMNO, leading to the formation of a new political party—Parti Keadilan Nasional (National Justice Party)—providing the stimulus for ideologically diverse opponents and critics of the BN to cooperate in advancing reform demands.[12] Whatever the differences among these forces, the use and abuse of state power to protect specific elite business and political interests now prompted united calls for Mahathir's resignation and an end to corruption and cronyism.[13]

This was the context of Prime Minister Mahathir's announcement that an NECC II was necessary to formulate a new strategy to enable Malaysia to face the challenges of economic globalization and liberalization (L. T. Lee 1999). The methodology of NECC II was comparable to its predecessor, incorporating 154 representatives from political parties, other organizations, and individuals in ways that married notions of consultative with particularist ideologies of race and ethnicity. However, there were a few notable differences in the composition of, and official pronouncements about, this council.

First, in obvious reference to *reformasi* mobilizations, Transport Minister Ling Liong Sik highlighted the emergence of a "riot culture" among Malaysian youth that needed to be addressed through the NECC to protect tourism and foreign investment. "When youth come out and throw stones and injure policemen, the foreign press takes advantage of the situation and gives us bad publicity," argued Ling (quoted in *New Straits Times* 1999). Accordingly, the EPU of the Prime Minister's Office and the Ministry of Education selected five youth representatives for the NECC II (Abdul 1999). Notwithstanding genuine worries about the economy, these additions to the NECC II underlined the BN's concern to redirect and/or discourage independent political activism away from public demonstrations altogether—however peacefully they were conducted.

Second, from the outset, key party political and NGO actors boycotted NECC II. The opposition DAP, Parti Keadilan Nasional (National Justice Party), Parti Islam Se-Malaysia (PAS, Pan-Malaysian Islamic Party, or simply Islamic Party nowadays), and Parti Rakyat Malaysia (Malaysian People's Party) all refused to take part. Since its suggestions were disregarded in the previous NECC, the DAP dismissed the NECC II as a "government gimmick" (Tay 1999). BN leaders roundly and bitterly condemned the opposition boycotts, revealing how important it was to them to try and project the NECC as truly representative of divergent views. Abdullah Badawi, by now out of the political doldrums and deputy prime minister, declared: "This showed that the Opposition is not interested in formulating plans and ideas for the development of the country" (quoted in Ramian, Ainon, and Sennyah 2001).

The government also failed in its attempt to incorporate representatives from possibly the most significant NGO reform group that had emerged within the *reformasi* movement—the Malaysian Chinese Organizations' Election Appeals Committee, Suqiu. Suqiu comprised eleven associations and produced a seventeen-point policy appeal that was endorsed by over two thousand other organizations (Weiss 2006, 135), most of which were middle-class–led organizations based in the urban centers of Kuala Lumpur and Penang that had expanded under Malaysia's rapid capitalist development.[14] The appeal included recommendations to curb corruption; improve transparency in, and a review of, privatization; achieve equitable economic policy; promote national unity; improve social services; respect workers' rights; ensure environmental protection; promote women's rights; and enhance electoral democracy through institutional change (*New Straits Times* 2000a). Many of these issues had been raised in NECC I but not acted upon.

Suqiu's proposals generated much controversy, some perceiving them as striking at ethnic Malay political dominance and affirmative action. However, MCA leaders worked hard to try and have Suqiu's demands steered through the NECC II, with strong and eventually successful advocacy to that effect within the BN

Cabinet.[15] MCA president and transport minister Ling Liong Sik subsequently directed senior party colleagues to discuss potential candidates with association leaders (Izatun 1999). However, the overture was rejected, further denting BN claims that NECC II would be representative of Malaysia's diverse policy viewpoints.

Despite the absence of opposition parties and NGOs, NECC II was still somewhat controversial. Views on affirmative action expressed by NECC deputy chairman David Chua, reported in the *Far Eastern Economic Review*, generated consternation. Chua was quoted as saying: "The current policy is not doing anybody any good. . . . We want to see increased liberalization and competition in our society based on merit" (quoted in Gilley 2000). Various options for partially or completely phasing out Bumiptera business, education, housing, and public sector employment benefits were reportedly being countenanced within NECC II. Ethnic Chinese voters had played a decisive role in keeping the BN in government at the November 1999 polls, and the interview also coincided with the anniversary of the lodging of the Suqiu appeal. This raised speculation that ethnic Chinese elites now felt empowered to push for significant reform through NECC II.

The front page of the Malay-language daily *Utusan Malaysia* glossed Chua's comments as "abolish Malay privileges." In an attempt to calm the waters, Chua explained a distinction between "rights" and "policies." The former were not being questioned, he emphasized, adding nevertheless that economic, trade, and industrial policies could be phased out when the time was right (quoted in *New Straits Times* 2000b). He declined, however, to indicate whether NECC II had discussed the issue of special assistance for Malays.

The next day, Malay businessperson Hasrul Faisal Mat lodged a police report against the *Far Eastern Economic Review*, its journalist Bruce Gilley, and Chua, claiming the article questioned the constitutional rights of Malays and the Bumiputera. Hasrul stated: "I urge police to investigate if anyone had contravened the Official Secrets Act 1972 by divulging contents of the council's documents" (quoted in *New Straits Times* 2000c). The behind-closed-doors discussions of the NECC II only exacerbated fears that Malay political supremacy could be compromised in seemingly rational policy dialogue over development plans. Forces benefitting from racial and ethnic affirmative action, embedded in national development plans from the NEP onward, constrained the range of policy proposals UMNO could accept. It thus resisted even relatively modest reform demands voiced through the NECC II.

Apart from this controversy, media coverage of NECC II was limited compared with NECC I. The NECC II report was never made publicly available either. Indeed, by the time the exercise had concluded, it appeared that the government had lost enthusiasm for this particular model of consultative representation. The

combined experiences of the two NECCs had not only failed to effectively incorporate regime and government critics to discourage their mobilization through
more independent MOPs. They had also created opportunities for particularist
ideologies to be questioned from within the ruling coalition. This raised anxieties from within UMNO's support base—not least among ethnic Malays outside the elite who had become increasingly materially and ideologically reliant on
special privileges as Malaysian capitalist development deepened. This was not sur-
prising, given how authoritarian rule had systematically curtailed the opportunities for collective organizations and coalitions thereof to emerge with alternative
redistributive rationales and programs.

Najib's Transformative Agenda

Precisely because of the failure of the NECCs to affect reforms to prevailing systems of resource distribution and governance, ruling elites would find it necessary to periodically reassure Malaysians that particularist institutions of political
representation could be reconciled with inclusive social and economic development. Mahathir's concept of *Bangsa Malaysia* (A Malaysian Nation) was one such
appeal, introduced in his Vision 2020 project in 1991 but given particular emphasis amidst the political turmoil of the late 1990s and early 2000s.

However, in 2008, the BN suffered its worst electoral result since Independence.
This was amidst escalating concerns about material inequalities and the integrity
of Malaysia's governance systems, problems compounded by declining economic
growth and private investment with the advent of the global financial crisis. Crucially, non-Malay voter support for the BN declined acutely, and there was a significant drift to the opposition from Malays as well. Particularist ideologies and
institutions of political representation appeared to be facing a new and more serious test.

When Najib Razak replaced Abdullah Badawi as prime minister in April 2009,
he immediately projected reform to address inequalities and provide nondiscrimi-
natory governance for all Malaysians irrespective of ethnicity and religion. Najib's
declared agenda was encapsulated in the slogan "One Malaysia. People First. Performance Now," often abbreviated to "1Malaysia." Najib projected himself as a
moderate Muslim and avoided explicit references to Islam to project the 1Malaysia
policy (Hamid and Razali 2015, 315).

Najib described himself at one stage as a "technocratic politician" (Khalid and
Abidin 2014, 407). However, while his background included an executive role with
state oil company Petronas and brief service with Malaysia's central bank, Bank
Negara, this did not place him outside the power structures of a state shaped by

political patronage, but at the core of them. He would also have to contend with rising ethno-nationalist and Islamic extremist forces within UMNO and its support base. Nevertheless, Najib seemed to have concluded that market-oriented reform was necessary to revitalize, so as to preserve, the economic and political sustainability of that state.

To this end, Najib appointed people with private sector backgrounds to Cabinet to steer reform, not least to the operations of the civil service and its relationship to government. In 2009, Najib also removed the 30 percent Bumiputera equity requirement for public-listed companies in twenty-seven services subsectors— including health and social services, tourism, transport, business, and computer and related services. Banking, energy, and telecommunications were excluded from this reform. In effect, Najib resumed the exercise Mahathir had earlier embarked on to harness selective economic liberalization and deregulation to facilitate new investment opportunities for domestic capital, but with an eye this time to attracting greater foreign investment as well (E. T. Gomez 2012a, 72).

Two more fundamental and complementary reform programs were connected to Najib's 1Malaysia rhetoric: the Government Transformation Program (GTP), announced in January 2010 to address the public's dissatisfaction with service delivery; and the Economic Transformation Program (ETP), announced in reports in March and September 2010, to usher in a New Economic Model (NEM) and finally propel Malaysia toward high-income status by 2020. Importantly, new mechanisms of policy consultation and feedback were integral to Najib's reform vision, with emphasis on administrative incorporation and explicit or implicit appeals to technocratic consultative ideologies of representation.

Accordingly, in 2009, the Performance Management and Delivery Unit (Pemandu) was established within the Prime Minister's Department, assuming and surpassing roles within the civil service hitherto undertaken by the EPU. Najib also created the National Economic Advisory Council (NEAC), entrusted with the task of defining the strategic direction and policy proposals for the NEM. The NEAC was not only a smaller body than either of the two NECCs, but its composition was also largely devoid of civil society actors and dominated by business people and professionals. These initiatives were intended to reframe contentious public policy issues as ones largely resolvable through enhanced state service delivery capacity and consultative mechanisms to refine strategic economic directions and implementation.

Yet this approach proved no more effective in containing or transcending fundamental political conflict over the prevailing capitalist model. As per the NECC experiences, interests aligned with existing privileges in state resource allocation and governance arrangements prevailed. Indeed, before long Najib would be reasserting the primacy of particularist ideologies and institutions of ethnicity and religion in defining the permissible limits to political conflict over Malaysia's public policy and development.

Pemandu's Administrative Incorporation

According to Najib, "the days of government knows best are over" (quoted in McCourt 2012). However, what transpired under his leadership drew inspiration from the private sector, not some model of participatory or deliberative democracy. In April 2009, Najib appointed Gerakan's Koh Tsu Koon to a special ministerial position, in order to identify a new "strategic direction" for the country, starting with the creation of business-like "performance indicators" for government (Lesley 2014, 2). Consequently, Koh called on Azman Mokhtar, head of the government-owned company Khazanah Nasional, and private sector consultants to conduct a number of Cabinet workshops in order to create National Key Result Areas (NKRAs).

This approach had resonances with the UK's Performance Management and Delivery Unit (PMDU) established during the Blair government. Not coincidentally, Britons with PMDU links were among the McKinsey private sector consultants integral to Koh's team (Xavier, Siddiquee, and Mohamed 2016, 84). This included Michael Barber, who headed the PMDU during 2001–2005.

The first Cabinet workshop was in May 2009, concluding with a polling of ministers on what they saw as national public policy priorities.[16] In the next Cabinet workshop public surveys conducted by consultants were injected into deliberations. According to Lesley (2014, 6), at this workshop a McKinsey consultant made the point that Cabinet needed to consider "not only what the public *wanted* but also what the public *needed* [italics in original]." Thus, Cabinet was never simply directed by public opinion but it was encouraged and supported by Koh and his team to strategically accommodate it.

As a result of this process, on July 27, 2009, Najib was able to announce six NKRAs: poverty eradication; crime prevention; corruption reduction; urban public transport; rural infrastructure; and education. In 2011, the cost of living was added as another NKRA.[17] Pemandu was created in September 2009 in order to implement the NKRAs. It was how these NKRAs were crafted into the GTP that largely defined the significance of new MOPs through Pemandu. In essence, Pemandu sought to enhance the information and strategies available to BN elites in determining and projecting its public policy. Public feedback and consultations were principally intended to contribute to refinement in the delivery of public goods and services rather than facilitate open-ended debate over policy options.

Najib attracted prominent business leader Idris Jala to take up the role as Pemandu's chief executive officer.[18] As Najib explained, Idris would "focus on sharing his expertise and experience in Shell [oil and gas company] and MAS [Malaysian Airlines]," where he had held very senior positions (quoted in *The Star* 2009a). Idris insisted, and Najib agreed, to the establishment of Pemandu as a corporation within the Prime Minister's Department so that it could pay the higher salaries needed to attract business consultants.[19] Transition to this new role was seamless in Idris' eyes: "It's just a different slant for how you tackle it— the public versus customers. You've got to deal with customers in a corporation. Here you deal with the general public, but you treat them as customers" (quoted in Daly and Singham 2011).

In this corporate conception of public engagement, Idris and others in Pemandu would also frequently refer to Malaysians as "stakeholders." This acknowledged that outcomes of public policy had an impact on Malaysians so they needed to be engaged, but not necessarily because as citizens they have rights to democratic representation. Consequently, the question of democratic authority to represent any particular section of the public was not central to Pemandu's considerations of whom to consult, how, or when. Furthermore, perceptions were at least as important as the substance of public policy. As Idris emphasized, engaging the public was critical to generating buy-in for government programs (Lesley 2014, 5).

Pemandu's processes of engagement were extensive, varied, and layered. Following the determination of broad NKRAs, Pemandu hosted labs of intense problem-solving focus lasting six-to-seven weeks—a methodology Idris learnt from his corporate experience. The aim was to establish concrete and measurable goals for the respective NKRAs. Each lab included approximately thirty to forty participants selected by Pemandu for their "experience and knowledge" (Lesley 2014, 8). According to Idris, "when you put people in labs, you had better put the best and the brightest" (quoted in Dichter, Lind, and Singham 2008).

It was only *after* this that town hall–style Open Days were conducted, in December 2009, providing opportunities for the general public to offer criticisms and suggestions concerning the identified NKRA priorities, goals, and means for achieving them (*The Star* 2009b). Idris emphasized the inclusive nature of these meetings thus: "We invite the entire Malaysian public to come and engage with us and see what we have produced in our labs" (quoted in Daly and Singham 2011). According to Pemandu, more than 13,000 people attended Open Days that were held in Kuala Lumpur, Kuching, and Kota Kinabalu (S. H. Yong 2010). However, these feedback sessions were, in effect, an opportunity to react to the government's agenda, rather than to help set it. They were also grounded in the ideological notion that the exercise was fundamentally a technical problem-solving one that made no distinction between input from democratically authorized representatives and anybody else.

At the end of this process of public consultations, Pemandu's principal attention turned to the evaluation of, and information about, concrete project implementation (Daly and Singham 2011; Futehally 2013). This would include further surveys and consultations, but also Pemandu peppering the public with information through its publications, website, and press copy to project the best possible light on the progress of the GTP (McCourt 2012, 2334). However, while this generated public interest in and awareness of the GTP and the ETP, a credibility problem emerged for Pemandu. The statistics it cited often lacked resonance with the public's experiences or perceptions, arousing suspicions among BN opponents as to the real purpose of Pemandu.

Data in Pemandu's annual reports were a particular source of controversy—not least as the basis to claim a 5 percent reduction in the overall crime index between 2009 and 2012. This provoked widespread public questioning, accompanied by Parti Keadilan Rakyat (PKR, People's Justice Party), PAS, and the DAP issuing a joint statement highlighting allegations that Pemandu's crime data were "manipulated" (Koon 2012; *Malaysiakini* 2012). There were also significant discrepancies between Pemandu's figures on corruption and those of Transparency International and other authoritative sources (Xavier, Siddiquee, and Mohamed 2016, 85). Contention surfaced too over Pemandu's methodology behind figures depicting reduced poverty between 2009 and 2012, including allegations that the gross national income figure for the base year of 2009 had been deliberately lowered. This prompted the DAP's Lim Kit Siang (2013) to declare that "Pemandu is now facing a crisis of its own making on its image as a credible, ethical and professional institution. It is fast gaining a reputation as a propaganda tool that cannot be taken seriously."

With a further drop in BN support at the 2013 election, and particularly the prominence of corruption and inequality issues in the campaigns by the BN's opponents, Lim's observation may not have been too wide of the mark. Moreover, there had been increasingly strident ethno-religious stances from within UMNO, its aligned NGOs, and state bureaucracies in the lead-up to the election (Hamid and Razali 2015).[20] As Hamid and Razali observed, rather than arrest this trend, Najib was "at pains to accommodate the stances adopted by Islamist conservatives" (316) to try to demonstrate what many regarded as his suspect Islamic credentials. Ethnic minorities' support for the BN thus bottomed in 2013.

Significantly, among the developments contributing to growing anxieties among elements of UMNO's base were NEM proposals generated from the NEAC. These forces would again prove influential in effectively blunting policy proposals linked to processes and ideologies of technocratic participation and representation.

NEAC and Consultative Representation

Following the two NECCs, the BN retreated from such consultative representation but it persisted with various small and less inclusive, high-level economic advisory committees.[21] The NEAC, established to advise on the development strategy for Vision 2020, was something of a return to consultative representation. However, it involved a different model of consultative representation from the NECCs—more technocrat-led and, in articulation with Pemandu's feedback mechanisms, seemingly more cohesively state sponsored. Was it better placed, then, to succeed where the NECCs had failed to instigate significant reforms?

The NEAC's composition did not reflect anything like the size or diversity of private sector, governmental organizations, and NGOs incorporated into the NECCs. Formed in May 2009, the ten-member body was chaired by Amirsham Aziz, who had been in charge of the EPU during Badawi's administration. Yet economic expertise and professional independence were more acute considerations this time. Council members comprised an impressive array of distinguished professional economists from major financial, government, and academic institutions from around the world and within Malaysia.[22] Indeed, such was the complexion of this new advisory body that it rekindled a measure of hope among reformist forces that some contentious issues that proved impossible to address in the past might be addressed this time.

Yet because of the composition of the NEAC it was primarily self-reliant in formulating its analysis and policy recommendations—both through their own expertise and their formal and informal networks of advisors.[23] Consequently, while there were overtures from various organizations and individuals seeking to have input in the lead-up to the NEAC's first report (NEAC 2010b), the NEAC exercised its discretion about whom it received or sought views from. There were selective consultations with business groups and the chambers of commerce, according to NEAC secretary Norma Binti Mansor. Later there was also an open call on the NEAC website for feedback through the Internet on issues concerning growth, the environment, and social structure. The input this attracted appeared to be largely from professionals, and was viewed by the NEAC as validating the direction the report was already taking.[24]

Following the release of that report, though, a wide range of consultations opened up to include forums, briefings, seminars, dialogues and online and in-person submissions.[25] A reported 11,000 Malaysians were involved through consultations with private companies, trade unions, political parties, executive councils of state legislatures, senior civil servants, and members of assorted civil society organizations (Lesley 2014, 9). During this time, Pemandu was tasked with refining the broad strategic directions of the NEM, referred to as Strategic

Reform Initiatives (SRI) in the first report.[26] To this end, after some directions from the NEAC, Pemandu conducted eight labs and a series of related sub-labs for each of the SRIs and determined who participated in these exercises.

Pemandu also embarked on a separate exercise facilitating the identification of the priority growth sectors for the ETP. The NEAC did not think it should be involved at this level of advice, lest it be seen to be involving itself in "picking winners."[27] Thus, in May 2010, Pemandu convened a "Thousand Person Workshop." This began with twenty mini-workshops, each comprising between thirty and seventy participants, covering twenty different sectors and including participants from the private sector, civil servants, and select civil society organizations (Pemandu 2010, 76). A subsequent series of labs beginning in June would lead not just to the announcement of the twelve National Key Economic Areas to drive the economic transformation,[28] but also to the launch of the ETP roadmap in October that year (Lesley 2014, 10–11).

However, not all consultations were equally significant or influential, and Pemandu gave special emphasis to engaging with the business community. Indeed, according to Idris, the ETP was "co-created by the private sector," explaining how 350 private sector and 150 public sector people worked together in an eight-week lab to fundamentally shape the reform program (quoted in Daly and Singham 2011). Only the best-resourced companies could commit their staff full-time to these labs.[29]

Crucially, in conjunction with the assorted consultative initiatives to refine sectoral priorities and related implementation strategies, a more fundamental dynamic had been precipitated by the NEAC's March report. Long-standing and rising conflicts over distributional and governance issues were reignited.

The report acknowledged the challenge of rising inequality, observing that the bottom 40 percent of Malaysian households experienced the slowest growth in average income. Echoing earlier NECC calls, it recommended a higher-productivity and higher-technology activities growth strategy involving consumer and producer subsidies, increased competition, and arresting corruption—but more extensively and effectively than implemented thus far. This meant "pushing ahead with liberalization will need to be complemented by a system that recognizes and rewards merit" (NEAC 2010b, 89).

The NEAC also revisited the most sensitive of issues that embroiled the NECCs, regarding the need to "strike a balance between the special position of *Bumiputera* and legitimate interests of different groups" (10). This required "market-friendly affirmative action programmes" targeting the bottom 40 percent in ways boosting "the capacity and capability of low-income households and small businesses, instead of imposing conditions to meet specific quotas or targets" (10). Phasing out the 30 percent target for Bumiputera equity ownership was part of this reform direction. Ethnic-based quotas, the report argued, have "given rise to unhealthy and pervasive rent seeking and patronage activities which has overshadowed and irreparably harmed the meritorious performance of key affirmative action programmes" (92). An Equal Opportunities Commission was proposed, which would provide a basis for claims of discrimination against ethnic minorities.

Malay ethno-nationalists denounced such proposed departures from core NEP policies. The Malay Consultative Council—established in anticipation of the NEM and comprising seventy-six Malay-rights organizations and 1,500 members—emphatically rejected the direction chartered by NEAC technocrats (J. M. Nelson 2012, 50). The Council passed a 31-point resolution demanding the retention of the NEP's main policies. Ibrahim Ali, leader of the most strident and influential Malay nationalist NGO within the Council, Persatuan Pribumi Perkasa (Perkasa, Mighty Native Organization), declared the vote as also one of no confidence in Najib (*Malaysiakini* 2010b).

The threat to Najib's leadership and sustained lobbying did not fall on deaf ears. Most of the contentious proposals were not included in the *Tenth Malaysia Plan 2011–2015*, tabled in parliament on June 10, 2010. Among those omitted were the creation of an Equal Opportunities Commission and changes to affirmative action to "consider all ethnic groups fairly and equally as long as they are in the low income 40% households" (NEAC 2010b, 24). Part Two of the NEM, published in December 2010 (NEAC 2010a), also significantly watered down recommendations in Part One. It now recommended the retention of affirmative action for Bumiputeras, although with revisions and reformulations to render it more effective. The report sought "to encourage reward based on performance and to foster greater competition by removing excessive protection and promoting sectoral liberalisation" (80). However, there were no references to policies for ensuring meritocracy, to guarantee open tenders for government projects or changes to Bumiputera quotas (*Malaysiakini* 2010c).

NEAC member Zainal Aznam provided some insight into the pressure the council felt following the release of Part One and public attacks on key proposals. "This was the government's litmus test at this time," observed Zainal (quoted in Aidila 2011b). However, Cabinet instead failed the test, according to Zainal, listening to Malay nationalist groups and demonstrating no political will for required reforms. In this context, Part Two had reportedly been heavily censored, with some members particularly unhappy about removing the 30 percent Bumiputera equity reform proposal. Zainal also revealed that political reform that was meant to be in the NEM did not make it into print. He reflected: "I joined NEAC with hesitancy . . . I had serious doubts about how far the *BN* government is willing to go" (quoted in Aidila 2011b). The NEAC dissolved on May 31, 2011, handing over the task of reform implementation to Pemandu.

Against this background, underlying social and political conflicts over Malaysia's development model and governance would increasingly find expression through other, more independent, civil society expressions. This process would accelerate with Najib at the center of a scandal from early 2015 over alleged corruption involving One Malaysia Development Bank (1MDB). This scandal was possible in no small part due to the failures of the NECCs and the NEAC to result in reforms to governance institutions shaping Malaysia's particular variant of state capitalism and related political patronage practices.

Elites in Malaysia have periodically looked to new state-sponsored MOPs in an endeavor to contain conflict linked to capitalist development, its governance, and the social distribution of its costs and benefits. This has not only included friction between popular forces and elites over rising inequalities, but also among elites as the interests of different fractions of capital have diversified. However, these new MOPs have taken distinctive paths in Malaysia, involving less sustained initiatives in societal incorporation and more problematic attempts to harness technocratic consultative ideologies of representation compared with Singapore and the Philippines.

The NECCs were carefully crafted with the aim of ensuring that societal incorporation reinforced prevailing structures of particularist representation. Indeed, elite appeals to technocratic consultative ideologies of representation were less rhetorical and more pragmatic. Nevertheless, forces inside and outside the ruling coalition attempted to exploit these new MOPs for more expansive reforms than BN leaders anticipated. Various interests served by the idea that Malay political dominance and state promotion of a Bumiputera business class are essential to redressing social and material inequalities perceived this as threatening and responded accordingly.

Yet the subsequent retreat from NECC consultative representation institutions and some of the contentious reform agendas generated by them did not mean the disappearance of underlying tensions over policy directions and governance regimes. Indeed, these intensified to such a point that the BN's electoral position had become seriously threatened by 2008. Moreover, this was accompanied by an escalation of Malaysians adopting civil society expression through mass demonstrations to try and advance reform.

In this context, resolving constraints to Malaysia's transition to a higher value-added and higher-wage economy became a BN priority. This resulted in a new strategy under Prime Minister Najib to try to harness technocratic consultative representation, both through feedback mechanisms of administrative incorporation and through establishing a new economic advisory council dominated by internationally reputed business experts. Yet while these initiatives made it possible for a revisiting of contentious policy issues hitherto unaddressed, the same Malay nationalist coalitions that thwarted reform under the NECCs again prevailed. Najib and his Cabinet colleagues demonstrated no more political will for major reform than his predecessors.

In Malaysia, state-sponsored extraparliamentary MOPs have thus emerged but never consolidated, extended, or diversified on anything like the same scale as in Singapore and the Philippines. In these regimes, consultative and particularist ideologies and institutions of representation have been more easily reconciled with the coalitions of interest embedded in relationships of state power.

This contrast is especially evident when comparing Malaysia with Singapore, where authoritarianism coexists with a different variant of state capitalism. In Singapore, a more cohesive set of politico-bureaucratic elite material and political interests have been collectively well served by institutions and ideologies of consultative representation championing policy consultation processes. Existing technocratic elite power and related ideas about meritocracy have been rationalized and shored up by these institutions and ideologies. It helps also that ethnic Chinese account for three-quarters of Singapore's population and dominate economic, political, and social power. Consequently, particularist ideologies of ethnicity and religion have been relatively easily accommodated to further entrench political fragmentation without risking serious challenges to existing power relations.

Importantly, the greater difficulty of institutionalizing state-controlled societal incorporation in Malaysia increased the likelihood of independent MOPs emerging to contest the limits of political contestation intended by the BN. As the next chapter explains, this has profoundly shaped the struggle over political representation in Malaysia.

9

CIVIL SOCIETY AND ELECTORAL REFORM IN MALAYSIA

The Malaysian political regime and capitalist model are premised on the notion of ethnic Malay political supremacy. This has made it difficult to depoliticize conflict through broad-based societal incorporation and consultative representation, as was emphatically demonstrated by the experiences of the National Economic Consultative Councils (NECCs) in 1989–1990 and 1999–2000. The political significance of this became more evident in the mid-2000s as contradictions between official ideologies and concrete outcomes of sustained capitalist growth intensified. Urbanization, rising material inequalities, and heightened public concern about state corruption and power abuses translated to growing support for opposition parties.

It was in this context that new reformist coalitions emerged to challenge the strategic selectivity of electoral and related political institutions. One such coalition was the Bersih (Gabungan Philihantaya Bersih dan Adil, Coalition for Clean and Fair Elections) movement. From 2007, Bersih demanded reforms to improve the integrity of national electoral institutions. During this time, a coalition of civil society groups also began mobilizing for the reintroduction of local government elections. Both coalitions were, to differing degrees, multiracial but Bersih was particularly worrying for the ruling coalition, Barisan Nasional (BN, National Front), because it deployed mass public mobilization in defiance of restrictive regulations on such forms of political participation. The significance of the Bersih challenge increased after the BN only retained government at the 2008 elections due to electoral malapportionment.

Bersih and the local elections coalitions were a product of a political crisis that the BN coalition framework of racial and ethnic representation could no longer manage or contain. The roots of this crisis reflected deep structural changes in the post-Mahathir political economy, including the social impacts of the privatization of services and more precarious employment opportunities as technological upgrading proved elusive. Such developments fostered more critical reflection about the particularist ideologies rationalizing institutions critical to the prevailing distribution of political and economic power in Malaysia.

Social and material inequalities also posed new challenges for the political management of capitalism in Singapore and the Philippines. However, Malaysian elites were acutely dependent on particularist ideologies of representation to fragment competing political forces. They had learned from the NECC experiments in particular that seemingly technocratic institutions and ideologies of consultative representation risked debate over governance reforms at fundamental odds with the defining aspect of the post-1969 political regime: Malay political supremacy founded on patronage politics and related discretionary powers of state officials.[1]

In the ensuing struggle over ideologies and institutions of political representation, though, there would be no simple divide between the BN and its civil society and party political opponents, nor a clear contest between nondemocratic and democratic ideological camps. Instead, particularist and technocratic consultative ideologies had some currency among reformist forces, including in shaping competing notions of democracy. This complexity reflected the historical institutionalization of particularism and the continuing systematic obstruction of ideological challenges to it under authoritarian rule and a specific variant of state capitalism in Malaysia. Yet as capitalist development generated more socially diversified societies, political identities would multiply and single-issue politics proliferate. These forces could periodically combine to advocate for changes to political and governance institutions.

However, such coalitions also contained serious contradictions. It would thus become increasingly evident that Bersih's own social foundations—and its political origins in a limited initiative to recover cooperation among opposition parties—rendered it unable to link its push for institutional political reforms to a coherent alternative address of inequalities to the BN. Similarly, contrasting ideologies of representation—including particularist and discursive democratic— played a role in fragmenting the opposition coalition and civil society over the reform of local government.

National Electoral Reform Unites Civil Society

The failure of broad societal incorporation to take root in Malaysia meant that, as tensions associated with Malaysia's capitalist development intensified, other modes of participation (MOPs) became more important sites of struggle over the permissible limits to conflict. What emerged was doubly troubling for the country's authoritarian leaders: growing recourse by BN critics and opponents to independent civil society expression, with strategic emphasis on street demonstrations, and a harnessing of this MOP by Bersih to demand reforms ensuring the democratic integrity of parliamentary elections and representation. These dynamics were all the more threatening to the regime because of the unprecedented degree to which different ethnic groups collectively mobilized around institutional reform demands.

Mass mobilization through street demonstrations had, of course, been a feature of *reformasi* (reformation), but that movement also contained tensions. Uniform disgust at systemic corruption and power abuse under the United Malays National Organization (UMNO) coexisted with both particularist and democratic ideologies of political representation. Consequently, infighting was periodic and peaked following September 11, 2001, and the advent of the War on Terror. Issues of religion and race were adeptly exploited by the BN to convincingly defeat the Barisan Alternatif (Alternative Front) opposition electoral coalition at the 1999 and 2004 polls (Weiss 2006, 127–61).[2] Yet emphatic reassertion of BN political hegemony also prompted opposition soul searching.

Against the background of the 2004 elections and a growing skepticism about Prime Minister Abdullah Badawi's rhetoric about governance reform, the leader of PKR (Parti Keadilan Rakyat, People's Justice Party), Anwar Ibrahim, brought together the three major opposition parties—Parti Islam Se-Malaysia (PAS, Pan-Malaysian Islamic Party), Democratic Action Party (DAP), and Parti Keadilan Rakyat (PKR, People's Justice Party)—toward a shared agenda across secularist and Islamic groups. Meetings began in July 2005 in search of what DAP participant Liew Chin Tong described as "some common denominator, some lowest hanging fruit, where all parties could agree."[3] The outcome was the establishment of the Joint Action Committee for Electoral Reform, officially launched as Bersih in November 2006 by a coalition comprising five opposition parties, twenty-four nongovernmental organizations, and the Malaysian Trades Union Congress. As PKR vice-president Chua Tian Chang (popularly known as Tian Chua) explained, these groups "put aside their ideological differences, put aside complex governance issues, to say: 'we just want free and fair elections.'"[4]

Impediments to free and fair elections were deep, systemic, and longstanding (H. H. Lim 2005). As Tsun Hang Tey observed, the BN "enlists a multi-pronged approach to stack the decks in its favor: legislative sculpting, behavioral conditioning in the Election Commission [EC] and exploitative use of the state machinery to aid its campaigning efforts" (Tsun 2010, 5). This included gross electoral malapportionment and gerrymandering favoring BN parties and UMNO in particular. The former is fundamental to the way that electoral institutions are strategically selective, systematically biased to favor ethnic political representation.

The Malaysian constitution provides for an unspecified "measure of weightage" toward rural votes.[5] This has led to massive discrepancies between urban and rural seats, in some cases up to tenfold.[6] While weightage does not formally favor any particular party, support for UMNO is strongest among ethnic Malay and other Bumiputera voters, who are especially concentrated in many rural districts. In practice, variable electorate weightings by the EC have decidedly partisan effects resulting consistently in smaller, overrepresented BN districts (Ostwald 2013; H. G. Lee 2015).

Bersih began its campaign in 2007, with four limited reform demands: a cleanup of the electoral roll; the use of indelible ink to identify electors who have voted; the abolition of postal voting; and equal access to government-controlled media for opposition parties (Aeria 2012, 340–41). Following unproductive meetings with the EC, activists from PAS argued successfully within Bersih that only through popular action would their demands be taken seriously. PAS boasted the most extensive, albeit religious-based, collective organizational capacity for mass action. Subsequent to a five-month road show to prepare the ground for mass mobilization, demonstrations at four different locations in Kuala Lumpur on November 11 attracted an estimated 40,000–60,000 supporters to what authorities deemed an illegal gathering. Police employed tear gas and water cannons, arresting forty-six protesters during or following the assemblies (H. G. Lee 2008, 198). PAS's organizational role in this mobilization was pivotal,[7] but a hallmark of the demonstrations now was the far greater extent of cross-ethnic participation compared to the earlier *reformasi* movement (Case 2010, 109).

Within weeks, another banned rally by the newly formed Hindu Rights Action Front (HINDRAF) attracted around 30,000 protesters.[8] HINDRAF's concerns were not explicitly about electoral institutions, including instead the demolition of Hindu temples and acute general structural discrimination and socioeconomic marginalization among ethnic Indians. Yet HINDRAF's emergence and modus operandi raised further questions about the effectiveness of the BN's framework of ethnic political representation.[9] Crucially, by endorsing this struggle, Anwar rejected "the prevailing Malay-Muslim sentiment which treated the HINDRAF challenge as a threat to the dominance of Islam" (Mohamad 2008, 452). A Malay leader standing up for the rights of the most marginalized non-Malays power-fully symbolized how an address of concerns by a particular ethnic group need not require ethnic representation (455) but might instead be achieved through democratic representation.

Meetings between the EC and Bersih then resumed, resulting in a commitment to introduce indelible ink at the next general elections. However, when this undertaking was reneged on just four days ahead of the March 2008 polls, suspicions of planned cheating intensified (Liew 2013, 302). This aided the opposition cause, adding to popular concerns about rising living costs, reduced government fuel subsidies, highway toll charges, job insecurity, corruption, rising crime in urbanized areas, and the rights of minority ethnic communities (H. G. Lee 2008; Welsh 2013b).

The 2008 election returned stunning results, the BN losing its two-thirds par-liamentary majority for the first time,[10] while the opposition's seats jumped from just 10 percent to more than a third of the 222 federal seats. The opposition also secured a record five state governments. It also won ten out of eleven seats in Kuala Lumpur, but the city is administered as a federal territory by the federal govern-ment. The BN's vote dropped in all states, but the drift of non-Malay and urban voters accounted for the most decisive swings against it.[11] This would result in a further strengthening of UMNO's ascendancy within the BN, and its subsequent adoption of more assertive Islamic and ethnic Malay particularist ideologies and policies (Hamid and Razali 2015). By contrast, Maznah Mohamad (2008, 443) argued that the opposition's capacity to obtain "optimum multiethnic con-sensus" was fundamental to its gains, opening up "unprecedented political possibilities."

Anwar was ineligible to contest the March elections owing to his earlier pros-ecution, but when that ban expired he entered federal parliament in August 2008 through a by-election. With Anwar now leading the Pakatan Rakyat (PR, People's Alliance) opposition coalition in parliament, the political possibilities thus be-came more worrying for the ruling coalition. Berih would also be integral to ex-ploring those possibilities, but this would entail a new division of labor between party political and civil society activists in the strategy for electoral institutional reform. However, the most important measure of this strategy's challenge to the prevailing political regime would be the extent to which Bersih could build a move-ment juxtaposing a democratic ideological alternative to ethnic and religious par-ticularism. Or would Bersih be unable to go beyond agreement on low-hanging fruit?

Contention over Local Elections

Apart from Bersih and its national electoral reform agenda, there was also cooperation among civil society actors for the reintroduction of local elections—though follow-through with this commitment would see some of the first signs of contention between reformers. In the 1960s, the ruling Alliance, headed by UMNO, found it hard to reproduce its federal and state electoral successes at local government level—especially in areas with ethnic Chinese concentrations supporting the DAP. Consequently, local elections scheduled for 1965 and 1966 were suspended (B. L. Goh 2005, 56). Confrontation with Indonesia, following the formation of Malaysia, was the official reason given by the federal government for this move. Subsequently, twenty councils were discontinued and taken over by state governments (Tennant 1973, 355; B. L. Goh 2005, 57).[12]

The Local Government Act, introduced in 1976 by the federal government—now led by UMNO's new Barisan Nasional coalition—did not seek to restore local elections, against the recommendation of a 1968 Royal Commission of Enquiry into local government chaired by Senator Athi Nahappan. Instead, appointment of local government councilors became important to political patronage dispensed by the ruling coalition and a mechanism by which federal and state bureaucracies and political parties exerted control locally (Wong, Chin, and Othman 2010, 941). In the process, ethnic and racial-based systems of control and distribution of economic and social resources were ideologically and structurally promoted. The DAP long maintained its opposition to the suspension of local elections. However, the expansion of urban-based middle class NGOs in ensuing decades generated additional pressure for local elections reform in the approach to the 2008 general elections. Yet there would be contention between PR and NGOs over how and why any reforms would take place.

The PKR 2008 manifesto stated that "in line with creating greater accountability, local elections will be immediately restored to take back the constitutional right of Malaysians to choose only the best and most responsible leaders for their local municipalities." PAS's manifesto omitted reference to local elections; however, it joined the DAP and PKR in endorsing *The People's Declaration*, penned by civil society actors, which included demands that government "re-introduce elections for local government so that leaders can be made accountable" (Centre for Public Policy Studies 2008).

Following large gains at the 2008 polls by the BN's opponents, the formation of PR coalition governments in Penang and Selangor appeared a perfect opportunity for NGO-party cooperation on local representation reform. Instead, it became evident that the attractions for political parties and NGOs in such reform differed. Who local governments should be accountable to and exactly what checks and balances were required to achieve this proved contentious. This was reflected not just in contrasting degrees of urgency about local elections and strategies for achieving them, but also in the role of party-political versus civil society actors in accountability processes.

Malaysia's evolving and complex federalism significantly shapes the context within which state governments and political parties adopt positions on how local government councilors are determined. Under the BN, there has been growing centralization of power by federal authorities at the expense of state governments, whose tax bases are generally narrow and primarily linked to land (Phang 2008). Meanwhile, development funds have gravitated toward local authorities entrusted with administering basic services delivery, some of which is the result of privatizations enacted by the federal government. Consequently, some local authority budgets constitute a substantial portion of total state government budgets and commercial contracts awarded (A. Khoo 2010, 76). Relations with local government therefore significantly mediate access to, and control over, resources by state governments and their component parties. Understandably, for PR state governments, therefore, the complexion of local councils would be pivotal both to curtailing corruption and to implementing development plans and policies.

By contrast, for middle class NGOs, the principal aim was to subject governance reforms and development plans to wider societal accountability and influence, wherein they would play a critical role. As Bersih steering committee member Maria Chin Abdullah (2008, 5) explained, "By not having elected councilors, this effectively takes away the right of the citizen to have some form of local check and balance." Significantly, she elaborated that "election is only a form towards accountability but the substantive change will really depend on how effectively civil society remains the eyes and ears of council" (6).

Consequently, claims about the importance of nonparty-political and so-called independent actors at local government level were to become central to NGO criticisms of the PR's handling of local government reform. Not only did NGOs see themselves as transcending ethnic-based notions of political representation, but also as best placed to scrutinize party orthodoxies on development to produce a decisive break from the BN. For NGOs, party-political appointments to local councils could all too easily translate to cadre control.

A possible PR postelection reappraisal of local government reform was foreshadowed in its Common Policy Platform in December 2009. There was no specific mention of elections but of the need to "strengthen local government democracy and democratically enhance the competency and effectiveness of the delivery system and guarantee transparency at all levels" (*Pakatan Rakyat* 2009). A subsequent policy direction statement on priorities, should PR eventually secure federal power, also lacked explicit reference to local elections (*Pakatan Rakyat* 2010).

Speculation was rife that PAS was a leading reason for PR's lessening support for local elections (C. H. Wong 2009). In urban areas of PAS-held states, where a higher proportion of the population was Chinese, there was an increased chance that DAP rather than PAS candidates would be voted in.

Nevertheless, if the apparent watering down of the PR's position on local elections reflected differences within the coalition nationally, this didn't necessarily mean PR state governments in Penang and Selangor could not act more concertedly. In 2008, for instance, the Selangor government commissioned leaders of the Coalition for Good Governance (CGG), which comprised a membership of forty-eight NGOs, to investigate and recommend on how local elections could be implemented. The report was submitted in June 2009 (Khoo, Wong, and Chin Abdullah 2009). Chow Kon Yeow, the Penang State executive councilor responsible for local government elections, also created the Local Government Elections Working Group for a similar purpose, membership of which included an activist from the human rights and social justice NGO Suara Rakyat Malaysia (SUARAM, Voice of the Malaysian People), and whose report was finalized by April 2009 (B. L. Goh 2009).

However, these reports were neither speedily nor comprehensively acted on. Instead, the Penang and Selangor governments participated in a protracted legal dispute over whether the federal EC could be required to conduct local elections in these states (Aidila 2010). Advocates of local elections pondered why so much faith was placed in the legal route. One *Malaysiakini* (2010a) contributor described how many in civil society felt: "We are tired of your lame excuses. If the Election Commission cannot help to organize these elections, then go and get some other people to monitor it. There are so many other independent watchdogs around the world."[13]

Meanwhile, the EC maintained that although it could not be involved in local elections, how state governments select councilors was up to them (Himanshu 2012). While the legal process ran its course, PR governments in Penang and Selangor embarked on landmark decisions to depart from BN tradition and include NGOs and professionals among its appointments in 2008 and beyond.

Penang

As early as April 2008, a coalition of more than forty Penang-based NGOs formed to engage the DAP-dominated PR state government over attempts to promote principles of popular political participation, transparency, accountability, sustainability, and social justice. The appointment of NGOs representatives to the

two Penang municipal councils, it was contended, would assist in this. It was observed by councilor Francis Loh that the most valuable role of NGOs was in
"highlighting issues," many of which can only be addressed at federal and state
rather than municipal levels.[14] Essentially, the NGO pitch was for a role in discursive
representation (Dryzek and Niemeyer 2008).

NGOs in Penang proposed that council appointments should be equally split
between three categories, namely, NGOs, professionals, and politicians. Although
this was an ambitious claim, the government indicated that ten NGO representatives would be incorporated in the first appointments in April 2008. By the government's own calculations, it subsequently made just seven NGO appointments
across the two councils.

The appointments were criticized by the CGG as "undemocratic and non-
transparent, and lacking public consultation." It contended not only that the
qualifications of partisan political appointments were unclear, but "further,
amongst the small contingent of seven non-partisan representatives, the over-
representation of commercial interests (five members) *vis-à-vis* non-commercial
non-governmental organisations (two members) is completely unacceptable"
(quoted in *Star* 2008). The 2009 appointments were equally disappointing for
NGOs. SUARAM lamented that the PR government had diminished rather than
enhanced the "participation of local, independent people" and missed an opportunity to implement a "transparent system of appointment of councillors"
(SUARAM 2009).

Against the background of such disappointing council appointment rounds,
the NGO coalition conducted the Penang Forum 3 in November 2010. This involved a mock election for Penang residents to vote for ten civil society nominees
to serve as councilors in 2011, a process that incorporated a modest 284 voters
(S. H. Tan 2010). Significantly, each candidate was required to declare that they
neither held office in a political party nor in a chamber of commerce (Hector 2010).

However, in January 2011 only two of the ten successful Penang Forum nominees were appointed to the councils. Meanwhile, party political appointments
totaled forty-one of the forty-eight appointees. Five of the seven NGO appointments continued to involve business representatives (*The Star* 2011). Chow had
earlier alluded to divergences within PR on the NGO representation: "It is not
that I do not want to fulfill the quota, but you must know that I do not run the
government alone" (quoted in Loone 2010). Internal government debate was likely
not just to have given expression to pressures to consolidate or extend party political appointments, but also reflected which nonparty-political appointments
made most strategic sense for economic development plans.

This was precisely what alarmed many NGO activists. According to one such
activist and councilor, Lim Kah Cheng, "PR wasn't trying to block NGOs but they

share the same economic vision of what they want for the state . . . same framework and ideology as business when it comes to development."[15] Disquiet about the shared development model of the government and business interests in Penang was thematic among contestants' manifestos in the Penang Forum 3 mock election (*Aliran* 2010). It was also the focus of the December 2011 Penang Forum 4.

However, increasing NGO criticisms and scrutiny inside and outside the council over development projects did not result in any revision of the logic and character of its NGO appointments by the Penang government. On the contrary, Chief Minister Lim Guan Eng responded by challenging claims to political independence by some NGOs. Meanwhile, Chow contended that nobody has a "monopoly as to what an NGO is" (quoted in Loone 2010), with commerce-related NGOs representing "an important section of society."[16]

Significantly, public debate did not extend to more extensive scrutiny of what specific issues or social segments might be best served through particular NGOs on councils or local government. This would be required to fully evaluate NGO claims to authentic representation of wider interests. English-educated middle-class actors dominated the NGOs debating Chow and other government politicians. But what were the issues that mattered to members of the many Chinese-educated associations of the working class and to petit bourgeois elements in the Penang society? Did they simply mirror the concerns presented at the Penang Forum? This was more difficult to ascertain. Questioned about the importance of local elections to these communities, councilor Lim Kah Cheng, for instance, admitted to not having any confidence about it: "We live in two different worlds."[17] It was this separation of NGO demands from such social bases that limited NGOs' ability to effectively counter the influence of either intraparty or private business interests over the complexion of local government appointments.

Selangor

In Selangor, the PR government committed to a quota of 25 percent NGOs and professionals for its 288 appointments to local councils. However, as NGO activists saw it, this target would prove increasingly illusory. According to Tan Jo Hann, chairman of the Coalition of Non-Governmental Organisations and Professional Appointed Councilors (CONPAC), formed in November 2009, just seventeen NGO representatives were appointed councilors in the first term (2008–2009), rather than the anticipated seventy-two, and that number fell to just ten in the subsequent term (Henry 2011).

Disenchantment with the process was so strong that in July 2010 CGG and CONPAC publicly handed Selangor's chief minister, Khalid Ibrahim, a memo describing the level of NGO/professional appointments as a "far cry" from the promised quota (J. H. Tan 2010). CGG's chairman, Jeffrey Phang, asserted that "if we do not respect this NGO quota, what we are really saying is that we are taking this voice of conscience out of the council. There will be no person that is independent inside it" (Pusat Komas 2010). The underlying premise was that party political appointees are less likely to look at issues on merit.

However, the latitude for NGO seats was necessarily conditioned by what Ronnie Liu, state executive councilor for Local Government, Research, and Development, explained as the overarching formula by which his government allocated council seats among component parties.[18] This took into account the proportion of state seats won by the DAP, PAS, and PKR; gender representation; and ethnic composition of appointments. CONPAC's Tan Jo Hann observed that "political parties are under a lot of pressure from grassroots leaders who are suggesting their people for positions and threatening to withdraw their support otherwise" (quoted in Aidila and Wong 2010). In this context, the "parties cannot touch each other's quotas so they dig into the NGO quota" (J. H. Tan, quoted in Aidila and Wong 2010). Owing to their limited social bases, NGOs were ill-equipped to issue countervailing threats.

What civil society actors did instead was harness the Local Government Act 1976 to their cause. Derek Fernandez, Petaling Jaya city councilor and CONPAC committee member, highlighted that the act makes no mention of political party eligibility. Rather, it refers to experience in local government affairs; having achieved distinction in any profession, commerce, or industry; or demonstrated ability to represent the interests of local communities. Indeed, Fernandez maintained that local government problems were primarily the result of a lack of professionals such as accountants, engineers, lawyers, and others capable of scrutinizing decisions and giving independent judgment guided by professional ethics (Pusat Komas 2010). Richard Yeoh, Petaling Jaya city councilor and Transparency International Malaysia activist, also protested that eligibility requirements of the Local Government Act 1976 and associated emphasis on meritocracy were being sidestepped.[19]

Consequently, some NGO activists submitted technocratic or instrumentalist arguments to advance their case for different representation. Whether this was a tactical or ideological approach is not clear, but what was being advocated was expertise to ensure effective governance rather than political authority derived from constituencies' endorsement to act on their behalf. Either way, from Liu's perspective, such arguments open a Pandora's box of unsustainable expectations: "If you insisted there must be an NGO there then how about the lawyers, how about the doctors, how about the architects? No end to it."[20]

Mirroring the pattern of contestation in Penang, NGO complaints extended to councilor appointment processes. Proposals by the CGG on how the Selangor government could circumvent the EC to hold elections emphasized a "people-oriented selection process" (Khoo, Wong, and Chin Abdullah 2009, 22). It was envisaged that a Selangor Local Government Selection Commission would be formed, comprising academics and nonpartisan civil society activists, as an interim measure prior to full council elections (23–24). This measure never transpired.

Unsuccessful attempts to conduct trial elections in both Selangor and Penang further underlined reticence within the respective PR governments about any dilution of party control over council appointments.[21] Apprehension about elections—trial or otherwise—was most intense within PAS, where concerns about the implications for ethnic representation compound anxieties over party patronage issues.

Kelantan and Kedah

In the PAS-dominated PR governments of the predominantly Malay rural states of Kelantan and Kedah, where middle-class NGOs were less prominent, there was nothing like the controversies in Selangor and Penang over local elections. NGOs were active but not on this issue, and also more closely aligned to political parties than in Selangor and Penang.

Despite PAS having been in office since 1990 in Kelantan, it had shown no interest in local elections during this time. Moreover, some in PAS pointed to Kelantan as purported evidence that local elections were not essential for good government in Selangor (C. Chan 2010). There was NGO pressure on the Kelantan government after the 2008 elections. However, this mainly came from pro-BN groups who mobilized around civil service employment priorities, water management, housing, religious laws, and land administration (Kaos 2012; *Bernama* 2012).

There was no local elections push either from the new Kedah government, whose chief minister, Azizan Razak, declared: "I do not see the need to restore local council elections. It's easier to get things done as councillors are our own people" (*New Straits Times* 2010). According to Azman Ismail, PKR federal member of parliament (MP) for Kuala Kedah, when the local elections issue is raised within the Kedah government, "we are told UMNO used to do this, there were quotas for MIC and MCA etc. We are too scared to run away from these (old policies)" (quoted in Aidila 2011a).

Meanwhile, PAS central committee member Khalid Samad maintained that any move to revive local elections must address the issue of Malay and non-Malay councilors: "I do not agree with racial politics but this will be the area that Barisan will attack us" (quoted in Al Jafree 2013). However, while Khalid asserted that he did not support "racial politics," others within PAS were more sympathetic to BN-fostered particularist representation. Indeed, this was an early public indication of a looming fragmentation of PAS into progressive and conservative factions.[22]

The attempted reintroduction of local elections was therefore accompanied by tensions not only between NGOs and PR, but also within and between the PR parties. NGOs harbored elements of technocratic and discursive ideologies of representation. These worldviews contrasted with pragmatic considerations internal to the PR, born of the need to contend with the pervasive effects of a political economy shaped by decades of BN federal rule. Importantly, tension within and between PR parties over race and religion as bases for electoral representation would become more evident as Bersih's rise failed to address the very inequalities Malaysia's particular variant of capitalism helped to create.

Bersih Gains Momentum

While the opposition's state electoral wins in 2008 led to some conflict between NGOs and PR over local government, it would also lead to NGOs being given a greater role in the national electoral reform movement. In the immediate aftermath of the 2008 elections, there was a lull in Bersih activity, despite it having grown by this time to incorporate over sixty religious, ethnic, consumer, student, women's, and pro-governance reform organizations (Weiss 2009, 755). Many of the leading party political and civil society activists involved were now members of state or federal parliament. Debate over how best to progress the agenda of electoral reform concluded that Bersih should become formally nonpartisan. A period of significant activism would follow, involving a broadening of the Bersih coalition, a ramping up of its national and federal electoral reform demands, and a reduced ability by authorities to blunt mass mobilizations. The extent to which these developments reflected or facilitated ideological opposition to particularist representation was unclear, however.

The strengthening and diversification of popular support that accompanied Bersih's new strategy was fueled in significant part by conflicts generated by unfolding social, economic, and political contradictions of Malaysian capitalist development. This included raised utilities and services costs acutely felt by working and lower middle classes of all ethnicities as a result of privatizations boosting UMNOputera capital accumulation strategies. Conflict over these contradictions added impetus to the range and causes of middle-class NGOs expanding with urbanization arising from Malaysia's economic growth—especially in Kuala Lumpur and Penang.

PR parties would still be critical support bases for any Bersih demonstrations. However, PKR's Tian Chua explained that it was decided that national "electoral reform should be taken up by civil society as we are now running governments."[23] From early 2009, opposition parties were thus less directly involved with Bersih, officially relaunched in April 2010 as Bersih 2.0. Crucially, the key drafter of the communiqué for Bersih 2.0, Wong Chin Huat, emphasized how the reform agenda had to be limited to pursuing procedural democracy: "It is not our job to go into the field of policy because that's the room for parties to compete."[24]

It was on this basis that Bersih 2.0 sought to reengage the EC, but again with little progress, despite the government being led from April 2009 by new prime minister Najib Razak. Moreover, the conduct of the April 2011 Sarawak state election led Bersih 2.0 organizers to schedule a March for Democracy demonstration for July 9 that year. Reform demands were now increased to eight, adding a minimum of twenty-one days for campaigning; a strengthening of public institutions; no corruption; and no dirty politics. These demands were endorsed by sixty-two NGOs, a coalition of advocacy groups for an assortment of causes—including good governance, environmentalism, consumer rights, women's rights, education, welfare and feminism—encompassing secular organizations and others organized around discrete ethnic, religious, and cultural identities.

The demands and the modus operandi of this coalition promoted democratic ideologies of representation and accountability in calling for less constrained electoral competition and insisting on the right to civil society protest action. However, the extent to which a democratic regime should ideologically and structurally facilitate challenges to existing inequalities of power was not debated while Bersih's focus remained confined to electoral institution reforms. What united this coalition was a shared desire to ensure that voters could hold the BN to account, a position that could be arrived at from a variety of liberal, democratic, and moral ideological perspectives (Rodan and Hughes 2014).

Although authorities refused a rally permit for the March for Democracy, in a seeming act of conciliation the government subsequently suggested approving a meeting in Kuala Lumpur's Merdeka Stadium, away from central city streets. However, it then abandoned this proposal, arresting 270 people for wearing Bersih's distinctive yellow T-shirts, printing or possessing Bersih posters, or promoting Bersih demands at public gatherings. On July 1, 2011, Bersih was also declared an illegal organization. To limit access to inner city Kuala Lumpur, roads were blocked and train stations closed, while civil servants were warned not to participate in the march. Despite such intimidation, demonstrators fronted the streets, contending with water cannons, tear gas, and other police aggression. Organizers

estimated 50,000 demonstrators, which was likely closer to reality than the police estimate of 10,000. Police arrested 500 demonstrators, with at least the same
number estimated to have been injured (Y. H. Khoo 2015).[25]

No less striking than protesters' courage was the increased diversification in
Bersih's support base. The re-arrest of Anwar on sodomy charges leading up to
the rally contributed to a spike in urban—especially Malay—youth participation
in seemingly spontaneous action, including extensive use of social media (Aeria
2012, 343; Weiss 2013). PAS grassroots organizations continued to be most important to mobilizations, but urbanized Malay students played a significant role
through smaller and less structured groups, which, according to one Bersih organizer, "are like mushrooms—very seasonal. They will not be there forever, but
if you have a good cause they will come out again."[26] Meanwhile, Bersih also
attracted increased participation from non-Malay students and middle-class
elements (K. M. Ong 2011).

Moreover, this rally saw the transformation of Bersih from a "very small coalition" to "a movement" that "woke a lot of people up," according to Maria Chin
Abdullah,[27] who became the head of Bersih 2.0 in 2013. The DAP's Liew Chin Tong
concurred, contending that of all the rallies before and including Bersih since the
mid-1990s, this "was the most effective in shaking the government."[28]

So shaken was the government that Prime Minister Najib subsequently announced a nine-member Parliamentary Select Committee (PSC) to recommend
on electoral reforms.[29] This appeared promising, despite five of the nine PSC members coming from the BN. The PSC report, tabled in April 2012, was also followed
by the EC indicating it would implement seven of the ten proposals, including
introducing indelible ink and cleaning up electoral rolls (Aeria 2012, 345; Ufen
2013, 7).

However, Bersih 2.0 leaders claimed the report neither adequately addressed
citizenship-for-votes deals nor roll manipulation, and lacked a reform implementation timetable. Following the refusal by the speaker of parliament to accept a
minority report by opposition members of the PSC, a third Bersih rally, backed
by eighty-four NGOs, was therefore held in April 2012 in Kuala Lumpur. Calls
extended now to the implementation of all previous eight demands before the next
general election, the introduction of international observers for that election, and
the resignation of the existing EC (Ufen 2013, 7). In a change of tactic, authorities abandoned extreme measures to block the rally, which attracted at least 100,000
demonstrators (Gooch 2012). Notwithstanding a Malay swing back to UMNO,
further decline in the BN's vote at the May 5, 2013, elections reduced the ruling
coalition's total vote share to just 47 percent, so that only extreme electoral malapportionment kept it in government.

Bersih had evolved into a formidable political movement, but also one that contained a complex array of social forces with varying grievances and goals. Indeed, asked how central the reform of electoral institutions was to rally attendees, Bersih organizer Wong remarked that "I'm not sure that would make up 10 percent: people who know clearly what that is, or would form a main part [of their motivation]. Then you have people who are generally not happy with the system . . . [as well as] people who want to end UMNO's rule."[30]

Conflicts over the uneven benefits of Malaysia's capitalist development had intensified. This created an opportunity for new political coalitions and mobilizations. This did not translate, though, to a coalescing of the government's opponents and critics around a shared democratic reform agenda and a subordination of particularist ideologies of representation to this.

Inequalities Intensify, PR Collapses

In the approach to, and following, the 2013 general election, rising material inequalities and costs of living were particularly important in generating anxieties among low and middle-income earners. As Weiss (2015) observed, opposition gains owed much to "rising costs of living, fear of declining opportunities, and an awareness of a growing chasm between those with an abundance and those with not enough." Bersih benefited from this dynamic, but the political limits of its exclusive focus on institutional reform, bypassing internal differences of material and ideological interests, would also be increasingly exposed.

By 2012, the total wealth of Malaysia's forty richest people was equivalent to 22 percent of the country's GDP, up from 15.7 percent in 2006 and boasting greater wealth than counterparts in Singapore and the United States (UNDP 2014, 48–49). In recognition of growing popular disquiet over rising inequalities, though, the BN introduced the Bantuan Rakyat 1 Malaysia cash assistance scheme for lower income households prior to the 2013 election. The amounts involved and the eligibility for this aid expanded over the next three years,[31] principally because many of the gains of this aid were being cancelled out or reduced by the effects of other government policies.

Public subsidies for electricity, tertiary education, petrol, and sugar were cut. Meanwhile, healthcare was being increasingly privatized, increased highway tolls were authorized, and retailers in city centers were contending with rising rental costs imposed by UMNO-linked conglomerates (P. Lee 2011; Rasiah, Abdullah, and Tumin 2011; H. G. Lee 2014, 9). A 6 percent goods and services tax (GST) was also introduced as heavy government borrowing prompted international ratings agency Fitch to downgrade Malaysia's fiscal outlook from stable to negative (Reuters 2013). Clamping down on state corruption and related political patronage was not part of the BN strategy to restore public finances (Netto 2014). In this atmosphere, street protests independent of Bersih occurred, including a 15,000 strong May 2014 anti-GST rally addressed by Anwar (Y. N. Yong 2014).

However, neither the PR coalition nor Bersih were equipped or inclined to harness this groundswell of popular concern about distributional issues to decisively blunt particularist ideologies and institutions of political representation. Indeed, particularist ideologies exerted significant influence among elements of the BN's opponents that did not diminish as Bersih progressed and the BN's electoral support declined. On the contrary, following the 2013 election, tensions grew within PAS and between PAS and the DAP. The latter now surpassed PKR as the largest opposition PR party by winning thirty-eight seats, while PAS had lost ground to BN in rural electorates and among the working class against a background of intensified UMNO communalist rhetoric (Welsh 2013b).

This, in turn, precipitated a reassertion of traditional Islamic religious values by PAS conservatives to shore up a declining Muslim vote base (Noor 2013, 99–103). The push was emboldened by the death in February 2015 of revered PAS spiritual leader Nik Aziz. Aziz had played a key role in limiting the influence of conservative *ulama* factions in the party, helping to bolster solidarity within the opposition bloc (*Malaysiakini* 2015c).[32] The jailing of Anwar in the same month now also robbed the PR of the requisite leadership and authority to contain tensions inherent to it.

The corollary was a successful strategy by PAS conservatives to take executive control of the party in June 2015 from progressives committed to the PR and Bersih.[33] PAS conservatives' opposition to the proposal that a woman, Wan Aziza Wan Ismail (Anwar's wife), take over as chief minister of Selangor's PR government combined with their increased resistance to the reintroduction of local elections to cause friction within the PR. Conservative PAS leader Abdul Hadi Awang directly invoked particularist ideologies to reject local elections, claiming they would "worsen racial inequality," "trigger instability," and lead to a repeat of the 1969 "race riots" (quoted in *FMT News* 2015). It was, however, the declared intention of PAS conservatives to enact the Islamic criminal code of *hudud* in Kelantan that brought an end to the PR in mid-2015.[34]

By September 2015, a reconstituted informal opposition coalition called Pakatan Harapan (PH, or Coalition of Hope) was established. This comprised the PKR, DAP, and the newly formed Parti Amanah Negara (Amanah/PAN, National Trust Party) set up by progressives who left PAS.[35] Meanwhile, UMNO sought to exploit this rift by encouraging PAS leaders to cooperate with it, playing up the centrality of ethnic and religious interests and identity as the basis of effective political representation (*The Star* 2015). Indeed, UMNO leaders had since the 2013 election indicated for the first time that if PAS wanted to push for *hudud* the government would seriously consider it (see R. K. Yang 2014; Hasbullah 2015).

The fragmentation among the BN's party political opponents had important implications for Bersih. The movement's strength and weakness had been its focus on institutional reforms emphasizing electoral fairness. Yet while some pro-testors sought to replace state political patronage and power abuse with merito-cratic governance systems, social and material inequality could not be effectively addressed by governance reforms alone. Indeed, potentially these inequalities might be exacerbated without more effective means of social redistribution to replace those of the New Economic Policy (NEP) based on ethnic discrimination.

Crucially, the proliferation of small single-issue NGOs alongside established religious and ethnic-based organizations involved in Bersih and the PR had shown no signs of providing social foundations for coalitions committed to a redistrib-utive agenda favoring the most disadvantaged. Class-based mobilization was not pursued because of the dominance of particularist ideologies and identities, re-flecting the success of UMNO over several decades in structuring social relation-ships and promoting worldviews that normalized this dominance. The biggest membership-based organizations involved were religious based, the rest a pleth-ora of small single-issue organizations led by the urban middle class. Conspicu-ously absent were sizeable or influential organizations representing the working class, or the influential involvement of such organizations in cross-class alliances.

The significance of this would become more evident with the advent in 2015 of Malaysia's biggest ever corruption scandals, involving Malaysian state capital-ism and Prime Minister Najib. Would the scandal prove a catalyst for decisively dis-crediting not just the ruling party but also the regime's defining power relationships and legitimating ideologies?

Fragmentation Hampers Response to 1MDB Scandal

Shortly after Najib became prime minister in April 2009, he established the gov-ernment company One Malaysia Development Bank (1MDB), projected as a creative state capitalist response to pressing structural economic challenges. However, by mid-2015, allegations of corrupt practices on a massive scale precipitated another episode of internal UMNO friction and a further round of Bersih demands and mass mobilizations. Yet, paradoxically, Bersih's largest ever mobilization would be marked by a diminished capacity for multiethnic participation. The scandal exposed Bersih's limitation as a democratic movement in the context of the Malaysian political economy: the lack of a socially redistributive reform agenda to address structural inequalities. The absence of such meant that UMNO's particularist ideologies of race and ethnicity would remain seductive for many disadvantaged Malays at this time of intense political crisis and polarization.

The scandal that embroiled Najib and 1MDB arose at a particular juncture in the structural evolution of Malaysian capitalist development. The manufacturing sector's share of gross domestic product declined from over 30 percent by the mid-1990s to 24 percent in 2008. It remained approximately at that level thereafter, consolidating a growing dependence on low-cost—especially foreign—labor as a basis of profits.[36] This low-skilled, low-productivity route reduced the expansion of better-paid, more skilled and professional employment, a problem Rasiah (2015, 95–96) attributed to policymakers being "mired in ethno-patronage politics and preoccupied with raising ethnic corporate ownership over upgrading technological capabilities." Impacts of the 2007–2008 global financial crisis further exposed how unlikely the official vision of Malaysia reaching developed country status by 2020 was (UNDP 2014).

Part of Najib's response was to establish 1MDB as a wholly government-owned company of the Ministry of Finance in 2009, its purported strategic function being to foster long-term economic development opportunities through global partnerships and foreign investment. Najib would exert a key influence as the chair of 1MDB's advisory board. From its inception, though, there were criticisms about a lack of transparency in 1MDB accounts, which later intensified amidst massive losses by the company (Pua 2010).[37] Far from forging new ground in higher value-added activities, 1MDB invested heavily in real estate and energy.

Major controversy erupted following reports in July 2015 by the *Sarawak Report* and the *Wall Street Journal* alleging that US$700 million originating in 1MDB had been deposited in Najib's personal bank accounts before the 2013 general election. An Australian Broadcasting Corporation documentary (ABC 2016) later revealed further transactions, concluding a total of US$1.03 billion was deposited in Najib's accounts one month prior to the election (see also Hope and Wright 2016). Investigations by crime authorities in the United States, Switzerland, and Hong Kong were also under way by early 2016, with Swiss investigators estimating that US$4 billion had been misappropriated by 1MDB (Hodge 2016). By mid-2017, estimates of alleged embezzlement and money-laundering had reached US$6.0 billion (*Straits Times* 2017).

The July 2015 reports sparked a sharp decline in the Malaysian ringgit and a BN political crisis.[38] Attorney General Abdul Gani Patail, who led the initial official investigation into the scandal, and Deputy Prime Minister Muhyiddin Yassin were soon replaced after calling on Najib to explain how such sums entered his accounts.[39] More extreme measures subsequently unfolded to contain challenges to Najib from inside and outside the ruling party. Meanwhile, Najib strategically shored up patronage networks within UMNO and the state to protect his own power (Amnesty International 2016; Berthelsen 2016; Case 2017).

Among the first responses to the scandal by opposition politicians was the filing of a suit against Najib and 1MDB for corrupt practices that compromised parliamentary elections, calling for the results of the 2013 election to be set aside. Bersih had already conducted a People's Tribunal in late 2013, compiling evidence of irregularities in the 2013 election. However, so outraged were many Malaysians by the new corruption allegations that Bersih's reform demands would now be significantly extended to include free and fair elections; a transparent government; the right to demonstrate; strengthening parliamentary democracy; saving the national economy; and Najib's resignation as prime minister.

This expanded institutional reform agenda to wider aspects of the de facto one-party state now highlighted the nexus between political and economic power more strongly. Strengthening the anti-corruption commission was, for example, not just relevant to illegal siphoning of money to political parties for electioneering but for investor confidence and economic performance. Bersih leader Maria Chin Abdullah thus declared that this fourth demonstration "will demand real democratisation to end corruption and save the economy" (quoted in Kow 2015).

The scandal compounded and crystalized varying feelings of injustice over existing elite rule that Bersih sought to capitalize on. Hence, the demand that Najib resign as prime minister was described by Bersih activist Wong Chin Huat as "a rally cry to attract the public" and thus purely "tactical."[40] According to PKR politician Tian Chua, people were "not so concerned just about electoral representation; the concern now is the wrong directions of the country and also social instability, the gap of economics, the social disparity, the increasingly lower middle class feeling a very heavy burden."[41] This appeal to all sections of society ideologically aligned with democratic representation, depicting diverse social conflicts and disparities as beyond problems of particular—especially ethnic—groups. However, Bersih's solutions remained principally institutional in nature, and this would prove insufficient to take full advantage of the BN political crisis to supplant particularist ideologies of representation.

Despite another rally ban and the blocking of websites, Bersih's fourth rally—during August 29–30 in the cities of Kuala Lumpur, Penang, Kuching, and Kota Kinabalu—attracted massive crowds over the two days. Estimated demonstrator numbers again varied wildly, put at 500,000 by Bersih organizers and 50,000 by police. Most independent estimates were at least well in excess of 100,000 in Kuala Lumpur alone (see Blakkarly 2015; *Malaymail* 2015). Nevertheless, PAS's refusal to mobilize support was politically costly for Bersih. According to one estimate, the Malay turnout was less than a fifth of the total, compared with more than half in the three previous rallies. UMNO leaders and supporters exploited this to depict Bersih as fundamentally a DAP-led ethnic Chinese exercise aimed at usurping power from Malays (Ikhwan 2015; *Malaysiakini* 2015b; Teoh 2015a). Meanwhile, some urban middle class Bersih supporters took to social media to question, and even mock, the commitment of ethnic Malays to reform (Hafidz 2015).

This rally was held prior to the formation of Amanah or the opportunity for ex-PAS progressives to develop new organizational bases. Indeed, according to one of those progressives, Dzulkefly Ahmad, "I still believe that the rank and file of PAS are with Bersih." Yet he also explained that, despite attempts to democratize PAS, it has a culture "of obedience and allegiance which are very tied up to cardinal doctrinal belief in Islam that you must respect—not just respect, you must obey your leader."[42] With conservative Islamists in firm control of PAS, Bersih's capacity to mobilize ethnic Malays—especially among the rural poor—was thus unlikely to return to earlier levels.

In any case, the failure of the fourth Bersih rally to maintain a high proportion of Malay participation prompted the most extreme elements of UMNO and defenders of the regime and its ideological rationale to ratchet up their efforts to combat and discredit Bersih—including by also taking to the streets. On September 16, 2015, authorities authorized a "red shirt" rally organized by the Malaysian National Silat Federation chaired by senior UMNO member Mohd Ali Rustam.[43] With at least 45,000 people in attendance,[44] speakers depicted Bersih as an unacceptable challenge to Malay political supremacy and religious beliefs, a view reinforced by Najib, who declared, "Malays have rights too . . . and we can rise up when our leaders are insulted, condemned and embarrassed" (quoted in Teoh 2015b).

Najib's rhetoric was soon backed by the passing in December 2015 of one of the most draconian measures ever in Malaysia—the National Security Council (NSC) Bill. Security is ill defined under the Bill, power concentrated in the prime minister as its chair, and any location can be declared a security area on suspicion of an offence within that area. The council could potentially contain various challenges to the prime minister—including from within UMNO—but was especially concerning for Bersih activists. It opened up new possibilities for blocking public meetings. Bersih was also concerned that declarations of security zones could potentially affect the conduct of elections (*Aliran* 2016b). Meanwhile, authorities intensified their recourse to assorted repressive legislations, not least the Sedition Act, to more generally intimidate critics and opponents of Najib, as well as journalists and public servants whose professional work was viewed as threatening to his political preservation (Nelson 2015).

The unfolding political polarization was all the more acute precisely because Bersih's Achilles' heel as a democratic movement was its separation from any substantive agenda, or serious debate thereof, to address inequality. This rendered both rural and urban Malays vulnerable to ruling elite pitches about the prospect of losing the benefits of special treatment in keeping with the spirit of the NEP. Despite the official end of the NEP, special treatment of Malays had in fact continued to expand since 1990 to include discounts and quotas for housing important to the poor, as well as preferential treatment for government procurement deals meted out to politically connected business elites (Pepinsky 2009, 120–21; Teoh 2015a).

Interviews with Bersih activists reveal an increasing awareness of this problem, but also formidable constraints to addressing it. Bersih leader Maria Chin Abdullah conceded that an alternative economic and social program was needed to assure the largest number of Malaysians that political change is in their interest. However, she also observed that "the movement is not going in that direction," but instead it was "focusing on civil liberties and not the economic issues."[45] Similarly, Liew observed that the limits to Bersih's strategy have been reached, because while "you can push and push and push on the democratization front. You will be confronted with this economic reality."[46] Moreover, according to Wong, Bersih activists remain committed to the "conscious decision not to take on institutional reform and political reform in one, which is in fact very attractive to some NGO activists."[47]

Resistance among NGOs to addressing the economic issue, despite its importance, reflects the dominance of liberal ideological notions of good governance and individual liberties as the basis of the critique of the BN regime. This dominance is understandable given the earlier decimation of organizational bases for social democratic and socialist critiques of the regime.

One departure from this division of labor involves Gabungan Bertindak Malaysia, established in 2011 specifically to address a wider range of issues than is common to most Malaysian civil society organization (CSOs) and NGOs. This nonpartisan, multiethnic, multifaith coalition comprises twenty-eight predominantly membership-based CSOs, dominated by middle-class professionals. Gabungan Bertindak Malaysia's fifteen-point charter embodies liberal values, with commitment to good governance topping the list. It also commits to "equitable distribution of wealth to eradicate poverty, end marginalization and ensure the welfare of the People," adding that "any affirmative action should be based on needs and not ethnicity" (quoted in Kamaruddin 2013). Absent, though, is any strategy for, or advocacy of, redistribution acknowledging the class basis of Malaysian society.

The inclination and capacity of opposition political parties to develop a comprehensive redistributive alternative program to the race-based NEP approach remained problematic too. The party whose support base is the most ethnically diverse is the PKR, but it was yet to develop any detailed nonracial redistributive alternative to the NEP either. This was despite Anwar Ibrahim having called for an end to the NEP before 2008 and repeatedly calling for this before his 2015 imprisonment. Meanwhile, the now leading opposition party, the DAP, principally champions liberal values of good governance, emphasizing merit against political patronage in resource allocation. Yet, as Liew poignantly notes of his own party, "The DAP has talked about meritocracy. But meritocracy is something that is not music to the ears of many Malays."[48] That was true during the proceedings of the 1989–1990 NECC and remained so.

These contradictions within the opposition and Bersih movement made it possible for Mahathir to lead a bipartisan group—comprising disaffected former UMNO MPs, opposition, and civil society figures—of signatories to a Citizens' Declaration calling for Najib's replacement as prime minister. Najib was grappling with the structural problems of a state capitalist model largely shaped by Mahathir. According to E. T. Gomez (2016), the resulting shifts in the sectors and interests emphasized were "extremely unproductive corporate activities" accompanied by more brazen corruption than ever alleged of Mahathir. Yet Najib's political discrimination in economic decision making was modeled fundamentally on Mahathir's development approach (Slater 2015; Lopez 2016).

Consequently, reformist forces were divided over the Citizens' Declaration, and whether the focus was now about reforming UMNO and the BN or the political regime and the exercise of state power (see Vekiteswaran 2016). To be sure, the declaration prescribed a host of institutional changes overlapping with Bersih's agenda to break down the one-party state. However, Mahathir had been instrumental in undermining the independence and integrity of most of those institutions—not least the judiciary and the EC.[49] The crucial point, though, was that Bersih's own limitations in advancing a democratic alternative to particularist ideologies had created the opportunity for Mahathir's attempted expropriation of the struggle precipitated by the corruption scandal.

Subsequent 2016 developments would see Mahathir and former deputy UMNO leader Muhyiddin link up with Bersih in its fifth rally to pressure Najib. The May Sarawak state election was shrouded in allegations of vote buying, gerrymandering, and malapportionment, but also abuse of government powers extending this time to banning PKR and DAP leaders from entering the state. Then in July the U.S. Department of Justice applied for seizure of US$1.4 billion of assets allegedly siphoned from 1MDB. This included more than US$700 million deposited in an account of a high-ranking official—referred to as "Malaysian Official 1." Confirming overwhelming public speculation, in early September the minister in the Prime Minister's Department, Ahmad Rahman Dahlan, conceded in interview that the official in question was Najib (Vaswani 2016).

Against this background, Bersih chief Maria Chin Abdullah announced on September 14 that there would be another street rally in Kuala Lumpur on November 19, preceded by a series of road shows across 246 cities and towns to raise aware-ness. Bersih's five demands again emphasized institutional changes and linked these to Najib's resignation.[50] Notwithstanding harassment from Red Shirt activists in the process (Kow 2016a), Bersih completed its convoy through Sabah and Sar-awak as well as Peninsula Malaysia. By now, the Red Shirts had also planned to rally in Kuala Lumpur on November 19 in opposition to Bersih's demands. Both rallies were banned, but it was Bersih that authorities concentrated their energies on, with at least thirteen of its activists detained on November 18—including Maria Chin Abdullah, who was detained under the Security Offences (Special Measures) Act (Kow 2016b).[51]

The Bersih demonstration nevertheless proceeded in defiance of authorities, as did that by the Red Shirts, albeit with some logistical challenges on the day as police blocked various roads (Kamal 2016). The Bersih turnout of around 40,000 fell short of aspirations, although it greatly exceeded estimated Red Shirt numbers of 4,000 (*Malaysiakini* 2016). Importantly, compared with the 2015 Bersih rally, there were more Malays in evidence, but not of the proportion achieved in earlier rallies. Projections of greater numbers of Malays in particular by Amanah and an-other new party established by Muhyiddin and Mahathir supported by others dis-illusioned with UMNO, Parti Pribumi Berastu Malaysia (PPBM, Malaysia United Indigenous Party), did not materialize. As *Malaysiakini* observed, "This once again proves that PAS is instrumental in mobilizing the rural heartland."

Significantly, as opposition parties looked to the next general elections, Ama-nah and PPBM expressed a desire to explore collaboration with PAS. However, while PAS indicated a preparedness to cooperate, it underlined its determination not to rekindle ties with the secularist DAP (*Malaysiakini* 2016). This underscored the continued tension between particularist and democratic ideologies of repre-sentation pervading party-political and civil society opponents of the BN. This was as much a consequence of the specifically liberal ideology of democracy on offer as it was the influence of historically embedded ideas about ethnicity and religion. Social democracy might theoretically coalesce different social and political forces opposed to the BN around a reform agenda to transcend this tension. However, there remained little or no prospect of that.

Instead, as speculation mounted about a general election being called well be-fore August 24, 2018, by which it had to be held, ethnic particularist representa-tion ideology assumed renewed importance in the opposition strategy to defeat the BN. The PPBM joined the PH and would run as a Malay—rather than multiracial—party in an attempt to woo support away from UMNO. Furthermore, Mahathir pointed out that he was the agreed chairman of PH; in effect, a "top dog" who would technically be prime minister-designate in the event of a PH victory

(Ghazali 2017a). He did qualify this, however, by indicating that if the people wanted Anwar as prime minister, he would accept that (Ghazali 2017b). Najib was sufficiently concerned about the ninety-two-year-old Mahathir's strategy to compete for the Malay vote that he set up a Royal Commission of Enquiry to investigate allegations of a cover-up pertaining to billions of dollars of foreign exchange losses by Malaysia's central bank in 1992, while Mahathir was prime minister.

As social and political conflicts associated with Malaysian development unfolded, heightened popular concerns about elite rule fueled a growing appetite for more independent extraparliamentary MOPs. Corruption and other abuses of state power and suppression of BN critics of such practices intensified. Importantly, the ideological rationale for ethnic Malay political supremacy also became increasingly at odds with concrete distributional realities. This laid the foundations for the Bersih movement and hopes among some social and political forces of a decisive break from particularist ideologies of political representation.

However, Bersih contained diverse and even contradictory reform aspirations that would limit its capacity and inclination to deliver on this promise. For some who supported Bersih, the good liberal governance and integrity of institutions were meant to ensure the triumph of individual merit as the basis for resource distribution. For others, this was problematic, as it equated merit with market utility and diminished or abandoned a social justice reform agenda to address inequality. The difficulty of Bersih in reconciling these agendas was no accident. It reflects the legacy of the Cold War and subsequent dynamics that militated against collective class-based organizations and social democracy gaining a foothold in the state, or outside it.

Yet as tensions and contradictions of Malaysian capitalism have mounted, a host of single-issue NGOs emerged alongside opposition parties to pose new challenges to the very institutions that define the prevailing MOP—including the local and national electoral systems. However, tensions remained between NGOs and their political partners and among the BN's party-political opponents. The technocratic and discursive forms of democracy promoted by NGOs in support of local elections did not sit well with either ideological or tactical exploitation of ethnic or religious particularism from within these parties. To be sure, there was significant liberal ideological alignment between reformist NGOs and the DAP, notably around the championing of meritocracy. However, this did more to block, than pave the way for, coalitions linking the amelioration of problems of social and material inequality with democratic ideologies and institutions of political representation. This problem Bersih had been unable yet to resolve or transcend.

Conclusion

CAPITALISM, INSTITUTIONS, AND IDEOLOGY

This book offers a new approach for comprehending struggles over political participation and representation as capitalism develops. Most distinctive about this framework, giving it potentially broad analytical purchase within and beyond Southeast Asia, is the way that it understands political institutions. These are viewed as inextricably related to broader societal struggles that define different capitalist systems and the complex of interests therein. In other words, the starting point of analysis must be how the political economy shapes institutions and their functioning.

It is this theoretical position that provides the basis of the book's most important contribution: *identifying*, *explaining*, and *evaluating* the significance of huge variations in the types of political participation, representation, and related accountability that have emerged in recent decades. Crucially, the modes of participation (MOP) framework advanced here is not constrained by notions of democratic or liberal transition through institutional reform, nor that regimes will either be democratic, authoritarian, or some suspended hybrid version of these ideal types. Instead, more open lines of enquiry enable it to observe that democratic and nondemocratic institutions and ideologies of participation and representation can be the basis of various political models, reflecting distinct power structures and interests linked to specific capitalist systems.

With focus on Singapore, the Philippines, and Malaysia, this book examined regime responses to emerging patterns in the many and varied conflicts accompanying capitalist transformations. A particularly striking theme is that the faster and more sustained capitalist development, the more pronounced and contentious material and social inequalities. This has generated real and potential regime legitimacy crises, creating pressures and opportunities, for elites and their opponents and critics alike, to push institutions of political participation and representation in new directions.

Indeed, institutional innovations that expand political space for participation and representation can also be instruments of elite control or vehicles of access and influence for political outsiders. Yet these different ends to which institutions are put are not simply because some institutions "work" while others do not. It is because institutions can work to protect the beneficiaries of existing power relations and related state structures, or work to open those relations up to contest and reform.

Moreover, everywhere specific histories mediate the ways that capitalism and political regimes articulate; and everywhere capitalist development generates new interests, threatens existing ones, and produces conflicts that require a political accommodation or response. Consequently, across a wide spectrum of authoritarian and democratic political regimes assorted new MOPs have been introduced.

The framework could thus equally be applied, for example, to explain the emergence and political significance of institutional initiatives and variations in Southeast Asian countries where capitalism has a more recent history, such as Cambodia, Vietnam, or Burma. It could also be more ambitiously drawn on to explain why similar political institutions serve different ends in Russia, Hungary, and the UK, for example. In all cases, we need to ask who promotes, supports, or opposes specific initiatives or reforms to political participation and representation, and why?

Applying the MOP framework to Singapore, the Philippines, and Malaysia concretely demonstrated *why* and *how* certain forms and ideologies of participation and representation emerged, involving different modes of political authority, cooption and control in each case. The wider relevance of these studies and the framework, though, is most apparent with regard to the institutional challenges posed by rising levels of inequality and related distributive conflicts inherent to capitalist development. This is a pressing and contentious reality across regime types, but it is conspicuously so for some of the most established liberal democracies. There disillusionment with existing political institutions and capitalist globalization has been reflected in increased support for populist ideologies of representation, especially those that seek strong political leadership at the expense of either new or old intermediary and representative political institutions.

Inequality and Institutions

Inequality is hardly a new problem in the political management of capitalism by elites. However, the advent and consolidation of neoliberal globalization marked a qualitatively new phase in market capitalism producing intensified inequalities. In the process, many of the redistributive social and economic policies that were a product of earlier reformist movements in liberal democracies have been diluted. The impact of state-initiated measures to contain inequalities in authoritarian regimes have also proven less effective in the face of new global capitalist dynamics.

And yet, heightened inequality is also forcing elites across all regime types to explore new institutional responses to protect their interests, as other social and political forces increasingly question or even reject existing political institutions of participation and representation. Indeed, some of the most creative explorations of new MOPs have been instigated by elites in authoritarian Singapore, where capitalist growth has been among the most dramatic and sustained in the world over recent decades.

The studies here of Singapore, the Philippines, and Malaysia not only demonstrated that the precise ways inequalities manifest and articulate with struggles over participation and representation necessarily vary. They also linked those differences to the social foundations and interests embedded in accumulation strategies of capitalism in each country. How capitalism is organized and controlled influences the way its costs and benefits are dispersed and ideologically rationalized or contested. Significant variations in the struggles over MOPs have sprung from these different political economy foundations.

Technocratic elites in Singapore were seen to be most active and creative in attempts to institutionalize consultative representation through both societal and administrative incorporation. The extensive powers of the politico-bureaucrats under state capitalism, and the broader political and social order crafted by the People's Action Party (PAP), have been consistently rationalized on the basis of technocratic merit. Little wonder that the mechanisms for incorporating groups and individuals through new parliamentary and nonparliamentary MOPs have been depicted as exercises in rational problem solving above politics. This has appealed, ideologically or tactically, to various social groups given constrained social and economic bases for independent civil society.

In a more contested struggle in the Philippines, a coalition of reformers sought to build institutions capable of arresting oligarchic power and related problems, not least of inequality, poverty, and corruption. However, oligarchs have been able to neutralize or hijack these institutions in ways that reflected their distinctive powers and interests through the state. Particularist ideologies of regionalism and ethnicity served oligarchs well in their strategies of exploiting the Party-List System to expand their dominance of Congress. Local patronage networks linking business and public administrative structures were exploited too by oligarchs in attempts to bypass participatory budgeting guidelines on civil society representation.

In Malaysia, elite-initiated consultative ideologies and institutions to contain conflict backfired. They inadvertently opened up scrutiny of race-based state political patronage and power abuses advancing and protecting the interests of business, bureaucratic, and political elites embedded in the prevailing model of capitalist development. Societal and administrative incorporation to inform and implement economic and social development strategies were dogged by inherent tensions between consultative and particularist ideologies of representation in Malaysia. Malaysia's failed consultative representation experiments helped to redirect reformers' energies more concertedly toward independent, civil society mobilization.

How can we draw on these theoretical insights from the book's case studies to better understand the dynamic relationships between political institutions and capitalism elsewhere—especially under liberal democracies where inequalities have also intensified?

Populist Representation Challenge

Chapter 1 explained how in many established liberal democracies the advent of neoliberal globalization was accompanied by the introduction of various new public consultative and feedback mechanisms embodying consultative representation ideologies. As elsewhere, while embraced by some social and political forces as vital supplements to representative democracy, they have been eschewed by others as political co-option designed to contain the scope of political contestation. However, recent increased appeal of populist ideologies of representation in liberal democracies in the UK, Western Europe, and the United States mark a new challenge for political institutions old and new as more people look to bypass intermediary institutions—irrespective of their ideological character—in favor of strong leaders. If this consolidates, assorted consultative and participatory mechanisms introduced in recent decades may be selective or wholesale casualties.

Crucially, alongside widening income and wealth inequalities under neoliberal globalization in liberal democracies, the social foundations of representative political institutions have also been transformed. With the advent of global production strategies and new technologies, class-based organizations have come under attack, and cohesive coalitions for social democracy have largely unraveled or been substantially diminished, even in previous strongholds of social democracy of the UK, Germany, and Scandinavia. This has been conducive to greater political fragmentation and compartmentalization of reform politics around single issues and identity politics including of environmentalism, feminism, ethnicity, and sexuality (Berman 2016; Crouch 2004, 2011; Schram 2015).

Meanwhile, for many of the biggest losers under advanced globalization—including blue-collar workers, fractions of national capital, and others whose material or ideological interests are perceived as threatened—effective political representation proved elusive. Various populist leaders have filled this political vacuum by offering direct representation of the "people" in opposition to an equally amorphous "establishment elite." As Mishra (2016, 51) observes: "In places where globalized capitalism has not fulfilled its promise of opportunity and prosperity, culturally and spiritually disoriented people have become increasingly susceptible to demagoguery and extremism."

To be sure, populist movements have differing complexions and political implications—some of which invest hope in plutocrats while others seek to arrest the powers of plutocrats and reboot social democracy. There are also significant normative divergences in the ways that progressive and conservative identity politics and related particularist ideologies—including of race, religion, and gender—articulate with populist movements or are the targets of resentment by them. Rising social and material inequalities generated by capitalist globalization create a context enabling nationalist, racist, and other worldviews and conflicts that predate neoliberal globalization to gain new political traction and constituencies (Gonzalez-Vicente and Carroll 2017). However, the MOP framework can contribute to an understanding of these complexities through its analytical emphasis on the dynamic social foundations underpinning the coalitions in support for, and opposition to, competing ideologies of representation.

Precisely because the focus in this study was new MOPs, it was founded on detailed analyses of consultative, particularist, and democratic ideologies and institutions rather than populist ideologies of representation. However, populist ideologies of representation are not entirely absent from struggles over representation in the region, or the case study countries. Significantly, though, it is the Philippines—where the complexion of economic and political elites, their interests and respective political modus operandi are less cohesive than in Singapore or Malaysia—where populist representation ideologies have periodically enjoyed important influence. This is reflected in the presidential election victories of Joseph Estrada and, more recently, Rodrigo Duterte.

Such has been the control of oligarchs and their allies over formal political institutions in the Philippines that serious reforms to address acute inequalities and systemic corruption have not been possible. Notwithstanding substantially increased social spending through conditional cash transfers to try and address poverty under President Benigno Aquino III, neither these nor the PLS or BUB initiatives evidently generated sufficient hope or expectations of substantive change among voters. Consequently, Duterte's anti-oligarchy rhetoric and declared anti-crime, pro-order agenda enjoyed wide cross-class appeal that capitalized on, but also transcended, the fragmentation of multiple political identities through the projection of himself as the authentic representative of "the people." Duterte's speedy dismantling of the BUB, the flagship initiative in popular political participation under Aquino, suggests that state-sponsored consultative bodies might more generally be wound back in future.

By contrast, we saw how the PAP in Singapore and the BN in Malaysia have historically presided over substantial initial material and social improvements for their respective populations. More recently the outcomes of development have been far less equitable and precipitated new chapters in struggles over representation. Yet this does not necessarily mean that voters have altogether lost faith in existing institutions or the possibility of reforming them to address inequalities, as apparently many have in the Philippines.

The PAP's cautious but significant recent return to greater policy and rhetorical commitment to social redistribution was strongly endorsed by voters in 2015, including from the working class. Through the considerable profits of government-linked companies and foreign reserves accumulated under Singapore's state capitalism, the PAP also has the capacity to further ameliorate the inequitable impacts of development if it chooses. Any such path, though, would be intended by the PAP to reinforce state political paternalism—not social citizenship rights. Similarly, the BN introduced new redistributive measures from 2013. Although it generally remains ideologically predisposed to systems of racially oriented state patronage that target its social and political base, it is clearly not averse to redistribution per se. The concept of redistribution—rationalized through distinct nondemocratic ideologies quite different from social democracy—is thus a legitimate and indeed institutionalized feature of these states. Authoritarian controls in Singapore and Malaysia also give authorities the means by which to intimidate and contain attempts to exploit populist ideologies by critics and opponents of ruling elites.

The general point is that there is no simple cause-and-effect relationship between inequality and the political traction of populist ideology, but neither are these unrelated. Links between capitalist development and institutions and ideologies of representation are dynamic, complex, and fundamental to shaping the conflicts that arise over what interests should and can be represented in political contestation and how.

Neoliberalism and Participation in Established Liberal Democracies

With the above insights in mind, let us return, then, to the earlier general obser-vation about the reinvigoration of populist ideologies of representation in estab-lished liberal democracies. This has occurred against the background of decades of neoliberal capitalist transformations, resulting in increased social and mate-rial inequalities generating new social conflicts and exacerbating existing ones. Yet new ideas and structures of political participation that have also emerged in attempts to contain or address those conflicts also continue to evolve. This plays out differently according to specific histories and political economies. Concrete examination of the UK—one of the oldest liberal democracies—illustrates the dy-namic, unresolved struggle over political participation and representation that can only be intensified by the populist challenge. This, necessarily limited, analysis nevertheless reinforces the case for extending the empirical application of the MOP framework beyond Southeast Asia.

Neoliberal reform in the UK in the 1980s and 1990s under Thatcher and Major Conservative governments was accompanied by a new ideological advocacy of "active citizenship." As Keith Faulks (quoted in Bee and Pachi 2014, 105) observed, though, the priority was "the development of a citizenship based upon the assertion of the individual and the market, rather than a genuine concern for the promotion of community values." Participation was linked to ideas of individual self-reliance, volunteer work, and improved local level service delivery (Fyfe 1993).

This New Right embrace of "active citizenship" rationalized the dilution of so-cial democratic notions of citizenship rights that emphasized obligations of the state to ensure equitable social distribution under market capitalism. Instead, improved service delivery to the public was linked to reform agendas of privati-zation and deregulation. Strong collective organizations—especially trade unions—that sought to contest this agenda were antithetical to the sort of active citizenship and attendant participation envisaged.

This was neatly captured in Prime Minister John Major's 1991 Citizen's Char-ter, under which the placement of the apostrophe assumed special significance. The Charter was meant to guarantee *individual* redress and quality of public services. And it was the individual as a consumer rather than politically orga-nized democratic participant that was championed. This ideology provided the rationale for channeling political participation through various service delivery complaints and redress mechanisms that would continue to expand under subse-quent Labour and Conservative governments (Mullen 2006; Bee and Pachi 2014, 105). Despite the appearance of a depoliticization of public policy, this was the administrative incorporation of politics into the state, bypassing civil society and collective political representation to limit the scope of political conflict and the means by which it could be conducted.

In other respects, though, the defeat of the Conservatives and advent in 1997 of the Blair, and subsequent Brown, Labour governments marked a new stage in the dynamic relationship between political participation and neoliberal transformation. "New Labour" pursued a "third way" that acknowledged and championed civil society's political importance through a different conception of "active citizenship." This even raised expectations of a move toward participatory democracy, encouraged by rhetoric from Labour leaders about "empowerment," "civic engagement," "civic participation," and "public/private partnerships" (Giddens 1998; Davies 2012; Bee and Pachi 2014, 106–7). Yet it was consultative ideologies and institutions of representation that flourished in tandem with deepening neoliberal reform and rising inequality. This included articulation with particularist ideologies, notably through incorporation of ethnic and religious minorities into various consultative bodies in attempts to foster assimilation and contain social conflict (Bee and Pachi 2014, 114).

By 2007, in England alone it was possible in any given month for a citizen to be invited to participate in one of the following avenues for informal political engagement: Participatory Budgeting; the Local Area Forum; Local Strategic Partnerships; the Local Involvement Network; the Citizens' Panel; as well as various citizen juries, service user panels, focus groups, and assorted school, hospital, and housing advisory boards (Potter 2008).

To be sure, these structures have provided opportunities for individuals and independent collective organizations to engage in public policy feedback. This includes some attempts by trade unions and other civil society organizations to exploit such societal incorporation to try to open up political conflict over neoliberal reform. Yet conflict containment has been a thematic feature of these institutions, many of which were conceived or rationalized through the ideological lenses of technocratic problem solving drawing a range of stakeholders into public policy consultations with authorities.

A detailed study of local strategic partnerships in the UK illustrates this point (Davies 2007). These consultative bodies were designed to incorporate local agencies, voluntary organizations, and business and community activists into the planning of public service delivery and related social, economic, and environmental needs. Davies concluded, however, that democratic partnerships were thwarted at two levels (792). First, local service delivery managers had predominantly internalized a "managerialist ethos" that arguably "hobbled" participation from the outset. Second, national governments were the main drivers of the restructuring guiding these partnerships. Consequently, the scope of policy deliberation was fundamentally constrained by the ideal of an efficient market economy.

More recently, a striking feature of various participatory budgeting exercises in the UK—and, indeed, elsewhere—is how they are often seeking public feedback on spending priorities in a context of severe public spending cutbacks. Here political participation can legitimize and facilitate the implementation of austerity drives contributing to increased inequality. This does not mean such political and ideological projects are always passively accepted. But they do invite serious analysis of where, when, and how it is possible to challenge elite interests through such innovations in political participation. The MOP framework is designed for such an analysis, providing a basis for drilling deep into the social foundations of struggles over who can participate, how, and on what through public consultation mechanisms. Moreover, the case for such insights only grows as struggles over participation and representation continue to evolve.

Indeed, even before the Brexit vote, and amidst mounting social tensions over neoliberal globalization, some UK politicians appeared to recognize the need to revitalize consultative representation to contain social and political conflict. In 2012, the government published a new civil service reform plan for "open policymaking" for engaging the public and experts from beyond the "Westminster village." An accompanying Contestable Policy Fund was established to "commission high quality advice from outside the civil service on ministers' priority policy areas; draw directly on the thinking, evidence and insight of external experts; and achieve a potentially broader and more radical range of options than ministers would receive internally" (GOV.UK 2013).

However, in its 2012–13 report, *Public Engagement in Policy-Making* (House of Commons 2013, 3), the cross-party House of Commons Public Administration Select Committee (PASC) seemed to up the ante. It warned of a risk of public disappointment and skepticism about the impact of their participation, and perceptions that the government listens principally to the media, lobbyists, and the "usual suspects" (5). The PASC argued there was a "need to use outsiders to debate issues and build consensus, and that the ability to think strategically depended, in part, on a willingness to listen to challenges and contrary views" (5).

The government's response contained significant qualifications about change it would countenance, distinguishing between open policy making and public engagement. The former, it argued, recognizes that the civil service does not have all the answers to all the questions. Yet this did not mean that the latter, understood as broad consultation and public deliberation, was the only way to be open. Depending on the question to be answered, the government argued that "it may be best to seek independent advice from an organization" (House of Commons 2014, 3). It also did "not believe that an insistence that all organisations contracted through the contestable policy-making fund should undertake public engagement is proportionate" (5).

This is just one indication of underlying differences between the PASC and government over the extent and purpose of new public engagement. A deeper probe through the MOP framework would, among other things, investigate the processes and interests shaping the incorporation of select organizations into policy advice or consultation. This would include analysis of the extent to which either broad consultation or more select engagement would help reinforce or erode notions and practices of democratic representation.

Evaluation of the political regime significance of this and broader societal struggles in the UK and everywhere else over participation and representation ultimately concerns a fundamental question: whether the limits to legitimate political conflict are being expanded or contained. The extent to which new forms of public policy engagement can accommodate political space for conflict over the control and distribution of the benefits and costs of capitalist development is pivotal to this evaluation. It is in these struggles that the contingent nature of support for political contestation within liberal democracies by some forces and interests becomes more evident.

A Different Convergence?

Carothers's (2002) pronouncement of the end of the democratic transitions paradigm was a critical intervention in debates about political regime directions. It distilled a growing skepticism and rejection of the resilient and influential idea that the paths of capitalism and democracy would naturally and ultimately converge. However, it did not instigate the sort of new theoretical enterprise that it warranted to adequately identify and explain divergent paths. The case for breaking the theoretical impasse has since become more urgent. Liberal democratic institutions against which political regimes are benchmarked in hybrid regime studies are coming under unprecedented pressure in some of the most advanced capitalist countries. The democratic convergence hypothesis has never seemed more implausible.

This does not mean that there have not been convergences of a sort between political regimes as capitalism's penetration has deepened across the globe. The diminished strength of social democratic movements in the established liberal democracies has been replaced by a political fragmentation of social and political forces. This was arrived at by market capitalism and technological transformations rather than Cold War authoritarian repression, as in many late developing countries. Broad-based reformist coalitions with organizational bases to challenge the power of capitalist elites and related interests have everywhere become more difficult to forge.

Yet, as much because of this as in spite of it, capitalist development everywhere continues to generate and compound conflicts that require political management by elites. This is precisely why across different regime types assorted new MOPs emerged in struggles over representation, leading in a variety of directions. These struggles are as dynamic and complex, though, as are the capitalist systems they are inseparable from. Consequently, the emergence of innovative institutional structures of participation and representation is no guarantee of their appeal or utility to elites and their opponents in competing attempts to define the permissible limits of political conflict.

Where consultative institutions of representation, for example, prove ineffective in depoliticizing the market or too effective for some elites' liking, different institutional structures and/or populist alternatives may emerge. The recent jettisoning of participatory budgeting with changes of governments in Brazil as well as the Philippines has illustrated that. Even in an established liberal democracy such as Australia this has been evident. For example, after taking office, Prime Minister Tony Abbott abolished a raft of policy advisory bodies in 2014, including on climate change, social inclusion, homelessness, corporate wrongdoing, firearms, and insurance reform.

Precisely because the MOP framework privileges the question of *why* political institutions emerge, it is uniquely placed to explain periodic transitions to new institutional structures. This is because it conceives of institutions as inseparable from dynamic societal conflicts, among which those concerning the way that capitalism is structured and its benefits and costs distributed are most pervasive and profound.

As recently as the early 1990s, following the end of the Cold War, Fukuyama (1992) speculated about the "end of history" and the triumph of liberalism. And yet just a few decades later it is anti-liberal populist ideologies that are most rapidly gaining support in a range of established liberal democracies. Ironically, interests well served by the intensified inequalities underpinning much of this populist disquiet see an opportunity here. This includes through the exploitation of libertarian ideologies—wherein it is the freedom of the market and the interests served by this idea, not the freedom of citizens to advance their interests through collective social and political organizations, that is paramount.

Indeed, where populist movements are sustained, it is not too fanciful to speculate about the possibility of selective attempts to institute new forms of authoritarian state power. This would be a very different sort of political convergence from what Huntington and modernization theorists had in mind. Whatever transpires will be better understood through some theorization of the dynamic social foundations of political institutions, which is what this study has sought to make a modest distinctive contribution to.

Notes

1. THEORIZING INSTITUTIONS OF POLITICAL PARTICIPATION AND REPRESENTATION

1. Much of the literature seems to have overlooked the earlier work of Barrington Moore (1966), who was concerned with explaining why capitalism led to autocracy in Germany. This had already highlighted the contingent nature of the link between capitalism and democracy in early and advanced industrializing capitalist countries.

2. The advent of the global financial crisis in 2008 and its aftermath added another dimension to critical reexamination of the presumed functional limits to authoritarianism. Thus, Plattner (2014, 14–15) raised concerns on the one hand about a "growing perception that the political institutions of the EU countries and the United States are functioning poorly"; on the other hand, he predicted that "the future performance and direction of China—whether it is able to maintain high economic growth without democratizing—will probably prove to be the single most important determinant of the outcome of the struggle between democracy and authoritarianism."

3. Huntington (1991, 12) also employed the concept of "semi-democracy" in distinguishing between those regimes that did and did not qualify among his generous list of third-wave transitions. See also Case (1996), who adopted the concept of "halfway house" regimes, and Karl's (1995) work on how regimes in Central America combined authoritarian clientelism and coercion at the local level with greater political pluralism at the national level.

4. See Morgenbesser 2016 for an analysis of the various rationales for regimes among leaders of authoritarian regimes in Southeast Asia.

5. Carothers (2002) was explicitly challenging a core transition theory assumption that processes of democratic opening, breakthrough, and consolidation would, however protracted, be the dominant pattern of regime change.

6. Mazzuca (2010) challenges hybrid regime categorizations for often conflating access to power—defining the character of a political regime—with the exercise of power—more concerned with administrative processes. Thus, focus on institutional quality highlighting corruption, clientelism, abuses of executive decree authority, and the absence of checks and balances on power are "best characterized not as indicators of authoritarianism and deficiencies in democratization but as reflecting—in Weberian terms—patrimonialism and failures in bureaucratization" (334). This distinction is no less relevant for critical evaluations of quality or qualities of democracy approaches to hybrid regime categorizations.

7. Gandhi's (2008) approach does include some consideration of attempts at broader institutional inclusivity to help sustain elite power. See Pepinsky 2014, 645 on this point.

8. Gandhi's study included Kuwait, Morocco, and Ecuador, while Brownlee examined regimes in Malaysia, Egypt, the Philippines, and Iran.

9. See Rodan and Hughes 2014 on nondemocratic ideologies of accountability and their importance to political regime directions in Southeast Asia.

10. Possibly the most expansive comparative work on new modes of participation is an edited collection by Törnquist, Webster, and Stokke (2009). This incorporates studies

of Latin America, Africa, Asia, and Norway, with special emphasis on distinguishing democratic popular representation.

11. The label "Murdoch School" derives from the fact that scholars at the fore of this approach have been based, for much of their careers, at Murdoch University in Australia. For a discussion of the origins and development of this approach since the 1980s, see Hameiri and Jones 2014.

12. A regime, by contrast, refers to a particular type of organization of the state apparatus. This organization is the basis of distinguishing, for example, between democratic, authoritarian, and totalitarian regimes as well as between different variants of each.

13. Examples cited by Schattschneider (1975, 70–74) included the way urban-rural conflict was exploited to contain the labor movement during the Cold War and the repeated use of religious conflict to deflect from a wide range of other cleavages.

14. The implications of this theoretical position are no less relevant for critically evaluating attempts to analyze the "quality of the state" (Fukuyama 2013; Holt and Manning 2014) than they are the quality of political institutions.

15. Other works adopting a similar approach in emphasizing capitalist dynamics to explain social and political change include Chaudhry 1997, Leys 1996, Bellin 2000, and King 2007.

2. IDEOLOGIES OF POLITICAL REPRESENTATION AND THE MODE OF PARTICIPATION FRAMEWORK

1. This is fundamentally different from the distinction between formal and informal institutions employed by Helmke and Levitsky (2004). See Jayasuriya and Rodan 2007, 779–80.

2. For a sample and survey of this now extensive and influential new institutionalist literature, see North 1990, Przeworski 2004, and Lowndes and Roberts 2013.

3. Some theorists argue that contemporary realities have rendered such authorization and accountability less feasible, as we will see below.

4. Hobbes, for example, highlighted the importance of formal authorization of representatives; Burke, by contrast, emphasized the expert knowledge and substantive virtue of the representative once authorized to represent; while Jefferson attributed more importance to active participation by the represented (see Gamble 1981). Pitkin (1967) herself identified four different perspectives on democratic representation: formalistic representation, descriptive representation, symbolic representation, and substantive representation.

5. Urbinati and Warren (2008, 405) draw this distinction when evaluating the political significance of "self-authorized" citizen representatives intended to increase the incorporation of the unorganized into political processes.

6. Examples include the Bids and Awards Committee in the Philippines responsible for awarding public sector contracts, and the Committee for Understanding and Religious Harmony Among Religious Adherents in Malaysia.

3. HISTORY, CAPITALISM, AND CONFLICT

1. The PAP's notion of a meritocracy is a highly formalistic and narrow one, almost exclusively based on educational and professional qualifications. See Barr 2014.

2. Privatization has generally been limited to rationalizations ensuring GLCs consolidate, strengthen, and internationalize rather than diminish their economic roles (see Asher 1994; Low 2001). Thus, in March 2017, the holding company for GLCs—Temasek Holdings—posted a record net portfolio value of US$203 billion (Chia 2017).

3. This figure excludes the impact of short-term low-paid guest workers.

4. In Lee Kuan Yew's early articulations on the rationality and problem-solving imperatives of politics there was a strong positivist ideological undertone consistent with what Hilary and Steven Rose referred to as "scientism." See Rodan 1989, 88–89.

5. Lee Kuan Yew's attacks on, and political persecution of, J. B. Jeyaretnam, who broke the PAP's monopoly in parliament with his 1981 by-election victory, had not prevented his reelection in 1984 and may have boosted public sympathy for him.

6. Indeed, PAP leaders would later press this claim ideologically, mounting an "Asian values" ideological campaign, depicting the institutionalized political conflict of liberal democracies as alien to Asians, who are supposedly predisposed to a "consensus politics" rooted in cultural traditions (Mahbubani 1994, 1995; Zakaria 1994).

7. The NCMP provision has been contentious within opposition parties, and initially there was a general reluctance to accept invitations to enter parliament by this route. Over time, though, more took up invitations for tactical reasons.

8. As Chua (2007) explains, the PAP's promotion of ethnic-based self-help organizations was also integral to the PAP's strategic political management of the poor.

9. According to Winters (2012, 54), the defining feature of oligarchs is that "they are individually and as a group more powerful than the laws and the system of legal enforcement. They are able to use their material power resources to block, deflect, or minimize the impact of laws."

10. However, the emphasis here is not on the dominance of particular families, per se, as in the important and influential work of McCoy (2009). It is instead on the way that the dynamic interests of powerful capitalists and political elites are mutually reinforced. The root of power resides in capitalist social relations rather than personalistic networks.

11. From early in the twentieth century through to the advent of the Marcos government in 1972, two almost indistinguishable elite parties dominated—the Nacionalista Party formed in 1907 and the Liberal Party established in 1946 by breakaway elements of the Nacionalista Party (Teehankee 2013, 190).

12. The Huk rebels were not completely opposed to electoral participation but selectively engaged in it. See Kerkvliet 1979.

13. The use of vigilantes and organized violence against independent trade unions never abated following the end of the Cold War. See Scipes 1996.

14. Scipes (1996) also emphasizes the continuing role of armed, physical violence by vigilantes and the state to repress the KMU.

15. Marcos was elected president in 1965 and 1969, subsequently declaring martial law in 1972.

16. However, this centralization was incomplete. For example, arresting patronage control from local oligarchs in Mindanao could only be partially achieved at best.

17. The first implemented element of Aquino's strategy to reduce poverty involved broadening the coverage of the conditional cash transfer (CCT) program inherited from the Arroyo administration. This provided direct cash subsidies to the poorest families under condition that children regularly attend school and health checkups.

18. For the period 2008–2012, GDP grew on average at 4.7 percent and reached 7.2 percent in 2013. This was second only to China (*Economist* 2014).

19. By 2005, only 7 percent of Malaysia's 10 million workforce was unionized (Loh 2012, 195).

20. These names subsequently changed to the Malaysian Chinese Association and Malaysian Indian Congress, both of which were part of the Alliance's successor coalition, the BN.

21. Between 1957 and 1970, income inequality generally increased, but especially between Malays (Sundaram 1988, 254).

22. Implementation of the NEP began in 1972, officially finishing in 1990.

23. In contrast with political parties in both Singapore and the Philippines, UMNO's structures significantly consolidated and grew following independence. By 2010 UMNO boasted a minimum of 17,000 branches and 191 divisions, and E. T. Gomez (2012b, 51) observed that "most local leaders rely on contracts from the government or GLCs [government-linked companies] for their livelihoods and to build and maintain support."

24. Non-Malay parties to join the coalition included the Gerakan Rakyat Malaysia (Malaysian People's Movement) and the People's Progressive Party. Among the Malay parties, PAS also joined early. Up to fourteen parties eventually joined the coalition (Mauzy and Barter 2008, 214).

25. Seats were also allocated to the unelected federal Senate and local government councils in ways that ensured benefits to the different ethnic-based coalition partners.

26. See Pepinsky 2009 for a detailed analysis of the struggle between Mahathir and Anwar and the former's superior coalitional politics therein.

27. This party merged in 2003 with the Parti Rakyat Malaysia (Malaysian People's Party) to form Parti Keadilan Rakyat (PKR, People's Justice Party).

4. NOMINATED MEMBERS OF PARLIAMENT IN SINGAPORE

1. This included the introduction in 1984 of non-constituency members of parliament (NCMPs), where between three to six (subsequently nine) of the best polled losing opposition candidates could be invited into parliament with reduced voting rights.

2. For analyses of the earlier political regime manifestations of this technocratic worldview, see H. C. Chan 1975.

3. In this respect, there is a parallel with the notionally competitive electoral institution of the elected president introduced in 1991. This involves stringent eligibility criteria, couched in terms of requisite capacities and talent (see Tan and Lam 1997). These criteria were further tightened in 2016 (Chia 2016).

4. Terms can be shorter, depending on when general elections are held. For example, the 2004 appointments served for only 1.5 years. Terms are also potentially renewable.

5. The Workers' Party subsequently increased its seats to seven with a by-election win in 2013.

6. In 1997, the Select Committee introduced Proposal Panels to facilitate and coordinate recruitment of candidates for the core functional groups targeted under the scheme: business and industry; the professions; and the labor movement. In 2002, three new functional groups were added: social and community service organizations; tertiary education institutions; and media, arts, and sports organizations. Then, in 2012, civic and people sector organizations were added.

7. Furthermore, not all NMPs rigidly adhere to the functional division of labor implied by these categories, some taking it upon themselves to have a wider brief than others. This is not always discouraged by the Select Committee.

8. This includes appointments from the Association of Small and Medium Enterprises, the Singapore National Employers' Federation, the Chinese Chamber of Commerce and Industry, and the Singapore Manufacturers' Federation.

9. Foreign labor grew to account for 1.1 million, or one-third of the total workforce, by 2010 (Chun 2013b).

10. Geh Min was yet another former AWARE president too.

11. Faizah Jamal (former NMP), interview by author, September 26, 2014, Singapore.

12. Ibid.

13. Audrey Wong (former NMP), interview by author, October 7, 2014, Singapore.

14. Ibid. Quotes from Wong in the following paragraph are all from the same interview.

15. Janice Koh (former NMP), interview by author, September 26, 2014, Singapore.

16. Ibid.

17. Viswa Sadasivan (former NMP), interview by author, October 1, 2014, Singapore. Quotes from Sadasivan in this and the following paragraph are all from the same interview.

18. Both Siew and Olsen were invited to apply to become NMPs by government ministers, underlining the importance the PAP attached to this new category of appointments.

19. Sadasivan interview by author.

20. Sylvia Lim (Workers' Party chairperson), interview by author, September 29, 2014, Singapore.

21. Fourteen current and former NMPs were interviewed by the author from 2006 to 2014. The one category of NMPs that did not cooperate with the project was appointments from the PAP-affiliated NTUC.

22. Thio Li-Ann (former NMP), interview by author, May 16, 2007, Singapore.

23. Janice Koh interview by author. Quotes from Koh in this and the following two paragraphs are all from the same interview.

24. NMP Sadasivan similarly saw himself discursively representing ideas rather than people, "generating discussion in areas that I feel are important in shaping the future of Singapore" (Sadasivan interview by author).

25. Edwin Khew (former NMP), interview by author, July 26, 2007, Singapore.

26. Geh Min (former NMP), interview by author, November 6, 2006, Singapore. Quotes from Geh in the rest of the paragraph are all from the same interview.

27. Goh Chong Chia (former NMP), interview by author, November 6, 2006, Singapore.

28. Goh was a past president of the Singapore Institute of Architects, chaired the Physical Development Feedback Group, and he had close links with the Handicapped Society.

29. Siew Kum Hong (former NMP), interview by author, May 17, 2007, Singapore.

30. Siew Kum Hong, interview by author, October 10, 2014, Singapore.

31. Eunice Olsen (former NMP), interview by author, May 14, 2007, Singapore.

32. Thio Li-Ann (former NMP), interview by author, May 16, 2007, Singapore.

5. PUBLIC FEEDBACK IN SINGAPORE'S CONSULTATIVE AUTHORITARIANISM

1. Another electronic channel involves indicative e-polls surveying between 500 and 1,000 respondents, again on issues or questions of interest to government departments and agencies. There are annual surveys but also more ad hoc e-polling exercises. Under the FU, the latter included such topics as marriage and procreation measures, racial integration in schools, and the White Paper on Terrorism.

2. In 2004, the government introduced the Portable Medical Benefits Scheme and the Transferable Medical Insurance Scheme.

3. Sadasivan became a nominated member of parliament in 2009.

4. At that time, only five of the sixty-eight registered unions in Singapore were not affiliated with the NTUC, and the secretary-general of the NTUC was Lim Boon Heng, also a PAP MP; this was not an uncommon joint status.

5. Citizens wishing to participate need to register in advance by filling in an online form requiring personal details such as name, age, and occupation, which REACH states are for statistical purposes only and will remain confidential.

6. In the deliberations of the 2009 PSW on the social integration of immigrants and foreign workers, for example, the Chairman Tan Ern Ser could recall no recruitment of "any oppositionists in any way," but added that "I don't think we were very restrained in what we proposed" (Tan Ern Ser [REACH Policy Study Workgroup], interview by author on integration issues, November 24, 2014, Singapore).

7. From June 2013, online news sites in Singapore exceeding a certain readership level needed a license under the Singapore Broadcasting Act.

8. The WP increased its numbers to seven with a subsequent by-election win in 2013.

9. Recurring breakdowns on the mass rapid transport system compounded these problems.

10. Opposition parties also deployed websites and Twitter accounts to good effect to promote their public rallies, and the government had lifted many of the restrictions on online campaigning that proved too difficult to enforce in 2006.

11. Reporters from GLCs were incorporated into dialogues as participants, and OSC committee members, volunteer facilitators, and community partners in the dialogues provided media interviews on radio and television. Two GLC media organizations—Lianhe Zaobao and Berita Harian—organized Dialogue Sessions for their readers and forum contributors (Khoo and Yee 2014, 9).

12. "OB markers" is a reference to the PAP government's distinction between permissible political discussion and activities and those that are "out of bounds."

13. Both worked in the prime minister's office.

14. Subsequent invitations to the Workers' Party to participate in the initial Dialogue Sessions of the OSC were rejected (see Chang 2012; *Temasek Times* 2012).

15. Dialogues were also supported by OSC committee members and various volunteer facilitators and note takers. The role of facilitators was not without controversy, some participants complaining that in their experience discussions were being steered toward particular ideas. See, for example, *TR Emeritus* (2013).

16. Melissa Khoo (director of the OSC program office), email correspondence to author, January 19, 2014.

17. Ibid.

18. Janice Koh (former NMP), interview by author, September 26, 2014, Singapore.

19. Kok Heng Leun (artistic director of Drama Box), interview by author, October 8, 2014, Singapore.

20. See also Minister Heng's comments on the budget-OSC connection in Quek 2013.

21. This concept was an attempt to distinguish the PAP's redistribution for what it pejoratively refers to as "western welfarism."

22. Actions by authorities included the conviction of popular blogger and Lesbian, Gay, Bisexual, and Transgender (LGBT) activist Alex Au for "scandalizing the judiciary" for comments about the way two constitutional challenges to Singapore's anti-sodomy law had been handled by Singapore's court; and the charging of sixteen-year-old blogger Amos Yee for "wounding religious feelings" and "obscenity" in an online video posted following Lee Kuan Yew's death, and a prosecution over an illegal assembly (see Koh 2015; Han 2016b).

6. THE PHILIPPINES' PARTY-LIST SYSTEM, REFORMERS, AND OLIGARCHS

1. On the history and evolution of different forms of "pork barrel" in the Philippines, see Gamala 2014.

2. The term "leftist reformers," or "progressives," as they are also referred to in this chapter, is inclusive of both radical and revolutionary reformers. Differences between these ideological camps are explored in detail in the next chapter, as they manifested in competing positions on combating poverty through state strategies of promoting grassroots participatory budgeting.

3. Sectoral representation refers to the representation of marginalized or disadvantaged groups via sectors. The Party-List System Act would later define the sectors as including "labor, peasant, fisherfolk, urban poor, indigenous cultural communities, elderly, handicapped, women, youth, veterans, overseas workers, and professionals" (Republic of the Philippines 1995, Sec. 5).

4. Sectoral representation was initially supported by Jaime Tadeo and Vilfrido Villacorta, who promoted exclusive sectoral representation for the marginalized and disadvantaged. While Villacorta eventually compromised with pluralist Christian Monsod, permanent sectoral representation exclusive to marginalized groups was further championed with a proposed "amendment" by Cory Aquino, Joaquin Bernas, and Jaime Tadeo (ConCom 1986, 574).

5. One of the few exceptions to this was Jaime Tadeo, national head of Kilusang Mag-bubukid ng Pilipinas (Philippine Peasant Movement), a leading leftist advocate for land reform. Significantly, the nomination of the Communist Party of the Philippines founder, José Maria Sison, was overlooked, while several oppositionists from the former Marcos administration were included (Rush 1987, 1–2).

6. By 2004, there were four Bayan Muna–aligned sectoral groups—along with Bayan Muna itself—contesting in the PLS elections: Anakpawis, representing peasants; the women's group Gabriela (General Assembly Binding Women for Integrity, Equality, Leadership, and Action); Migrante, representing overseas workers; and the youth group Anak ng Bayan (later renamed Kabataan). This would be expanded into the Makabayan coalition in 2009.

7. In 2010, the top vote getter Ako Bicol secured three seats with 1,524,006 votes, while 164,044 votes were enough to earn a seat for Alay Buhay Community Development Foundation Inc. (Alay Buhay).

8. In practice, this turned out to be twenty-nine new seats, owing to immediate disqualification cases faced by two groups and the dissolution of a legislative district in Mindanao.

9. These figures are based on data obtained from Comelec (2007, 2010), taking into account the disqualification of Alliance for Barangay Concerns in 2010.

10. Antonio Tinio (ACT Teachers representative), interview by author, March 28, 2014, Manila.

11. Ibarra "Barry" Gutierrez (Akbayan representative), interview by author, March 31, 2014, Manila.

12. The ruling also contradicted the eight-to-seven 2009 *Banarguay Association for National Advancement and Transparency vs. Comelec* ruling in favor of totally excluding any form of major political party participation in the party-list (Supreme Court 2009, "Participation of Major Political Parties in Party-List Elections").

13. Guttierrez interview by author.

14. Courage represents government employees; Piston represents drivers; Katribu represents indigenous peoples; Akap Bata represents children; Kalikasan represents the environment; Aking Bikolnon represents the poor and marginalized in Bicol.

15. Gutierrez interview by author.

16. Bayan is the leftist mass-based People's Organization, from which the political party Bayan Muna emerged.

17. Neri Colmenares (Bayan Muna representative), interview by author, April 1, 2014, Manila.

18. Gutierrez interview by author.

19. Renato Reyes (Secretary-General of Bayan), interview by author, May 8, 2013, Manila.

20. According to Walden Bello, this included the Reproductive Health Act bringing major benefits to women, the Kasambahay Act benefiting domestic workers, and the Marcos Compensation Act recouping public money.

21. Bello cited as reasons for his resignation the lack of progress by the administration in implementing an agrarian land reform law and the discretionary powers afforded Budget Secretary Abad under the Disbursement Acceleration Program to transfer funds from slow moving to fast-moving projects. See Bello 2015 and Gamil 2014.

22. For example, while the bill tabled in 2013 sought to prohibit "two or more people related within second degree of consanguinity or affinity to hold or run for national or local positions in successive, simultaneous, or overlapping terms" (Bacani 2013), the bill put forward by Belmonte in 2016 had increased this to "three or more" people, and the term "successive" had been dropped (see Diaz 2016a).

23. Gabriela was especially targeted by vote-buying tactics in Luzon and Bicol in 2013 according to its Congress representative Luzviminda Iligan (interview by author, July 23, 2013, Manila).

7. PARTICIPATORY BUDGETING IN THE PHILIPPINES

1. For an account of an exception to this pattern, in Naga City, see Brilliantes 2007.

2. This participatory budgeting had a number of name changes since its introduction in the Philippines: bottom-up budgeting; grassroots participatory budget process; enhanced bottom-up budgeting.

3. Dressel's (2012) focus was on initiatives begun in early 2011 to incorporate civil society groups into national budget planning, involving six national departments.

4. Dressel refers to works by Sabatier and Jenkins-Smith (1993), Jenkins-Smith and Sabatier (1994), Sabatier and Weible (2007), and Weible et al. (2011) as influential on his approach.

5. Dressel (2012) is not unaware of the possibility of intra-coalition tensions, but the framework he adopts is not equipped to interrogate this tension and draw out its political implications.

6. Kapit-Bisig Laban sa Kahirapan (Linking Arms Against Poverty)-Comprehensive and Integrated Delivery of Social Services.

7. There were, of course, differences among socdems on just how extensively the market needed to be tempered to achieve social justice.

8. This funding dependence influences the substantive agendas of NGOs and compounds their fragmentation into specialized advocacy and service delivery–oriented groups, reflecting the priority programs and projects of others.

9. The scandal was fueled by publicly released audio recordings of a phone conversation between Arroyo and electoral commissioner Virgilio Garcilliano, hence the "Hello Garci" reference.

10. This tag derived from the fact the ten made their announcement at the Hyatt Regency Hotel.

11. Akbayan was to subsequently become a minor party within the ruling Liberal Party–dominated coalition.

12. Joel Rocamora (NAPC secretary), interview by author, July 24, 2013, Quezon City.

13. LPRAT was initially composed of a chairperson (the local chief executive); a co-chairperson; government representatives; a representative from the business sector; and CSOs representatives (including a CCT program leader, a leader of a CSO accredited by the local government unit, a CSO leader accredited by any national government agency, a leader of a women's group, a leader of a basic sector organization, a leader of a basic sector organization accredited by NAPC, and a leader of another community or grassroots organization).

14. LGUs include independent elected assemblies at the city, municipality, and *barangay* (village, district, or ward) level.

15. The consistent definition of CSOs in the various Joint Memorandum Circulars was: "Civil Society Organizations (CSOs)—include nongovernment organizations (NGOs), People's Organizations (POs), cooperatives, trade unions, professional associations, faith-based organizations, youth organizations, media groups, indigenous peoples

movements, foundations, and other citizen's groups which are nonprofit and are formed primarily for social and economic development to plan and monitor government programs and projects, engage in policy discussions, and actively participate in collaborative activities with the government" (DBM-DILG-DSWD-NAPC 2012, 2).

16. The basic sectors were defined in the act that gave birth to the NAPC as "farmer-peasant, artisanal fisherfolk, workers in the formal sector and migrant workers, workers in the informal sector, indigenous peoples and cultural communities, women, differently-abled persons, senior citizens, victims of calamities and disasters, youth and students, children, and urban poor" (Republic of the Philippines 1997, sec. 3).

17. During Robredo's time as Naga City mayor, NAPC had been able to exert an influence through representatives on the City Development Council. See Ilago 2005, 66–67.

18. Joel Rocamora, interview by author, May 2, 2013, Quezon City.

19. Florencio "Butch" Abad (budget secretary), interview by author, August 2, 2013, Manila.

20. Despite BAYAN leadership claims to a centralized national movement, in practice there are some elements of the movement that are less integrated than others under national structures. Thus, there was potential to involve some ND-linked organizations in specific areas. Case studies in the Institute of Philippine Culture (2013) report illustrate this.

21. Marie Labajo (undersecretary and head of Empowerment Fund Management Program Management Office, NAPC), email interview by author, July 29, 2013.

22. Under the CCT, the poorest families are given monthly subsidies on condition that their children are sent to public schools, and that mothers and children regularly visit public health centers. As of May 29, 2013, nearly four million households and over nine million children were enrolled in the CCT (*Philippine Daily Inquirer* 2013).

23. In what is referred to under CEAC as the initial "social preparation" stage, community volunteers, chosen at a *barangay* assembly by their peers, analyze the community's social and economic conditions. Village residents are subsequently called to another *barangay* meeting to validate the results. Criteria for the selection and ranking of proposals are then determined at a workshop involving village representatives. The next step is the convening of an inter-village meeting—the municipal inter-*barangay* forum—at which project proposals are competitively ranked by those assembled.

24. Interview by author with anonymous former World Bank official, July 30, 2013, Manila.

25. On this point, see Labonne and Chase (2008, 6), who distinguish between formal and informal social capital through CDD programs, the former referring to ties between community and non-community members while the latter referring to ties between households and local and national governments.

26. Abad interview by author.

27. Camilo Gudmalin (DSWD assistant secretary), interview by author, August 1, 2013, Manila.

28. Joel Rocamora interview by author, July 24, 2013, Quezon City.

29. Marie Labajo (NAPC undersecretary), interview by author, July 25, 2013, Quezon City.

30. NAPC official, interview by author, November 12, 2015, Manila.

31. Francisco "Bimbo" Fernandez (DILG undersecretary), interview by author, August 2, 2013, Manila.

32. Rocamora interview by author.

33. Labajo interview by author.

8. MALAYSIA'S FAILED CONSULTATIVE REPRESENTATION EXPERIMENTS

1. In 1970, Prime Minister Abdul Razak (cited in Funston 1980, 225) made this quite clear when explaining where power resided in the ruling coalition: "This government is based on UMNO and I surrender its responsibility to UMNO in order that UMNO shall determine its form—the government must follow the wishes and desires of UMNO—and it must implement policies which are determined by UMNO."

2. Political parties and civil society organizations were generally asked by the government to nominate their NECC representatives, but there were also direct approaches from the government to other individuals to participate.

3. Toh Kin Woon, interview by author, December 17, 2015, Penang, Malaysia. All quotes in this and the following paragraph are from the same interview.

4. Ibid.

5. Lim Teck Ghee (NECC I representative and academic), interview by author, April 26, 2016, Kuala Lumpur.

6. Michael Yeoh (MCA representative), interview by author, April 28, 2016, Kuala Lumpur.

7. Ghee interview by author.

8. Jomo Kwame Sundaram, Skype interview by author, May 23, 2016.

9. Yong Poh Kon (business leader and MCA representative on the NECC I), interview by author, April 28, 2016, Kuala Lumpur, and email correspondence, July 11, 2017.

10. Sundaram interview by author.

11. Toh interview by author.

12. In 2003, this party would become Parti Keadilan Rakyat (PKR, People's Justice Party) when it merged with the Malaysian People's Party.

13. For more details on reform demands by NGOs and the Barisan Alternatif (Alternative Front) alliance of opposition parties, including on relaxing authoritarian controls over freedom of expression and access to information, see Weiss 2006, 133–41.

14. For full details of the eleven Chinese associations, see *New Straits Times* 2000a.

15. The three predominantly ethnic Chinese component parties of the BN—MCA, Sarawak United People's Party, and Gerakan—accepted the petition on the basis that the "appeal is non-racial and non-partisan" (Esther Tan 1999). This change in language from "demands" to an "appeal" in the English-language version of the petition was part of the strategy to try and reduce UMNO anxiety, according to B. T. Khoo (2003, 139).

16. Ministers identified crime, education, corruption, unity, the economy, and transportation (Lesley 2014, 7).

17. Ironically, this was in a context of intensified public disquiet over reduced government subsidies for various public services, a policy that was part of the broader transformation agenda under Najib.

18. To facilitate this, Najib appointed Koh and Idris as ministers in his government—an effective backdoor into parliament.

19. The initial cost of these consultants was reportedly RM66 million (~US$15 million) (R. Lee 2011).

20. This pattern was discernible before the 2008 election but it consolidated and extended under Najib. Calls for wider interpretations of Islamic codes and laws were thematic to many controversies. See Saleem (2016).

21. The longest-standing smaller elite-dominated committee was the National Economic Action Council that Mahathir set up in 1998, which was expanded and renamed the Economic Council by Badawi. The latter included economic ministers, the central bank governor, the government's chief secretary, and just one nongovernment member.

22. Council members included Mahini Zainal Abidin (director-general of Malaysia's Institute of Strategic Studies); Zainal Azman Yusof (deputy-director of the World Bank); Homi J. Kharas (Brookings Institution and World Bank economist); Danny Quah (London School of Economics professor); Yukon Huang (advisor to the World Bank and Asian Development Bank); Andrew Sheng (former Bank Negara chief economist and chairman of the Hong Kong Securities and Futures Commission); Nicholas S. Zeffreys (president of the American Malaysian Chamber of Commerce); Hamzah Kassim (a consultant on technology and public policy); Dzulkifli Abdul Razak (vice-chancellor of University Sains Malaysia).

23. The NEAC had a formal Advisory Group to the Secretariat.

24. Norma Mansor (secretary to the NEAC), interview by author, November 28, 2016, Kuala Lumpur.

25. For details, see the List of Key Engagements in NEAC 2010a, 121–27.

26. The NEM identified the following eight SRIs: reorganizing the private sector; developing a quality workforce and reducing dependence on foreign labor; creating a competitive domestic economy; transparent and market-friendly affirmative action; building the knowledge base infrastructure; enhancing the sources of growth; strengthening the public sector; re-energizing the private sector to drive growth; and ensuring the sustainability of growth.

27. Mansor interview by author.

28. These sectors were oil, gas, and energy; palm oil and rubber; wholesale and retail; financial services; tourism; electronics and electrical; business services; communications content and infrastructure; education; agriculture; healthcare; and Greater Kuala Lumpur and Klang Valley.

29. Pemandu invitations for the labs were sent to all commerce organizations with significant memberships.

9. CIVIL SOCIETY AND ELECTORAL REFORM IN MALAYSIA

1. In the pre-1969 period, UMNO relied to an extent on funds from Chinese business interests and the Malaysian Chinese Association. Subsequently, and especially with the advent of the New Economic Policy, a firmer base for Malay political supremacy was created. Political supremacy and political patronage were then mutually reinforcing. This included patronage to selected non-Malays.

2. BN's share of the popular vote in 2004 rose from 57 percent to 64 percent, and it won 90 percent of the seats in national parliament and control of eleven of the twelve state governments (Aeria 2012, 333).

3. Liew Chin Tong (DAP member of parliament), interview by author, December 11, 2015, Kuala Lumpur.

4. Tian Chua (PKR vice-president), interview by author, December 8, 2015, Kuala Lumpur.

5. In the original 1957 Constitution discrepancies were limited to 15 percent, but amendments in 1962 and 1973 removed this specific restriction on weightings.

6. In the 2013 general elections, for example, the electorate of Putrajaya had around 15,700 voters, while Kapar had about 145,000 (Ostwald 2013, 526).

7. This included bringing activists from Kelantan, Terengganu, and the northern states into the capital days ahead of the rally to bypass blockades by authorities (Liew 2013, 301).

8. Estimates ranged from 20,000–50,000 (H. G. Lee 2008, 190).

9. Under that framework, grievances by ethnic Indians should be channeled through the Malaysian Indian Congress (MIC) party, a member of the BN coalition government.

10. A two-thirds majority enables the government to enact constitutional change through legislation.

11. Losses by the MIC, the Malaysian Chinese Association (MCA) and Parti Gerakan Rakyat Malaysia (Malaysian People's Movement Party) were substantial (see Ufen 2009, 617–19).

12. Most analysts explained this in terms of the threat local elections posed for the ruling coalition and its racial political formula (see Rabushka 1970; Enloe 1975; Cheema and Hussein 1978), though some disagreed with this assessment (see Tennant 1973).

13. Indeed, the Federal Court would eventually rule, in August 2014, that the constitution does not allow for the EC to preside over local elections, but this would not stop state governments from using alternative mechanisms to select councillors using more democratic methods—an option that has not been adopted by the opposition (Himanshu 2014).

14. Francis Loh (Penang councilor, academic, and activist with the social justice-oriented Aliran NGO), interview by author, February 6, 2012, Penang.

15. Lim Kah Cheng (Penang councilor and activist with the Women's Centre for Change NGO), interview by author, February 7, 2012, Penang.

16. Chow Kon Yeow (Penang State executive councilor responsible for local government elections), interview by author, February 6, 2012, Penang.

17. Lim interview by author.

18. Ronnie Liu (Selangor state executive councilor for Local Government, Research, and Development and member of the DAP), interview by author, February 16, 2012, Kuala Lumpur.

19. Richard Yeoh (Selangor councilor and Transparency International NGO activist), interview by author, January 28, 2011, Kuala Lumpur.

20. Liu interview by author.

21. Tan Jo Hann (chairman of the Coalition of Non-Governmental Organisations and Professional Appointed Councilors), interview by author, February 10, 2012, Kuala Lumpur, and Chow Kon Yeow, interview by author, February 6, 2012, Penang.

22. An earlier and more serious indication, although not publicly known until November 2015, was that an UMNO-proposed "Malay unity government" incorporating PAS had been given quiet consideration after the 2008 general election by conservative PAS leader Abdul Hadi Awang (*Malaysiakini* 2015a).

23. Tian Chua, interview by author, December 8, 2015, Kuala Lumpur.

24. Wong Chin Huat (Bersih organizer and academic), interview by author, December 7, 2015, Kuala Lumpur.

25. Among those arrested was PKR vice-president, Tian Chua, whose five-year struggle in the courts led to his imprisonment in late September 2017. Amnesty International declared Chua a prisoner of conscience and called for his immediate release (Karim 2017).

26. Wong interview by author.

27. Maria Chin Abdullah (Bersih steering committee member and feminist and human rights activist), interview by author, December 9, 2015, Kuala Lumpur.

28. Liew interview by author.

29. Najib also pledged in September 2011 to repeal laws curtailing civil liberties, including the Internal Security Act (ISA), four emergency proclamations, and the police act covering public assemblies and printing permits (Aeria 2012, 344). These reforms would not materialize though.

30. Wong interview by author.

31. At its peak, around 60 percent of households became eligible for Bantuan Rakyat 1 Malaysia before declining commodity prices for Malaysian exports saw a retreat in 2016 from the generosity of the scheme.

32. This included Nik Aziz's vehement opposition to PAS leader Abdul Hadi Awang's willingness to consider working with UMNO in Perak and Selangor after March 2008. This infighting was publicly revealed in November 2015 (see *Malaysiakini* 2015a).

33. The progressives' inductive reading of the Quran was influenced by *maqasidic* theory, which contrasted with the more literal reading of the Quran adopted by the conservatives in PAS. See Dzulkefly 2015.

34. The joint program *Buku Jingga* of PR did not include any mention of *hudud*.

35. Amanah was established on September 16, 2015, and Pakatan Harapan on September 22, 2015.

36. According to Rasiah (2015, 91), legal and illegal foreign workers may have comprised around four million, or a quarter of the total employed workforce, by 2012.

37. By 2016, 1MDB would amass debts in excess of $US12.7 billion (Adam 2016).

38. The ringgit was trading at levels not seen since the Asian financial crisis of 1997–1998.

39. In the documentary *State of Fear* (ABC 2016), on September 4, 2015, Kevin Morais, one of Malaysia's most senior public prosecutors, was dragged from his car by unidentified men in traffic and found murdered twelve days later. Days prior to his abduction he had prepared the charge sheets against Prime Minister Najib.

40. Wong, interview by author.

41. Chua interview by author.

42. Dzulkefly Ahmad (former PAS member of parliament and member of the PAS central working committee, then parliamentary representative for Parti Amanah Negara), interview by author, December 10, 2015, Kuala Lumpur.

43. Most at this "United Citizens' Gathering," as it was called, wore Malay Dignity Gathering red T-shirts.

44. This was the estimate by *Malaysiakini*, while police estimates were around 50,000. UMNO Supreme Council member Mohd Shakar Shamsudin maintained that more than 100,000 people rallied while Selangor UMNO head Noh Omar estimated 200,000 (see *Malaysiakini* 2015e).

45. Chin Abdullah interview by author.

46. Liew interview by author.

47. Wong interview by author.

48. Liew interview by author.

49. For the full list of demands see *Aliran* (2016a).

50. The demands were for clean elections; clean government; strengthening parliamentary democracy; right to dissent; and empowering Sabah and Sarawak.

51. This act replaced the ISA in 2012.

References

Abad, Florencio. 2013. "Closing Remarks of the Secretary of Budget and Management." Speech delivered at the Philippine Economic Briefing, Manila, September 17. http://www.gov.ph/2013/09/17/closing-remarks-of-the-secretary-of-budget-and -management-at-the-philippine-economic-briefing.

ABAMIN (Abante Mindanao Party-List). n.d. "ABAMIN Homepage." Accessed June 30, 2014. http://abamin.webs.com.

ABC (Australian Broadcasting Corporation). 2016. "State of Fear: Murder and Money in Malaysia." *Four Corners*, March 28. Documentary. http://www.abc.net.au/4corners /stories/2016/03/28/4431284.htm.

——. 2017. "Rodrigo Duterte: Philippines President Presides over a Nation Divided as Opposition to Drug War Grows." August 28. http://www.abc.net.au/news/2017-08 -28/rodrigo-duterte-philippines-extrajudicial-killing-is-stronghold/8847614.

Abdul, Razak Ahmad. 1999. "NECC II 'An Effective Channel for Students.'" *New Straits Times*, August 8.

Abinales, Patricio N. 2013. "The Philippines under Aquino III, Year 2: A Ponderous Slog Continues." In *Southeast Asian Affairs*, edited by Daljit Singh, 221–239. Singapore: Institute of Southeast Asian Studies.

Abinales, Patricio N., and Donna J. Amoroso. 2005. *State and Society in the Philippines*. Lanham: Rowman & Littlefield Publishers.

ABS-CBN News. 2013. "SC Party-List Ruling Assailed." April 7, 2013. http://www.abs -cbnnews.com/nation/04/07/13/sc-party-list-ruling-assailed.

Adam, Shamim. 2013. "Singapore Protest Exposes Voter Worries about Immigration." *Bloomberg*, February 18. http://www.bloomberg.com/news/articles/2013-02-16 /singaporeans-protest-plan-to-increase-population-by-immigration.

——. 2016. "Malaysia's Troubled 1MDB at Risk of Default." *Australian*, April 20.

ADB (Asian Development Bank). 2012. *The KALAHI-CIDDS Project in the Philippines: Sharing Knowledge on Community-Driven Development*. Manila: Asian Development Bank. Accessed October 26, 2015. http://adb.org/sites/default/files/pub/2012 /kalahi-cidss-project-philippines.pdf.

Adel, Rosette. 2016. "Comelec Proclaims 46 Winning Party-lists." *Philippine Star*, May 19. http://www.philstar.com:8080/headlines/2016/05/20/1584908/comelec-proclaims -46-winning-party-lists.

Aeria, Andrew. 2012. "BERSIH! Expanding Democratic Space via Electoral Reform in Malaysia." In *From Unity to Multiplicities: Social Movements and Democratization in Asia*, edited by Hee-Yon Cho, Andrew Aeria, and Songwoo Hur, 331–50. Petaling Jaya: Strategic Information and Research Development Centre.

Africa, Sonny. 2013. "Philippine NGOs: Defusing Dissent, Spurring Change." *Pingkian: Journal for Emancipatory and Anti-Imperialist Education* 1 (2): 49–66.

Ahmad, Osman. 2000. "AMP Drops Idea for Separate Leaders." *Straits Times*, December 23.

Aidila, Razak. 2010. "EC Can't Hold Local Polls for Penang, S'gor." *Malaysiakini*, March 28. http://www.malaysiakini.com/news/127330.

——. 2011a. "Delegates Flay PAS-Led Kedah Gov't." *Malaysiakini*, November 26. http:// www.malaysiakini.com/news/182523.

——. 2011b. "Perkasa Hijacked NEM, Says NEAC Man." *Malaysiakini*, February 9. https://www.malaysiakini.com/news/155486.

Aidila, Razak, and Tek Chi Wong. 2010. "Confusion Abounds in S'gor Local Councils." *Malaysiakini*, July 8. http://www.malaysiakini.com/news/136815.

AKB (Ako Bicol Party-list). 2010. "AKB Party-list: About." Accessed June 30, 2014. https://www.facebook.com/akobicolpartylist.

Akbayan. 2010. "About Akbayan: Brief History." https://akbayan.org.ph/who-we-are.

Aliran. 2010. "Penang Forum: Expectations of the Elected." *Aliran Monthly* 30 (10): 13.

——. 2016a. "Demands of the Citizens' Declaration." *Aliran*, March 4. http://aliran.com /civil-society-voices/2016-civil-society-voices/demands-citizens-declaration.

——. 2016b. "National Security Council Must Go, Says Bersih 2.0." *Aliran*, March 16. http://aliran.com/coalitions/clean-and-fair-elections/national-security-council -bill-must-go-says-bersih-2-0.

Al Jafree, Md Yusop. 2013. "PAS Fears Racial Politics in Local Council Polls." *Ant Daily*, August 30. http://www.theantdaily.com/news/2013/08/30/pas-fears-racial-politics -local-council-polls.

Almén, Oscar. 2016. "Local Participatory Innovations and Experts as Political Entre-preneurs: The Case of China's Democracy Consultants." *Democratization* 23 (3): 478–97.

Alvarez, Kathrina. 2013. "Lawmakers Split on SC Party-List Ruling." *Sun Star*, April 6. http://archive.sunstar.com.ph/manila/local-news/2013/04/06/lawmakers-split-sc -party-list-ruling-276267.

——. 2016. "DBM Scraps Aquino Admin's Bottom-Up Budgeting, Says It's a 'Waste of Funds.'" *GMA News*, July 14. http://www.gmanetwork.com/news/story/573698 /money/economy/dbm-scraps-aquino-admin-s-bottom-up-budgeting-says-it-s-a -waste-of-funds.

Amnesty International. 2016. *Critical Crackdown: Freedom of Expression under Attack in Malaysia*. London: Amnesty International.

Anakbayan. 2012. "Letter to Comelec to DQ Akbayan." Press release, October 3. http:// www.anakbayan.org/letter-to-comelec-to-dq-akbayan.

Anderson, Benedict. 1988. "Cacique Democracy in the Philippines: Origins and Dreams." *New Left Review* 169 (3): 3–31.

Anderson, Theo. 2017. "The Right-Wing Machine behind the Curtain." *In These Times*, April 14. http://inthesetimes.com/features/trump_pence_heritage_foundation.html.

Añonuevo, Carlos Antonio Q. 2000. "Philippine Trade Union Profile." FES Online Pa-pers, July 12. Manila: Friedrich Ebert Stiftung Philippine Office. http://library.fes .de/pdf-files/bueros/philippinen/50082.pdf.

Aquino, Benigno III. 2010. "2010 State of the Nation Address." Speech delivered at the Congress of the Philippines, Batasan Pambansa Complex, Quezon City, July 26. http://www.gov.ph/2010/07/26/state-of-the-nation-address-2010-en.

Aram, Ziai. 2004. "The Ambivalence of Post-Development: Between Reactionary Popu-lism and Radical Democracy." *Third World Quarterly* 25 (6): 1045–60.

Arnson, Cynthia J., and Jose Raul Perales, eds. 2007. *The "New Left" and Democratic Gov-ernance in Latin America*. Washington, DC: Woodrow Wilson International Centre for Scholars.

Asher, Mukul. 1994. "Some Aspects of Role of State in Singapore." *Economic and Political Weekly* 29 (14): 795–804.

Asia Foundation. 2009. *The Mechanisms to Settle Administrative Complaints in Vietnam: Challenges and Solutions*. Prepared by the Policy, Law, and Development Institute, August. Vietnam: Asia Foundation. Accessed April 24, 2015. http://asiafoundation .org/resources/pdfs/VNAdminComplaintSettleReportEnglish.pdf.

Asrul, Hadi Abdullah Sani. 2010. "Umno Is Scared of US, Says Anwar." *Malaysian In-sider*, November 28. http://lite.themalaysianinsider.com/malaysia/article/umno-is-scared-of-us-says-anwar.

Avritzer, Leonardo. 2013. "Democratic Innovation and Social Participation in Brazil." *Taiwan Journal of Democracy* 9 (2): 153–70.

Aw, Melissa. 2012. "We Will Engage in National Conversation: Heng." Yahoo News, August 26. https://sg.news.yahoo.com/we-will-engage-in-a-national-conversation—heng.html.

Bacani, Louis. 2013. " 'Historic Moment': House Body OKs Anti-Political Dynasty Bill." *Philippine Star*, November 20. http://www.philstar.com/headlines/2013/11/20/1258900/historic-moment-house-body-oks-anti-political-dynasty-bill.

Baiocchi, Gianpaolo, Patrick Heller, and Marcelo K. Silva. 2011. *Bootstrapping Democracy: Transforming Local Governance and Civil Society in Brazil*. Stanford, CA: Stanford University Press.

Balderacchi, Claudio. 2016. "Problems and Contradictions of Participatory Democracy: Lessons from Latin America." *Contemporary Politics* 22 (2): 164–77.

Barr, Michael. 2006. "Beyond Technocracy: The Culture of Elite Governance in Lee Hsien Loong's Singapore." *Asian Studies Review* 30 (1): 1–18.

——. 2010. "Marxists in Singapore? Lee Kuan Yew's Campaign Against Catholic Social Justice Activists in the 1980s." *Critical Asian Studies* 42 (3): 335–62.

——. 2014. *The Ruling Elite of Singapore: Networks of Power and Influence*. London: I. B. Taurus & Co.

BBC News. 2011. "President Aquino Says Tackling Corruption Key to Growth." November 12. http://www.bbc.co.uk/news/world-asia-pacific-12708841.

Bee, Cristiano, and Dimitri Pachi. 2014. "Active Citizenship in the UK: Assessing Institutional Political Strategies and Mechanisms of Civic Engagement." *Journal of Civil Society* 10 (1): 100–117.

Beetham, David. 2004. "Towards a Universal Framework for Democracy Assessment." *Democratization* 11 (2): 1–17.

Bellin, Eva. 2000. "Contingent Democrats: Industrialists, Labor, and Democratization in Late-Developing Countries." *World Politics* 52 (2): 175–205.

Bello, Walden. 2015. "Power and Principle: The Vicissitudes of a Sociologist in Parliament." *Global Dialogue*, July 4. http://isa-global-dialogue.net/power-and-principle-the-vicissitudes-of-a-sociologist-in-parliament-july-4-2015.

Bello, Walden, and John Gershman. 1990. "Democratization and Stabilization in the Philippines." *Critical Sociology* 17 (1): 35–56.

Bensahel, Nora. 2004. "Political Reform in the Middle East." In *The Future Security Environment of the Middle East: Conflict, Stability, and Political Change*, edited by Nora Bensahel and Daniel L. Byman, 15–55. Santa Monica, CA: RAND Corporation.

Berman, Sheri. 2016. "The Lost Left." *Journal of Democracy* 27 (4): 69–76.

Bernama. 2012. "MTRK: People of Kelantan are Calling for a Change in Leadership." December 27. http://www.kualalumpurpost.net/mtrk-people-of-kelantan-are-calling-for-a-change-in-leadership.

Bernas, Joaquin G. 2007. "The Party-list Experiment." *Philippine Daily Inquirer*, April 30. https://global.factiva.com.

Berthelsen, John. 2016. "Power, Najib's Money and Malaysia's Corrupt System." *Asia Sentinel*, March 2. http://www.asiasentinel.com/politics/power-najibs-money-and-malaysias-corrupt-system.

Bird, Karen. 2005. "The Political Representation of Visible Minorities in Electoral Democracies: A Comparison of France, Denmark, and Canada." *Nationalism and Ethnic Politics* 11: 425–65.

Bird, Karen, Thomas Saalfeld, and Andreas M. Wüst, eds. 2011. *The Political Representation of Immigrants and Minorities: Voters, Parties and Parliaments in Liberal Democracies*. Abingdon: Routledge.

Blakkarly, Jarni. 2015. "Yellow Protesters Unafraid Calling for PM's Resignation." *Al Jazeera*, August 30. http://www.aljazeera.com/indepth/features/2015/08/yellow -protesters-defiant-calls-pm-resignation-150830094449440.html.

Boggards, Matthijs. 2009. "How to Classify Hybrid Regimes? Defective Democracy and Electoral Authoritarianism." *Democratization* 16 (2): 399–423.

Bordadora, Norman. 2012. "Aquino: Corona Ouster Brightens Democracy." *Philippines Daily Inquirer*, June 13. http://newsinfo.inquirer.net/210847/corona%E2%80%99s -ouster-proof-democracy-alive-in-ph.

Boudreau, Vincent. 2009. "Elections, Repression and Authoritarian Survival in Post-transition Indonesia and the Philippines." *Pacific Review* 22 (2): 233–53.

Brennan, Jason. 2016. *Against Democracy*. Princeton, NJ: Princeton University Press.

Brillantes, Alex B., Jr. 2007. "The Philippines: Civic Participation in Local Governance-Focus on Subnational Budgeting and Planning." In *Participatory Budgeting*, edited by Anwar Shah, 49–65. Washington, DC: The World Bank.

Brito Vieira, Monica, and David Runciman. 2008. *Representation*. Cambridge: Polity Press.

Brown, David. 2000. *Contemporary Nationalism: Civic, Ethnocultural and Multicultural Politics*. London: Routledge.

Brown, Mark B. 2006. "Survey Article: Citizen Panels and the Concept of Representation." *Journal of Political Philosophy* 14 (2): 203–25.

Brownlee, Jason. 2007. *Authoritarianism in an Age of Democratization*. New York: Cambridge University Press.

——. 2008. "Bound to Rule: Party Institutions and Regime Trajectories in Malaysia and the Philippines." *Journal of East Asian Studies* 8 (1): 89–118.

Bueza, Michael Joseph. 2013. "Sectoral? Party List Votes Come from Reg'l Bailiwicks." *Rappler*, June 14. http://www.rappler.com/nation/31314-party-list-votes-regional -bailiwicks.

Burgonio, T. J. A. 2012a. "Aquino Praises NGOs." *Philippine Daily Inquirer*, November 23. http://newsinfo.inquirer.net/311525/aquino-praises-ngos.

——. 2012b. "Aquino Signs P2-T 'Empowering Nat'l Budget.'" *Philippine Daily Inquirer*, December 20. http://newsinfo.inquirer.net/326887/aquino-signs-p2-0tr-budget -for-2013

——. 2013. "Sona Focus Is Growth for Everyone." *Philippine Daily Inquirer*, July 11.

Burke, Edmund. 1968. *Reflections on the Revolution in France*. London: Penguin.

Burnham, Peter. 2001. "New Labour and the Politics of Depoliticization." *British Journal of Politics and International Relations* 3 (2): 127–49.

——. 2014. "Depoliticisation: Economic Crisis and Political Management." *Policy and Politics* 42 (2): 189–206.

Business Daily. 2015. "New CRA Rules Seek Greater Public Input in Country Budgets." *Business Daily*, December 5. http://www.businesstoday.co.ke/news/money-and -markets/1427207692/new-cra-rules-seek-greater-public-input-county-budgets

Buur, Lars. 2009. "The Politics of Gradualismo: Popular Participation and Decentralised Governance in Mozambique." In *Rethinking Popular Representation*, edited by Olle Törnquist, Neil Webster, and Kristian Stokke, 99–118. London: Palgrave Macmillan.

Cai, Yongshun. 2005. "China's Moderate Middle Class: The Case of Homeowners' Resistance." *Asian Survey* 45 (5): 777–99.

Cameron, Maxwell A., and Kenneth E. Sharpe. 2010. "Andean Left Turns: Constituent Power and Constitution-Making." In *Latin America's Left Turns: Politics, Policies and Trajectories of Change*, edited by Maxwell A. Cameron and Eric Hershberg, 61–79. Boulder, CO: Lynne Rienner.

——. 2012. "Voice and Consequence: Direct Participation and Democracy in Latin America." In *New Institutions for Participatory Democracy in Latin America: Voice and Consequence*, edited by Maxwell A. Cameron, Eric Hershberg, and Kenneth E. Sharpe, 1–20. New York: Palgrave Macmillan.

Capoccia, Giovanni, and Daniel Ziblatt. 2010. "The Historical Turn in Democratization Studies: A New Research Agenda for Europe and Beyond." *Comparative Political Studies* 43 (8/9): 931–68.

Carothers, Thomas. 2002. "The End of the Transitional Paradigm." *Journal of Democracy* 13 (1): 5–21.

——. 2006. *Confronting the Weakest Link: Aiding Political Parties in New Democracies.* Washington, DC: Carnegie Endowment for International Peace.

Carroll, Toby. 2010. *Delusions of Development: The World Bank and the Post-Washington Consensus.* Basingstoke: Palgrave Macmillan.

Case, William. 1996. "Can the 'Halfway House' Stand? Semidemocracy and Elite Theory in Three Southeast Asian Countries." *Comparative Politics* 28 (4): 437–64.

——. 2002. *Politics in Southeast Asia: Democracy More or Less.* London: Curzon.

——. 2010. "Transition from Single-Party Dominance? New Data from Malaysia." *Journal of East Asia* 10 (1): 91–126.

——. 2017. "Stress Testing Leadership in Malaysia: The 1MDB Scandal and Najib Tun Razak." *Pacific Review* 30 (5): 633–54.

Cayabyab, Marc Jayson de Vera, and Mikhail Franz Espaldon Flores. 2012. "From Alternative to Traditional: An Investigative Study on Party-List Representation in the 15th Philippine Congress." Undergraduate thesis, College of Mass Communication, University of the Philippines Diliman.

Centre for Public Policy Studies. 2008. *Elections '08 Daily Policy Factsheet #7: Local Government.* Kuala Lumpur: CPPS Policy Fact Sheets. Accessed October 7, 2016. http://www.cpps.org.my/resource_centre/Local%20Government.pdf.

Chan, Christine. 2010. "PAS Leaders Pose Questions over Local Polls." *Malaysiakini*, March 12. http://www.malaysiakini.com/news/126396.

Chan, Heng Chee. 1971. *Singapore: The Politics of Survival 1965–1967.* Singapore: Oxford University Press.

——. 1975. "Politics in an Administrative State: Where Has the Politics Gone?" Occasional Paper Series. Singapore: Department of Political Science, University of Singapore.

Chan, Robin. 2013a. "GDP Growth Forecast Up, PM Lee Says Govt to Do More to Build Fair Society." *Straits Times*, August 8. http://www.straitstimes.com/singapore/gdp-growth-forecast-up-pm-lee-says-govt-to-do-more-to-build-fair-society.

——. 2013b. "Why Setting a Poverty Line May Not Be Helpful." *Straits Times*, October 23. http://www.straitstimes.com/singapore/why-setting-a-poverty-line-may-not-be-helpful-minister-chan-chun-sing.

——. 2014. "At the End of the Day, NMPs Make the House Better." *Straits Times*, August 8. http://news.asiaone.com/news/singapore/end-day-nmps-make-house-better.

Chandhoke, Neera. 2009. "What Is the Relationship between Participation and Representation?" In *Rethinking Popular Representation*, edited by Olle Törnquist, Neil Webster, and Kristian Stokke, 25–38. London: Palgrave Macmillan.

Chang, Rachel. 2012. "Framing THE Singapore Conversation." *Straits Times*, September 15. http://lkyspp.nus.edu.sg/ips/wp-content/uploads/sites/2/2013/06/ST_Framing-THE-Singapore-Conversation_150912.pdf.

——. 2013. "Our Singapore Conversation Enters Phase 2." *Straits Times*, March 3. https://0-global.factiva.com.prospero.murdoch.edu.au/ha/default.aspx#./!?&_suid=14440166481060197871334777771546.

——. 2015a. "A Unicorn's Identity Crisis." *Straits Times*, September 6. http://www.straitstimes.com/politics/a-unicorns-identity-crisis.

——. 2015b. "GE2015: Party Big Guns Draw Battle Lines for Coming Polls." *Straits Times*, August 27. http://www.straitstimes.com/politics/ge2015-party-big-guns-draw-battle-lines-for-coming-polls?login=true.

——. 2015c. "GE2015: PM Lee Urges Singaporeans to 'Vote in Good Conscience' as Campaign Hits Mid-Way Point." *Straits Times*, September 5. http://www.straits times.com/politics/ge2015-pm-lee-urges-singaporeans-to-vote-in-good-conscience-as-campaign-hits-mid-way-point.

Channel NewsAsia. 2012. "Panel Spearheading National Conversation on Singapore's Future Unveiled." September 8. http://www.channelnewsasia.com/news/panel-spearheading-national-conversation-on-singapore-s-future-unveiled/481660.html.

Chaudhry, Kiren Aziz. 1997. *The Price of Wealth: Economics and Institutions in the Middle East*. Ithaca, NY: Cornell University Press.

Cheema, Shabbir G., and Ahmad S. Hussein. 1978. "Local Government Reform in Malaysia." *Asian Survey* 18 (6): 577–91.

Chia, Lianne. 2016. "Elected Presidency Review: Bill to Amend Singapore's Constitution Tabled in Parliament." Channel NewsAsia, October 10. http://www.channelnewsasia.com/news/singapore/elected-presidency-review-bill-to-amend-singapore-s-constitution/3194646.html.

Chia, Yan Min. 2017. "Temasek's Net Portfolio Value Hits Record High." *Straits Times*, July 12, 1.

Chin Abdullah, Maria. 2008. "Local Government and Public Participation: The NGOs." Paper presented at the workshop Local Government in Malaysia: The Search for New Directions, University of Malaya, Kuala Lumpur, Malaysia, May 22.

Chong, Zi Liang. 2015a. "Entrench Opposition Presence, Urges WP Chief." *Straits Times*, August 27. http://www.straitstimes.com/singapore/entrench-opposition-presence-urges-wp-chief.

——. 2015b. "GE2015: PAP Saw Swing in Support from Middle-High-Income Earners, IPS Survey Finds." *Straits Times*, November 4. http://www.straitstimes.com/politics/ge2015-pap-saw-swing-in-support-from-middle-high-income-earners-ips-survey-finds.

Choo, Remy. 2016. "New Bill on Contempt of Court Proposes Unusually Harsh Punishment." *Online Citizen*, July 12. http://www.theonlinecitizen.com/2016/07/12/new-bill-on-contempt-of-court-proposes-unusually-harsh-punishment.

Chow, Jermyn. 2015. "Credit to Opposition? It's Just a Rooster's Boast: ESM Goh." *Straits Times*, August 27. http://www.straitstimes.com/politics/singapolitics/credit-to-opposition-its-just-a-roosters-boast-esm-goh.

Chua, Beng Huat. 1994. "Arrested Development: Democratization in Singapore." *Third World Quarterly* 15 (4): 655–68.

——. 1997. *Political Legitimacy and Housing: Stakeholding in Singapore*. London: Routledge.

——. 2007. "Political Culturalism, Representation and the People's Action Party of Singapore." *Democratization* 14 (5): 911–27.

Chun, Han Wong. 2013a. "In Singapore, Calls for Poverty Line Amid Rising Inequality." *Wall Street Journal*, November 11. http://blogs.wsj.com/searealtime/2013/11/11/in-singapore-calls-for-poverty-line-amid-rising-inequality.

——. 2013b. "Singaporeans Protest Immigration Plans." *Wall Street Journal*, February 16. http://www.wsj.com/articles/SB10001424127887324616604578308222594086686.

——. 2013c. "Singapore Strike: The Full Story." *Wall Street Journal*, August 31. http://blogs.wsj.com/indonesiarealtime/2013/08/31/singapore-strike-the-full-story/tab/print.

Chun, Han Wong, and Esther Fung. 2013. "Rare Riot Hits Singapore: Fatal Road Accident Angers Foreign Workers." *Wall Street Journal*, December 8. http://www.wsj.com/news/articles/SB10001424052702303330204579246540635617948?cb=logged0.9609431177377701.

Clutterbuck, Richard. 1973. *Riot and Revolution in Singapore and Malaya 1945–63*. London: Faber & Faber.

Collier, Ruth B., and Samuel Handlin. 2009. *Reorganizing Popular Politics: Participation and the New Interest Regime in Latin America*. University Park: Pennsylvania State University Press.

Comelec (Election Commission of the Philippines). 2007. "2007 National and Local Elections-Results: National Tally Sheet." *Party-list Canvass Report*, No. 33. Accessed February 11, 2015. http://www.comelec.gov.ph/?r=Archives/RegularElections/2007NLE/Results/07partyrpage.

——. 2010. "2010 Election Results." Accessed April 4, 2011. http://electionresults.comelec.gov.ph.

ConCom (Constitutional Commission). 1986. *Record of the Constitutional Commission, Proceedings and Debates*. Vol. 2. Manila: Republic of the Philippines.

Coronel, Sheila S., Yvonne T. Chua, Luz Rimban, and Booma C. Cruz. 2004. *The Rulemakers: How the Wealthy and Well-born Dominate Congress*. Manila: Philippine Center for Investigative Journalism.

Corpuz, Gerry Albert. 2004. "Partly-list Groups Deplore 'State-directed Fraud and Terrorism.'" *Bulatlat*, May 16. http://www.bulatlat.com/news/4-15/4-15-partylist.html.

Croissant, Aurel, and Wolfgang Merkel. 2004. "Introduction: Democratization in the Early Twenty-First Century." *Democratization* 11 (5): 1–9.

Crouch, Colin. 2004. *Post-Democracy*. Cambridge: Polity Press.

——. 2011. *The Strange Non-Death of Neoliberalism*. Cambridge: Polity Press.

Cruz, Elfren S. 2013. "Combating Judicial Corruption." *Philippine Star*, October 10. http://www.philstar.com/opinion/2013/10/10/1243554/combating-judicial-corruption.

——. 2014. "How the Left Must Evolve." *Philippine Star*, March 27. http://www.philstar.com/opinion/2014/03/27/1305525/how-left-must-evolve.

Cruz, Neal H. 2013. "Party-List System Is Being Abused." *Philippines Daily Inquirer*, April 15. http://opinion.inquirer.net/50735/party-list-system-is-being-abused.

Cuarteros, Gladstone A. 2005. "State and Civil Society Relations in Legislating Local Sectoral Representation." In *Policy Advocacy: Experiences and Lessons from the Philippines*, edited by Institute for Popular Democracy, 48–68. Quezon City: Institute for Popular Democracy.

Curato, Nicole. 2016. "Politics of Anxiety, Politics of Hope: Penal Populism and Duterte's Rise to Power." *Journal of Southeast Asian Affairs* 3: 91–109.

Dahl, Robert. 1956. *A Preface to Democratic Theory*. Chicago: University of Chicago.

Daily Mail. 2016. "Philippine Boxing Legend Pacquiao Punches Way into Senate." *Daily Mail*, May 10. http://www.dailymail.co.uk/wires/afp/article-3582491/Philippine-boxing-legend-Pacquiao-punches-way-Senate.html.

Daly, Eoin, and Seelan Singham. 2011. "Jump-Starting Malaysia's Growth: An Interview with Idris Jala." *McKinsey & Company: Insights and Publications*, October, 2011. http://www.mckinsey.com/industries/public-sector/our-insights/jump-starting-malaysias-growth-an-interview-with-idris-jala.

David, Randy. 2012. "Crumbs from the Master's Table." *Philippine Daily Inquirer*, October 17. http://opinion.inquirer.net/38946/crumbs-from-the-masters-table.

Davies, Jonathan S. 2007. "The Limits of Partnership: An Exit-Action Strategy for Local Democratic Inclusion." *Political Studies* 5 (4): 779–800.

——. 2012. "Active Citizenship: Navigating the Conservative Heartlands of the New Labour Project." *Policy and Politics* 40 (1): 3–19.

DBM (Department of Budget and Management). 2015. *People's Proposed Budget 2016.* August, 2015. Philippines: Department of Budget and Management. Accessed October 17, 2015. http://www.dbm.gov.ph/?page_id=13550.

DBM-DILG-DSWD-NAPC. 2012. *DBM-DILG-DSWD-NAPC Joint Memorandum Circular No. 2.* December 19. Manila: Republic of the Philippines, Department of Budget and Management. http://www.dbm.gov.ph/wp-content/uploads/Issuances/2012/Joint%20Memorandum%20Circular/JMC2012-2/JMC2012-2.pdf.

——. 2013. *DBM-DILG-DSWD-NAPC Joint Memorandum Circular No. 4.* November 26. Manila: Republic of the Philippines, Department of Budget and Management. http://www.dbm.gov.ph/wp-content/uploads/Issuances/2013/Joint%20Memorandum%20Circular/JMC-4.pdf.

de la Torre, Carlos. 2013. "Technocratic Populism in Ecuador." *Journal of Democracy* 24 (3): 33–46.

Della, Percy. 2016. "1Pacman's Practical Piggyback Ride." *Philippine Daily Inquirer*, May 27. http://sports.inquirer.net/213291/1pacmans-practical-piggyback-ride.

de Quiros, Conrado. 2013. "What the Right Hand Gives." *Philippines Daily Inquirer*, April 16. http://opinion.inquirer.net/50853/what-the-right-hand-gives.

Deyo, Frederic C. 1981. *Dependent Development and Industrial Order: An Asian Case Study.* New York: Praeger.

——. 2006. "South-East Asian Industrial Labour: Structural Demobilisation and Political Transformation." In *The Political Economy of South-East Asia: Markets, Power and Contestation*, edited by Garry Rodan, Kevin Hewison, and Richard Robison, 283–304. Melbourne: Oxford University Press.

Diamond, Larry. 1989. "Preface." In *Democracy in Developing Countries: Asia*, edited by Larry Diamond, Juan J. Linz, and Lynne Martin Lipset, ix–xxvii. Boulder, CO: Lynne Rienner.

——. 2002. "Thinking About Hybrid Regimes." *Journal of Democracy* 13 (2): 21–35.

Diaz, Jess. 2010. "Ako Bicol Vows to Support Aquino Administration." *Philippine Star*, July 2. http://www.philstar.com/nation/589109/ako-bicol-vows-support-aquino-administration.

——. 2016a. "Belmonte Files Anti-Dynasty Bill." *Philippine Star*, July 3. http://www.philstar.com/headlines/2016/07/03/1599038/belmonte-files-anti-dynasty-bill.

——. 2016b. "Duterte Urged to Reform Party-list System." *Philippine Star*, August 1. http://www.philstar.com/headlines/2016/08/01/1608898/duterte-urged-reform-party-list-system.

Dichter, Alex, Fredrik Lind, and Seelan Singham. 2008. "Turning around a Struggling Airline: An Interview with the CEO of Malaysia Airlines." *McKinsey & Company: Insights and Publications*, November. Accessed December 16, 2015. http://www.mckinsey.com/global-themes/leadership/turning-around-a-struggling-airline-an-interview-with-the-ceo-of-malaysia-airlines.

Diola, Camille. 2014. "Philippines 6th in World for Marcos Era-Like Crony Capitalism." *Philippine Star*, March 19. http://www.philstar.com/headlines/2014/03/19/1302693/philippines-6th-world-marcos-era-crony-capitalism.

Doorenspleet, Renske. 2000. "Reassessing the Three Waves of Democratization." *World Politics* 52 (3): 384–406.

Doronila, Amando. 2013. "Big Business, Church to Aquino: Perform More." *Daily Inquirer*, July 22, A20. http://opinion.inquirer.net/57095/big-business-church-to-aquino -perform-more.

Dressel, Björn. 2012. "Targeting the Public Purse: Advocacy Coalitions and Public Finance in the Philippines." *Administration and Society* 44 (6 Supplementary): 65s–84s.

Dryzek, John S. 2010. *Foundations and Frontiers of Deliberative Governance*. Oxford: Oxford University Press.

——. 2015. "Democratic Agents of Justice." *Journal of Political Philosophy* 23 (4): 361–84.

Dryzek, John S., and Simon Niemeyer. 2008. "Discursive Representations." *American Political Science Review* 102 (4): 481–93.

Dzulkefly, Ahmad. 2015. "My Say: Maqasid Syariah and a Better Malaysia." *Edge Markets*, November 9. http://www.theedgemarkets.com/my/article/my-say-maqasid-syariah- and-better-malaysia.

Easter, David. 2005. " 'Keep the Indonesia Pot Boiling': Western Covert Intervention in Indonesia, October 1965–March 1996." *Cold War History* 5 (1): 55–73.

Eaton, Kent. 2003. "Restoration or Transformation? Trapos versus NGOs in the Democratization of the Philippines." *Journal of Asian Studies* 62 (2): 469–96.

Economic Times. 2015. "Singapore Economy Would Fail without Foreigners: Lee Hsien Loong." August 23. http://economictimes.indiatimes.com/news/international/business /singapore-economy-would-fail-without-foreigners-lee-hsien-loong/articleshow /48643674.cms.

Economist. 2006. "Singapore's Election: Ten in a Row for the Men in White." May 11. http://www.economist.com/node/6919244.

——. 2013. "Regulating Singapore's Internet: Two Steps Back." June 5. http://www .economist.com/blogs/banyan/2013/06/regulating-singapores-internet.

——. 2014. "Coming Up Jasmine." August 23. http://www.economist.com/news /finance-and-economics/21613336-once-laggard-economy-philippines-starting -catch-up-coming-up.

Edwards, Vincent, and Anh Phan. 2008. "Trade Unions in Vietnam: From Socialism to Market Socialism." In *Trade Unions in Asia: An Economic and Sociological Analysis*, edited by John Benson and Ying Zhu, 199–214. Abingdon: Routledge.

Eley, Geoff. 2002. *Forging Democracy: The History of the Left in Europe, 1850–2000*. Oxford: Oxford University Press.

Enloe, Cynthia. 1975. "The Neglected Strata: States in the City-Federal Politics of Malaysia." *Publius* 5 (2): 151–70.

Epstein, David L., Robert Bates, Jack Goldstone, Ida Kristensen, and Sharyn O'Halloran. 2006. "Democratic Traditions." *American Journal of Political Science* 50 (3): 551–69.

Esguerra, Leila Salaverria C. V. 2007. "Party-List Groups Take Rule Fight to High Tribunal." *Philippine Daily Inquirer*, July 17. http://global.factiva.com.

Esmaquel, Paterno II. 2012. "Comelec Disqualifies Top Party-list Group." *Rappler*, October 10. http://www.rappler.com/nation/politics/elections-2013/13929-comelec -disqualifies-top-party-list-group.

Far Eastern Economic Review. 1963. "What Is at Stake?" February 21, 349–50.

Feedback Unit. 2004. *Building Bridges: The Story of Feedback Unit*. Singapore: Ministry of Community Development and Sports.

——. 2005. *Shaping Our Home: Turning Ideas into Reality*. Singapore: Ministry of Community Development and Sports.

Fernandez, Warren. 2013. "When Singapore Had a Dream . . . ." *Straits Times*, August 11. http://www.straitstimes.com/the-big-story/asia-report/singapore/story/when -singapore-had-dream-20130811.

Fiorina, Morris P., and Samuel J. Abrams. 2011. *Disconnect: The Breakdown of Representation in American Politics.* Norman: University of Oklahoma Press.

Fishkin, James, He Baogang, Robert Luskin, and Alice Siu. 2010. "Deliberative Democracy in an Unlikely Place: Deliberative Polling in China." *British Journal of Political Science* 40 (2): 435–48.

Flinders, Matthew, and Matt Wood. 2014. "Depoliticisation, Governance and the State." *Policy and Politics* 42 (2): 135–49.

FMT News. 2015. "Hadi Claims Local Elections Recipe for Another May 13." January 23. http://www.freemalaysiatoday.com/category/nation/2015/01/23/hadi-claims-local -elections-recipe-for-another-may-13.

Fong, Sip Chee. 1980. *The PAP Story—The Pioneering Years.* Singapore: Times Periodicals.

Franco, Jennifer Conroy. 2001. *Elections and Democratization in the Philippines.* New York: Routledge.

Frialde, Maike. 2016. "Duterte Camp Accuses Roxas of Buying Votes from Local Execs." *Philippine Star,* February 13. http://www.philstar.com/headlines/2016/02/13/15526 49/duterte-camp-accuses-roxas-buying-votes-local-execs.

Fukuyama, Francis. 1992. *The End of History and the Last Man.* New York: Avon Books.

——. 2013. "Democracy and the Quality of the State." *Journal of Democracy* 24 (4): 5–16.

Fuller, Thomas. 2014. "Sedition Act in Malaysia Will Stand, Premier Says." *International New York Times,* November 28. http://www.nytimes.com/2014/11/28/world/asia /malaysian-premier-says-sedition-act-will-stand.html?_r=0.

Funston, N. John. 1980. *Malay Politics in Malaysia: A Study of the United Malays National Organisation and Party Islam.* Kuala Lumpur: Heinemann Education Books.

Futehally, Ilmas. 2013. "Malaysian Recipe for Good Governance." *Strategic Foresight Group,* October 14. http://www.strategicforesight.com/inner-articles.php?id=308# .WBhdKRbstCw.

Fyfe, Nicholas R. 1993. "Making Space for the Citizen? The (In)Significance of the UK's Citizen's Charter." *Urban Geography* 14 (3): 224–27.

Gamala, Ruben Magan. 2014. "Evolution of the Pork Barrel System in the Philippines." *UP Forum,* January 24. http://www.up.edu.ph/evolution-of-the-pork-barrel-system -in-the-philippines.

Gamble, Andrew. 1981. *An Introduction to Modern Social and Political Thought.* London: Macmillan.

Gamil, Jaymee T. 2014. "Congress Urged to Junk 2015 Budget Due to Pro-DAP Provisions." *Philippine Daily Inquirer,* October 21. http://newsinfo.inquirer.net/646082 /congress-urged-to-junk-2015-budget-due-to-pro-dap-provisions.

Gandhi, Jennifer. 2008. *Political Institutions under Dictatorship.* New York: Cambridge University Press.

Gandhi, Jennifer, and Adam Przeworski. 2007. "Authoritarian Institutions and the Survival of Autocrats." *Comparative Political Studies* 40 (11): 1279–301.

Geddes, Barbara. 2006. "Stages of Development in Authoritarian Regimes." In *World Order after Lenin,* edited by Vladimir Tismaneanu, Mac Morje Howard, and Rudra Sil, 149–70. Seattle: Washington University Press.

George, Cherian. 2011. "Internet Politics: Shouting Down the PAP." In *Voting in Change: Politics of Singapore's 2011 General Election,* edited by Kevin Y. L. Tan and Terence Lee, 145–60. Singapore: Ethos Books.

Ghazali, Rahman. 2017a. "Dr M: I'm Top Dog in Pakatan Harapan." *Star Online,* July 18. http://www.thestar.com.my/news/nation/2017/07/18/mahathir-mohamad-top -dog-in-pakatan/.

——. 2017b. "Dr M Says He'll Accept If People Wants [sic] Anwar as PM." *Star Online*, July 18. http://www.thestar.com.my/news/nation/2017/07/18/mahathir-mohamad -if-people-want-anwar-why-not/.

Giddens, Anthony. 1998. *The Third Way: The Renewal of Social Democracy*. Cambridge: Polity Press.

Gill, Graeme. 2013. *Symbolism and Regime Change in Russia*. Cambridge: Cambridge University Press.

Gilley, Bruce. 2000. "Affirmative Reaction." *Far Eastern Economic Review* 163 (32): 26–27.

Gills, Barry K., and Kevin Gray. 2013. *People Power in an Era of Global Crisis: Rebellion, Resistance and Liberation*. Abingdon: Routledge.

GMA News. 2012. "CBCP to Monitor New Aquino Appointees' Performances." *GMA News Online*, September 1. http://www.gmanetwork.com/news/story/272088 /news/nation/cbcp-to-monitor-new-aquino-appointees-performance.

Goh, Ban Lee. 2005. "The Demise of Local Government Elections and Urban Politics." In *Elections and Democracy in Malaysia*, edited by Mavis Puthucheary and Norani Othman. Bangi: Penerbit Universiti Kebangsaan Malaysia.

——. 2009. *Report of the Local Government Elections Working Group*. Penang, Malaysia: Local Government Elections Working Group, April 20. http://penanginstitute.org /v3/files/reports/Local_Government_Election_Working_Group_Report.pdf.

Goh, Chin Lian. 2013. "Meritocracy Works but Beware of Elitism: ESM Goh." *Straits Times*, July 28. http://www.straitstimes.com/breaking-news/singapore/story/guard -against-elitism-and-sense-entitlement-esm-goh-20130727.

Goh, Chok Tong. 1986. "A Nation of Excellence." Address at *Alumni International Singapore*, Ministry of Communications and Information, Singapore, December 1.

——. 1989. *Session No. 1, Volume No. 54, Sitting No. 8, Parliament No. 7*. November 29. Singapore: Singapore Parliament Reports.

——. 2013. "Averting a Mid-Life Crisis." *Today Online*, August 12. http://www.todayonline .com/singapore/averting-mid-life-crisis.

Goldfrank, Benjamin, and Aaron Schneider. 2006. "Competitive Institution Building: The PT and Participatory Budgeting in Rio Grande do Sul." *Latin American Politics and Society* 48 (3): 1–31.

Gomez, Edmund Terence. 2002. "Political Business in Malaysia: Party Factionalism, Corporate Development, and Economic Crisis." In *Political Business in East Asia*, edited by Edmund Terence Gomez, 82–114. London: Routledge.

——. 2012a. "The Politics and Policies of Corporate Development: Race, Rents and Redistribution in Malaysia." In *Malaysia Development Challenges: Graduating from the Middle*, edited by Hal Hill, Tham Siew Yean, and Ragayah Haji Mat Zin, 63–82. Abingdon: Routledge.

——. 2012b. "Targeting Horizontal Inequalities: Ethnicity, Equity and Entrepreneurship in Malaysia." *Asian Economic Papers* 11 (2): 31–57.

——. 2016. "Politics and Business: Fundamental Differences between Mahathir and Najib." *Aliran*, March 23. http://aliran.com/web-specials/2016-web-specials/politics -business-fundamental-differences-dr-m-najib.

Gomez, Edmund Terence, and Johan Saravanamuttu, eds. 2013. *The New Economic Policy in Malaysia: Affirmative Action, Ethnic Inequalities and Social Justice*. Singapore: National University of Singapore Press.

Gomez, James. 2006. " 'Citizen Journalism': Bridging the Discrepancy in Singapore's Election News." *Sudostasien Aktuell* 6: 3–34.

——. 2008. "Online Opposition in Singapore: Communications Outreach without Electoral Gain." *Journal of Contemporary Asia* 38 (4): 591–612.

Gonzalez-Vicente, Ruben, and Toby Carroll. 2017. "Politics after National Development: Explaining the Capitalist Rise under Late Capitalist Development." *Globalizations* (online): 1–23. Accessed June 30, 2017. doi: 10.1080/14747731.2017.1316542.

Gooch, Liz. 2012. "Police Clash with Malaysia Protestors Seeking Electoral Reforms." *New York Times*, April 28. http://www.nytimes.com/2012/04/29/world/asia/malaysian-capital-braces-for-rally-by-democracy-activists.html?_r=0.

GOV.UK (Government of the United Kingdom). 2013. *Contestable Policy Fund.* Accessed June 4, 2017. https://www.gov.uk/guidance/contestable-policy-fund.

Graeber, David. 2013. *The Democracy Project: A History, A Crisis, A Movement.* London: Penguin.

Gramsci, Antonio. 1971. *Selections from the Prison Notebooks of Antonio Gramsci.* Edited by Quintin Hoare and Geoffrey Nowell Smith. London: Lawrence and Wishart.

Grant, Jeremy. 2015. "Rights Groups Condemn Malaysia Sedition Arrests." *Financial Times*, March 31. www.ft.com/cms/s/0/eb892e36-d777-11e4-94bl-00144feab7de.html#axzz3fwhOIW43.

Greenslade, Roy. 2014. "Vietnamese Blogger Arrested for 'Anti-State' Articles." *Guardian*, December 4. http://www.theguardian.com/media/2014/dec/04/vietnamese-blogger-arrested-for-anti-state-articles.

Hadiz, Vedi R., and Richard Robison. 2013. "The Political Economy of Oligarchy and the Reorganization of Power in Indonesia." *Indonesia* 96: 35–58.

Hafidz Baharom. 2015. "Those Missing Malays? Look All around You." *Free Malaysia Today*, August 30. http://www.freemalaysiatoday.com/category/opinion/2015/08/30/those-missing-malays-look-all-around-you.

Hameiri, Shahar, and Lee Jones. 2014. "Murdoch International: The 'Murdoch School' in International Relations." Working Paper No. 178. Perth, Australia: Asia Research Centre, Murdoch University.

Hamid, Ahmad Fauzi Abdul, and Che Hamdan Che Mohd Razali. 2015. "The Changing Face of Political Islam in Malaysia in the Era of Najib Razak, 2009–2013." *SOJOURN* 30 (2): 301–37.

Han, Kirsten. 2016a. "Singapore's Contempt of Court Bill Has Far Reaching Implications for Press Freedom." *Hong Kong Free Press*, August 6. https://www.hongkongfp.com/2016/08/06/singapores-contempt-court-bill-far-reaching-implications-press-freedom.

——. 2016b. "Singapore's 'Light Touch' on the Internet Gets Heavier." *Byline*, January 27. https://www.byline.com/column/23/article/756.

Hasbullah, Awang Chik. 2015. "UMNO Never Rejected Hudud, Supreme Council Member Tells PAS." *Malaymail Online*, December 17. http://www.themalaymailonline.com/malaysia/article/umno-never-rejected-hudud-supreme-council-member-tells-pas.

Hawkins, Kirk A. 2010. *Venezuela's Chavismo and Populism in Comparative Perspective.* New York: Cambridge University Press.

Hawthorne, Amy. 2004. "Middle Eastern Democracy: Is Civil Society the Answer?" Carnegie Papers, Middle East Series No. 44, March. Washington, DC: Carnegie Endowment for International Peace.

Hay, Colin. 2007. *Why We Hate Politics.* Cambridge: Polity Press.

Haynes, Jeff. 2001. " 'Limited' Democracy in Ghana and Uganda. What Is Most Important to International Actors: Stability or Political Freedom?" *Journal of Contemporary African Studies* 19 (2): 183–204.

He, Baogang. 2014. "Deliberative Culture and Politics: The Persistence of Authoritarian Deliberation in China." *Political Theory* 42 (1): 58–81.

——. 2015. "Reconciling Deliberation and Representation: Chinese Challenges to Deliberative Democracy." *Representation* 51 (1): 35–50.

Hector, Charles. 2010. "People Vote for Civil Society Representatives to Local Councils in Penang–Will Selangor Follow?" November 18. http://charleshector.blogspot.com/2010/11/people-elect-civil-society.html.

Hedman, Eva-Lotta E. 2006. *In the Name of Civil Society: From Free Election Movements to People Power in the Philippines*. Ithaca, NY: Cornell University Press.

——. 2012. "Beyond Machine Politics? Reformism, Populism and Philippine Elections." *LSE Research Online*. London: London School of Economics. Accessed May 10, 2013. http://www.lse.ac.uk/IDEAS/publications/reports/pdf/SR005/Phil_Hedman.pdf.

Hedman, Eva-Lotta E., and John Thayer Sidel. 2000. *Philippine Politics in the Twentieth Century: Colonial Legacies, Post-Colonial Trajectories*. London: Routledge.

Helmke, Gretchen, and Steven Levitsky. 2004. "Informal Institutions and Comparative Politics: A Research Agenda." *Perspectives on Politics* 2 (4): 725–40.

Henderson, Karen. 2004. "The Slovak Republic: Explaining Defects in Democracy." *Democratization* 11 (5): 133–55.

Heng, Pek Koon. 1997. "The New Economic Policy and the Chinese Community in Peninsula Malaysia." *The Developing Economies* 35 (3): 262–92.

Henry, Edward. 2011. "NGO Reps in Selangor Feel Cheated Over Broken Promise." *Star Online*, June 24. http://thestar.com.my/news/story.asp?file=/2011/6/24/nation/8966871&sec=nation.

Hewison, Kevin. 2014. "Thailand: The Lessons of Protest." *Asian Studies: Journal of Critical Perspectives on Asia* 50 (1): 1–15.

Hewison, Kevin, and Garry Rodan. 1994. "The Decline of the Left in Southeast Asia." In *The Socialist Register 1994*, edited by Ralph Miliband and Leo Panitch, 235–62. London: Merlin Press.

——. 2012. "Southeast Asia: The Left and the Rise of Bourgeois Opposition." In *Routledge Handbook of Southeast Asian Politics*, edited by Richard Robison, 25–39. London: Routledge.

Hewison, Kevin, Garry Rodan, and Richard Robison. 1993. "Introduction: Changing Forms of State Power in Southeast Asia." In *Southeast Asia in the 1990s: Authoritarianism, Democracy and Capitalism*, edited by Kevin Hewison, Richard Robison, and Garry Rodan, 2–8. Sydney: Allen & Unwin.

Heydarian, Richard Javad. 2015. "Philippines' City of Illusions: Time for an Economic 'EDSA Revolution.'" *Huffington Post*, March 16. http://www.huffingtonpost.com/richard-javad-heydarian/philippines-city-of-illus_b_6869618.html.

Hilhorst, Dorothea. 2003. *The Real World of NGOs: Discourses, Diversity and Development*. London: Zed Books.

Hilley, John. 2001. *Malaysia: Mahathirism, Hegemony and the New Opposition*. London: Zed Books.

Himanshu Bhatt. 2012. "Penang and Selangor Can Hold Local Government Elections Minus EC." *Sun Daily*, January 31. http://www.thesundaily.my/news/281776.

——. 2014. "Penang Reaches the End of the Road in Local Elections Bid." *Malaysian Insider*, December 12. http://www.themalaysianinsider.com/malaysia/article/penang-reaches-the-end-of-the-road-in-local-elections-bid.

Ho, Khai Leong. 1992. "Dynamics of Policy-Making in Malaysia: The Formulation of the New Economic Policy and the National Development Policy." *Asian Journal of Public Administration* 14 (2): 204–27.

Hodge, Amanda. 2016. "Najib Has Mahathir in the Frame for Sedition." *Australian*, April 13.

Holden, William N. 2009. "Ashes from the Phoenix: State Terrorism and the Party-List Groups in the Philippines." *Contemporary Politics* 15 (4): 377–93.

Holt, Jordan, and Nick Manning. 2014. "Fukuyama Is Right about Measuring State Quality: Now What?" *Governance* 27 (4): 717–28.

Hope, Bradley, and Tom Wright. 2016. "IMDB Scandal: Deposit in Malaysian Leader Najib's Accounts Said to Top $1 Billion." *Wall Street Journal*, March 1. http://www.wsj.com/articles/deposits-in-malaysian-leaders-accounts-said-to-top-1-billion-1456790588.

Horsley, Jamie P. 2006. "Public Participation and the Democratization of Chinese Governance." In *Political Civilization and Modernization: The Political Context of China's Reform*, edited by Yang Zhong and Shiping Hua, 207–50. Singapore: World Scientific Press.

House of Commons. 2013. *Public Administration Select Committee. Public Engagement in Policy-Making.* Second Report of Session 2013–14. London: Statutory Office Limited.

——. 2014. *Public Administration Select Committee. Public Engagement in Policy-Making and Engaging the Public in National Strategy: Government Responses to the Committee's Second and Fourth Reports of Session 2013–14.* Sixth Special Report of Session 2013–14. London: Statutory Office Limited.

Houtzager, Peter P., and Adrian Gurza Lavalle. 2010. "Civil Society's Claims to Political Representation in Brazil." *Studies in Comparative International Development* 45 (1): 1–29.

Human Rights Watch. 2014. *Thailand: Theatre Activists Jailed for Insulting Monarchy.* August 20. http://www.hrw.org/news/2014/08/20/thailand-theater-activists-jailed-insulting-monarchy.

Huntington, Samuel P. 1991. *The Third Wave: Democratization in the Late Twentieth Century.* Norman: University of Oklahoma Press.

Hutchcroft, Paul D. 1998. *Booty Capitalism: The Politics of Banking in the Philippines.* Ithaca, NY: Cornell University Press.

Hutchcroft, Paul D., and Joel Rocamora. 2012. "Patronage-Based Parties and the Democratic Deficit in the Philippines: Origins, Evolution and the Imperatives of Reform." In *Routledge Handbook of Southeast Asian Politics*, edited by Richard Robison, 97–119. London: Routledge.

Hutchison, Jane. 2001. "Crisis and Change in the Philippines." In *The Political Economy of South-East Asia: Conflicts, Crises and Change*, edited by Garry Rodan, Kevin Hewison, and Richard Robison, 42–70. New York: Oxford University Press.

——. 2006. "Poverty of Politics in the Philippines." In *The Political Economy of South-East Asia: Markets, Power and Contestation*, edited by Garry Rodan, Kevin Hewison, and Richard Robison, 39–73. Melbourne: Oxford University Press.

——. 2007. "The 'Disallowed' Political Participation of Manila's Urban Poor." *Democratization* 14 (5): 853–72.

——. 2015. "Authoritarian Labor Legacies in the Philippines." In *Working Through the Past: Labor and Authoritarian Legacies in Comparative Perspective*, edited by Teri L. Caraway, Mariana Lorena Cook and Stephan Crowley, 64–81. Ithaca, NY: Cornell University Press.

Hutchison, Jane, and Andrew Brown, eds. 2001. *Organising Labour in Globalising Asia.* London: Routledge.

Ikhwan, Zulkaflee. 2015. "Bersih 4 Proved DAP in Control." *Berita Daily*, September 1. http://www.beritadaily.com/news/2015-09-01/21017/bersih-4-proved-dap-in-control.

Ilago, Simeon Agustin. 2005. "Participatory Budgeting: The Philippine Experience." In *Participatory Planning and Budgeting at the Sub-National Level*, edited by Department of Economic and Social Affairs of the United Nations, 63–78. New York: United Nations.

INCITEGov (International Center for Innovation, Transformation and Excellence in Governance). 2008. *Crossover Leadership in Asia: Staying Whole in Two Halves:*

From Civil Society to Government. Pasig City: INCITEGov. Accessed October 26, 2015. http://incitegov.org/wp-content/uploads/2011/05/Crossover-Leadership-in -Asia-Staying-Whole-in-Two-Halves-preview.pdf.

Institute of Philippine Culture. 2013. *Bottom-up Budgeting Process Evaluation. Final Report.* May. Manila: Ateneo de Manila University. Accessed October 27, 2015. http:// www.ipc-ateneo.org/content/bottom-budgeting-process-evaluation.

Ionescu, Ghita, and Ernest Gellner, eds. 1969. *Populism: Its Meaning and National Characteristics.* London: Weidenfeld and Nicolson.

Iriye, Akira. 1974. *The Cold War in Asia: A Historical Introduction.* Englewood Cliffs, NJ: Prentice-Hall.

Izatun, Hamim Shari. 1999. "Leaders from Chinese Groups on NECC II." *New Straits Times*, October 7.

Jacobs, Ben. 2017. "Trump Disbands Business Councils as CEOs Flee after Charlottesville Remarks." *Guardian*, August 17. https://www.theguardian.com/us-news/2017/aug /16/donald-trump-advisory-councils-disbanded-ceos-charlottesville.

Jamal, Faizah. 2013. *Session No. 1, Volume No. 90, Sitting No. 4. Motion: A Sustainable Population for a Dynamic Singapore, Parliament No. 12.* February 6. Singapore: Singapore Parliamentary Reports. http://sprs.parl.gov.sg/search/report.jsp?current PubID=00078619-WA.

Jayasuriya, Kanishka, and Garry Rodan. 2007. "Beyond Hybrid Regimes: More Participation, Less Contestation in Southeast Asia." *Democratization* 14 (5): 773–94.

Jenkins-Smith, Hank C., and Paul A. Sabatier. 1994. "Evaluating the Advocacy Coalition Framework." *Journal of Public Policy* 14 (2): 175–203.

Jessop, Bob. 1982. *The Capitalist State: Marxists Theories and Methods.* Oxford: Martin Robertson.

——. 1983a. "Accumulation Strategies, State Forms and Hegemonic Projects." *Kapitalistate* 10 (11): 89–111.

——. 1983b. "Capitalism and Democracy: The Best Possible Shell." In *States and Societies*, edited by David Held, James Anderson, Bram Gieben, Stuart Hall, Laurence Harris, Paul Lewis, Noel Parker, and Ben Turok. New York: New York University Press.

——. 1983c. "The Capitalist State and the Rule of Capital: Problems in the Analysis of Business Associations." *West European Politics* 6 (2): 139–62.

——. 1990. *State Theory: Putting the Capitalist State in its place.* University Park: Pennsylvania State Press.

——. 2008. *State Power: A Strategic-Relational Approach.* Cambridge: Polity Press.

Jiao, Diane Claire J. 2011. "Expanded Budget Role for Civil Society Groups." *Business World*, July 17. http://incitegov.org/expanded-budget-role-for-civil-society -groups.

Jones, Lee. 2014. "The Political Economy of Myanmar's Transition." *Journal of Contemporary Asia* 44 (1): 144–70.

Josey, Alex. 1974. *The Struggle for Singapore.* Sydney: Angus & Robertson.

Kamal, Shazwan Mustafa. 2016. "Three Things We Learned from: Bersih 5." *Malaymail Online*, November 20. http://www.themalaymailonline.com/malaysia/article/three -things-we-learned-from-bersih-5#BIEZhsXsktrzy9HB.97.

Kamaruddin, Zaid. 2013. "Civil Society Organisations and Change: A Collaborative Approach." October 21. http://suaramjb1.blogspot.com.au/2013/10/civil-society -organisations-andchange.html.

Kaos, Joseph. 2012. "Kelantan NGOs Demand State Fulfill Election Promises." *Star Online*, February 22. http://www.thestar.com.my/News/Nation/2012/02/22/Kelantan -NGOs-demand-state-fulfill-old-election-promises.aspx.

Karim, Khairah N. 2017. "Tian Chua Goes to Jail for Trespassing into Pulapol." *New Straits Times*, September 29. https://www.nst.com.my/news/crime-courts/2017/09 /285485/tian-chua-goes-jail-trespassing-pulapol.

Karl, Terry Lynn. 1995. "The Hybrid Regimes of Central America." *Journal of Democracy* 6 (3): 72–86.

Katz, Richard S., and Peter Mair. 1995. "Changing Models of Party Organization and Party Democracy: The Emergence of the Cartel Party." *Party Politics* 1 (1): 5–28.

Kawanaka, Takeshi, and Yuki Asaba. 2011. "Establishing Electoral Administration Systems in New Democracies." IDE Discussion Paper No. 305, August. Chiba, Japan: Institute of Developing Economies.

Kerkvliet, Benedict J. 1979. *The Huk Rebellion: A Study of Peasant Revolt in the Philippines.* Quezon City: New Day Publishers.

Khalid, Khadijah M., and Mahani Zainal Abidin. 2014. "Technocracy in Economic Policy-Making in Malaysia." *Southeast Asian Studies* 3 (2): 383–413.

Khoo, Andrew. 2010. "Local Government: Managing Expectations." In *The Road to Reform: Pakatan Rakyat in Selangor*, edited by Tricia Yeoh. Petaling Jaya: Strategic Information and Research Development Centre.

Khoo, Boo Teik. 2003. *Beyond Mahathir: Malaysian Politics and Its Discontents.* London: Zed Books.

——. 2005. "Ethnic Structure, Inequality and Governance in the Public Sector: Malaysian Experiences." Democracy, Governance and Human Rights Programme Paper No. 20, December 15. Geneva: United Nations Research Institute for Social Development. http://www.unrisd.org/__80256b3c005bccf9.nsf/0/19309421df6d65d3c1 2570fa00392e12?OpenDocument&cntxt=3553A&cookielang=fr&Click=.

——. 2006. "Malaysia: Balancing Development and Power." In *The Political Economy of South-East Asia: Markets, Power and Contestation*, edited by Garry Rodan, Kevin Hewison, and Richard Robison, 170–96. Melbourne: Oxford University Press.

——. 2010. "Social Movements and the Crisis of Neoliberalism in Malaysia and Thailand." IDE Discussion Paper No. 238, June. Chiba, Japan: Institute of Developing Economies. http://ir.ide.go.jp/dspace/handle/2344/899.

——. 2012. "Social Change and the Transformation of Islamic Dissent: The Parti Islam of Malaysia." Paper presented at Islam and Political Dissent: Studies and Comparisons from Asia and the Middle East, Institute of Developing Economies and Asia Research Centre, Murdoch University, Chiba, Japan, November 7–8.

Khoo, Chin Hock Andrew, Chin Huat Wong, and Maria Chin Abdullah. 2009. *An Advocacy Paper: Bring Back Local Government Elections.* Petaling Jaya: Coalition for Good Governance.

Khoo, Melissa, and Lai Fong Yee. 2014. "Redefining Engagement: Lessons for the Public Service from Our Singapore Conversation." *Ethos* 13: 7–17.

Khoo, Ying Hooi. 2015. "Malaysia's Bersih 5 Rally: Protesters Weigh the Cost of Action under a Repressive Regime." *The Conversation*, November 18. https://theconversation .com/malaysias-bersih-5-rally-protesters-weigh-the-cost-of-action-under-a -repressive-regime-68723.

Khor, Amy. 2006. "Feedback Unit's 21st Anniversary Dinner Speech." Speech delivered at the *Feedback Unit's 21st Anniversary Dinner*, Pan Pacific Hotel, Singapore, October 12, 2006.

——. 2013. "Notes from Amy." *REACHNews*, February–May 2013.

——. 2015. "Welcome Address by Senior Minister of State (Health and Manpower) and REACH Chairman." Address at the REACH Contributors' Forum, Holiday Inn, Orchard City Centre, Singapore, August 3.

Kiernan, Ben, and Chantal Boua. 1982. *Peasants and Politics in Kampuchea 1942–1981.* London: Zed Press.

King, Gary, Jennifer Pan, and Margaret E. Roberts. 2013. "How Censorship in China Allows Government Criticism but Silences Collective Expression." *American Political Science Review* 107 (2): 326–43.

King, Stephen J. 2007. "Sustaining Authoritarianism in the Middle East and North Africa." *Political Science Quarterly* 122 (3): 433–59.

Koh, Valerie. 2015. "Govt Orders Shutdown of the Real Singapore." *Today Online*, May 3. http://www.todayonline.com/singapore/mda-suspends-licence-socio-political-website-real-singapore.

Kontra Daya. 2012. "Initial Review of Some Incumbent Partylist Groups Seeking Reelection in 2013." Accessed June 24, 2014. http://kontradaya.org/kontra-dayas-initial-review-of-some-incumbent-partylist-groups-seeking-reelection-in-2013.

——. 2013. "SC Decision Puts Final Nail on Coffin of Party-List System." April 8. http://www.kontradaya.org/sc-decision-puts-final-nail-on-coffin-of-partylist-system.

Koon, Yew Yin. 2012. "Doctored Crime Statistics: Answers Needed Now." *Malaysiakini*, August 24. https://www2.malaysiakini.com/news/207036.

Kor, Kian Beng. 2015. "Battle Lines Drawn to Differentiate Opposition from PAP." *Straits Times*, September 2. http://www.straitstimes.com/politics/battle-lines-drawn-to-differentiate-opposition-from-pap.

Kow, Gah Chie. 2015. "Bersih 4 Will Be a Show of No Confidence in Najib." *Malaysiakini*, August 15. https://www.malaysiakini.com/news/308638.

——. 2016a. "Maria Believes More BN Supporters Will Join in Bersih 5." *Malaysiakini*, November 18. http://www.malaysiakini.com/news/363383.

——. 2016b. "Maria Chin Released after 10-day Detention." *Malaysiakini*, November 28. http://www.malaysiakini.com/news/363383.

Kuah, Adrian W. J., and Hui Lim Seok. 2014. "After Our Singapore Conversation: The Future of Governance." *Ethos* 13: 18–23.

——. n.d. *"It's Good to Talk": The Rationale, Design and Processes behind "Our Singapore Conversation."* Zurich: Zurich University of Applied Sciences. Accessed March 1, 2014. http://www.zhaw.ch/fileadmin/user_upload/engineering/_Institute_und_Zentren/INE/veranstaltungen/Papers_IFA/Kuah_Adrian.pdf.

Kuper, Andrew. 2004. *Democracy beyond Borders: Justice and Representation in Global Institutions.* Oxford: Oxford University Press.

Labonne, Julien, and Robert S. Chase. 2008. "Do Community-Driven Development Projects Enhance Social Capital: Evidence from the Philippines." Policy Research Working Paper No. 4678. Washington, DC: World Bank.

La Botz, Dan. 2001. *Made in Indonesia: Indonesian Workers Since Suharto.* Cambridge, MA: South End Press.

Laclau, Ernesto. 2007. *On Populist Reason.* London: Verso Books.

Lane, Max R. 1990. *The Urban Mass Movement in the Philippines, 1983–87.* Singapore: Institute of Southeast Asian Studies.

Lasswell, Harold. 1936. *Politics: Who Gets What, When and How.* New York: Whittlesey House.

Lau, Albert, ed. 2012. *Southeast Asia and the Cold War.* Abingdon: Routledge.

Law, Melissa. 2013. "We Need to Guard against Elitism: ESM Goh." Yahoo News, July 28. https://sg.news.yahoo.com/we-need-to-guard-against-elitism—esm-goh-024750768.html.

Lee, Hock Guan. 2008. "Malaysia in 2007: Abdullah Administration under Siege." In *Southeast Asian Affairs 2008*, edited by Daljit Singh and Tin Maung Maung Than, 188–206. Singapore: Institute of Southeast Asian Studies.

———. 2014. "Malaysia's Funding System for Higher Education not Sustainable." *ISEAS Perspective*, vol. 2. Accessed August 7, 2015. https://www.iseas.edu.sg/images/pdf /ISEAS_Perspective_2014_02.pdf.

———. 2015. "Mal-apportionment and the Electoral Authoritarian Regime in Malaysia." In *Coalitions in Collision: Malaysia's 13th General Election*, edited by Johan Saravanu-mutta, Lee Hock Guan, and Mohamed Nawab Mohamed Osman, 63–90. Petaling Jaya: Institute of Southeast Asian Studies and Strategic Information and Research Development Centre.

Lee, Hsien Loong. 1999. "Speech by Deputy Prime Minister Lee Hsien Loong." Speech delivered at the Administrative Services Dinner and Promotion Ceremony, Mandarin Hotel, Singapore, March 29. http://www.singapore21.org.sg/speeches_290399.html.

———. 2004. "Speech by Deputy Prime Minister Lee Hsien Loong." Speech delivered at the Harvard Club of Singapore's 35th Anniversary Dinner, Singapore, January 6. http:// unpan1.un.org/intradoc/groups/public/documents/APCITY/UNPAN015426.pdf.

———. 2007. *Session No. 1, Volume No. 83, Sitting No. 15, Parliament No. 11*. October 23, 2007. Singapore: Singapore Parliament Reports.

———. 2012. "Prime Minister Lee Hsien Loong's National Day Rally Speech." Speech delivered at the 2012 National Day Rally, Singapore, August 26. http://www.pmo.gov .sg/mediacentre/prime-minister-lee-hsien-loongs-national-day-rally-2012-speech -english.

———. 2013a. "Prime Minister Lee Hsien Loong's National Day Rally Speech." Speech delivered at The 2013 National Day Rally, Singapore, August 18. http://www.pmo .gov.sg/mediacentre/prime-minister-lee-hsien-loongs-national-day-rally-2013 -speech-english.

———. 2013b. "Speech at Zaobao 90th Anniversary and Launch of Zaobao.sg." Speech delivered at The Zaobao Forum 2013, Singapore, November 22. http://www.pmo.gov .sg/media-release/speech-prime-minister-lee-hsien-loong-zaobao-90th -anniversary-and-launch-zaobaosg.

Lee, Lam Thye. 1999. "NECC II to Consult All Segments of Society." *New Straits Times*, August 16.

Lee, Patrick. 2011. "Big Problem in Little India." *Free Malaysia Today*, February 12. http:// www.freemalaysiatoday.com/category/nation/2011/02/12/big-problems-in-little -india.

Lee, Regina. 2011. "Pemandu Explains RM64 Mil Expenditure." *Malaysiakini*, June 18. https://www.malaysiakini.com/news/167327.

Lee, Yoolim, and Effie Chew. 2015. "Scandal Rocks Malaysia." *Australian Financial Review*, July 23.

Legaspi, Amita. 2013. "At Comelec, Election Lawyer Luie Guia Vows to Pursue Electoral Reforms." GMA News Online, April 19. http://www.gmanetwork.com/news/story /304627/news/nation/at-comelec-election-lawyer-luie-guia-vows-to-pursue -electoral-reforms.

Leib, Ethan J., and He Baogang, eds. 2006. *The Search for Deliberative Democracy in China*. New York: Palgrave Macmillan.

Lesley, Elena. 2014. *Mapping a Transformation Journey: A Strategy for Malaysia's Future, 2009–2010*. Princeton, NJ: Woodrow Wilson School of Public and International Affairs, Princeton University. Accessed September 1, 2016. https://www.pemandu .gov.my/assets/publications/academic-reports/Mapping_a_Transformation _Journey.pdf.

Levitsky, Steven, and Lucan A. Way. 2002. "The Rise of Competitive Authoritarianism." *Journal of Democracy* 13 (2): 51–65.

——. 2010. *Competitive Authoritarianism: Hybrid Regimes After the Cold War*. New York: Cambridge University Press.

Leys, Colin. 1996. *The Rise and Fall of Development Theory*. Oxford: James Currey.

Liew, Chin Tong. 2013. "An Opposition's Transformation—an Interview with Liew Chin Tong." In *Awakening: The Abdullah Badawi Years in Malaysia*, edited by Bridget Welsh and James U. H. Chin. Petaling Jaya: Strategic Information and Research Development Centre.

Lijphart, Arend. 1968. *The Politics of Accommodation: Pluralism and Democracy in the Netherlands*. Berkeley: University of California Press.

——. 1977. *Democracy in Plural Societies: A Comparative Exploration*. New Haven, CT: Yale University Press.

Lim, Hong Hai. 2005. "Making the System Work: The Electoral Commission." In *Elections and Democracy in Malaysia*, edited by Mavis Puthucheary and Norani Othman, 249–91. Bangi: Penerbit Universiti Kebangsaan Malaysia.

Lim, Kit Siang. 2013. "Feeble Denial by Pemandu on Its GNI Figure." *Malaysiakini*, April 9. https://www.malaysiakini.com/news/226217.

Lim, Lydia. 2013. "PM Outlines 'New Way Forward' at National Day Rally Speech." *Straits Times*, August 19. http://www.straitstimes.com/breaking-news/singapore/story/pm-outlines-new-way-forward-20130819.

——. 2015. "GE2015: Can PAP Crack Its Performance Paradox." *Straits Times*, August 26. http://www.straitstimes.com/politics/ge2015-can-pap-crack-its-performance-paradox.

Lim, Yan Liang. 2014. "Aim to Be 'Democracy of Integrity and Deeds.'" *Straits Times*, October 18. http://news.asiaone.com/news/singapore/aim-be-democracy-integrity-and-deeds.

Linz, Juan J. 1997. "Some Thoughts on the Victory and Future of Democracy." In *Democracy's Victory and Crisis*, edited by Alex Hadenius, 404–26. Cambridge: Cambridge University Press.

Llamas, Ronaldo M. 2001. "The 2001 Party-list Elections: Winners, Losers and Political/Legal Contradictions." FES Online Papers, September. Manila: Friedrich Ebert Stiftung Philippine Office. Accessed September 1, 2014. http://library.fes.de/pdf-files/bueros/philippinen/50073.pdf.

Loh, Chee Kong, and Dai Lin Ong. 2009. "A Brand New Slate." *Today Online*, July 7. http://sgforums.com/forums/10/topics/367127.

Loh, Francis. 2012. "Organized Groups, Development Strategies and Social Policies." In *Policy Regimes and the Political Economy of Poverty Reduction in Malaysia*, edited by Khoo Boo Teik, 183–216. Basingstoke: Palgrave Macmillan.

Loone, Susan. 2010. "10 'Elected' for NGO Quota in Penang Municipal Councils." *Malaysiakini*, November 14. http://www.malaysiakini.com/news/148195.

Lopez, Leslie. 2016. "Mahathir's Politics of Fatigue." *Straits Times*, March 7. http://www.straitstimes.com/asia/se-asia/mahathirs-politics-of-fatigue.

Low, Donald, and Sudhir Vadaketh. 2014. "Preface." In *Hard Choices: Challenging the Singapore Consensus*, edited by Donald Low and Sudhir Vadaketh, ix–xiii. Singapore: National University of Singapore Press.

Low, Linda. 2001. "The Singapore Developmental State in the New Economy and Polity." *Pacific Review* 14 (3): 411–41.

——. 2006. *The Political Economy of a City-State Revisited*. Singapore: Marshall Cavendish Academic.

Lowndes, Vivien, and Mark Roberts. 2013. *Why Institutions Matter: The New Institutionalism in Political Science*. Basingstoke: Palgrave Macmillan.

Luci, Charissa. 2016. "Speaker Supports Duterte on Abolition of Party-List System." *Manila Bulletin*, August 14. http://mb.com.ph/?p=467110.

Luebbert, Gregory M. 1991. *Liberalism, Fascism or Social Democracy: Social Classes and the Political Origins of Regimes in Interwar Europe*. New York: Oxford University Press.

Lydgate, Chris. 2003. *Lee's Law: How Singapore Crushes Dissent*. Melbourne: Scribe.

Macasaet, Sixto Donato C. 2013. "Bottom-up Budgeting: Moving up, but a Long Way to Go." *Rappler*, April 14. http://www.rappler.com/move-ph/issues/budget-watch/25594-budgetwatch-bottom-up-budgeting.

Mahbubani, Kishore. 1994. "The United States: 'Go East Young Man.'" *Washington Quarterly* 17 (2): 3–23.

——. 1995. "The Pacific Way." *Foreign Affairs* 74 (1): 100–111.

Mair, Peter. 1997. "E. E. Schattschneider's 'The Semisovereign People.'" *Political Studies* 45 (5): 947–54.

——. 2013. *Ruling the Void: The Hollowing Out of Western Democracies*. London: Verso.

Malaymail. 2015. "So How Many People Were in Kuala Lumpur for Bersih 4?" *Malaymail Online*, September 2. http://www.themalaymailonline.com/malaysia/article/so-how-many-people-were-in-kuala-lumpur-for-bersih-4.

Malaysiakini. 2010a. "Local Polls: Stop Giving Excuses Pakatan." March 26. http://www.malaysiakini.com/letters/127619.

——. 2010b. "Najib in for a Tough Time with NEM." June 3. https://www.malaysiakini.com/news/133492.

——. 2010c. "NEM Promises 'Improved' Affirmative Action." December 3. https://www.malaysiakini.com/news/149914.

——. 2012. "Gov't Urged to Clarify Crime Data Manipulation Claim." August 23. https://www.malaysiakini.com/news/206944.

——. 2015a. "Ex-PAS Leader Confirms Husam's Unity Gov't Claim." November 8. http://www.malaysiakini.com/news/318834.

——. 2015b. "Malay NGOs Slam Labelling of Bersih as 'Chinese.'" September 9. https://www.malaysiakini.com/news/311686.

——. 2015c. "PAS Spiritual Leader Nik Aziz Dies at 84." February 12. http://www.malaysiakini.com/news/289138.

——. 2015d. "Selangor PAS: Those in Harapan No Longer with Us." July 14. http://www.malaysiakini.com/news/305047.

——. 2015e. "UMNO Man Denies Red Shirt Rally Racist, Only Meant to 'Teach Lesson.'" September 17. https://www.malaysiakini.com/news/312598.

——. 2016. "40,000 for Bersih, 4,000 for Red Shirts." November 19. http://www.malaysiakini.com/news/363454.

Malloy, James M. 1977. *Authoritarianism and Corporatism in Latin America*. Pittsburgh, PA: University of Pittsburgh Press.

Manalansan, Ely H., Jr. 2007. "The Philippine Party List System: Opportunities, Limitations and Prospects." In *Oligarchic Politics: Elections and the Party-list System in the Philippines*, edited by Bobby M. Tuazon, 47–93. Quezon City: CenPEG Books.

Manila Standard. 2012. "LP Promoting New Political Patronage." September 6. http://thestandard.com.ph.

Mansbridge, Jane. 2004. "Representation Revisited: Introduction to the Case against Electoral Accountability." *Democracy and Society* 2 (1): 12–13.

——. 2009. "A Selection Model of Political Representation." *Journal of Political Philosophy* 17 (4): 369–98.

MARUAH. 2013. *Defending the Legitimacy of Singapore Elections: MARUAH Position Paper on the GRC System*. Singapore: MARUAH Working Group for ASEAN Human

Rights Mechanism. Accessed October 20, 2014. https://maruahsg.files.wordpress
.com/2013/08/maruah-position-paper-on-the-grc-system1.pdf.

Matsuzawa, Mikas. 2015. "20 Lawmakers Accused of Malversation in New PDAF Scam."
CNN News, September 3. http://www.newsjs.com/url.php?p=http://cnnphilippines
.com/news/2015/09/02/PDAF-pork-barrel-scam-complaint-fake-NGOs-not
-operated-by-Janet-Napoles.html.

Mauzy, Diane K. 1995. "The Tentative Life and Quiet Death of the NECC in Malaysia." In
Managing Change in Southeast Asia: Local Initiatives, Global Connections, edited by
Jean de Bernardi, Gregory Forth, and Sandra Niessen, 77–92. Montreal: University
of Montreal.

Mauzy, Diane K., and Shane J. Barter. 2008. "Learning to Lose? Not if UMNO Can Help
It." In *Political Transitions in Dominant Party Systems: Learning to Lose*, edited by
Edward Friedman and Joseph Wong, 211–30. Oxon: Routledge.

Mauzy, Diane K., and Robert Stephen Milne. 2002. *Singapore Politics under the People's
Action Party*. London: Routledge.

Mazzuca, Sebastian L. 2010. "Access to Power Versus Exercises of Power Reconceptualizing
the Quality of Democracy in Latin America." *Studies in Comparative International
Development* 45 (3): 334–57.

McCargo, Duncan. 2011. *Mapping National Anxieties: Thailand's Southern Conflict*. Co-
penhagen: NIAS Press.

McCourt, Willy. 2012. "Can Top-Down and Bottom-Up Be Reconciled? Electoral Competition and Service Delivery in Malaysia." *World Development* 40 (11): 2329–41.

McCoy, Alfred. 2009. *An Anarchy of Families: State and Family in the Philippines*. Madi-
son: University of Wisconsin Press.

McNulty, Stephanie. 2011. *Voice and Vote: Decentralization and Participation in Post-
Fujimori Peru*. Stanford, CA: Stanford University Press.

McRae, Kenneth. 1974. *Consociational Democracy: Political Accommodation in Segmented
Societies*. Toronto: McLelland and Stewart.

Mena, Mary Triny. 2014. "Venezuela's Growing Middle-Class Revolt." CBC News,
March 1. http://www.cbc.ca/news/world/venezuela-s-growing-middle-class-revolt
-1.2555786.

Merkel, Wolfgang. 2004. "Embedded and Defective Democracies." *Democratization* 11
(5): 33–58.

Micklethwait, John. 2011. "'Taming Leviathan.' A Special Report on the Future of the State."
Economist, March 17. https://mansueto.files.wordpress.com/2011/03/the-future-of
-the-state.pdf.

Milne, Robert Stephen, and Diane K. Mauzy. 1999. *Malaysian Politics under Mahathir*.
London: Routledge.

Mishra, Pakaj. 2016. "The Globalization Rage." *Foreign Affairs* 95 (6): 46–54.

Mizuno, Kosuke, and Phongpaichi Pasuk, eds. 2009. *Populism in Asia*. Singapore: National University of Singapore Press.

Mohamad, Maznah. 2008. "Malaysia-Democracy and the End of Ethnic Politics?" *Australian Journal of International Affairs* 62 (4): 441–59.

——. 2009. "Politics of the NEP and Ethnic Relations in Malaysia." In *Multiethnic Malay-
sia: Past, Present and Future*, edited by Teck Ghee Lim, Alberto Gomes, and Azly
Rahman, 113–39. Petaling Jaya: Strategic Information and Research Development
Centre.

——. 2010. "The Authoritarian State and Political Islam in Muslim-Majority Malaysia."
In *Islam and Politics in Southeast Asia*, edited by Johan Saravanamuttu, 65–105.
Abingdon: Routledge.

——. 2013. "The New Economic Policy and Poverty at the Margins: Family Dislocation, Dispossession and Dystopia in Kelantan." In *The New Economic Policy in Malaysia: Affirmative Action, Ethnic Inequalities and Social Justice*, edited by Edmund Terence Gomez and Johan Saravanamuttu, 61–86. Singapore: National University of Singapore Press.

Møller, Jørgen. 2013. "When One Might Not See the Wood for the Trees: The 'Historical Turn' in Democratization Studies, Critical Junctures, and Cross-Case Comparisons." *Democratization* 20 (4): 693–715.

Møller, Jørgen, and Svend-Erik Skaaning. 2013. *Democracy and Democratization in Comparative Perspective: Conceptions, Causes, and Consequences*. London: Routledge.

Moore, Barrington. 1966. *The Origins of Dictatorship and Democracy: Lord and Peasant in the Making of the New World*. Boston, MA: Beacon Press.

Morgenbesser, Lee. 2016. *Behind the Façade: Elections under Authoritarianism in Southeast Asia*. Albany: State University of New York Press.

Morlino, Leonardo. 2004. "What Is a 'Good Democracy'?" *Democratization* 11 (5): 10–32.

——. 2012. *Changes for Democracy: Actors, Structures, Processes*. Oxford: Oxford University Press.

Morlino, Leonardo, Björn Dressel, and Ricardo Pelizzo. 2011. "The Quality of Democracy in Asia-Pacific: Issues and Findings." *International Political Science Review* 32 (5): 491–511.

Mouzelis, Nicos. 1985. "On the Concept of Populism: Populist and Clientelist Modes of Incorporation into Semiperipheral Polities." *Politics & Society* 14 (3): 329–48.

Muga, Felix P., II. 2007. "How the Allocation Formulas Disenfranchise Millions of Voters." In *Oligarchic Politics: Elections and the Party-list System in the Philippines*, edited by Bobby M. Tuazon, 82–100. Quezon City: CenPEG Books.

Mullen, John. 2006. "John Major's Citizen's Charter—Fifteen Years Later." In *Citoyen ou Consommateurs? Les Mutations rhétoriques et Politiques au Royaume-Uni*, edited by Raphaële Espiet-Kilty and Timothy Whitton, 33–53. Clermont-Ferrand: Presses Universitaires de Clermont-Ferrand.

Munro-Kua, Anne. 1996. *Authoritarian Populism in Malaysia*. Basingstoke: Macmillan.

Mydans, Seth. 2006. "Singapore's Young Challengers Beg to Differ." *International Herald Tribune*, May 6. http://www.singapore-window.org/sw06/060506IH.HTM.

——. 2011. "Opposition Makes Inroads in Singapore." *New York Times*, May 7. http://www.nytimes.com/2011/05/08/world/asia/08singapore.html?_r=0.

NEAC (National Economic Advisory Council). 2010a. *New Economic Model for Malaysia. Concluding Part: Strategic Policy Measures*. December 3. Putrajaya, Malaysia: NEAC. https://www.pmo.gov.my/dokumenattached/NEM_Concluding_Part.pdf.

——. 2010b. *New Economic Model for Malaysia. Part 1: Strategic Policy Directions*. March 30. Putrajaya, Malaysia: NEAC. https://www.pmo.gov.my/dokumenattached/NEM_Report_I.pdf.

Nelson, Colleen McCain. 2015. "In Malaysia, Obama Presses for Human Rights and Government Accountability." *Wall Street Journal*, November 20. http://www.wsj.com/articles/in-malaysia-obama-presses-for-human-rights-and-government-accountability-1448030205.

Nelson, Joan M. 2012. "Political Challenges in Economic Upgrading: Malaysia Compared with South Korea and Taiwan." In *Malaysia's Development Challenges: Graduating from the Middle*, edited by Hal Hill, Tham Siew Yean, and Ragayah Haji Mat Zin, 43–62. Abingdon, Oxon: Routledge.

Netto, Anil. 2014. "Seven Reasons Why Malaysians Are Struggling to Put Food on the Table." *Aliran*, March 22. http://aliran.com/aliran-monthly/2013/2013-9/seven-reasons-malaysians-struggling-put-food-table.

New Straits Times. 1999. "NECC II Will Have Some Reps from Chinese Associations." September 30.

———. 2000a. "Committee's Appeal Sparked Controversy." September 16.

———. 2000b. "NECC Deputy Chairman Clarifies 'Utusan' Report." August 15.

———. 2000c. "Report Lodged Over Article." August 16.

———. 2010. "Kedah Says No to Local Polls." March 15.

Ng, Jing Yng. 2012. "Opposition Slams Make-Up of 'National Conversation' Committee." *Today Online*, September 10. http://www.todayonline.com/singapore/opposition-slams-make-up-of-committee.

———. 2015. "At Least 20 Seats Needed for a More Effective Opposition, Says WP." *Today Online*, August 27. http://www.todayonline.com/singapore/least-20-seats-needed-more-effective-opposition-says-wp.

Nilles, Giovanni. 2016. "Rody Wants Party-List System Abolished." *Philippine Star*, July 31. http://www.philstar.com/headlines/2016/07/31/1608503/rody-wants-party-list-system-abolished.

Nonini, Donald. 2015. *"Getting By" Class and State Formation among Chinese in Malaysia*. Ithaca, NY: Cornell University Press.

Noor, Farish A. 2013. "The Malaysian General Elections of 2013: The Last Attempt at Secular-inclusive Nation-building?" *Journal of Current Southeast Asian Affairs* 32 (2): 89–104.

Nordlinger, Eric A. 1972. *Conflict Regulation in Divided Societies*. Cambridge, MA: Centre for International Affairs, Harvard University.

North, Douglas C. 1990. *Institutions, Institutional Change and Economic Performance*. Cambridge: Cambridge University Press.

Nur Asyiqin, Modamad Salleh. 2015. "Political Websites Creating a Buzz in Singapore." *Straits Times*, May 2. http://www.straitstimes.com/singapore/political-websites-creating-a-buzz-in-singapore.

Nye, John V. C. 2011. "Taking Institutions Seriously: Rethinking the Political Economy of Development in the Philippines." *Asian Development Review* 28 (1): 1–21.

O'Donnell, Guillermo. 1994. "Delegative Democracy." *Journal of Democracy* 5 (1): 55–69.

O'Donnell, Guillermo, Philippe C. Schmitter, and Laurence Whitehead. 1986. *Transitions from Authoritarian Rule*. 4 vols. Baltimore, MD: Johns Hopkins University Press.

Office of External Affairs. 2006. *Memorandum for the President*. October 16. Malacañang: Office of the President of the Philippines. http://kontradaya.wordpress.com/2007/04/26/memorandum-on-malacanang-sponsored-partylist-groups.

Ofreneo, Rene E. 2009. "Developmental Choices for Philippines Textiles and Garments in the Post-MFA Era." *Journal of Contemporary Asia* 39 (4): 543–61.

Ong, Andrea. 2014a. "Consider What Compassionate Meritocracy Entails." *Singapolitics (Straits Times)*, January 8. http://www.singapolitics.sg/news/consider-what-compassionate-meritocracy-entails-lim-siong-guan.

———. 2014b. "Elevate Political Discourse Beyond Credit-Blame Match." *Straits Times*, June 14. http://news.asiaone.com/news/asian-opinions/elevate-political-discourse-beyond-credit-blame-match.

Ong, Kian Ming. 2011. "Bersih 2.0 Rally in Malaysia Stirs Discontent with Ruling Party." *East Asia Forum*, August 13. http://www.eastasiaforum.org/2011/08/13/bersih-2-0-rally-in-malaysia-stirs-discontent-with-ruling-party.

Ortmann, Stephan. 2015. "Political Change and Civil Society Coalitions in Singapore." *Government and Opposition* 50 (1): 119–39.

OSC (Our Singapore Conversation) Committee. 2013. *Reflections of Our Singapore Conversation: What Future Do We Want? How Do We Get There?* Singapore: Our Singapore Conversation Secretariat.

Ostwald, Kai. 2013. "How to Win a Lost Election: Malapportionment and Malaysia's 2013 General Election." *The Round Table* 102 (6): 521–32.

Ottaway, Marina. 2003. *Democracy Challenged: The Rise of Semi-Authoritarianism.* Washington, DC: Carnegie Endowment for International Peace.

Padua, Reinier. 2013. "Cops, Anti-SONA Rallyists Clash." *Philippine Star,* July 23. http://www.philstar.com/headlines/2013/07/23/1002271/cops-anti-sona-rallyists-clash.

Pakatan Rakyat. 2009. *PR Common Policy Platform.* December 19. http://www.tindakmalaysia.com/threads/1282-PR-Common-Policy-Platform-%28PR-CPP%29-Contents.

——. 2010. *Baku Jingga—Change Now, Save Malaysia!* December 14. http://www.pakatanrakyat.info/wp-content/uploads/2010/12/Buku-Jingga-English-Abridged.pdf.

Pang, Chen Lian. 1971. *Singapore's People's Action Party.* Kuala Lumpur: Oxford University Press.

Panganiban, Artemio V. 2013. "Sad Day for the Poor." *Philippine Daily Inquirer,* April 13. http://opinion.inquirer.net/50641/sad-day-for-the-poor.

Panti, Llanesca. 2013a. "Party Listers Divided over SC Purge." *Manila Times,* April 4. http://www.manilatimes.net.

——. 2013b. "Top Party-List Loses Popularity." *Manila Times,* April 15. http://www.manilatimes.net.

Pasuk, Phongpaichit, and Chris Baker. 2004. *Thaksin: The Business of Politics in Thailand.* Chang Mai: Silkworm Books.

Pateman, Carole. 2012. "Participatory Democracy Revisited." *Perspectives on Politics* 10 (1): 7–19.

PCIJ (Philippine Centre for Investigative Journalism). 2006. "Can Comelec Reform?" *PCIJ Blog,* June 16. http://pcij.org/blog/2006/06/16/can-comelec-reform.

Pemandu. 2010. *Economic Transformation Programme: A Roadmap for Malaysia.* Putrajaya: Pemandu.

Pepinsky, Thomas. 2009. *Economic Crises and the Breakdown of Authoritarian Regimes: Indonesia and Malaysia in Comparative Perspective.* New York: Cambridge University Press.

——. 2014. "The Institutional Turn in Comparative Authoritarianism." *British Journal of Political Science* 44 (3): 631–53.

Perry, Elizabeth J., and Merle Goldman, eds. 2007. *Grassroots Political Reform in Contemporary China.* Cambridge, MA: Harvard University Press.

Phang, Siew Nooi. 2008. "Decentralisation or Recentralisation? Trends in Local Government in Malaysia." *Commonwealth Journal of Local Governance* 2008 (1): 126–32.

Philippine Daily Inquirer. 2009. "How 'Hyatt 10' Was Formed." July 9. http://newsinfo.inquirer.net/inquirerheadlines/nation/view/20090709-214576/How-Hyatt-10-was-formed.

——. 2013. "In the Know: Conditional Cash Transfer Scheme." June 25. http://newsinfo.inquirer.net/432371/in-the-know-conditional-cash-transfer-scheme.

Philippine Star. 2016. "Con-com OK with Duterte." August 4. http://www.philstar.com/headlines/2016/08/04/1609951/con-com-ok-duterte.

Phua, Mei Pin. 2012. "Opposition Keen to Join SG Dialogue." *Straits Times,* October 18. http://newshub.nus.edu.sg/news/1210/PDF/SG-st-18oct-pA8.pdf.

Pinches, Michael. 1996. "The Philippines' New Rich: Capitalist Transformation amidst Economic Gloom." In *The New Rich in Asia: Mobile Phones, McDonalds and Middle Class Revolution,* edited by Richard Robison and David Goodman, 105–37. London: Routledge.

Pitkin, Hanna Fenichel. 1967. *The Concept of Representation.* Berkeley: University of California Press.

Plattner, Marc F. 2014. "The End of the Transitions Era?" *Journal of Democracy* 25 (3): 5–16.

Porcalla, Delon. 2009. "Clarification Sought on Party-List." *Philippine Star*, April 23.

Potter, Dominic. 2008. "Public Participation in the UK: Lessons from the UK Experience." Background paper for a SIGMA workshop on consultation, Bucharest, Romania, October 14. http://www.sigmaweb.org/publicationsdocuments/41838063.pdf.

Poulantzas, Nicos. 1973. *Political Power and Social Classes*. Translated by Timothy O'Hagan. London: New Left Books.

——. 1974. *Fascism and Dictatorship*. Edited by Jennifer and Timothy O'Hagan. Translated by Judith White. London: New Left Books.

Protsyk, Oleh. 2010. *The Representation of Minorities and Indigenous People in Parliament*. Inter-Parliamentary Union and United Nations Development Programme. Accessed May 12, 2017. http://www.ipu.org/splz-e/chiapas10/overview.pdf.

Przeworski, Adam. 2004. "Institutions Matter?" *Government and Opposition* 39 (4): 527–40.

Przeworski, Adam, Michael E. Alvarez, José Antonio Cheibub, and Fernando Limongi. 2000. *Democracy and Development: Political Institutions and Well-Being in the World, 1950–1990*. New York: Cambridge University Press.

Pua, Tony. 2010. "Pua Says 1MDB Profits Suspect." *Malaysian Insider*, October 18.

Punay, Edu. 2013. "Groups Picket SC over Ruling on Party-list Groups." *Philippine Star*, April 9. http://www.philstar.com/headlines/2013/04/09/928551/groups-picket-sc-over-ruling-party-list-groups.

Pusat Komas. 2010. "CGG & CONPAC Hands Memo Part2." July 13. http://www.youtube.com/watch?v=DVOe2bITUyM&noredirect=1.

Puthucheary, James. 1960. *Ownership and Control of the Malayan Economy*. Singapore: Eastern University Press.

Quek, Tracey. 2013. "Ministries to Discuss Follow-up to National Dialogue." *Straits Times*, June 12. http://yourhealth.asiaone.com/content/ministries-discuss-follow-national-dialogue.

Quimpo, Nathan Gilbert. 2008. *Contested Democracy and the Left in the Philippines after Marcos*. New Haven, CT: Yale University Press.

Rabushka, Alvin. 1970. "The Manipulation of Ethnic Politics in Malaya." *Polity* 2 (3): 345–56.

Rahim, Lily Zubaidah. 1994. "The Paradox of Ethic-Based Self-Help Groups." In *Debating Singapore*, edited by Derek Da Cunha, 46–50. Singapore: Institute of Southeast Asian Studies.

——. 2001. *The Singapore Dilemma: The Political and Educational Marginality of the Malay Community*. Kuala Lumpur: Oxford University Press.

Rajah, Jothie. 2012. *Authoritarian Rule of Law: Legislation, Discourse and Legitimacy in Singapore*. Cambridge: Cambridge University Press.

Ramian Said, Ainon Mohd, and Patrick Sennyah. 2001. "Abdullah Takes Opposition to Task." *New Straits Times*, April 11.

Ramzy, Austin. 2015. "Malaysian Security Bill Invites Abuses, Rights Groups Say." *International New York Times*, December 4.

Rappler. 2013. "Bottom-up Budgeting Needs Work." April 6. http://www.rappler.com/move-ph/issues/budget-watch/30667-bottom-up-budgeting-needs-work.

——. 2016. "Official Tally of Votes for the 2013 Party-list Race." June 26. http://www.rappler.com/nation/politics/elections-2013/features/rich-media/29634-official-election-results-2013-party-list-race.

Raquiza, Antoinette R. 2014. "Changing Configurations of Philippine Capitalism." *Philippine Journal of Political Science* 35 (2): 225–50.

Rasiah, Rajah. 2015. "Industrialization and Labour in Malaysia." *Journal of the Asia Pacific Economy* 20 (1): 77–99.

Rasiah, Rajah, Nik Rosnah Wan Abdullah, and Makmor Tumin. 2011. "Markets and Health Services in Malaysia: Critical Issues." *International Journal of Institutions and Economics* 3 (3): 467–86.

Rasiah, Rajah, and Johannes Dragsbaek Schmidt. 2010. "Introduction." In *The New Political Economy of Southeast Asia*, edited by Rajah Rasiah and Johannes Dragsbaek Schmidt, 1–43. Cheltenham: Edward Elgar Publishing.

REACH (Reaching Everyone for Active Citizenry @ Home). 2007. *Citizen Engagement Handbook*. Singapore: Singapore Government.

———. 2013. *Reflections on Our Singapore Conversation*. Singapore: Singapore Government. Accessed August 20, 2014. http://www.reach.gov.sg/Portals/0/Microsite/osc/OSC_Reflection.pdf.

Real Singapore. 2012. "Heng Swee Keat Explains Why the 'National Conversation' Committee Did Not Include the Opposition." September 11. Accessed September 30, 2013. http://therealsingapore.com (URL no longer available).

———. 2013. "Only PAP Trolls Allowed." November 25. Accessed December 1, 2014. http://therealsingapore.com.

Reid, Ben. 2004. "EDSA II, the Arroyo Government and the 'Democratic Left' in the Philippines." *Links* 25 (January–June): 185–99.

———. 2005. "Poverty Alleviation and Participatory Development in the Philippines." *Journal of Contemporary Asia* 35 (1): 29–52.

———. 2008. "Developmental NGOs, Semiclientism, and the State in the Philippines: From 'Crossover' to Double-crossed." *Kasarinlan: Philippine Journal of Third World Studies* 23 (1): 4–42.

Reilly, Benjamin. 2007. *Democracy and Diversity: Political Engineering in the Asia-Pacific*. New York: Oxford University Press.

Remitio, Rex. 2016. "DBM Presents Proposed P3.35 Trillion Budget for 2017." CNN News, July 15. http://cnnphilippines.com/news/2016/07/14/dbm-2017-budget.html.

Remmer, Karen L. 2012. "The Rise of Leftist-Populist Governance in Latin America: The Roots of Electoral Change." *Comparative Political Studies* 45 (8): 947–72.

Republic of Singapore. 1990. *Fourth Schedule Amendment: Appointment of Nominated Members of Parliament, Constitution of the Republic of Singapore*. Singapore.

Republic of the Philippines. 1987. *Constitution of the Philippines, Article VI*. Philippines.

———. 1995. *Party-List System Act, Republic Act No. 7941*. Philippines.

———. 1997. *Social Reform and Poverty Alleviation Act, Republic Act No. 8425*. Philippines.

———. 2013a. *Anti-Political Dynasty Act, House Bill No. 837*. Philippines.

———. 2013b. *Genuine Party-List Group and Nominee Act, House Bill No 179*. Philippines.

Requejo, Ray E. 2013. "Party-List Bucks Criticisms vs High Court." *Manila Standard*, April 12. http://manilastandardtoday.com/2013/04/12/party-list-bucks-criticisms-vs-high-court.

Reuters. 2013. "RPT-Fitch Revises Malaysia's Outlook to Negative; Affirms at 'A–'/'A.'" July 30. http://www.reuters.com/article/fitch-revises-malaysias-outlook-to-negat-idUSFit66566620130730.

———. 2015. "Malaysia's Opposition Forms New Alliance Against Scandal-Hit Najib." September 22. http://www.businessinsider.com/r-malaysias-opposition-forms-new-alliance-against-scandal-hit-najib-2015-9?IR=T.

Rich, Gary. 2002. "Categorizing Political Regimes: New Data for Old Problems." *Democratization* 9 (4): 1–24.

Rivera, Temario C. 2011. "In Search of Credible Elections and Parties: The Philippine Paradox." In *Chasing the Wind: Assessing Philippine Democracy*, edited by Felipe B.

Miranda, Temario C. Rivera, Malaya C. Ronas, and Ronald D. Holmes, 46–94. Quezon City: Commission on Human Rights, Philippines.

Roberts, Andrew. 2005. "Review Article: The Quality of Democracy." *Comparative Politics* 37 (3): 357–76.

Roberts, Kenneth M. 2007. "Latin America's Populist Revival." *SAIS Review* 27 (1): 3–15.

Robinson, Neil. 2003. "The Politics of Russia's Partial Democracy." *Political Studies Review* 1 (2): 149–66.

Robison, Richard. 1986. *Indonesia: The Rise of Capital*. North Sydney: Allen & Unwin.

Robison, Richard, and Vedi R. Hadiz. 2004. *Reorganising Power in Indonesia: The Politics of Oligarchy in an Age of Markets*. London: Routledge.

Rocamora, Joel. 2011. "Poverty Reduction and Good Governance." Unpublished paper, November 24. Microsoft Word file.

——. 2012. "Participatory Budgeting and Democratic Deepening: Notes for a Frame." Unpublished paper, May 19, 2012. Microsoft Word file.

——. 2013. "Power and Longing: The Burdens and Challenges of Government." Paper presented at the Philippines Political Science Association Conference, Manila, March 29.

Rodan, Garry. 1989. *The Political Economy of Singapore's Industrialization: National State and International Capital*. London: Macmillan.

——. 1993. "Preserving the One-Party State in Contemporary Singapore." In *Authoritarianism, Democracy and Capitalism: Southeast Asia in the Nineties*, edited by Kevin Hewison, Richard Robison, and Garry Rodan, 75–108. Sydney: Allen & Unwin.

——. 1996a. "State-Society Relations and Political Opposition in Singapore." In *Political Oppositions in Industrialising Asia*, edited by Garry Rodan, 95–127. London: Routledge.

——. 1996b. "The Internationalization of Ideological Conflict: Asia's New Significance." *Pacific Review* 9 (3): 328–35.

——. 2003. "Embracing Electronic Media but Suppressing Civil Society: Authoritarian Consolidation in Singapore." *Pacific Review* 16 (4): 503–24.

——. 2004. "International Capital, Singapore's State Companies, and Security." *Critical Asian Studies* 36 (3): 479–99.

——. 2006a. "Lion City Baits Mousy Opposition." *Far Eastern Economic Review*, May, 11–17.

——. 2006b. "Singapore: Globalisation, the State, and Politics." In *The Political Economy of South-East Asia: Markets, Power, and Contestation*, edited by Garry Rodan, Kevin Hewison, and Richard Robison, 137–69. Melbourne: Oxford University Press.

——. 2008. "Singapore 'Exceptionalism'? Authoritarian Rule and State Transformation." In *Political Transitions in Dominant Party Systems: Learning to Lose*, edited by Edward Friedman and Joseph Wong, 231–51. London: Routledge.

——. 2009. "New Modes of Political Representation and Singapore's Nominated Members of Parliament." *Government and Opposition* 44 (4): 438–62.

——. 2012. "Competing Ideologies of Political Representation in Southeast Asia." *Third World Quarterly* 33 (2): 311–32.

——. 2013. "Southeast Asian Activism and Limits to Independent Political Space in Southeast Asia." In *Social Activism in Southeast Asia*, edited by Michele Ford, 22–39. Abingdon: Routledge.

——. 2016. "Capitalism, Inequality and Ideology in Singapore: New Challenges for the Ruling Party." *Asian Studies Review* 40 (2): 211–30.

Rodan, Garry, Kevin Hewison, and Richard Robison, eds. 1997. *The Political Economy of South-East Asia: An Introduction*. Melbourne: Oxford University Press.

——. 2001. *The Political Economy of South-East Asia: Conflict, Crises and Change*. Melbourne: Oxford University Press.

——. 2006. "Theorising Markets in South-East Asia: Power and Contestation." In *The Political Economy of South-East Asia: Markets, Power and Contestation*, edited by Garry Rodan, Kevin Hewison, and Richard Robison, 1–38. South Melbourne: Oxford University Press.

Rodan, Garry, and Caroline Hughes. 2012. "Ideological Coalitions and the International Promotion of Social Accountability: The Philippines and Cambodia Compared." *International Studies Quarterly* 56 (2): 367–80.

——. 2014. *The Politics of Accountability in Southeast Asia: The Dominance of Moral Ideologies*. Oxford: Oxford University Press.

Rodan, Garry, and Kanishka Jayasuriya. 2007. "The Technocratic Politics of Administrative Participation: Case Studies of Singapore and Vietnam." *Democratization* 14 (5): 795–815.

——. 2009. "Capitalist Development, Regime Transitions and New Forms of Authoritarianism in Asia." *Pacific Review* 22 (1): 23–47.

——. 2012. "Hybrid Regimes: A Social Foundations Approach." In *Routledge Handbook of Democratization*, edited by Jeffrey Haynes, 175–89. Abingdon: Routledge.

Rodis, Rodel. 2015. "After Mamaspano, Can Filipinos Still Rally to the Flag?" *Philippine Daily Inquirer*, February 21. http://globalnation.inquirer.net/118894/after-mamaspano-can-filipinos-still-rally-to-the-flag.

Rodriguez, Agustin Martin G. 2009. *Governing the Other: Exploring the Discourse of Democracy in a Multiverse of Reason*. Quezon City: Ateneo de Manila University Press.

Ronda, Rainier Allan. 2014. "DSWD to Expand Anti-Poverty Programs." *Philippine Star*, January 5. http://www.philstar.com/nation/2014/01/05/1275146/dswd-expand-anti-poverty-programs.

Rood, Steven. 2013. "Families, Not Political Parties Still Reign in the Philippines." *In Asia*, May 22. http://asiafoundation.org/in-asia/2013/05/22/families-not-political-parties-still-reign-in-the-philippines.

Runciman, David. 2007. "The Paradox of Political Representation." *Journal of Political Philosophy* 15 (1): 93–114.

Rush, James. 1987. "The Cory Constitution." *Universities Field Staff International Reports, Asia, No. 4*. Indianapolis, IN: Universities Field Staff International.

Saad, Imelda. 2014. "PM Lee Offers His Definition of 'Constructive Politics.'" Channel NewsAsia, May 28. http://www.channelnewsasia.com/news/specialreports/parliament/news/pm-lee-offers-his/1125558.html.

Sabatier, Paul A., and Hank C. Jenkins-Smith, eds. 1993. *Policy Change and Learning: An Advocacy Coalition Approach*. Boulder, CO: Westview Press.

Sabatier, Paul A., and Christopher M. Weible. 2007. "The Advocacy Coalition Framework: Innovations and Clarifications." In *Theories of the Policy Process*, 2nd ed., edited by Paul A. Sabatier, 189–222. Boulder, CO: Westview Press.

Salamat, Marya. 2013. "Is There a Concerted Effort to Crowd out the Poor, Remove Progressives from Party-List Elections?" *Bulatlat*, April 8. http://bulatlat.com/main/2013/04/08/is-there-a-concerted-effort-to-crowd-out-the-poor-remove-progressives-from-partylist-elections.

Salaverria, Leila B. 2012. "Akbayan Defends Party-List Stand." *Philippine Daily Inquirer*, October 23. http://newsinfo.inquirer.net/293908/akbayan-defends-party-list-stand.

Saleem, Saleena. 2016. "Malaysia's Secular Versus Religious Divide." *APPS Policy Forum*, October 10. http://www.policyforum.net/malaysias-secular-versus-religious-divide.

Sangmpam, S. N. 2007. "Political Rules: The False Primacy of Institutions in Developing Countries." *Political Studies* 55 (1): 201–24.

Santuario, Edmundo, III. 2001. "High Time for Bayan Muna—Or Why It Topped the May Party-List Polls." *Bulatlat*, June 15–21. http://www.bulatlat.com/archive1 /018high_time_for_bayan_muna.htm.

Saxena, Naresh C. 2011. *Virtuous Cycles: The Singapore Public Service and National Development*. Singapore: United Nations Development Programme.

Saxer, Marc. 2014. "Middle Class Rage Threatens Democracy." *New Mandala*, January 21. http://asiapacific.anu.edu.au/newmandala/2014/01/21/middle-class-rage-threatens -democracy.

Schattschneider, Elmer E. 1975. *The Semi-Sovereign People: A Realist's View of Democracy in America*. Boston, MA: Wadsworth.

Schedler, Andreas. 2002. "Elections without Democracy: The Menu of Manipulation." *Journal of Democracy* 13 (2): 36–50.

———. 2006. *Electoral Authoritarianism: The Dynamics of Unfree Competition*. London: Lynne Rienner.

Schmitter, Philippe, and Gerhard Lembruch, eds. 1979. *Trends towards Corporatist Intermediation*. Beverly Hills, CA: Sage.

Schram, Sanford F. 2015. *The Return of Ordinary Capitalism: Neoliberalism, Precarity, Occupy*. New York: Oxford University Press.

Scipes, Kim. 1996. *KMU: Building Genuine Trade Unionism in the Philippines, 1980–1994*. Quezon City: New Day Publishers.

———. 2011. *AFL-CIO's Secret War against Developing Country Workers: Solidarity or Sabotage?* Plymouth: Lexington Books.

Seah, Chee Meow. 1973. *Community Centres in Singapore: Their Political Involvement*. Singapore: National University of Singapore Press.

Searle, Peter. 1999. *The Riddle of Malaysian Capitalism: Rent-Seekers or Real Capitalists?* Honolulu, HI: Asian Studies Association of Australia in association with Allen & Unwin and University of Hawai'i Press.

Seeberg, Michael. 2014. "Mapping Deviant Democracy." *Democratization* 21 (4): 634–54.

Selee, Andrew, and Enrique Peruzzotti, eds. 2009. *Participatory Innovation and Representative Democracy in Latin America*. Washington, DC: Woodrow Wilson International Centre for Scholars.

Shalom, Stephen Rosskamm. 1986. *The United States and the Philippines: A Study of Neocolonialism*. Quezon City: New Day Publications.

Shibani, Mahtani. 2013. "Singapore Likes a Crowd." *Wall Street Journal*, January 29. http://blogs.wsj.com/indonesiarealtime/2013/01/29/singapore-likes-a-crowd.

Sidel, John Thayer. 1999. *Capital, Coercion and Crime: Bossism in the Philippines*. Stanford, CA: Stanford University Press.

Silverio, Ina. 2012a. "Corruption in Party-List System in the Philippines." *Wikamagazine: The Filipino American Online Magazine*, September 13. http://wikamag.com /corruption-in-party-list-system-in-the-philippines.

———. 2012b. "More Groups Urge Comelec to Disqualify Akbayan." *Bulatlat*, October 26. http://bulatlat.com/main/2012/10/26/more-groups-urge-comelec-to-disqualify -akbayan.

Sim, Walter. 2015a. "PAP Will Do Even More to Engage Public: Heng Swee Keat." *Straits Times*, September 14. http://www.straitstimes.com/politics/singapolitics/pap-will -do-even-more-to-engage-public-heng.

———. 2015b. "Young Singaporeans Throw Up Ideas for Country's Future at Dialogue." *Straits Times*, November 30. http://www.straitstimes.com/politics/young-singaporeans -throw-up-ideas-for-countrys-future-at-dialogue.

Simon, Thomas W. 2012. *Ethnic Identity and Minority Representation: Designation, Discrimination and Brutalization.* Plymouth: Lexington Books.

Singapore Department of Statistics. 2015. *Time Series: Annual GDP at 2010 Market Prices and Real Economic Growth. National Accounts.* Singapore: Singapore Government. Accessed August 21, 2015. http://www.singstat.gov.sg/statistics/browse-by-theme /national-accounts.

Slater, Dan. 2010. *Ordering Power: Contentious Politics and Authoritarian Leviathans in Southeast Asia.* New York: Cambridge University Press.

——. 2015. "Malaysia's Mess Is Mahathir-made." *East Asia Forum,* July 29. http://www .eastasiaforum.org/2015/07/29/malaysias-mess-is-mahathir-made.

Slater, Dan, and Erica Simmons. 2010. "Informative Regress: Critical Antecedents in Comparative Politics." *Comparative Political Studies* 43 (7): 886–917.

Soin, Kanwaljit. 1999. "Woman Doctor in the House." *Singapore Medical Journal* 40 (4): 228–29.

Soliman, Sandino. 2016. "Ministries to Discuss Follow-up to National Dialogue." CODE-NGO News, October 17. http://code-ngo.org/2016/10/csos-across-nation-call-conti nuation-bottom-budgeting.

Star Online. 2008. "Group Hits out at Penang Government." April 30. http://thestar.com .my/news/story.asp?file=/2008/4/30/nation/21107308&sec=nation.

——. 2009a. "Airlines Chief Appointed Malaysian Minister." August 28. http://news .asiaone.com/News/AsiaOne+News/Malaysia/Story/A1Story20090828-164062.html.

——. 2009b. "Govt Seeks Public Feedback." December 17.

——. 2011. "Almost Half of MPPP and MPSP Line-up of Councillors Are New Faces." January 6. http://thestar.com.my/metro/story.asp?file=/2011/1/6/north /7742349&sec=north.

——. 2015. "Delegate: DAP Is the Real Enemy." December 12. http://www.thestar.com .my/news/nation/2015/12/12/delegate-dap-is-the-real-enemy.

Straits Times. 2005. "Mr. Feedback: You Have His Ear Even When You Mouth Off." January 28.

——. 2014. "Role for NMPs in Deliberative Democracy." June 2. http://www.straitstimes .com/opinion/role-for-nmps-in-deliberative-democracy.

——. 2015. "New Group Plans to Bring Pakatan Back." July 14. http://www.straitstimes .com/asia/se-asia/new-group-plans-to-bring-pakatan-back.

——. 2017. "1MDB Pays Abu Dhabi Fund S$477 Million Ahead of Aug 12 Deadline while US Intensifies Criminal Probe." August 11. http://www.straitstimes.com/asia /se-asia/1mdb-pays-abu-dhabi-fund-s477-million-ahead-of-aug-12-deadline

Streeck, Wolfgang. 2014. *Buying Time: The Delayed Crisis of Democratic Capitalism.* London: Verso.

STWOE (Straits Times Weekly Overseas Edition). 1989. "Nothing to Lose from Having Nominated MPs, says BG Lee." *Straits Times,* December 9.

SUARAM (Suara Rakyat Malaysia). 2009. "SUARAM Urge State Government to Practice Democracy." Press Release, March 7. http://suarampg.blogspot.com.au/2009/03 /suaram-urge-state-government-to.html.

Sundaram, Jomo Kwame. 1988. *A Question of Class: Capital, the State, and Uneven Development in Malaya.* New York: Monthly Review Press.

——. 1994. *U-Turn? Malaysian Economic Development Policies after 1990.* Townsville: James Cook University.

Sundaram, Jomo Kwame, and Wee Chong Hui. 2014. *Malaysia@50: Economic Development, Distribution, Disparities.* Petaling Jaya: Strategic Information and Research Development Centre.

Sun Star. 2013a. "123 Party-Lists to Be Listed in Official Ballots." January 27. http://archive.sunstar.com.ph/breaking-news/2013/01/27/123-party-lists-be-listed-official-ballots-265025.

——. 2013b. "SC Paves Way for Proclamation of Senior Citizens Party-List." July 23. http://archive.sunstar.com.ph/breaking-news/2013/07/23/sc-paves-way-proclamation-senior-citizens-party-list-293971.

Supreme Court. 2001. *Ang Bagong Bayani-OFW Labor Party vs. Comelec et al. (G.R. No. 147589) and Bayan Muna vs. Comelec et al. (G.R. No.147613)*. Philippines.

——. 2009. *BANAT vs. Comelec (G.R. No.179271) and Bayan Muna et al. vs. Comelec (G.R. No. 179295)*. Philippines.

——. 2013. *Atong Paglaum vs. Comelec (G.R. No. 203766)*. Philippines.

Surowiecki, James. 2013. "Middle Class Militants." *New Yorker*, July 8. http://www.newyorker.com/magazine/2013/07/08/middle-class-militants.

Tan, Esther. 1999. "Three BN Components Accept Hua Tuan Appeal." *New Straits Times*, September 24.

Tan, Eugene. 2011. "Election Issues." In *Voting in Change: Politics of Singapore's 2011 General Election*, edited by Kevin Y. L. Tan and Terence Lee, 27–48. Singapore: Ethos Books.

Tan, Jo Hann. 2010. "Letter to Y. A. B. Tan Sri Dato' Seri Abd Khalid Bin Ibrahim from CONPAC." Pusat Komas, July 12. http://komas.org/news_events_12july.htm.

Tan, Kevin Y. L., and Peng Er Lam, eds. 1997. *Managing Political Change in Singapore: The Elected Presidency*. London: Routledge.

Tan, Netina. 2013. "Manipulating Electoral Laws in Singapore." *Electoral Studies* 32 (4): 632–43.

Tan, Oscar Franklin B. 2007. "Party-List System: Mathematical Absurdity." *Philippine Daily Inquirer*, June 24. http://www.scribd.com/doc/120137260/Party-List-System-Mathematical-Absurdity-Oscar-Franklin-Tan-Jun-24-2007-PDF.

——. 2008. "The Party-List System Revised." *Philippine Law Journal* 82: 181–232.

Tan, Seng Hai. 2010. "Historic Pilot Local Council Polls." *Aliran Monthly* 30 (10): 2.

Tan, Tony. 2014. "Singapore President Tony Tan Keng Yam Opens New Session of Parliament: His Address in Full." *Straits Times*, May 16. http://www.straitstimes.com/singapore/singapore-president-tony-tan-keng-yam-opens-new-session-of-parliament-his-address-in-full.

Tan, Wah Piow. 2012. *Smokescreens & Mirrors: Tracing the "Marxist Conspiracy."* Singapore: Functions 8 Limited.

Tay, David. 1999. "Opposition Should Forget Differences." *New Straits Times*, August 12.

Teehankee, Julio C. 2002. "Electoral Politics in the Philippines." In *Electoral Politics in Southeast and East Asia*, edited by Aurel Croissant, 149–202. Singapore: Friedrich Ebert Stiftung.

——. 2013. "Clientelism and Party Politics in the Philippines." In *Party Politics in Southeast Asia: Clientelism and Electoral Competition in Indonesia, Thailand and the Philippines*, edited by Dirk Tomsa and Andreas Ufen, 186–214. Abingdon: Routledge.

Temasek Times. 2012. "Lawrence Wong Appeals to Workers Party to Join 'Singapore Conversation.'" October 27. https://temasektimes.wordpress.com/2012/10/27/lawrence-wong-appeals-to-workers-party-to-join-singapore-conversation.

Tennant, Paul. 1973. "The Decline of Elective Local Government in Malaysia." *Asian Survey* 13 (4): 347–65.

Teoh, Shannon. 2015a. "Bersih Rally Turning into Racial Issue." *Straits Times*, August 31. http://www.straitstimes.com/asia/se-asia/bersih-rally-turning-into-racial-issue.

——. 2015b. "'Red Shirt' Rally Brings Out Malaysians' Insecurities." *Straits Times*, September 30. http://www.straitstimes.com/opinion/red-shirt-rally-brings-out-malaysians -insecurities.

Tham, Yuen-C. 2014. "NMP Scheme Sparks Less Controversy Than Before." *Straits Times*, August 16. http://www.singapolitics.sg/views/nmp-scheme-sparks-less-controversy.

Thompson, Mark R. 1995. *The Anti-Marcos Struggle: Personalistic Rule and Democratic Transition in the Philippines*. New Haven, CT: Yale University Press.

——. 2010. "Populism and the Revival of Reform: Competing Political Narratives in the Philippines." *Contemporary Southeast Asia: A Journal of International and Strategic Affairs* 32 (1): 1–28.

——. 2016. "Bloodied Democracy: Duterte and the Death of Liberal Reformism in the Philippines." *Journal of Current Southeast Asian Affairs*, 3: 39–68.

Toh, Elgin. 2013. "Kenneth Paul Tan: 'OSC Committee Made Difficult Interventions.'" *Asia One*, August 17. http://news.asiaone.com/news/singapore/kenneth-paul-tan -osc-committee-made-difficult-interventions?page=0%2C0.

Tolosa, Benjamin T., Jr., ed. 2012. *Socdem: Filipino Social Democracy in a Time of Turmoil and Transition*. Quezon City: Ateneo de Manila University Press.

Tomsa, Dirk, and Andreas Ufen, eds. 2013. *Party Politics in Southeast Asia: Clientelism and Electoral Competition in Indonesia, Thailand and the Philippines*. Abingdon: Routledge.

Tormey, Simon. 2015. *The End of Representative Politics*. Cambridge: Polity Press.

Törnquist, Olle. 2009. "Introduction: The Problem Is Representation! Towards an Analytical Framework." In *Rethinking Popular Representation*, edited by Olle Törnquist, Neil Webster, and Kristian Stokke, 1–24. London: Palgrave Macmillan.

——. 2013. "Democracy and the Philippine Left." In *Introduction to Philippine Politics: Local Politics and State Building and Democratization*, edited by Maria Ela Atienza, 170–219. Quezon City: University of the Philippines Press.

Törnquist, Olle, Neil Webster, and Kristian Stokke, eds. 2009. *Rethinking Popular Representation*. London: Palgrave Macmillan.

TR Emeritus. 2013. "Another Reader Shares First-Hand Experience of OSC." August 9. http://www.tremeritus.com.

Tremewan, Christopher. 1994. *The Political Economy of Social Control in Singapore*. London: Macmillan.

Trocki, Carl A. 2006. *Singapore: Wealth, Power and the Culture of Control*. Abingdon: Routledge.

Tsun, Hang Tey. 2010. "Malaysia's Electoral System: Government of the People?" *Asian Journal of Comparative Law* 5 (1): 1–32.

Tuazon, Bobby M. 2007. "The Future of Oligarchic Politics and the Party-List System." In *Oligarchic Politics: Elections and the Party-List System in the Philippines*, edited by Bobby M. Tuazon, 134–49. Quezon City: CenPEG Books.

——. 2011. "Analyzing the May 2010 Election Results: Clans Use the Party-List System to Remain Dominant in 15th Congress." In *12 Years of the Party-List System*, edited by Bobby M. Tuazon, 152–57. Quezon City: CenPEG Books.

Turnbull, C. 1982. *A History of Singapore 1819–1975*. Kuala Lumpur: Oxford University Press.

Ufen, Andreas. 2009. "The Transformation of Political Party Opposition in Malaysia and its Implications for the Electoral Authoritarian Regime." *Democratization* 16 (3): 604–27.

——. 2013. "The 2013 Malaysian Electoral System: Business as Usual or Part of a Protracted Transition?" *Journal of Current Southeast Asian Affairs* 32 (2): 3–17.

Umil, Anne Marxze D. 2010. "Millionaires, Allies of GMA, Lead Nominees of Dubious Party-List Groups." *Bulatlat*, April 12. http://bulatlat.com/main/2010/04/12/millionaires-allies-of-gma-lead-nominees-of-dubious-party-list-groups.

UNDP (United Nations Development Program). 2014. *Malaysia Human Development Report 2013: Redesigning an Inclusive Future.* Kuala Lumpur: United Nations Development Program.

Update. PH. 2016. "Akbayan, Magdalo Lawmakers: Reform Party-list System, Not Abolish." August 1. http://www.update.ph/2016/08/akbayan-magdalo-lawmakers-reform-party-list-system-not-abolish/8105.

Urbinati, Nadia. 2000. "Representation as Advocacy: A Study of Democratic Deliberation." *Political Theory* 28 (6): 758–86.

———. 2002. *Mill on Democracy: From the Athenian Polis to Representative Government.* Chicago: University of Chicago Press.

Urbinati, Nadia, and Mark E. Warren. 2008. "The Concept of Representation in Contemporary Democratic Theory." *Annual Review of Political Science* 11: 387–412.

Uy, Jocelyn R. 2012. "Comelec Disqualifies 17 Party-List Groups." *Philippine Daily Inquirer*, September 29. http://newsinfo.inquirer.net/279260/comelec-disqualifies-17-party-list-groups.

Van Gelder, Sarah, ed. 2011. *This Changes Everything: Occupy Wall Street and the 99% Movement.* San Francisco, CA: Berrett-Koehler Publishers.

van Reybrouck, David. 2016. *Against Elections: The Case for Democracy.* London: Bodley Head.

Vaswani, Karishma. 2016. "Who Is 'Malaysian Official 1'?" BBC News, September 1, 2016. http://www.bbc.com/news/business-37234717.

Vekiteswaran, Gayathry. 2016. "Why I Reject the Citizens' Declaration." *Malaymail Online*, March 6. http://www.themalaymailonline.com/what-you-think/article/why-i-reject-the-citizens-declaration-gayathry-venkiteswaran.

Venudran, Charlotte. 2000. "Goh Has Come Down Hard on Us." *New Straits Times*, November 8. https://groups.yahoo.com/neo/groups/bmalaysia/conversations/messages/12790.

Verzola, Roberto. 2010. "Chronic Fraud in Philippine Elections." In *Project 2010: Confronting the Legacy of the GMA Regime*, edited by Aya Fabros, 5–15. Quezon City: Focus on the Global South.

Viet Nam News. 2010. "Complaints Draft Bill to Be Revised Before Submission." August 23, 2010. http://vietnamnews.vn/politics-laws/202836/complaints-draft-bill-to-be-revised-before-submission.html.

Visscher, Sikko. 2007. *The Business and Politics of Ethnicity: A History of the Singapore Chinese Chamber of Commerce and Industry.* Singapore: National University of Singapore Press.

Visto, Cecille S. 1999. "Supreme Court Ruling on Party-List Controversy Expected This Week." *Business World*, July 19. https://global.factiva.com.

Vitug, Marites Dañguilan. 2010. *Shadow of Doubt: Probing the Supreme Court.* Quezon City: Newsbreak.

———. 2011. "Powerful People and a Book They Almost Stopped." *Nieman Reports* 65 (4): 56–8.

———. 2012. *Hour before Dawn: The Fall and Uncertain Rise of the Philippine Supreme Court.* Quezon City: Cleverheads Publishing.

———. 2014. "Aquino Successor to Appoint 11 SC Justices." *Rappler*, December 6. http://www.rappler.com/newsbreak/in-depth/77160-aquino-successor-supreme-court-justices.

Volpi, Frederic. 2004. "Pseudo-Democracy in the Muslim World." *Third World Quarterly* 25 (6): 1061–78.

von Vorys, Karl. 1975. *Democracy without Consensus: Communalism and Political Stability in Malaysia.* Princeton, NJ: Princeton University Press.

Wampler, Brian. 2007. *Participatory Budgeting in Brazil: Contestation, Cooperation and Accountability.* University Park: Pennsylvania State University Press.

Warren, Mark E., and Dario Castiglione. 2004. "The Transformation of Democratic Representation." *Democracy and Society* 2 (1): 5–22.

Weible, Christopher M., Paul A. Sabatier, Hank C. Jenkins-Smith, Daniel Nohrstedt, Adam D. Henry, and Peter de Leon. 2011. "A Quarter Century of Advocacy Coalition Framework: An Introduction to the Special Issue." *Policy Studies Journal* 39 (3): 349–60.

Weiss, Meredith L. 2003. "Malaysia NGOs: History, Legal Framework and Characteristics." In *Social Movements in Malaysia: From Moral Communities to NGOs*, edited by Meredith L. Weiss and Saliha Hassan, 17–44. London: RoutledgeCurzon.

——. 2006. *Protest and Possibilities: Civil Society and Coalitions for Political Change in Malaysia.* Stanford, CA: Stanford University Press.

——. 2009. "Edging Toward a New Politics in Malaysia: Civil Society at the Gate?" *Asian Survey* 49 (5): 741–58.

——. 2013. "Parsing the Power of 'New Media' in Malaysia." *Journal of Contemporary Asia* 43 (4): 591–612.

——. 2014a. "New Media, New Activism: Trends and Trajectories in Malaysia, Singapore and Indonesia." *International Development Planning Review* 36 (1): 91–109.

——. 2014b. "Of Inequality and Irritation: New Agendas in Activism in Malaysia and Singapore." *Democratization* 21 (5): 867–87.

——. 2015. "Mobilizing around Inequality in Malaysia and Singapore." *Kyoto Review of Southeast Asia.* Accessed April 18, 2016. https://kyotoreview.org/issue-17/mobilizing-around-inequality-in-malaysia-and-singapore.

Welsh, Bridget. 2013a. "Malaysia's Election and Najib's Challenged Mandate." *Asia Pacific Bulletin No. 216.* Washington, DC: East West Centre Publication.

——. 2013b. "Malaysia's Elections: A Step Backward." *Journal of Democracy* 24 (4): 136–50.

Weyland, Kurt. 2013. "The Threat from the Populist Left." *Journal of Democracy* 24 (3): 18–32.

Weymouth, Lally. 2013. "An Interview with Singapore Prime Minister Lee Hsien Loong." *Washington Post*, March 15. https://www.washingtonpost.com/opinions/an-interview-with-singapore-prime-minister-lee-hsien-loong/2013/03/15/5ce40cd4-8cae-11e2-9838-d62f083ba93f_story.html.

Winters, Jeffrey A. 2012. "Oligarchs and Oligarchy in Southeast Asia." In *Routledge Handbook of Southeast Asian Politics*, edited by Richard Robison, 53–68. Abingdon: Routledge.

Wong, Audrey. 2011. "One Foot In: An 'Arts NMP' on Politics and Activism in Influencing Cultural Policy." Paper presented at Institute of Policy Studies Seminar, Singapore, June 15. http://lkyspp.nus.edu.sg/ips/wp-content/uploads/sites/2/2013/06/sp_Andrey-Wong_Seminar_One-Foot-In_150611.pdf.

Wong, Chin Huat. 2009. "PR's Spin on Local Elections." *Nut Graph*, December 23. http://www.thenutgraph.com/prs-spin-on-local-elections.

Wong, Chin Huat, James Chin, and Noraini Othman. 2010. "Malaysia—Towards a Typology of an Electoral One-Party State." *Democratization* 17 (5): 920–49.

Wong, Chin Huat, and Noraini Othman. 2009. "Malaysia at 50—An 'Electoral One-Party State'?" In *Governing Malaysia*, edited by Abdul Razak Baginda, 1–58. Kuala Lumpur: Malaysian Strategic Research Centre.

Wong, Tessa, and Bryna Sim. 2012. " 'No Sacred Cows' in review of policies." *Straits Times*, August 9. https://www.facebook.com/notes/reachsingapore/no-sacred-cows-in -review-of-policies/10151012580338795.

Wong, Wee Nam. 2012. "Is There a Need to Stage a Conversation?" *Singapore Democratic Party Articles*, October 19. http://yoursdp.org/publ/perspectives/is_there_a_need _to_stage_a_conversation/2-1-0-1144.

World Bank. 2009. *Philippines—Community Driven Development and Accountable Local Governance: Some Lessons from the Philippines.* October 15. Washington, DC: World Bank. http://documents.worldbank.org/curated/en/2009/10/16332762/philippines -community-driven-development-accountable-local-governance-some-lessons -philippines.

———. 2011. *Philippines—The KAALAHI-CIDDS Impact Evaluation: A Synthesis Report.* Washington, DC: World Bank.

———. 2013. *National Community-Driven Development Program (NCDDP) Final Aide Memoire.* March 12. Pasig: World Bank. http://www.dswd.gov.ph/download /national_community-driven_development_project/NCDDP%20Pre -Appraisal%20Aide%20Memoire.pdf.

Worthington, Ross. 2003. *Governance in Singapore.* London: RoutledgeCurzon.

Wright, Tom, and Simon Clark. 2015. "Investigators Believe Money Flowed to Malaysian Leader Najib's Accounts amid IMDB Probe." *Wall Street Journal*, July 2. http:// www.wsj.com/articles/SB10130211234592774869404581083700187014570.

Wurfel, David. 1997. "The Party List Elections: Sectoral or National? Success or Failure?" *Kasarinlan: Philippine Journal of Third World Studies* 13 (2): 19–30.

Xavier, John Antony, Noore Alam Siddiquee, and Mohd Zin Mohamed. 2016. "The Government Transformation Programme of Malaysia: A Successful Approach to Public Service Reform." *Public Money & Management* 36 (2): 81–7.

Yan, Xiajun, and Ge Xin. 2016. "Participatory Policy Making under Authoritarianism: The Pathways of Local Budgetary Reform in the People's Republic of China." *Policy & Politics* 44 (2): 215–34.

Yang, Calvin. 2015. "GE 2015: Opposition Can Continue to Contribute to Singapore, Says DPM Tharman." *Straits Times*, September 14. http://www.straitstimes.com /politics/opposition-can-continue-to-contribute-to-singapore-dpm-tharman.

Yang, Razali Kassim. 2014. "Islamic Governance in Malaysia: Taking the Cue from Brunei?" *RSIS Commentaries*. Accessed May 10, 2016. https://www.rsis.edu.sg/wp -content/uploads/2014/07/CO14020.pdf.

Yong, Charissa. 2015. "PAP: Be Open to More Diverse Views." *Straits Times*, September 20. http://www.straitstimes.com/politics/be-open-to-more-diverse-views.

Yong, Soo Heong. 2010. "Idris Jala Sheds Light on Pemandu's Functions and ETP Issues." *New Straits Times*, November 1. http://www.nst.com.my.

Yong, Yen Nie. 2014. "Thousands March in KL against GST." *Straits Times*, May 2.

Youngs, Richard. 2015. "Exploring 'Non-Western Democracy.' " *Journal of Democracy* 26 (4): 140–55.

Yu-Jose, Lydia N., ed. 2011. *Civil Society Organizations in the Philippines, A Mapping and Strategic Assessment.* Quezon City: Civil Society Resource Institute.

Zakaria, Fareed. 1994. "Culture is Destiny: A Conversation with Lee Kuan Yew." *Foreign Affairs* 73 (2): 109–26.

———. 1997. "The Rise of Illiberal Democracy." *Foreign Affairs* 76 (6): 22–43.

———. 2003. *The Future of Freedom: Illiberal Democracy at Home and Abroad.* New York: W. W. Norton & Company, Inc.

Zakir, Hussain. 2015. "No Walkovers, 2.46m to Vote on Sept 11." *Straits Times*, September 11. http://www.straitstimes.com/politics/no-walkovers-246m-to-vote-on-sept-11.

Zinecker, Heidrun. 2009. "Regime-Hybridity in Developing Countries: Achievements and Limitations of New Research on Transitions." *International Studies Review* 11 (2): 302–31.

Zurbano, Joel E. 2013. "3 More Party Lists Join House." *Manila Standard*, July 21. http://manilastandardtoday.com/news/-main-stories/112630/3-more-party-lists-join-house.html.

Index

Note: Page numbers in italics indicate figures; those with a *t* indicate tables.